Note on Photos

Many of the illustrations and photographs used in this book are old, historical images. The quality of the prints is not always up to current standards, as in some cases the originals are from old or poor quality negatives or are damaged. The content of the illustrations, however, made their inclusion important despite problems in reproduction.

Library of Congress Cataloging-in-Publication Data

Aaseng, Nathan
African-American religious leaders / Nathan Aaseng.
        p. cm.
Includes bibliographical references and indexes.
ISBN 0-8160-4878-9 (alk. paper)
1. African American religious leaders—Biography. 2. Religious
leaders—United States—Biography. I. Title.
  BL72.A27 2003
  200'.92'396073—dc21   2002156645

Facts On File books are available at special discounts when purchased in bulk quantities for businesses, associations, institutions, or sales promotions. Please call our Special Sales Department in New York at (212) 967-8800 or (800) 322-8755.

You can find Facts On File on the World Wide Web at http://www.factsonfile.com

Text design by Joan M. Toro
Cover design by Nora Wertz

Printed in the United States of America

VB FOF 10 9 8 7 6 5 4 3 2 1

This book is printed on acid-free paper.

A TO Z

OF AFRICAN AMERICANS

AFRICAN-AMERICAN
RELIGIOUS LEADERS

Nathan Aaseng

Facts On File, Inc.

CONTENTS

LIST OF ENTRIES

INTRODUCTION

Any book on African-American religious leaders is going to have a distinctly different emphasis than a book on religious leaders in general. The African-American religious experience has been uniquely shaped by the institution of slavery and the racial discrimination that both supported the institution and succeeded it.

Religion and spirituality have been key elements of life for blacks in the United States from the earliest days of the slave trade. Although much of their culture was destroyed in the wrenching transition to servitude in a foreign culture on a continent far from their homeland, and their masters in the United States had little tolerance for any cultural carryover from Africa, some African religious beliefs and behaviors survived. As one example, the spiritual songs of the field workers helped keep alive the flame of human dignity under the most degrading, oppressive, and hopeless conditions.

In the meantime, European Americans had little interest in imparting any of their religious traditions to the slaves. Despite the evangelical zeal that compelled many devout Christians to follow the instruction of Jesus in the book of Matthew and elsewhere in the New Testament, to go out and make disciples of all the Earth, there was initially great reluctance to apply this dictate to African slaves. The idea of proselytizing slaves never occurred to some of them, as they did not really consider blacks to be people in the strict sense of the word. Others were hindered by the common understanding that Christians were not to hold other Christians in bondage. Believing this, they had no choice but to withhold Christianity from slaves if they were to continue to benefit from their labor. This objection, however, was eventually dispensed with by governmental and ecclesiastical laws and opinions that sanctioned the ownership of black Christians by white Christians. This left one final objection—the fear that becoming Christian tended to make blacks less amenable to slavery. Many slave owners felt that, not only would Christian slaves be less inclined to work, but they might actually foment uprisings.

Nonetheless, the religious convictions of many white Christians who felt it their duty to save lost souls no matter how unworthy gradually overrode any objections, and slaves became a primary mission field, beginning in the late 18th century. The African slaves, however, did not take readily to this new brand of religion. W. E. B. DuBois estimated that perhaps as few as one in 10 slaves responded to the invitation to accept Christianity; others put the figure at only slightly higher. Their objections ranged from discomfort with an entirely new religious paradigm to resentment of this imposed religion as simply another part of their lives that their white masters were attempting to control.

There was one element of the Judeo-Christian tradition, however, that struck a strong chord with black slaves, and that was the book of Exodus in the Old Testament of the Bible. They could not help but be drawn to the story of God's dramatic deliverance of the Israelites from the oppression of slavery in the land of Egypt and make the obvious connection to their own situation. Once Christianity did gain a foothold among blacks, whether free blacks from the North or plantation slaves from the South, blacks came to regard slavery as an issue of Christian morals and of salvation. In their view, unless white America repented of the evil that they were doing in perpetuating the institution of slavery, a just God would soon take vengeance on them and set his black children free from bondage. As early as the 18th century, African Americans were preaching on the subject of slavery from an Old Testament perspective. Richard Allen and Absalom Jones in 1794 wrote in their "Address to Those Who Keep Slaves and Approve the Practice,"

We do not wish to make you angry, but excite your attention to consider; how hateful slavery is in the sight of God, who hath destroyed kings and princes, for their oppression of poor slaves; Pharaoh and his princes with the posterity of Saul, were destroyed by the protector and avenger of slaves.

A generation later David Walker would make a similar reference to the God of the Christian religion in decrying "how much more cruel we are treated by the Americans than were children of Jacob by the Egyptians." Freedom from oppression, as achieved in the Old Testament, has been a major theme of African-American religions ever since.

Even when the practice of slavery was abolished at the end of the Civil War, African Americans found themselves shut out from much of the white world, including white religion. Although churches such as the Methodist, Episco-palian, Congregationalist, Baptist, and Presbyterian had accepted blacks into their religion since the mid-18th century, none of them welcomed blacks with open arms. Even in congregations that allowed blacks and whites to worship in the same building, the races were divided either by assigned seating or by separate times of worship for blacks and whites. Sharing power or decisions with blacks was something few white churchgoers were willing to grant. Well past the middle of the 20th century, Benjamin Mays characterized the Sunday morning worship time as "the most segregated hour in America."

As a result, the African-American religious community flourished separately from the white religious community. African Americans found that religion was the only area in which they could exercise complete control over their affairs. According to black critic Martin Delany,

Among our people generally, the church is the Alpha and Omega of all things. It is their only source of information—their only acknowledged public body—their state legislature . . . their only acknowledged advisor.

Furthermore, in the words of Benjamin Mays,

The opportunities found in the Negro church to be recognized, and be "somebody" has stimulated pride and preserves the self-respect of many Negroes who would have been entirely beaten by life.

The importance of the church to African Americans meant that their religious leaders became the leaders of the entire African-American community. According to Mays, writing in the 1930s, "The Negro pastor is one of the freest as well as most influential men on the American platform today."

The importance of the biblical Exodus imagery in regards to slavery and oppression and the status of the African-American clergy have combined to make African-American leaders far more socially conscious than their average white counterparts. As civil rights activist Lawrence Guyot declares, "There could not have been a civil rights movement without the black church . . . That was the only institution controlled, run, financed, and dictated by black folks."

One of the results of this reality is that the distinct separation that white-dominated religions tend to observe between church and state as far as vocation is concerned do not apply so easily in the world of African-American religious leaders. As the most respected, most powerful figures in the community, African-American religious leaders have tended to accept secular roles alongside their sacred roles without hesitation. A book on religious leaders in general would not have anywhere near the political involvement found in this book.

While the political and social character of many African Americans sometimes obscures their function as religious leaders, it has had little effect on who was included in this book. Although they may also have been important political and social leaders, such people as Martin Luther King, Jr.; Ralph Abernathy; Ben Chavis; and Malcolm X are or were ordained ministers, and therefore religious leaders. The same holds true even of politicians such as Floyd Flake, William Gray, and Walter Fauntroy. The few entries on people who have not been ordained or worked in some aspect of organized religious ministry are those such as David Walker and Marcus Garvey, who appealed to or influenced the religious beliefs of others.

African-American women in religious leadership have experienced a double dose of discrimination. Many of the African-American churches have traditionally regarded religious leadership as strictly a male prerogative. Although that has changed somewhat in recent years, it has made leadership more difficult for women to achieve; hence the preponderance of entries on men.

The book presents influential African-American religious leaders, with special consideration given to those who were pioneers or innovators. The book profiles a range of leaders from the most famous (Martin Luther King, Malcolm X, Elijah Muhammad) to those whose influence has been generally ignored (Jehu Jones). Those profiled come from a vast range of pursuits and include civil rights scions, founders of the African-American churches, compassionate lay leaders, dynamic preachers, pioneers in the ecclesiastical realms previously reserved for whites, workers for social justice, missionaries, and even ordained celebrities from the entertainment world who carry a spiritual message in their interactions with the public. Leaders from a wide variety of persuasions are included: mainstream Christian denominations, African-American Christian denominations, Islam, Black Muslim, voodoo, and mystic religions. The book makes no attempt to evaluate the worthiness of the subjects' religious convictions, the only exceptions being to report cases where controversy has been noted.

Abernathy, Ralph
(David Abernathy)
(1926–1990) *Baptist clergy, political activist*

Ralph Abernathy spent most of his career overshadowed by his friend and associate MARTIN LUTHER KING, JR. But he worked side by side with King to provide crucial direction to the southern church movement that succeeded in breaking down many of the racial barriers in the United States.

David Abernathy was born on March 11, 1926, in Marengo County, Alabama. His father, W. L. Abernathy, was a hardworking, prosperous cotton farmer who exuded moral authority. His mother, Louivery, was also active in their local Baptist church. Abernathy was a bookish sort who showed no aptitude for farming. Instead, he remembered, "From the time I knew my name, I knew I was going to be a preacher." He took on the name "Ralph" when one of his 11 siblings kept calling him Ralph David, after a teacher she admired.

Abernathy attended Linden Academy, the local black high school. In 1944, he enlisted in the U.S. Army and served in a segregated unit overseas during the final months of World War II. Upon returning, he enrolled at Alabama State University in Montgomery, where he was voted president of the student council. Carrying

through on his childhood ambition, he was ordained in the Baptist tradition in 1948. After graduation in 1950, he moved on to Atlanta University where he obtained a master's degree.

Abernathy then returned to his hometown, where he served as part-time pastor of Eastern Star Baptist Church. He filled a temporary vacancy at First Baptist in Montgomery, Alabama, where he performed so well that he was invited to take over permanently in 1952. Three months later, Martin Luther King, Jr., was called to a different Baptist church in Montgomery. The two, who had met at King's father's church in Atlanta, became good friends.

In 1955, when Rosa Parks was arrested for refusing to give up her seat on the bus for a white person, King and Abernathy responded by calling for nonviolent confrontation. Their church-based Montgomery Improvement Association organized a black boycott of the city's buses. This 381-day boycott gained national attention for the Civil Rights movement and ended in triumph when the courts issued an injunction against the discriminatory policy.

The success demonstrated both the power of nonviolent confrontation and the effectiveness of the churches as leaders in the fight for racial equality. In January 1957, Abernathy joined King and others in Atlanta to extend their strategy into a larger sphere of influence by forming the

Southern Christian Leadership Conference (SCLC). While he was there, Abernathy's church and home were firebombed, and his family barely escaped with their lives. It was far from the last sacrifice required of him for the cause. Over the next decade, Abernathy and King would be jailed more than a dozen times as they organized and participated in a series of marches, rallies, and sit-in demonstrations for voting rights, economic justice, and equal housing and employment opportunities. In 1961, Abernathy answered King's request to move to Atlanta to join him in coordinating the activities of the SCLC. While serving as vice president of the organization, Abernathy accepted a call as minister at West Hunter Street Baptist in Atlanta.

Those who fought in the vanguard of the Civil Rights movement described a symbiotic relationship between King and Abernathy. King was the strategist of the movement, outlining a vision and ideals. Abernathy was considered the tactician, more concerned with the organization of local events. While King wore a traditional clerical collar and spoke in eloquent tones that stirred the soul, Abernathy wore African prayer beads and spoke in more down-to-earth tones. With his thick Alabama accent, he communicated more effectively than King did with rural and less educated blacks. He often met with hostile groups and won them over prior to King's arrival in a community. King's and Abernathy's efforts culminated in the 1965 Voting Rights Act that struck down long-standing laws restricting black voting rights.

According to an associate quoted by the *New York Times*, "They were the greatest team and Ralph was the unsung hero of the civil rights movement. Martin wouldn't make a decision without him." There was, however, disagreement over the amount of influence each exercised. Some said that Abernathy was the man who held an often chaotic organization together, while others argued that it was King's magnetic presence that did so.

Although far less acclaimed than his friend and coworker Martin Luther King, Jr., Ralph Abernathy exerted a major influence on the Civil Rights movement. *(Birmingham Public Library Department of Archives and Manuscripts)*

King realized that he had created violent opposition and ran the risk of assassination. To head off a potential power struggle in such an event, he named Abernathy his successor should he die. That eventually came to pass when King was shot while standing on a motel balcony in Memphis, Tennessee, in 1968. Abernathy escaped harm that day when he returned to the room to retrieve some items at the time the shooting occurred. It was Abernathy who prayed over King and held his head in the ambulance as it sped to the hospital.

King's assassination thrust Abernathy into the spotlight. Despite his grief, Abernathy stepped up to the challenge. "No man can fill Dr. King's shoes," he admitted. But he added, "Don't ever get it into your mind it was Martin Luther King's dream only. It was Ralph Abernathy's dream, too."

His first order of business was to bring to fruition the Poor People's Campaign in Washington, D.C. This was followed by more desegregation protests, voter registration drives, a 100-mile march in Georgia to protest police brutality, and Operation Breadbasket, an effort to fight hunger in the country.

Abernathy, however, did not have King's charisma. Despite his efforts, the SCLC began to lose momentum in the early 1970s. King's associates began to go their own way; for example, JESSE JACKSON left in December 1971 to form his own Operation PUSH (People United to Save Humanity). By 1973, the SCLC's income had dropped to one-fourth of its peak level, and it was forced to cut back staff. Abernathy attempted to resign in 1973, an action that the board would not accept. He continued in his position until 1977. At that time he ran for Congress from an Atlanta district, but he was defeated.

He experienced a falling out with most civil rights leaders at that time, partially because of his complaints that King was being glorified at the expense of other black leaders who had contributed to the civil rights effort. Abernathy's relations with the civil rights leadership reached bottom in 1980, when he supported conservative candidate Ronald Reagan for president. But he mended fences somewhat by strongly supporting Jesse Jackson's presidential campaigns in 1984 and 1988.

Abernathy continued to preach at Hunter Baptist and stayed active in social campaigns such as the Foundation for Economic Enterprises Development. He died in 1990, a somewhat neglected figure given his nearly equal status with King during the early years of the civil rights campaign.

Further Reading

Abernathy, Donzaleigh. *Partners to History: Martin Luther King, Jr., Ralph Abernathy, and the Civil Rights Movement.* Los Angeles: General Publishing Group, 1999.

Abernathy, Ralph. *And the Walls Came Tumbling Down: An Autobiography.* New York: HarperCollins, 1991.

Fairclough, Adam. *To Redeem the Soul of America: The SCLC and Martin Luther King, Jr.* Athens: University of Georgia Press, 1987.

Powledge, Fred. *Free at Last? The Civil Rights Movement and the People Who Made It.* Boston: Little, Brown, 1991.

Adams, Charles
(1936–) *Baptist pastor*

Charles Adams is a pastor who has been influential in the Civil Rights movement and is widely regarded as one of the most gifted African-American preachers in the country.

He was born on December 13, 1936, in Detroit, Michigan, to Charles and Clifton Verdella Adams. Charles Adams attended Fisk University in Nashville, Tennessee, from 1954 to 1956, but he completed his bachelor's degree at the University of Michigan in 1958. He was ordained by the National Baptist Convention USA in 1961, the year when that body engaged in a spirited struggle between the conservative forces of incumbent president JOSEPH JACKSON of Chicago and supporters of MARTIN LUTHER KING, JR.'s more socially active stance toward civil rights issues. Adams sided with King and the Progressive National Baptist Convention, which broke away from Jackson's group.

In 1962, Adams accepted a call to serve Concord Baptist Church in Boston. A year later, he married Florence Layne; the couple eventually had two children. While serving this congregation, he studied for his advanced divinity degree, which he obtained from the Harvard Divinity School in 1964. Adams built a reputation as a strong preacher and social activist, highlighted by his founding of a community housing project in 1967.

In 1969, Adams returned to his hometown to lead Hartford Memorial Baptist Church, a largely middle-class congregation in Detroit. He took an active role in a wide variety of church and civic positions. Showing a gift for writing, he began editing the *Baptist Progressive* magazine in 1970 and a few years later began writing a regular column for the *Michigan Chronicle* newspaper. In 1971, Adams took over the leadership of the Michigan branch of the Southern Christian Leadership Conference (SCLC), the organization's largest branch. Two years later, he headed the efforts of Operation PUSH (People United to Save Humanity) in Detroit.

Adams's preaching style was somewhat unusual for an African-American preacher in that he read his sermons from carefully prepared manuscripts. Yet his powerful delivery and the eloquent words made his style effective. One fellow minister described Adams as having "the unusual gift of setting a manuscript on fire." Adams also wrote a book entitled *Equality under the Law,* published in 1976. In 1982, he received Harvard Divinity School's prestigious Katzenstein Award for "passionate and helpful interest in the lives of others." From time to time during his career he taught seminary courses at Boston University, Andover Newton Theological Seminary, and Central Baptist Seminary.

Adams was frequently a passionate speaker on political issues relating to moral and religious perceptions. He once addressed the United Nations in opposition to South African apartheid. During the early 1990s, he was a vocal critic of President George H. W. Bush and his Supreme Court nominee conservative justice Clarence Thomas. He was especially critical of what he

saw as Republican Party attempts to claim God's support in the 1992 national elections. "Some of us are trying to make this election a referendum on God," he complained, "as if God belongs to Bush and his party and his ideology."

Adams continues to serve Hartford Baptist and remains in great demand throughout much of the nation as both a preacher and a lecturer.

Further Reading
"Moravian's MLK Program to Feature Rev. Dr. Charles Adams." Moravian College Available online. URL: http://www.moravian.edu/news/releases/2001/003.htm. Downloaded February 17, 2003.

Murphy, Larry G., ed. *Encyclopedia of African American Religious Biography.* New York: Garland Publishing, 1993.

Agyeman, Jaramogi Abebe (Albert Buford Cleage, Jr.)
(1911–2000) *founder of the Pan African Orthodox Christian Church*

Jaramogi Abebe Agyeman was a Congregationalist pastor who broke from mainstream Christianity to found the Pan African Orthodox Christian Church. The success of this effort in the 1970s propelled him into national prominence as a leading theologian in the Black Christian National Movement.

One of seven children of Pearl and Albert Cleage, Sr., he was born Albert Buford Cleage, Jr., on June 13, 1911, in Indianapolis, Indiana. A few years after his birth, the family moved to Kalamazoo, Michigan, and then to Detroit. There his father became the first black physician on the city staff at Detroit General Hospital, in addition to operating his own private practice.

Albert Jr. studied sociology at Wayne State University in Detroit, obtaining his degree in 1937. He worked for a time as a caseworker for the Detroit Department of Public Health until he experienced a call to the ministry and went on to earn his divinity degree at Oberlin School of Theology in Ohio in 1943. Ordained as a minister in the Congregational Church, he served as a pastor in Lexington, Kentucky, and San Francisco, California, before taking over the leadership of St. John's Congregational Church in Springfield, Massachusetts, one of the oldest African-American churches in New England, in 1946. It was there that he became involved in social activism, an interest that increased when he moved back to Detroit in 1951 as pastor at St. Mark's Community Presbyterian church on the city's west side.

At St. Mark's he began to wrestle with racial issues in religion. He started to meld ideas of black nationalist MARCUS GARVEY and the tenets of the Nation of Islam (NOI) with the Bible to create a new theology. In Cleage's view, the Hebrews of the Old Testament were black, and Jesus was the Black Messiah, "the nonwhite leader of a nonwhite people struggling for national liberation against the rule of a white nation."

While moving this direction theologically, Cleage led 300 members of his church to form a new church, Central Congregational Church in 1953. As he developed his ideas in this setting, he became increasingly political and militant in his stances. In 1963, he worked with MARTIN LUTHER KING, JR., to organize a protest "Walk to Freedom" through the city. His most dramatic action occurred on Easter Sunday, 1967, when he displayed an 18-foot painting, "The Black Madonna," in the church sanctuary.

Riots in Detroit that summer and the backlash that followed helped solidify Cleage's increasingly radical views. In 1968, he renamed his church the Shrine of the Black Madonna and espoused his views in the book *The Black Messiah*. In April 1970, he organized the first convention of the Black Christian Nationalist

movement, which he saw as a vehicle to make the church a revolutionary force in social change. By then well out of the mainstream of Christian thought, he severed connections with the United Church of Christ in 1972, and he created a new denomination, the Pan African Orthodox Christian Church. At that time, he changed his name to Jaramogi Abebe Agyeman, a Swahili name meaning "liberator, blessed man, savior of the nation."

During the 1970s and early 1980s, the Shrine of the Black Madonna reached a peak of some 1,000 members, and Agyeman gained recognition as a widely quoted spokesperson on religion and Black Power issues. Religious militancy among blacks waned, however, in the years that followed. By the time of his death on February 20, 2000, the movement he had begun had declined significantly.

Further Reading

Cleage, Albert, Jr. *Black Christian Nationalism.* New York: William Morrow, 1972.
———. *The Black Messiah.* New York: Sheed & Ward, 1968.
"Jaramogi Abebe Agyeman," African American Publishing. Available online. URL: http://www.africanpubs.com/Apps/bios/0273Agyeman Jaramogi.asp. Posted July 2, 2002.
Moses, Wilson Jeremiah. *Black Messiahs and Uncle Toms: The Social and Literary Manipulations of a Religious Myth.* University Park: Pennsylvania State University Press, 1982.

Ali, Noble Drew
(Timothy Drew)
(1886–1929) *founder of the Moorish Science Temple of America*

Noble Drew Ali was the founder of a briefly influential group of African Americans who reawakened pride in their heritage during the 1920s. They disregarded standard history in their claim to be descendants of an ancient Biblical people, though not of the Hebrews.

Timothy Drew was born on January 8, 1886, in North Carolina. Little is known of his early years. Despite growing up in poverty and with little education, he somehow acquired the means to travel across the world. He was particularly intrigued by the relative lack of racial prejudice he found in Islamic and Asian philosophy. Drew became convinced that the path to salvation for blacks lay in rediscovering their proud ethnic origins.

His study of cultures led him to conclude that the ancestors of the black population of the United States were the Moabites of Canaan described in the Bible. These people eventually emerged as the Moors. They created an empire in Morocco, and from there a large group of them immigrated to the United States. In Drew's view, these blacks had lived as a proud people, flying the Moorish flag, until the United States's Continental Congress condemned them to slavery in 1779. Since that time, the truth of the Moorish heritage had been expunged in an effort to rob blacks of their memory and identity.

Drew was working in Newark, New Jersey, when he compiled his research and theories into a religious paradigm. He changed his name to Noble Drew Ali as an expression of his heritage, and he began preaching his views to black passersby on street corners. By 1913, he had gained enough of a following to found the Moorish Science Temple of America in that city. The movement spread rapidly to other cities, although it did not attract great numbers. It found its greatest acceptance in Chicago, where Ali established his headquarters. By 1928, there were 17 Moorish temples in 15 states. Membership required acceptance of the Moorish identity as defined by Ali.

Ali summarized his views in a short work called *The Holy Koran of the Moorish Holy Temple of Science,* not to be confused with Islam's Koran, or Qur'an. His book was intended only for members and was not to be shown to those outside the group. Ali's movement grew to the point where he began to experience problems both in doctrine and in organization. At one point, many members became convinced that the group's Moorish identity cards possessed magical powers and acted defiantly toward civil authorities on that basis. Ali tried hard to discourage the practice. He also brought in a group of more educated blacks to help him run the organization. However, some of them appeared interested only in exploiting the group, marketing Moorish products and reaping the profits. Ali was forced to expel his business manager from the group for such practices. When the manager was killed in 1929, suspicion fell on Ali despite evidence that he was out of town at the time of death, and he was arrested. While in jail, he indicated the extent of his beliefs about his power, when he wrote to his followers, "Though I am now in custody for you and the cause, it is all right and is well for all who believe in me and my father, God."

Ali was released on bond but died a few weeks later on July 20, 1929, under circumstances that have never been explained. His movement faded away soon after.

Further Reading

Baer, Hans A., and Merrill Singer. *African American Religion: Varieties of Protest and Accommodation.* Knoxville: University of Tennessee Press, 2002.

Faucet, Arthur Huff. *Black Gods of the Metropolis: Negro Religious Cults of the Urban North.* New York: Octagon Books, 1970.

Garrity, John A., and Mark C. Carnes, eds. *American National Biography.* Vol. 1. New York: Oxford University Press, 2002.

Moses, Wilson Jeremiah. *Black Messiahs and Uncle Toms: The Social and Literary Manipulations of a Religious Myth.* University Park: Pennsylvania State University Press, 1982.

Allen, Richard

(1760–1831) *cofounder of the African Methodist Episcopal Church*

There was no more influential religious leader in the black community during the formative days of the United States than Richard Allen. An ex-slave who became an itinerant Methodist preacher, Allen was instrumental in forming the first separate African-American religious denomination, the African Methodist Episcopal Church (AME Church), and he served as its first bishop.

Allen was born on February 14, 1760, in Philadelphia, where his family were slaves of a prominent lawyer, Benjamin Chew. When Richard was a child, his family was sold to Stokely Sturgis, who farmed near Dover, Delaware. Sturgis was a relatively humane master, but he eventually ran into financial problems that caused him to sell Richard's mother and three siblings (his father had apparently died by then), separating them from Richard, a brother, and a sister.

At some point, the three remaining siblings were converted to the Methodist faith by an itinerant preacher. Sturgis allowed them to attend religious classes and meetings, which drew scorn from neighbors who predicted that such preoccupation with religion would ruin them as servants. Richard worked extra hard to prove them wrong, which convinced Sturgis that religion made better workers of slaves. He gave permission for Richard to evangelize friends and neighbors and to invite Methodist preachers to speak on his property.

One such preacher, a former slave owner named Freeborn Garretson, gave a stirring antislavery sermon called "Thou Art Weighed in the Balance and Found Wanting," which convinced Sturgis that slavery was wrong. He agreed to let Richard hire himself out for work so that he could buy his freedom. It took Richard several years of hard work, sawing logs and driving a

Richard Allen was the founder and first bishop of the African Methodist Episcopal Church, the first African-American religious denomination. *(Library of Congress)*

wagon for the Continental army to raise the necessary $2,000. Sometime around 1781, he purchased his freedom, taking on the last name of Allen to indicate his free status.

One attractive feature of the Methodist Church for blacks was that it allowed them to serve as "licensed exhorters," who were basically unordained preachers. After gaining his freedom, Allen spent the next six years walking through the countryside exhorting on the Methodist circuit. He went as far south as South Carolina and then back up to New Jersey, New York, and Pennsylvania, preaching to both black and white audiences. When he needed money, he would simply take up jobs such as sawing wood and shoemaking.

While he was working near Philadelphia, Allen was asked to preach to the black members of racially mixed St. George's Episcopal Church in the city. He had viewed Philadelphia as just one stop in his wandering ministry, but he soon found a calling among the large unchurched black population of the city. Using St. George's as a headquarters for his ministry, he would preach as often as four or five times a day in public places throughout the city. This ministry earned him a position as assistant minister at St. George's in 1786, although he had to work as a shoemaker to support his family. By the end of the year, black membership at the church had risen to 42 members.

Although St. George's had mixed membership, it was far from integrated. Blacks were not allowed to be buried in the church's cemetery, and they had to worship at 5 A.M. on Sunday so as not to interfere with the white services. Concerned about this second-class status, Allen proposed forming a separate black church. This met with heated opposition from the white elder of the church who, according to Allen, "used very degrading and insulting language to us to try and prevent us from going." Since few of his supporters backed a separate church, Allen set aside the idea.

He did, however, continue discussions about the needs of African-American church people with his friend ABSALOM JONES. In April 1787, the two of them joined a group of ex-slaves and Quaker philanthropists to form the Free African Society, a nondenominational group that offered fellowship and social assistance to free blacks. But when the group adopted some Quaker practices, such as 15 minutes of silence at all meetings, Allen, a staunch Methodist, withdrew from the society.

Meanwhile, conditions at St. George's grew more oppressive. The rapid increase in African-American members made the white membership uncomfortable. They ended the practice of black services and then undertook a major remodeling of the church that included a new gallery that would provide separate seating for blacks. This led to a famous incident in which Allen, Jones, and several other blacks were interrupted in

midprayer during a service and forced to move to the new gallery.

The outrage among the black community revived interest in the idea of a separate black church. The Free African Society led the fundraising for the proposed African Church of Philadelphia. A committee was formed to implement the plan, and Allen was authorized to find a lot for the new church. He did so, but after he agreed to a sale price, the committee found a more favorable location. Allen refused to renege on the agreement and so had to purchase the property in his own name. His final break with the project came over a disagreement as to the affiliation of the new church. Most of the black churchgoers had grown up in the Episcopalian community, which had been active among blacks in Philadelphia since the 1740s. They voted to retain their affiliation with this church, with only Allen and Jones dissenting. "I informed them that I could not be anything but a Methodist, as I was born and awakened under them," declared Allen. Furthermore, he firmly believed the less rigid, more expressively emotional Methodist Church was better suited to the needs and temperament of African Americans. When the new church, known as St. Thomas's African Episcopal Church, offered him its pastorate, he declined.

Instead, he gathered his small group of Methodist stalwarts and organized a black Methodist church. On May 5, 1794, they completed plans to purchase an old blacksmith shop and move it to the location that Allen had bought. After a little remodeling, Bethel Methodist Episcopal Church was ready for worship. Allen's influence helped the membership to grow rapidly in this predominantly black neighborhood. Francis Asbury, the first bishop of the Methodist Church in the United States, lent his blessing to the operation by dedicating the church in July of that year. The church prospered, growing from a handful of members at its inception to 121 in 1795 and 457 by 1803. The converted wooden blacksmith shop was replaced by a permanent wood structure in 1805.

For a time, Bethel submitted to the governance of the white-dominated national denomination. On June 6, 1798, Bishop Asbury ordained Allen, making him the first officially ordained black deacon in the church. As late as 1807, the Bethel congregation declared its loyalty to the Methodist Church. Over time, however, Allen and his followers grew uncomfortable under this system, particularly when the Methodists began to soften some of their abolitionist positions. The precariousness of black existence among whites was demonstrated when Allen was captured in 1806 under the harsh provisions of the Fugitive Slave Law and nearly sold into slavery. Allen came to see the need to break away from the national Methodist body to free blacks from possible prejudice, so that they could "call any brother that appears to us adequate to the task to preach or exhort as a local preacher, without the interference of the Conference."

Over the next decade, Allen led the fight to separate from the Methodists. Opposition from the white church led to a legal battle over church ownership that was resolved in Allen's favor in 1816. Bethel then hosted representatives of four other congregations from Maryland, New Jersey, Delaware, and Pennsylvania that year to form the AME Church. On April 11, 1816, Allen was consecrated as the first bishop of the denomination.

This first black denomination in the United States was significant in its establishment of a separate identity for African-American churchgoers. Since their disagreements with the Methodists were not based on doctrinal issues, they used the Methodist Episcopal Church's Book of Discipline with a few alterations, such as increased emphasis on the struggle against slavery. Allen hewed strictly to the Methodist views on strict religious discipline and rejection of activities such as drinking and gambling, yet allowed for a wider range of emotions in worship for a people who had long been repressed by slavery.

Under Allen's leadership, the AME Church established a solid foundation. It was able to develop a strong group of young pastors and to expand throughout the North and eventually into the southern United States, Canada, the West Indies, and Africa. It gave blacks a free and independent voice in society and set up a recognized organization to provide social welfare, nurture spiritual development, and give aid to runaway slaves. Allen's leadership was also crucial to the establishment of schools for African Americans. In 1795, he opened a day school that accommodated 60 children. In 1804, he founded the Society of Free People of Colour for Promoting the Instruction and School Education of Children of African Descent. By 1811, 11 black schools were operating in Philadelphia. After initially promoting plans for settling free blacks in Africa, Allen came to reject such schemes and urged blacks to make a place for themselves in American society. In 1827 he declared, "This land which we have watered with our tears and our blood is now our mother country."

Because of his aggressive nature and uncompromising views, Allen could be difficult to work with. It was largely because of him that an angry group split off from the AME Church, forming the African Methodist Episcopal Zion Church (AMEZ Church). But he also served the church for many years without a salary and paid the church's debts from his own pocket. Long before his death on March 26, 1831, he was regarded as among the most influential black leaders in the nation.

Further Reading

Allen, Richard. *The Life, Experience, and Gospel Labors.* Nashville, Tenn.: Abingdon Press, 1960.

Allen, Richard, and Absalom Jones. "A Narrative of the Black People During the Late Awful Calamity in Philadelphia (1794)." In *Pamphlets of Protest: An Anthology of Early African American Protest*

Literature, 1790–1860, edited by Richard Newman et al. 32–43. New York: Routledge, 2001.

Cheek, H. Lee. "Original Diversity: Bishops Allen,
Asbury and Black Methodism." *Methodist History*
(April 1997): 188–91.

George, Carol V. R. *Segregated Sabbaths: Richard Allen
and the Emergence of Independent Black Churches,
1760–1840*. New York: Oxford, 1973.

Litwack, Leon, and August Meier, eds. *Black Leaders
of the Nineteenth Century*. Urbana: University of
Illinois Press: 1988.

Young, Henry J. *Major Black Religious Leaders,
1755–1940*. Nashville, Tenn.: Abingdon, 1977.

Anderson, Leafy
(Mother Leafy Anderson)
(1887–1927) *Spiritualist movement leader*

One of the more enigmatic figures in African-
American religion was Leafy Anderson, commonly known to followers as Mother Leafy
Anderson. She was influential in establishing a
fast-growing movement of Spiritualist churches
in the South in the early 20th century.

Few details are known of Anderson's personal life. Evidence exists that she was born in
Wisconsin in 1887, and was of mixed Native
American and African-American blood. By the
time she reached her 20s she was heavily involved in what came to be known as the Spiritualist movement. Introduced in the mid-19th
century, Spiritualism involved some form of edi-
fication through communication with spirits of
the dead. A version of this religion became popular among a small group of blacks in the first
two decades of the 20th century.

Anderson is known to have established the
Eternal Life Christian Spiritual Church in
Chicago around 1913. Seven years later, she
moved to New Orleans to lay the groundwork
for the church in the South. One of the most
prominent features of her church was a reliance
on a spiritual contact with a Native American

named Black Hawk, who had at least some connection with the historical Indian leader of that
name. Black Hawk was revered by her church
and included among rituals and other religious
observances. Anderson taught that Black Hawk
was the saint for the South while White Hawk
was the saint for the church in the North. She
also invoked other spiritual guides, such as a
doctor and minister called Father John, Queen
Esther, and the Virgin Mary.

On October 25, 1920, Anderson obtained
a Louisiana state charter for her group. Acceptance in New Orleans was a different matter,
however. Anderson and her group were ostra-
cized and put under police surveillance in
the church's formative months. At one point,
Mother Anderson was arrested. The climate
soon changed, according to supporters, because
of her accurate spiritual reading of the life of
the judge who was trying her case. Her New
Orleans church developed a large membership,
and she established an association of Spiritualist churches by personally forming congregations in Biloxi, Mississippi; Houston, Texas;
Little Rock, Arkansas; Memphis, Tennessee;
and Pensacola, Florida.

Part of the movement's appeal had to do
with demographics. Hers was one of the few
churches at the time that provided significant
leadership opportunities for women. During her
lifetime, virtually all the leaders of the movement, most of whom she trained, were women.
As one of her students reported,

> She taught healin' and prophesyin' and callin'
> up spirits. Of course, most of 'em didn't ever
> finish cause everybody ain't got the power.
> But most of the Mothers in New Orleans
> now learned what they know from Mother
> Anderson.

The Spiritualist movement was also unique
in that it eliminated many racial barriers—both
whites and blacks joined her movement and
sought her out for personal readings.

Anderson's enterprise was financially rewarding. She charged $1 per lesson to her students and made much more on spiritual readings. When she died suddenly of complications from a cold in December 1927, her church rapidly faded away. However, the more mystical religious impulses of Spiritualism that she fostered were infused into a number of churches after her death.

Further Reading

Murphy, Larry G. *Down by the Riverside: Readings on African American Religion.* New York: New York University Press, 2000.

Smith, Jesse Carney, ed. *Notable Black American Women.* Vol. 2. Detroit, Mich.: Gale Research, 1996.

Anthony, Wendell

(1950–) *clergy, leader of the National Association for the Advancement of Colored People*

Wendell Anthony has been a dynamic force for religious renewal and social justice in Detroit and has served as head of the largest National Association for the Advancement of Colored People (NAACP) branch in the United States.

He was born in St. Louis, Missouri, in 1950, to parents who divorced when he was two. His mother, Ida, married James Patton and moved to Detroit, where both worked for the post office and enjoyed a comfortable home on the city's west side. Anthony's involvement as an activist leader began in elementary school when he led a student walkout over what they considered an unfair punishment. As president of the Central High School student body he was an outspoken advocate for inclusion of an African-American history curriculum. He also took an active part in African-American efforts to help the city recover from the devastating riots and resulting racial wounds that scarred Detroit in 1967.

Anthony graduated from high school the following year and enrolled at Wayne State University in Detroit. During that time, he took a trip to Ghana and Liberia that was a turning point in his life. "It just struck me so powerfully," he recalled. "Here were black folks running the government, the schools, everything. . . . I had never seen black folks in charge of everything before." Inspired, Anthony began to develop ideas on promoting black self-reliance while working as a coordinator of community outreach during his college years.

He obtained a degree in social work from Wayne State in 1976. However, influenced by Rev. James Wadsworth, his mentor and pastor of the Fellowship Chapel that Anthony attended, he pursued a career in ministry. Married and a father by this time, he achieved ordination in 1981. Shortly thereafter, he was called as an associate pastor to Fellowship Chapel to work with Wadsworth. At the same time, he continued his studies at Marygrove College in Detroit, with special emphasis on using the church as a vehicle for reform and uplifting the black community. Anthony obtained a master's degree in 1984, but the effort contributed to the breakup of his marriage and a resulting bitter custody battle over their two children.

When Wadsworth died of cancer in 1986, Anthony took over the congregation. He proved to be an inspirational speaker. "You wring yourself out to drain yourself so that the people can absorb you," he once said of his preaching style. Anthony initiated a major renewal at the church, key to which was the creation of Isutha, a male mentoring program. Due to this and other programs aimed at this group, Fellowship Chapel drew an unusual number of young men and quadrupled its membership over the course of Anthony's ministry. In later years, he initiated a similar program for young women.

Anthony's reputation as a minister of action led to increasingly high-profile responsibilities. In 1990, he was selected to be among a small group of pastors to meet with newly released South African leader Nelson Mandela. At about the same time, he took a leadership role in a boycott of the *Detroit Free Press* and the local American Broadcasting Corporation (ABC) television affiliate for sensationalist stories that he felt exacerbated racial tensions in the city. Many observers credited the boycott with helping to usher in a new sensitivity among the press and an easing of racial hostilities.

In 1993, Anthony was elected head of the Detroit chapter of the NAACP. He has continued to command a high profile in the city, taking black Detroit residents on an annual pilgrimage to Africa, leading a march in Detroit (reportedly drawing 250,000 people) to commemorate a similar march led by the late MARTIN LUTHER KING, JR., actively recruiting businesses to the inner city, and being arrested in 1998 while protesting the U.S. Supreme Court's failure to hire black law clerks.

Further Reading

"Detroit NAACP Reacts to Lott Resignation," *Detroit Now News.* Available online. URL: http://www.detnow.com. Posted December 20, 2002.

Oblander, David G. *Contemporary Black Biography.* Vol. 25. Detroit, Mich.: Gale Research, 2000.

Arnett, Benjamin William

(1838–1906) *African Methodist Episcopal Church historian, educator, bishop*

Despite limited formal education, Benjamin Arnett enjoyed a remarkable career as a teacher, politician, historian, and the 17th bishop of the African Methodist Episcopal (AME) Church. He was commonly recognized as the most influential African American in the administration of President William McKinley (1897–1901).

Arnett was born on March 6, 1838, in Brownville, Pennsylvania. He described his eth-

nic background as "8 parts Negro, 6 parts Scotch, 1 part Indian, and 1 part Irish." His education took place in a one-room school taught by his uncle. Arnett's father was an active AME Church member who bought the lot on which the local church was constructed. Benjamin joined the church a few weeks before his 18th birthday, about the time he began working as a laborer on wagons and steamboats.

At the age of 20, Arnett's occupational opportunities were limited when a malignant tumor resulted in a leg being amputated. He decided to become a teacher, and over the next several years he taught himself the profession without benefit of college. He qualified for a teacher's certificate in 1863, which made him the only black teacher in Fayette County, Pennsylvania. The following year, Arnett became active in Frederick Douglas's Faith and Hope League of Equal Rights, organizing six branches in Pennsylvania. He then moved on to teach in Washington, D.C., where he experienced a call to the ministry.

Arnett obtained a preaching license in the AME Church in 1865 and worked his way up to deacon and elder while serving various urban parishes in Ohio. During the 1860s, he became active in both state politics, as a member of the Republican Party, and the national church organizations. In 1872, he was chosen as a delegate from Ohio to the AME Church's first general conference. Four years later he was elected general secretary of that body, and, in 1880, he added the duties of financial secretary. It was in that capacity that he produced his most lasting contribution, a report called simply *The Budget.* Arnett filled his report not only with financial data but also with facts and cultural history of the AME Church. Subsequent annual issues followed his lead and provided similar useful historical information.

At a time when few blacks were granted positions of authority over whites, Arnett's competence and conciliatory manner were so evident that in 1872 his white peers voted him foreman of a jury. In 1879, he was named chaplain of the Ohio State Legislature. That whetted his appetite for taking the bold step of running for political office himself. In 1886, he ran for the state legislature in Ohio and won election by six votes. During his single term, he played a key role in writing legislation that abolished Ohio's discriminatory laws against blacks.

At the end of his term, he moved back into the ecclesiastical world, taking on the duties as a bishop of the AME Church in South Carolina. While there, he was portrayed as an inspirational figure in a popular biography entitled *Poor Ben: A Real Life Story*. He went on to serve as a bishop in the Midwest, East, and Northwest. A longtime friend of William McKinley from their early days in Ohio politics, Arnett presented President McKinley with the Bible upon which he took his oath of office. This friendship led to

Arnett's reputation as the most powerful black influence in the administration.

Arnett was active in the International Sunday School Convention and served as a chaplain in the Spanish-American War before his death from urinary poisoning on October 9, 1906.

Further Reading

Dickerson, Dennis. *The Historiographers of the African Methodist Episcopal Church.* Nashville, Tenn.: AME Publishing House, 1992.

Haskins, Jim. *Distinguished African-American Political and Government Leaders.* Phoenix, Ariz.: Oryx Press, 1999.

Kealing, H. T. "Bishop Arnett." *AME Church Review* (January 1907): 282.

Melton, J. Gordon. *Religious Leaders of America.* 2d ed. Detroit, Mich.: Gale Research, 1999.

Smith, Jesse Carney, ed. *Notable Black American Men.* Vol. 1. Detroit, Mich.: Gale Research, 1999.

B

Barnes, Carnella Jamison
(1911–1997) *Disciples of Christ clergy, community leader*

Carnella Barnes was a pioneer in achieving ordination two decades before women were generally accepted into the ministry. She went on to give a lifetime of distinguished service to her community and her denomination.

Barnes was born Carnella Jamison on January 11, 1911, in Edward, Mississippi. She was the youngest of eight children of Anna and Samuel Jamison, who had little money but grew ample supplies of food on their small farm. After her mother's death when Carnella was five, she was raised by her father, who eventually remarried. Jamison was steeped in the Baptist religion; she later remembered her first library books as collections of Bible stories.

At the age of 14, she was sent to the Southern Christian Institute, a mostly white boarding school. Although he could afford to pay her tuition, her father insisted that his youngest daughter work through school in preparation for the realities of life. She made butter and cream in the school's dairy through most of her schooling. Jamison received an associate degree in education and began teaching elementary school. The pay was so poor for someone with her qualifications, however, that after three years she returned to school at Talledega College in Alabama on scholarship. The degree she obtained allowed her to increase her salary when she returned to teaching.

As a young adult, Jamison became active in the predominantly white Disciples of Christ Church. Her work as president of the denomination's first national youth movement provided her with contacts that led to a job with the United Christian Mission Society in Indianapolis. While working there, she anticipated by two decades the celebrated Montgomery bus boycott of the mid-1950s when, despite being repeatedly threatened with arrest, she refused to move from a whites-only railroad car to a "colored" car. At about this time, Jamison also enrolled at Chicago Theological Seminary. She earned a master's degree in religious education, and in 1939 was one of the few women of her time to be ordained.

Jamison's life, however, took a turn toward the secular in 1945, when she moved to Los Angeles to accept a position as executive secretary of the Avalon Community Center, the city's first such center. While performing that job, she met and married Anderson Barnes, with whom she had a set of triplets. She continued her education at the University of California, Los Angeles, and the University of Southern California, and in 1952 created a stir by running for the Los Angeles School Board. Despite race baiting by opponents, she garnered more than 100,000 votes in a losing effort.

Barnes embarked on yet another new career in 1962 when she joined the newly created Department of Senior Citizens Affairs in Los Angeles, where she worked her way up to deputy director. In that capacity she organized the first American Association of Retired Persons (AARP) chapter in Los Angeles. She left the job in 1976 and served as a program consultant for Los Angeles County and then program director for Respite Care/Transportation, another program for seniors. Barnes died on January 4, 1997.

During her lifetime, Barnes was inundated with honors, including Disciples of Christ Disciple of the Year, and the Rosa Parks Award from the Southern Christian Leadership Conference. Her work as president of the Los Angeles Church Women United and of the International Christian Women's Fellowship bore witness to her remark, "Service to and with others has been my way of life."

Further Reading

Melton, J. Gordon. *Religious Leaders of America.* 2d ed. Detroit, Mich.: Gale Research, 1999.

Murphy, Larry G., ed. *Encyclopedia of African American Religious Biography.* New York: Garland Publishing, 1993.

Barrow, Willie B.
("The Little Warrior," Willie Taplan)

(1924–   ) *Church of God clergy, religious organizer, executive*

Willie Barrow, one of the first black women to earn a doctor of divinity degree, was one of the most visible religious leaders in the fight against hunger and poverty in the United States.

She was born Willie Taplan on December 7, 1924, in Burton, Texas, where her father, Nelson Taplan, served a rural parish as a Church of God

minister. She grew up in Texas through high school, where she was active in her father's church, and then attended Warner Pacific School of Theology in Portland, Oregon. Far ahead of her time as a woman exercising leadership, she was elected president of the school's student council, and along with her studies, found time to start a black Church of God congregation. Taplan went on to attend the Moody Bible Institute in Chicago, spent some time at the Central Conservatory of Music, and traveled to Liberia, where she earned her doctorate from the University of Monrovia.

Returning to the United States, she worked as a social justice activist with the National Urban League in 1943, with the National Council of Negro Women in 1945, and in various parishes in the Church of God. In the late 1940s, she married Clyde Barrow, national labor leader from Honduras, with whom she had one son.

While serving as an associate pastor at Vernon Park Church of God in Chicago, Barrow became a leader in Christian social action causes. She began working with JESSE JACKSON in the 1960s and fought so tenaciously for social justice that she earned the nickname "the Little Warrior." Her top priority was hunger, and in 1969 she and Jackson organized a campaign to publicize the existence of hunger in Chicago. Her efforts won the admiration of the city, and she was named 1969 Chicago Woman of the Year. Barrow continued her fight against hunger by serving as the state coordinator of the Illinois Coalition Against Hunger and as project director of the Special Hunger Task Force of Operation Breadbasket, a service of the Southern Christian Leadership Conference.

In December 1971, Jesse Jackson formed Operation PUSH (People United to Save Humanity). Barrow threw herself wholeheartedly into this effort to promote the rights of the poor and to invest in the black community. She provided leadership in a boycott of a national chain of grocery stores over its hiring practices and in a 1973 protest against budget cuts in social services by the Nixon administration. Barrow rose to the position of national vice president of Operation PUSH in the mid-1970s. She served as Jackson's national deputy campaign and road manager in his presidential campaigns of 1984 and 1988, and was one of several who took over from Jackson as acting head of Operation PUSH during his 1984 campaign for the U.S. presidency. Two years later, she accepted the position on a permanent basis and served as president until her retirement in 1989.

At that point, she continued to work as a consultant on social justice issues. In describing her motivation, she said, "My life's breath is dealing with problems before these problems become crises."

Further Reading

Smith, Jesse Carney, ed. *Notable Black American Women*. Vol. 1. Detroit, Mich.: Gale Research, 1992.

"Willie Barrow." The History Makers. Available online. URL: http://www.thehistorymakers.com. Downloaded February 17, 2003.

Bell, Ralph S.

(1934–   ) *Evangelical Free Church evangelist*

Ralph Bell has been a major force in one of the nation's longest lived and best-known national ministries, the Billy Graham Association.

He was born in St. Catharines, Ontario, on May 13, 1934, to Archibald and Cecilia Bell. For most of his childhood, he harbored dreams of being a professional athlete, a dream made even more enticing by Jackie Robinson's sensational shattering of major league baseball's color barrier in 1947. Bell's high school baseball team played for the Canadian national title, and professional scouts followed his progress. At the age

of 16, against the wishes of his parents, Bell left home to play in the minor leagues.

Shortly thereafter, however, he listened to a sermon by an evangelist that pierced him to the core. When the preacher spoke of sinners in need of salvation, Bell has said, "I realized God was talking to me." Bell decided to dedicate his life to bringing the message he had heard to other people. He enrolled at the Moody Bible Institute in Chicago in 1954 and completed his course work there in 1957. After marrying Jean Overstreet that year, he pursued further studies at Taylor University in Upland, Indiana. He remained there until called to be pastor of West Washington Community Church in Los Angeles, in 1960.

Three years later, he learned that the famous Billy Graham Crusade was planning a visit to Los Angeles. Bell involved himself in the coordination of the crusade with local churches. Inspired by the quality of the crusade, he kept in contact with the organization even after it left town. Later that year he completed work on his master's degree at Fuller Theological Seminary in Pasadena, California.

In 1964, Bell took on a huge new challenge when he accepted a call to be chaplain at the Los Angeles County Jail. The work started him on a lifelong career of ministry to prison inmates around the county. At the same time, freed from the duties that went with parish ministry, he began to involve himself in a great number of community projects and ecumenical Christian programs.

Looking to expand his ministry, Billy Graham personally recruited Bell to join him as an associate minister in his organization in 1965. Bell traveled all over the world for Graham, joining him on larger crusades and going off on his own for smaller efforts. At the same time, he headed the association's expansion of its ministry into prison work.

Bell's style of ministry follows the standard framework of Billy Graham. The focus is on helping people discover a personal relationship with Jesus Christ. Inspirational sermons and music are followed by calls for public confession of the newfound faith. At the same time, Bell is concerned that the crusades be more than a short-lived spiritual high. He has spent weeks on location of upcoming campaigns, helping to coordinate local efforts with the national organization, and laying the groundwork for community action. "I have developed a strong belief in the important role the local church should play in meeting the needs of the sick, elderly, disadvantaged, and handicapped in the community," he has said.

Although a member of the Evangelical Free Church, he has no interest in promoting his denomination; instead he encourages people to find a church that best fits their own needs. In contrast to highly publicized scandals involving other high-profile evangelists, Bell has lived modestly and maintains a reputation for open and honest service.

Further Reading

Bigelow, Barbara Carlisle. *Contemporary Black Biography.* Vol. 5. Detroit, Mich.: Gale Research, 1994.
"Ralph Bell Celebration." The Billy Graham Evangelistic Association. Available online. URL: http://www.billygraham.org. Posted March 25, 2003.

Beman, Amos
(1812–1874) *pioneer Congregational clergy*

Amos Beman was one of the first African Americans active in the Congregational Church, serving as a pastor in New England for more than 35 years.

Beman was born in 1812 in Colchester, Connecticut, where his father, Jehiel Beman, worked as shoemaker and later as a preacher in the newly formed African Methodist Episcopal Zion Church (AMEZ Church). In 1830, the church assigned Jehiel Beman to the Cross Street AMEZ Church in Middletown, Connecticut. Amos took an active part in his father's favorite causes, particular during his late teens. In 1831, he joined an organization opposed to the American Colonization Society's efforts to relocate American blacks to Liberia. Two years later, he served as secretary of his father's Black Home Temperance Society.

Following the admission of a black student to Wesleyan University in Middletown, Connecticut, Beman planned to enroll at the school. His hopes were dashed, though, when Wesleyan abruptly reversed course and barred blacks from class just before Beman could begin. One Wesleyan student, Samuel Doyle, tried to right the injustice by tutoring Beman in his room. But hostility from fellow students forced him to move the lessons off campus and then to halt them altogether.

Instead, Beman walked to Hartford and obtained certification to teach in the city's only school for blacks, run by black members of the Congregational Church. During his four years as a teacher he debated going into the ministry. Finally, with encouragement from AMEZ minister Hosea Easton, he enrolled at Oneida Theological Seminary, near Utica, New York. Among his classmates at the school were ALEXANDER CRUMMELL and HENRY HIGHLAND GARNET. Beman, however, could not keep pace with his class due to lack of funds, and he dropped out after one year.

Beman returned to his teaching job but continued to pursue other avenues to ministry. He obtained a license to preach in 1838 and was sent to Temple Street African Congregational Church in New Haven, Connecticut, which had been founded in 1829 as the first black Congregational church in the country. He was ordained as an evangelist the following year and, despite his lack of theological education, was installed as the congregation's pastor in 1841.

Although he had changed denominations, Beman carried on his father's strict moral code and abhorrence of drinking. He required abstinence from drinking as a condition of membership in his church and served as vice president of the Connecticut State Temperance and Moral Reform Society. His skills as a leader and public speaker were recognized nationally, and he was chosen president of the 1843 National Black Convention in Buffalo, New York. He was a regular columnist in black newspapers and a social activist who made his church a part of the Underground Railroad. Yet despite his high profile and abolitionist views, he managed to keep on such good terms with whites that he experienced no incidents of the anti-black violence so common in Connecticut at that time.

Beman was much in demand as a speaker and traveled frequently in New England. He helped organized black Congregational churches in Portland, Maine, and Pittsfield, Massachusetts. After losing his wife and two children to a typhoid epidemic in 1856–57, he finally moved on to the Abyssinian Congregational Church that he had founded in Portland. There he married a white widow, which caused a temporary storm of outrage that he calmly weathered with no long-term effects. In his first two years at the church, membership tripled.

Beman left soon afterward to take a position with the American Missionary Association. In 1861, he returned to parish ministry, serving small congregations in Long Island, New York, and Cleveland, Ohio, before returning to Connecticut in 1869. He served as chaplain of the Connecticut Senate in 1872 and died in 1874.

Further Reading

Swift, David E. *Black Prophets of Justice: Activist Clergy before the Civil War.* Baton Rouge: Louisiana State University Press, 1989.

Ben-Israel, Ben Ami
(Ben Carter)
(1940–   ) *founder of the Black Hebrews*

Ben Ami Ben-Israel is the founder of the largest contemporary group of adherents of the Black Hebrew religious movement.

He was born Ben Carter in 1940 in Chicago, Illinois. Although he was raised in the Baptist faith, as a young man he became intrigued by the Black Hebrew teachings that gained popularity among some African Americans in the late 19th century. According to this point of view, people of African descent, not Jews, are the true descendants of the Israelites of the Bible. The argument was based on a sociological theory that West African cultures were of Hebrew origin. Largely confined to large urban centers, the Black Hebrews practiced traditional Jewish rituals and celebrated Jewish holidays.

While employed in Chicago as a bus driver and foundry worker, Carter became deeply involved in this movement. In 1966, he reported that an angel came to him in a vision and told him that he was to lead African Americans back to the promised land. Carter was not convinced at first that this was indeed his destiny, but as he shared the vision with the Black Hebrews of the A-Beta Cultural Center on Chicago's South Side, he came to believe this was his calling.

"We are the Messianic people whom the prophecies have foretold would return to the land," he declared. He cited Genesis 15:13: "Then the LORD said to Abram, Know of a surety that your descendants will be sojourners in a land that is not theirs, and will be slaves there, and they will be oppressed for four hundred years." For Carter, who changed his name to Ben Ami Ben-Israel, that prophesy had been fulfilled in the African bondage in the Americas. Now it was time for black Americans to redeem God's promise.

Ben-Israel saw a return to the West African empire as the first step on the way to redemption. In 1967, between 200 and 300 people answered his call to move to Liberia to set up a kibbutz. The attempt was short-lived, however; within two years, more than half the group had returned to the United States.

But Ben-Israel continued to the next step—the return to the Promised Land of Israel. Again, he experienced major problems as the group had difficulty obtaining residency visas from Israel. But Ben-Israel and 38 followers persevered until they obtained temporary work permits. Eventually they were joined by others, and about 100 of them founded a colony known as Dimona in the Negev desert.

By 1971, the colony had grown to more than 300 members. Many of them had come over from the United States on tourist visas and then stayed. The rapidly growing colony was virtually ignored by the authorities until 1979, when reports circulated that Ben-Israel was the leader of a dangerous cult. The Israeli government then opposed the colony and in the early 1980s won a Supreme Court ruling that the Black Hebrews had no legal standing as Jews, and so had no automatic citizenship or work permits. The group appealed to the U.S. government for help. In 1994, an agreement was negotiated granting the group permanent resident status. The colony has remained stable at about 1,500 members, and the Black Hebrews number several thousand in the United States.

Further Reading

Mabunda, L. Mpho. *Contemporary Black Biography.* Vol. 11. Detroit, Mich.: Gale Research, 1996.

Melton, J. Gordon. *Religious Leaders of America.* 2d ed. Detroit, Mich.: Gale Research, 1999.

Moses, Wilson Jeremiah. *Black Messiahs and Uncle Toms: The Social and Literary Manipulations of a Religious Myth.* University Park: Pennsylvania State University Press, 1982.

Murphy, Larry G., ed. "Black Judaism in the United States." In *Down by the Riverside: Readings on African American Religion.* New York: New York University Press, 2000.

Bethune, Mary McLeod
(1875–1955) *educator*

Few African-American women of any era achieved more national recognition and influence than Mary McLeod Bethune. She transformed a thwarted desire to be a missionary into a career of service in education.

Mary Jane McLeod was born on July 10, 1875, the 15th of 17 children of ex-slaves Samuel and Patsy McLeod. She was raised on the small Mayesville, South Carolina, farm they had purchased from their owners, in the midst of a large extended family. Hard work was expected of the children, and at the age of nine, Mary picked 250 pounds of cotton a day, and pulled a plow after the death of the family mule.

Education was important to Samuel and Patsy, but the public schools in their area did not admit black children. Although the family was Methodist, they sent Mary to Trinity Presbyterian Mission School for Negroes, the only available school in the area. Talented both musically and in formal speaking, she attracted the interest of school founder Emma Wilson, who put her in contact with a benefactor, Mary Crissmon. Crissmon, a teacher by profession, supported McLeod as she went on to Scotia Seminary in Concord, North Carolina, from which she graduated in 1894.

Convinced that her life's work was to be a missionary, she enrolled at the Moody Bible Institute in Chicago. But upon completing the course work, she was rejected for duty because of her age. Dejected, she settled for a teaching job at the Haines Institute in Augusta, Georgia. The school was run by Lucy Laney, who convinced McLeod that she could serve God as well in southern U.S. schools as in Africa.

After a brief stint at Haines, she moved on to teach at Kendall Institute in Sumter, South Carolina. There she met and married Albertus Bethune. When he was offered a teaching position in Savannah, Georgia, Mary followed him. Although they had a young son, she persuaded her husband to let her take a teaching position at a missionary school in Palatka, Florida. There she began a long career of organizing and administering schools, starting at a Presbyterian school in 1900, and an independent school two years later.

On a subsequent visit to Daytona Beach, Florida, Mary McLeod Bethune discovered a

Thwarted in her dream to be a missionary, Mary McLeod Bethune made the education of blacks her new mission field. *(Library of Congress)*

woeful lack of educational opportunities for black children. She responded by founding the Daytona Normal and Industrial Institute for Negro Girls, which she patterned after her own experience at Scotia Seminary. The venture required courage and a strong faith, especially when only five girls enrolled for the first session. Bethune, however, proved a magnificent saleswoman and fund-raiser. She enlisted the help of two black churches and made successful appeals to a number of wealthy individuals who wintered in Daytona Beach. With a zeal that consumed her marriage, she gathered money, bought land, and constructed buildings. Within two years, the school boasted 250 students, including its first boys. Bethune presided over her school with a gentle but firm hand. Insisting on proper respect, she refused to answer when addressed as "Mary."

Bethune's efforts created a ripple effect that benefited the entire community. Many of her students taught in mission schools in camps for turpentine workers. When she discovered that the local hospital would not admit black patients, much less help train her students to be nurses, Bethune started the McLeod Hospital. As with her other endeavors, it met with phenomenal success. By 1914, the hospital/school had expanded to more than 300 students and was one of the few black schools in the area to offer a high school curriculum. Several years later, her school merged with a nearby men's school to form Bethune-Cookman College, which continues to thrive today. Indicative of Bethune's religious emphasis in education, the college's motto was: Enter to Learn, Depart to Serve. So highly regarded was Bethune that Presidents Coolidge and Hoover both enlisted her as an adviser on black educational issues.

A woman of boundless energy, Bethune expanded her service efforts from education into a vast array of public service. Over the years she accepted major volunteer positions with the Red Cross, War Relief, and patriotic organizations.

She served two terms as president of the *National Association of Women* from 1924 through 1928. Sensing a need for women to be more active politically, she founded the National Council of Negro Women in 1935, and served as its president for more than a decade.

Bethune's work caught the attention of Eleanor Roosevelt, and the two became friends. This friendship led to Bethune's appointment as director of Minority Affairs in President Franklin Roosevelt's National Youth Administration. It also provided her with greater access to the president than any previous black woman. Her influence on the Roosevelt administration led to the increased hiring of blacks in the federal government and more federal interest in racial issues. She exerted her own influence in challenging some of the injustices of her time. When, due to her prominent status, she was admitted to prestigious Johns Hopkins University Hospital for sinus surgery, she used the occasion to break the school's color barrier by insisting that black physicians be on hand to observe the procedure.

Bethune suffered increasingly from asthma, which forced her to curtail her activities and travels, and to eventually relinquish her post as president of Bethune-Cookman College in 1942. She officially retired from public service in 1950, but retirement did not cause her to abandon her life's mission, as she devoted much of her time to establishing the Bethune Foundation.

Bethune died of a heart attack on May 18, 1955. As evidence of the esteem in which she was held, she received a dozen honorary degrees. On July 10, 1974, the federal government unveiled a statue of her at Lincoln Park in Washington D.C. This made her the first African American and the first woman honored with a public monument in the nation's capital.

Further Reading

Franklin, John Hope, and August Meier, ed. *Black Leaders of the Twentieth Century.* Urbana: University of Illinois Press, 1982.

Haskins, Jim. *Distinguished African-American Political and Government Leaders.* Phoenix, Ariz.: Oryx Press, 1999.

McCluskey, Audrey Thomas et al, eds. *Mary McLeod Bethune: Building a Better World.* Bloomington: Indiana University Press, 2002.

Blake, Charles Edward, Sr.
(1940–) *Church of God in Christ bishop*

Charles Blake has accomplished one of the most remarkable congregational success stories in modern history, transforming his West Los Angeles Church of God in Christ parish from a barely surviving congregation into the largest church in his denomination.

Blake was born on August 5, 1940, in North Little Rock, Arkansas, the son of Junious and Lula Mae Blake. He grew up steeped in the culture of the Church of God in Christ, as his father was a senior bishop in the denomination. Blake showed early signs of ministerial promise, preaching his first sermon at the age of 16 and obtaining his preaching license a year later. He attended California Western University in San Diego, where he earned his B.A. degree in 1962. Following his ordination the same year, he served as a copastor in San Diego, then moved on to Interdenominational Theological Seminary in Atlanta. Blake served a parish in Marietta, Georgia, while working toward his master of divinity degree, which he achieved in 1965. While in school, he married Mae Lawrence, with whom he would have three children.

Blake served for four years as copastor of the Greater Jackson Church of God in Christ in Mississippi. He wasted no time in becoming an active force within his denominational circles. While beginning his pastorate in Mississippi in 1965, he wrote a history of his church called *The Church of God in Christ: Its Organizing Crisis.* That same year, he was chosen as vice president of the national publication board, and he eventually became chair of the Christian Education Board in the Youth Department.

In 1969, Blake moved to the West Los Angeles Church of God in Christ, which at that time numbered little more than 50 members. While continuing his leadership role on a national level, Blake transformed the church through his organizational skills and a preaching talent that *Ebony* magazine rated as one of the top 15 among black preachers in the nation. Since that time, the congregation has swelled to the point where it boasts a membership of nearly 20,000 members, and has gained some notice for attracting celebrity members such as basketball star Earvin "Magic" Johnson and actor Denzel Washington. It developed a widely respected choir and initiated more than 80 programs, ranging from HIV awareness to crisis counseling, which were led by more than 200 full-time staff members. In 2001, the congregation moved from its outgrown facilities to a spacious new sanctuary capable of seating 5,000 people.

Blake, who was elected bishop of Southern California in 1985, explains how his church has managed to maintain its phenomenal growth: "We aim for contemporary and relevant worship. We have to be socially conscious and politically aware. We try to maintain the human touch, even with growing size."

Yet in the middle of his astounding success story, Blake remains focused on trying to find ways to make further inroads in urban culture. "Our nation is in trouble, our cities are in trouble," he said recently, "and unless influence can be exerted in the inner city, I don't see any hope for our denomination."

Further Reading

Blake, Charles E., Sr. *Free to Dream: Discover Your Divine Destiny.* Tulsa, Okla.: Albury Press, 2000.

Melton, J. Gordon. *Religious Leaders of America.* 2d ed. Detroit, Mich.: Gale Research, 1999.

Boyd, Richard Henry
(Dick Gray)
(1843–1922) *Baptist publisher, administrator*

With his savvy business skills, Richard Henry Boyd established one of the largest and most influential publishing houses for black religious materials, and retained control despite concerted efforts to drive him out.

He was given the name Dick Gray when he was born on March 15, 1843, on a slave plantation near Nexubee City, Mississippi. In 1849, he moved along with his owners to their new plantation in Washington City, Texas. Gray accompanied his master to the Civil War battlefields until the master was killed in fighting at Chattanooga, Tennessee.

The family rewarded his loyalty by making him plantation manager after the war. Gray changed his name to Richard Boyd, and began educating himself in his spare time. At the age of 24, he learned to read and write, and eventually learned enough to enroll at Bishop College in 1869. Shortly thereafter, he became a Baptist preacher. Boyd formed the first black Baptist organization in Texas, consisting initially of six churches. An active evangelist, he roamed throughout the state, founding six churches over the next 26 years.

Boyd had become a widely respected member of the black clergy by the time that the National Baptist Convention, a national organization of black Baptists, was formally established in 1895. The following year he moved to the national headquarters in Nashville, Tennessee, where he served as secretary of the group's Home Missions Board. While there, he founded the National Baptist Publications Board (NBPB). This publishing house produced a wide variety of religious materials that were especially important in countering the stereotypes found in white Baptist materials and affirming black pride and dignity. Technically, Boyd was merely the secretary-treasurer of the NBPB, but he exercised almost complete control over its operations.

While the publishing board prospered, Boyd ventured into a number of entrepreneurial concerns, most of which were remarkably successful. He helped found the Citizens Savings Bank and served as its president beginning in 1904. Two years later he started the Nashville Globe Publishing Company, which produced secular print materials. In 1911, Boyd founded the National Negro Doll Company, which was a pioneer in the creation of black dolls.

Boyd's influence over the NBPB became so great that the National Baptist Convention grew concerned in the mid-1910s. There were other issues involved, including Boyd's strong advocacy of cooperation with white Baptist groups. But the primary concern was his lack of accountability to the denomination. When National Baptist Convention president E. C. Morris demanded that Boyd produce financial records to account for his spending, Boyd balked. The dispute between the two ended in a lawsuit, in which the National Baptist Convention attempted to wrest control from Boyd. The court, however, supported Boyd when it found that, at the NBPB's inception, he had built the publishing house on his own property and incorporated it in his own name.

The court decision did not end the controversy, however. Although Boyd retained the publishing house, he and his supporters left the National Baptist Convention and operated independently until Boyd's death in Nashville on August 19, 1922.

Further Reading

Bowden, Henry Warden. *Dictionary of American Religious Biography.* Westport, Conn.: Greenwood Press, 1993.
Garrity, John A., and Mark C. Carnes, eds. *American National Biography.* Vol. 3. New York: Oxford University Press, 2002.
"Richard Henry Boyd." Annual Local Conference on Afro-American Culture and History web site. Available online. URL: http://www.tnstate.edu/library/digital/RHBoyd.htm. Downloaded March 25, 2003.

Bragg, George Freeman
(1863–1940) *Episcopal priest*

George Freeman Bragg enjoyed a long and productive ministry and earned a reputation as the historiographer of the Afro-American Episcopal Church.

He was born on January 25, 1863, in Warrenton, North Carolina, and raised in Petersburg, Virginia, where the family moved when he was two. His parents, George Freeman and Mary Bragg, were strong Episcopalians, dating back to his grandmother's days as a house slave of an Episcopalian rector. That grandmother was one of the founders of St. Stephen's Church for Negroes in Petersburg, Virginia, where Bragg was steeped in the faith and attended the Parish and Normal School. He supported himself by delivering newspapers and working as a valet.

In 1879, he entered the Theological Seminary for Negroes in Petersburg, a branch of Virginia Theological Seminary. He was suspended after just one year by the rector, an old Confederate officer with whom he repeatedly clashed, on the grounds that he was "not humble enough." Historians speculated that Bragg's active involvement in the Readjuster Party, which advocated increasing taxes on corporate wealth, played a role in his dismissal.

Bragg began teaching school in Staunton, Virginia, while hiring private tutors for his own education. He began a lifelong fascination with publishing in 1882, when he printed a weekly newspaper called *The Lancet,* which he printed in his own home. After recovering from a serious case of typhoid in 1883, he learned that the rector at his old school had left. Bragg reapplied and was admitted to the school, now renamed Bishop Payne Divinity School. While studying there, he started a new magazine called *Afro-American Churchman*, later renamed *The Church Advocate*.

He finished course work at the school and was ordained a deacon in 1887, the same year he married Nellie Hill, the mother of his four children. Bragg was ordained into the priesthood on December 19, 1888, at St. Luke's Church, in Norfolk, Virginia, where he was involved in a whirlwind of activity. In addition to presiding over a thriving church, he founded the Industrial School for Colored Girls and two mission churches, and served as chaplain of the Second Battalion of Colored Militia as well as secretary of the National Colored Association.

In November 1891, he was called to St. James Church in Baltimore, which was in serious decline with only 69 members, hopelessly in debt, and operating out of rented facilities. Bragg led the church to an astounding recovery. Within a few years, St. James was not only self-supporting but able to build a new sanctuary. He served that congregation for the remainder of his career.

Among his community accomplishments were starting the Maryland Home for Friendless Children in 1899, and leading the fight for black teachers in Baltimore's Negro Schools. He believed strongly that the Episcopal Church was the best institution for fostering cooperation and understanding among races. Nearly two dozen men went into the ministry as a result of his influence. Bragg's most lasting contribution was as a church essayist, publisher, editor, and historian. In 1922, he published his major work, *History of the Afro-American Group of the Episcopal Church.* The Rev. Theodore DeBose Bratten described him as "a historian who loves facts but loves still more the life which lived them." He died on March 12, 1940, after 48 years as rector of St. James.

Further Reading

Bragg, George F. *History of the Afro-American Group of the Episcopal Church.* Baltimore, Md.: Church Advocate Press, 1921.

Rodman, Edward W. "Walk about Zion." *Anglican Theological Review* (fall 1994): 444–464.

Shattuck, Gardiner H., Jr. *Episcopalians and Race.* Lexington: University Press of Kentucky, 2000.

Broughton, Virginia E. Walker
(ca. 1856–1934) *Baptist missionary*

Virginia Walker was a missionary working in the Deep South who was particularly creative in finding ways of surmounting opposition to educated women's leadership in church matters.

She was born Virginia E. Walker around 1856, named for her father's home state. Nelson Walker had been a slave who, through many years of overtime work, had been able to purchase his freedom and that of his wife, Eliza. Virginia Walker spent her childhood in Nashville, Tennessee. She was a brilliant student and entered the newly launched Fisk University, a school whose curriculum spanned a vast range, in 1866. Walker spent 10 years at the school and, in 1875, was one of four in its first graduating class, and was one of the first black women to graduate from college.

She moved on to Memphis, Tennessee, where she taught for 12 years in the city's segregated black schools. Never one to tolerate gender discrimination, Walker complained when a less experienced man was named assistant principal at Kortrecht Grammar School. Her protest was successful, and she won the position at the school, which offered the only high school curriculum for blacks in the city. While in Memphis, she met and married John Broughton, a Republican lawyer who later won election as a state representative. The couple had five children.

In 1882, Virginia Broughton met Joanna Moore, a white missionary widely respected by blacks for her views on racial equality. A few years later, she became a member of one of Moore's "Bible bands," a group of women who met daily to study the Bible. Her expertise in Bible study led the Midwestern auxiliary of the American Baptist Missionary Society to sponsor her as a missionary in the South. Secure and happy in her teaching career, Broughton declined. But the death of her mother and feelings of mortality brought on by her own severe illness changed her priorities. When Broughton recovered her health, she accepted the challenge and worked full time, traveling through Mississippi, Arkansas, Missouri, and Tennessee. A woman of strong views who tended to consider all who disagreed with her as in league with the devil, she threw herself into the work so vigorously that she neglected her family. When John Broughton objected, she told him, "I belong to God first, and you next; so you two must settle it." Eventually, John came to support her work.

Broughton soon narrowed the scope of her work to Tennessee. By 1894, she had created Bible bands in 57 cities in the state and had organized 20 schools. The bands were a particularly effective way of providing women with religious education while defusing growing white opposition to formal schools for blacks. Although some of the bands were dissolved due to male opposition, most survived. Broughton also garnered support for the Howe Institute, a Memphis school for blacks that included a Bible training class for women. During the 1890s she taught Bible study at the school and gained a reputation as a top biblical expositor. The strength of her reputation in the community at large was evident when she became the first black appointed by the Associated Charities of Memphis to assist in flood relief.

Part of Broughton's success was the result of finding ways to provide religious leadership outside of the pulpit, which most Baptists considered strictly a male privilege. At the same time, she was active in working for meaningful inclusion of women in the church. In 1900, she helped organize a separate state convention for black Baptist women and gained recognition for the Women's Convention as an official body of the National Baptist Convention. An active writer with strong feminist views, she wrote *Woman's Work, as Gleaned from the Women of the Bible,* published in 1904. Broughton died on May 21, 1934, from complications of diabetes.

Further Reading

Broughton, Virginia. *Twenty Years Experience of a Missionary.* Chicago: Pony Press, 1907.

Higginbothom, Evelyn Brooks. *Righteous Discomfort.* Cambridge, Mass.: Harvard University Press, 1993.

Brown, Morris
(1770–1849) *African Methodist Episcopal bishop*

Morris Brown survived an explosive racial incident that led to his banishment from South Carolina, and despite virtually no education, he advanced to become the second bishop of the African Methodist Episcopal Church (AME Church). Little is known of Brown's early life other than that he was born free, of mixed-race parents, in Charleston, South Carolina, on January 8, 1770. Accounts vary as to whether he received any education, but one of his associates reported that Brown had no schooling and was illiterate. He made a living as a shoemaker in Charleston, where he enjoyed some privilege among whites because of his mixed parentage.

Like many African Americans, Brown joined the Methodist Church, whose antislavery leanings were especially attractive. At some point, Brown acquired a license to preach, and married a woman named Maria, with whom he had six children. The church's modification of its slavery position in 1815 to accommodate white Southerners' views led to a mass exodus of blacks from the church; 4,000 black Methodists in the Charleston area withdrew that year and formed three separate groups. Under Brown's leadership, one of these groups joined the AME Church, making it the first AME Church affiliate in the state. He was ordained a deacon in the AME Church in 1817. The following year, he circumvented South Carolina's travel restrictions on free blacks to attend the AME Church's annual conference in Philadelphia, where he was ordained an elder.

Brown's Charleston congregation, known as Emanuel AME Church, worshiped in an old sanctuary given to them by a group of white Methodists. Brown used both his church and his prosperous shoe business to help slaves purchase their freedom and move to the North. There were reports that he went so far as to hide fugitive slaves in the church. A number of white neighbors were displeased by the blacks' withdrawal from the Methodist Church and their rumored activities, and they harassed Brown and his congregation. Arrests for disorderly conduct were common, and Brown himself was imprisoned briefly in 1821.

His world was shattered in June 1822, when a minister who worked closely with his church, DENMARK VESEY, was arrested for conspiring to foment a major slave revolt. As nearly all of Vesey's coconspirators were members of Emanuel, suspicion fell on Brown as an accomplice, if not a leader in the revolt. Brown was saved from prosecution and possible death by his influential white friends, but he was convicted of violating South Carolina's law prohibiting free blacks from entering the state. The 1,800-member church was shut down, and Brown and his family were forced to leave South Carolina.

They fled to Philadelphia, where Brown fell back on his shoemaking skills to earn a living.

He soon resumed his ministry, traveling on an AME circuit in western Pennsylvania and Ohio. His work so impressed his fellow AME clergy that in 1826 he was elected assistant bishop to help out the ailing RICHARD ALLEN. Allen's continued decline led to Brown's consecration as bishop in 1828.

Allen's death in 1831 left Brown in charge of the denomination. He served ably for 13 years until he suffered a stroke while attending a conference in Toronto in 1844. This forced Brown's retirement, and he was largely housebound until his death on May 9, 1849. During his tenure, the AME Church doubled its membership to more than 17,000. Brown was particularly effective in organizing the church's movement into Pennsylvania, Ohio, Indiana, and Canada, and in arguing for increased education for pastors. In honor of his contributions, Morris Brown College in Atlanta has been named after him.

Further Reading

Garrity, John A., and Mark C. Carnes, eds. *American National Biography.* Vol. 3. New York: Oxford University Press, 2002.

"Morris Brown." PBS Online: Africans in America. Available online. URL: http://www.pbs.org/wgbh/aia/part3/3h96.html. Downloaded March 28, 2003.

Murphy, Larry G., ed. *Encyclopedia of African American Religious Biography.* New York: Garland Publishing, 1993.

Walker, John S. "Morris Brown: Crisis Leadership of the AME Church, 1830–1850." *Perspective* (1972): 136–155.

Brown, Oliver

(1919–1961) *African Methodist Episcopal pastor, civil rights pioneer*

Oliver Brown was a quiet part-time pastor whose name has been branded into U.S. history as the lead plaintiff in the landmark *Brown v. Topeka Board of Education* Supreme Court case.

He was born in 1919 in Topeka, Kansas, and lived there all of his life, except for his years of military service during World War II. According to one of his school teachers, "He was an average pupil and a good citizen—he was not a fighter in his manner."

Brown lived a life of quiet respectability, marrying the beauty queen of his black high school and working as a welder for the Santa Fe railroad. He became a member of St. John's African Methodist Episcopal Church, the black establishment church in town, and eventually became its assistant minister.

In 1951, his life changed when civil rights advocates sought a test case to challenge segregated education policies. One of Brown's three daughters, Linda, was a third grader who had to walk six blocks through a bad neighborhood to catch a bus that drove her to Monroe Elementary School, a mile away. Concerned for her safety, Brown attempted to enroll her in Summer Elementary, a school only seven blocks away that was reserved for whites. Brown was denied.

As a union member, minister, and respectable citizen with no ties to any civil rights advocacy group, Brown was an ideal candidate to test the constitutionality of the policy. Under the direction of civil rights lawyers, he and 12 other plaintiffs filed suit on behalf of 20 children against the Topeka School Board on February 28, 1951. As the first person listed on the suit, he became the point man of the endeavor.

The lawsuit was not popular among blacks at his church, and at first, Brown went along with it reluctantly. On the witness stand he was visibly uncomfortable and spoke so softly he could hardly be heard. But at some point in the proceedings, according to author Richard Kluger in *Simple Justice,* "He was no longer willing to accept second class citizenship. Oliver Brown wanted to be a whole man." Brown came

to see his involvement in the suit as God's will for him.

Under federal law, "separate but equal" facilities for blacks and whites were allowable. In a key strategic move, Brown's lawyers did not argue that the facilities at Monroe were inferior to those at Sumner. Their key argument was that the policy inherently discriminated against blacks simply by its refusal to allow blacks to mix with whites. They cited psychologists to show the damage to self-esteem and learning that such a policy created.

In 1953, the case came before the U.S. Supreme Court, which ruled in Brown's favor and initiated the dismantling of school segregation in the United States. According to legal analyst Paul E. Wilson, "From many standpoints, *Brown* may be the most important decision rendered by the Supreme Court during the twentieth century." Oliver Brown, however, retreated to a life of anonymity. He died in 1961 without ever giving a public account of his role or his thoughts during his historic lawsuit.

Further Reading

Kluger, Richard. *Simple Justice: The History of* Brown v. Board of Education *and Black America's Struggle for Equality.* New York: Vintage Books, 1977.

Patterson, James T. Brown v. Board of Education: *A Civil Rights Milestone and Its Troubled Legacy.* New York: Oxford University Press, 2001.

Wilson, Paul E. *A Time To Lose: Representing Kansas in* Brown v. Board of Education. Lawrence: University Press of Kansas, 1995.

Bryan, Andrew
(ca. 1737–1812) *pioneer Baptist clergy*

Andrew Bryan was the founder of the first black Baptist church built on U.S. soil and was one of the rare African Americans of his time who was widely respected by his white neighbors in the Deep South.

Bryan was born into slavery on a plantation at Goose Creek, South Carolina, 20 miles outside of Charleston. His date of birth is unknown, but the year has been conjectured at anywhere from 1718 to 1737. No information exists about Bryan's early life.

In 1783, late in his life, Bryan was converted by pioneer black Baptist preacher GEORGE LIELE. Bryan and his wife, Hannah, then began leading prayer meetings among the plantation workers. In 1785, Bryan felt called to preach, and began by bringing his brother Sampson to the faith. Eventually he expanded his preaching to larger audiences, including curious whites.

His owner, Jonathan Bryan, saw nothing wrong with his ministry and allowed it to continue. But when Bryan began to experience remarkable success, including 43 converts in a single day on a plantation southwest of Savannah, his success raised suspicion as well as envy from neighboring whites. These neighbors so disrupted Bryan's work that he was forced to hold prayer meetings deep in a swamp.

Since Bryan was not a licensed minister, he could not baptize his converts. But a white Baptist minister named Abraham Marshall took on this task for him. On January 20, 1788, this mass of new converts was organized into the first black Baptist church in the nation. Bryan was then ordained as its pastor.

Both Bryan and the church prospered over the next two years. Bryan earned his freedom and that of his wife and daughters, and was thus able to devote the rest of his life to ministry. Meanwhile, the church membership rolls grew rapidly. This revived envy and suspicion among his neighbors. In 1789 or 1790, he and about 50 of his parishioners were beaten, whipped, and imprisoned on charges of plotting insurrection. Helped by the intercession of Bryan's former master, Bryan and his parishioners were found innocent and were released. For a time, the congregation retreated to the plantation barn so they could worship in safety. One of Bryan's most virulent antagonists stalked him in hopes of catching him in the act of a punishable offense. But when he overheard Bryan praying specifically for him, his heart was turned and he became a supporter. Such incidents spread Bryan's fame among both blacks and whites. The persecution ended when state Chief Justice Henry Osborne issued a ruling granting blacks legal right to worship between sunrise and sunset.

In 1790, Bryan's church joined the Georgia Baptist Association. In the same year, Bryan bought a lot on which he hoped to build a permanent house of worship. That dream was finally fulfilled in 1795, when the congregation, now boasting 381 members and known as the First Colored Baptist Church, moved into the structure. The church continued to grow at such a rate that a second black Baptist church was built in the area in 1799, and a third a few years later.

Bryan was a stickler on church discipline—he required couples to present a certificate of marriage before he would baptize their children. In his later years, Bryan was an easily recognizable figure in Savannah, as he dressed like a bishop and rode around in a chariot. He was so widely respected that his death, on October 6, 1812, drew the races together in the community for a brief time. More than 5,000 people, white and black, attended his funeral.

Further Reading

Montgomery, William E. *Under Their Own Vine and Fig Tree: The African-American Church in the South, 1865–1900.* Baton Rouge: Louisiana State University Press, 1993.

Sernett, Milton, ed. *African-American Religious History: A Documentary Witness.* Durham, N.C.: Duke University Press, 1999.

Wagner, Clarence M. *Profiles of Black Georgia Baptists.* Gainesville, Ga.: privately published, 1980.

Burgess, John Melville
(1909–   ) *Episcopal bishop*

While other African Americans before him had been consecrated as bishops in the Episcopal Church, John Burgess was the first assigned to head a regular diocese in the United States.

He was born John Melville Burgess on March 11, 1909, in Grand Rapids, Michigan. His father, Theodore, worked as a waiter on a railroad dining car, while his mother, Ethel, was trained as a kindergarten teacher. While attending Henry Street Elementary and Central High School in Grand Rapids, Burgess was impressed by the patience and care of several of his teachers. Influenced by their example, he went on to school at the University of Michigan, where he supported himself by waiting on tables at a fraternity house. Burgess graduated from Michigan in 1930 and obtained his M.A. degree in sociology there the next summer.

While working a summer job in social work, he decided that Christianity was the surest solution to the abundant problems of racism and other societal ills. He began studying for the ministry of his parents' denomination at the Episcopal Theological School in Cambridge, Massachusetts. Burgess earned his degree there in 1934, was ordained a deacon on June 29, 1934, and was assigned to his home church, St. Philips of Grand Rapids. He was ordained into the priesthood on January 25, 1936.

Burgess served in Grand Rapids until 1939 and then moved to a parish in Cincinnati. As a parish priest, he was a reasoned advocate of black concerns within his denomination and a pillar of compassion for the downtrodden. During his later years there, he married Esther Taylor, the mother of his two children.

In 1946, he was called to be a chaplain at Howard University in Washington, D.C. During his decade in that position, Burgess also served as director of the Episcopal Student Center, as a canon at Washington's National Cathedral, and as a delegate to the World Council of Churches meeting in India.

Burgess moved on to Boston in 1956 to serve as his denomination's archdeacon in the city and as supervisor of the Episcopalian City Mission. This largely inner-city ministry allowed him to make use of his sociology background. Six years later, he was appointed assistant to the Bishop of Massachusetts and given jurisdiction over the eastern part of the state. This was a major breakthrough in the Episcopal Church, as its only previous assistant bishops had been restricted to supervision of black parishes in Arkansas and North Carolina. In 1967, he broke more new ground as the first African American elected to the Church Pension Fund Board of Trustees.

Burgess was then elected bishop in first-ballot voting, and on January 12, 1970, he became the bishop of the Massachusetts diocese. Again, the only previous black bishop had been limited to oversight of black congregations in Liberia. Burgess served as bishop for six years, placing major emphasis on shepherding black Episcopalians into the mainstream of their church, and raising awareness of black and inner-city issues.

He resigned as bishop in 1976 and joined the faculty of Yale University's Berkeley Divinity School, where he taught pastoral care. One of his major accomplishments in that post was the editing of *Black Gospel, White Church*, a collection of sermons given by black priests from the 1800s to contemporary times, published in 1982.

Further Reading

Bishop, John J. "Bishop Who 'Took Positions' Honored by His Place in History." The Episcopal Times. Available online. URL: http://www.diomass.org/Epistim/BpBurgess_Celebration.htm. Posted March 1998.

Murphy, Larry G., ed. *Encyclopedia of African American Religious Biography*. New York: Garland Publishing, 1993.

Burroughs, Nannie Helen
(1878–1961) *Baptist educator*

Nannie Burroughs was a pioneer in providing educational opportunities for African-American women. Her devout Baptist beliefs moved her to found an influential school seeking "the highest development of Christian womanhood."

Nannie Helen Burroughs was born on May 2, 1878, in Orange, Virginia, the older of two daughters of John and Jennie Burroughs. Her younger sister died in infancy, and her father, a farmer and preacher, died a few years later. At that time, Nannie and her mother moved to Washington, D.C., where Jennie Burroughs supported them as a cook.

Nannie was a fine student who organized the Harriet Beecher Stowe Literary Society and graduated with honors in 1896 from M Street High School (later Dunbar High School) in Washington, D.C. Her goal was to teach in the Washington school system, but despite her obvious abilities and achievements, she was unable to gain employment. Upset that the administration's reputation for hiring lighter-skinned blacks may have been the cause of her failure, Burroughs dreamed of someday righting the injustice by founding her own school.

After spending a year in Philadelphia working as an editorial assistant, she returned to Washington to apply for a government job as a clerk. Although she achieved a high score on the civil service exam, she was told there were no openings for "colored" women. Burroughs ended up in Louisville, Kentucky, working as a secretary for the Foreign Mission Board of the National Baptist Convention. An inspiring speaker, Burroughs made a deep impression on members of the National Baptist Convention with an address at their annual meeting. She was subsequently chosen to be corresponding secretary of the newly formed National Baptist Woman's Convention. Burroughs worked tire-

Nannie Burroughs's devout Baptist faith fueled her drive to provide educational opportunities for young black women. *(Library of Congress)*

lessly for this group, traveling around the country, raising money, and promoting its work. She retained her position of secretary until 1948, when she assumed presidency of the organization. Late in life, she remarked, "I have given my entire life to the Woman's Convention and have proudly built it and watched it grow from the humblest beginnings to world service and security."

In this position, Burroughs found a way to take up her educational dream by creating the Woman's Industrial Club. This Washington,

D.C., school, which opened in 1908, provided evening classes for members, who had nowhere else to turn for education. Burroughs taught the classes herself to the 31 students who enrolled in the first year. But the quality of the instruction attracted such interest in the school that applications soared. Within a few years, Burroughs hired teachers and took over the administrative functions.

Burroughs's goals in education were to help women achieve self-sufficiency by combining vocational training, domestic training, and higher education. She maintained a close connection between religion and education, emphasizing "the three B's—the Bible, the bath, and the broom," which symbolized a clean life, clean body, and clean home. At a time when few acknowledged any contributions of African Americans to society, she created a department of Negro history and required students to take courses in that area. Among Burroughs's other contributions were producing a quarterly devotional called *The Worker*, writing regular columns, and organizing a self-help cooperative in Washington during the leanest years of the depression.

By the time Burroughs died of a stroke in 1961, thousands of black women had graduated from her school. In 1964, the school was renamed in her honor, and in 1975, Mayor Walter Washington passed a declaration setting aside May 10 as "Nannie Helen Burroughs Day" in the District of Columbia.

Further Reading

Carpenter, Delores. *A Time for Honor.* St. Louis, Mo.: Chalice Press, 2001.

Easter, Opal V. *Nannie Helen Burroughs.* New York: Garland Publishing, 1995.

Johnson, Karen Ann. *Uplifting the Women and the Race: The Lives, Educational Philosophy and Social Activism of Anna Julia Cooper and Nannie Helen Burroughs.* New York: Garland Publishing, 2000.

Butts, Calvin Otis
(1949–) *Baptist clergy, community leader*

Calvin Butts rejuvenated one of the most prestigious black churches in the nation, Abyssinian Baptist in Harlem, at a time when it was stagnating. A tireless and highly visible leader in the community, his influence has been felt in the community on religious, economic, and political levels.

He was born Calvin Otis Butts on July 19, 1949, in New York City. His mother, Patricia, worked as a city welfare supervisor, and his father, Calvin, was a chef in Manhattan. The family lived in a public housing project on the Lower East Side for the first eight years of Calvin's life and then moved to a middle-class black neighborhood in Queens. He often spent summers with his devoutly religious grandmothers in Georgia.

Butts was bused to predominantly white schools beginning in junior high. He was a model student who had a gift for working with whites as well as blacks, a trait that helped him become student body president during his senior year at Flushing High School.

In 1967, he entered Morehouse College in Atlanta, where he attracted notice both with his probing intelligence and his habit of dressing in suits and carrying a briefcase. Butts's reason for becoming interested in religious studies was more practical than spiritual. He had ambitions of high position and influence, having dreamed of being mayor of New York City since the third grade, and he noted that in the black community it was the ministers who commanded the most respect and clout.

Butts's father had instilled in him a high degree of black solidarity. "My father was the kind who would say, 'If a black man opens a store, go shop in it,'" he recalled. The racial tensions within him exploded in 1968 with the assassination of MARTIN LUTHER KING, JR. Butts joined a group of rioters in firebombing a neighborhood store. But after seeing a police gun aimed at him, he reconsidered and renounced violence. His career plans had shifted toward psychology, but after encountering seminary recruiters on campus three consecutive days, he began to believe he was being called into the ministry.

Butts graduated from Morehouse in 1972 and enrolled at Union Theological Seminary in New York. There he displayed his fiercely independent spirit with a sermon denouncing homosexuality in front a largely liberal faculty. However, Butts eventually came to be a strong defender of the civil liberties of gays.

Calvin Butts has served as a dynamic pastor of historic Abyssinian Baptist Church in Harlem and as president of State University of New York, College at Old Westbury. *(Dr. Calvin Butts III)*

During his first year at Union, the legendary ADAM CLAYTON POWELL, JR., whom Butts called "a man bigger than life," died. During Powell's later years, controversies surrounding his political career had detracted from his ministry at Abyssinian Baptist Church. His successor, Dr. Samuel Proctor, was determined to bring in new blood to rejuvenate the church. He asked his associates to recruit some dynamic young associate pastors. One of them approached Butts, who had impressed him with his passion to accomplish something worthwhile, and offered him a position as youth pastor. Butts accepted and began his long service at the church, which he balanced with his continuing education. Eventually, Butts would earn his master's degree from Union as well as a doctorate in church and public policy from Drew Theological Seminary in New Jersey. He also served as an adjunct professor at City College of New York and at Fordham University in the Bronx in the late 1970s.

In his early years at Abyssinian Baptist, Butts expanded his role into social and political arenas and created a stir in the church community with his aggressive and outspoken tactics. He criticized politicians for being too timid in addressing the real problems of the inner city. "Stop being so damn cautious," he railed, "because we are living in critical times and caution will result in all of us literally being wiped out." In 1983, he spoke before a congressional hearing on police brutality, which led to changes in police policy. In 1987, he claimed that racism in New York City was "worse than it was in Alabama and Mississippi 35 or 40 years ago."

Occasionally his rhetoric went too far for Proctor, who advised him to try and find more common ground with people rather than demonizing enemies. Nonetheless, Proctor had no reservations about recommending Butts to take over upon his retirement in 1989. The church board agreed, waiving a bylaw that required an outside search for a pastor and instead calling Butts.

Once Butts took over as head pastor, with the weight of one of the black community's most venerable institutions on his shoulders, his approach changed markedly. He looked around at the neighborhood and saw that despite decades of social action and advocacy, there had been no real change—it was continuing to deteriorate. Looking for practical solutions, he began to mix in the world of business and politics and found himself an adept player. "It's time to move from hope to making what we hoped about and dreamed about real," he said.

Butts began to spend more time building alliances rather than denouncing politicians and businesspeople. He quietly engaged in behind-the-scenes deal-making to bring millions of dollars' worth of economic development into Harlem. He helped create and operate the Abyssinian Development Corporation, which invested more than $65 million in neighborhood restoration, renovation, and commercial development. This strategy even led him to seek alternatives to the Democratic Party, which, although the traditional supporter of black progress, appeared to him to be taking black support for granted. He occasionally opposed the Democrats, throwing his support to independent candidate Ross Perot in the 1992 presidential election (he later called this the biggest mistake of his life) and supporting Republican George Pataki in the gubernatorial New York race.

On the other hand, he engaged in direct confrontation when he felt it necessary. In the late 1980s, he led a campaign to paint over billboards that aimed their tobacco and liquor ads at blacks. In 1993, he led a widely publicized campaign against foul lyrics in rap music, dumping a pile of offending compact discs on the doorstep of a record company. Five years later, he accused Mayor Rudolph Giuliani and the New York Police Department of racism.

Political experts often speculated that Butts was primed to run for high political office. Butts did not discourage such speculation, saying that he was prepared to serve wherever God called him. But in 1999 he temporarily cut off any possible political draft by accepting the presidency of the State University of New York, College at Old Westbury.

Further Reading

Dreyfuss, Joel. "Harlem's Ardent Voice." *The New York Times Magazine*, January 20, 1998, 19–39.

Gore, Bob, Robert L. Gore, Jesse Jackson, and Calvin O. Butts. *We've Come This Far: Abyssinian Baptist Church: A Photo Journal.* New York: Stewart, Tabori and Chang, 2001.

Thompson, Clifford, ed. *Current Biography 2000.* New York: H. W. Wilson, 2000.

C

Cannon, Katie Geneva
(1950–) *Presbyterian clergy and theologian*

Katie Cannon is a Christian ethicist and ordained Presbyterian minister who has gained recognition as one of the nation's foremost feminist theologians.

Cannon was born in Kannapolis, North Carolina, on January 30, 1950, to Carin and Esau Cannon. Hers was one of the few families in her area equipped with such basics as a telephone and television. She was no stranger to discrimination, as the local library and swimming pool were segregated. Her mother was a great influence on her life. Along with her career as an Avon representative, Carin Cannon was active in the Parent-Teacher Association and started a church in their home.

Katie Cannon's intellectual gifts were apparent at an early age. She was encouraged by teachers to enroll at Barber-Scotia College, a school founded in 1887 by freed women slaves, near her hometown. Teaching was the only acceptable professional job for a black woman in those days, and Cannon set out on that career course in school. She had an interest in religion and ethics, having been raised in a very devout household and having experienced a roller coaster of emotions on the subjects while at school. For a time she lost faith in God after going through the pain of losing a boyfriend and noting inconsistencies in Christian teaching and in the conventions of society. She got over that to the point where she decided to enroll at Interdenominational Theological Seminary after college.

Before that happened, however, Cannon experienced a powerful exhilaration during a trip to West Africa. "We believed that we had returned to Africa in honor of our ancestors who wanted to but could never return home," she declared. That was followed by a miserable archeology dig on which she was the only black. Her second-class status was obvious in the housing arrangements, the unwillingness of others to interact with her, and the racial slurs that she heard for the first time. The result of this buffeting was a floundering for anchors in her life. Eventually, she came to see God as the Creator who sustains life. "Knowing God is being able to relax, slow down, and live life," she decided.

Cannon completed her B.S. degree in 1971, and followed through on her plan to attend Interdenominational Theological Seminary. She was one of only four females in her class. Her love of her grandmother's Old Testament stories prompted her to major in Hebrew. After obtaining her master of divinity degree in 1974, she spent three years as a pastor at Ascension Presbyterian Church in New York City, followed by a stint as an administrator at New York Theological Seminary.

While studying for her Ph.D., she experienced a bias greater than any she had previously known. Angry young male students demanded to know what made her think God would call her, a woman, to leadership in the church. Crushed by the hostility, she sought refuge in the Woman's Caucus, where she discovered she was the only black member.

Cannon persevered in her effort to become the first woman to get a Ph.D. in Old Testament studies, an elite bastion of the male professors. She went on to hold respected faculty positions at Yale Divinity School, Wellesley College, Radcliffe College, and Harvard Divinity School, before settling into a position as professor of Christian Ethics at Temple University in Philadelphia. Cannon is widely regarded as a distinguished feminist theologian. She explains her ethical approach by saying, "I try to help people understand what it means to live as a moral agent, when you have to live with racism, classism, and sexism every day of your life."

Further Reading

Cannon, Katie. *Black Womanist Ethics.* Atlanta: Scholars Press, 1988.

Cannon, Katie, et al., eds. *God's Fierce Whimsy: Christian Feminism and Theological Education.* New York: Pilgrim Press, 1985.

———. *Inheriting Our Mother's Gardens: Feminist Theology in Third World Perspective.* Philadelphia: Westminster Press, 1988.

Mabunda, L. Mpho. *Contemporary Black Biography.* Vol. 10. Detroit, Mich.: Gale Research, 1996.

Cary, Lott
(ca. 1780–1828) *Baptist missionary*

Lott Cary was one of the first black Christian missionaries to Africa. He was largely responsible for establishing the Baptist Church in Liberia and holding the colony together in its formative years.

Cary was born in about 1780 on the plantation of William Christian in Charles County, Virginia, near Richmond. He was the only child of slaves, about whom nothing is known except that his father was a member of the Baptist Church. That connection had no apparent influence on Cary, who described himself as a person of "profane and vicious habits" during his youth.

In 1804, Cary's master hired him out to work at a Richmond tobacco warehouse. While working there, he experienced a religious conversion, was baptized in 1807, and joined the First Baptist Church in Richmond. While sitting in the gallery reserved for blacks at the church, he heard a sermon that so inspired him that he bought himself a copy of the New Testament and learned to read.

Cary's religious awakening led him to become an exemplary employee. He worked long hours until by 1813 he had saved enough money to purchase his freedom and that of his two children by a deceased wife. Cary continued working and saving at the warehouse until he was able to buy a plot of land. In the meantime, he began preaching the gospel at plantations near Richmond. Despite poor grammar and an unimpressive delivery, he eventually became pastor of the African Baptist Church.

In 1815, he and 16 other blacks joined a religious night school started by two white members of First Baptist. The group's enthusiasm spilled over into the founding of the Richmond African Baptist Missionary Society, along with the dream of carrying the gospel to Africa. Although both the American Baptist Missionary Society and the American Colonization Society agreed to sponsor their effort, they did not provide funds, and the group had to raise the money by itself.

They finally were able to do so, and on January 23, 1821, the newly ordained Cary and his friend Colin Teague left for Sierra Leone. After a period of time spent working on a farm to support themselves, Cary departed for a settlement in what was to become Liberia. He joined a colony discouraged by squalid conditions and the threat of attacks from hostile Africans. Cary played a major role in inspiring the group to stay, and he demonstrated courage in fighting off the Africans' attacks in November and December of 1822.

He then started from scratch to establish a Baptist church in the city of Monrovia. When his fledgling congregation grew from six converts in 1823 to nearly 70 members in 1825, he supervised the building of a meetinghouse. That same year, Cary opened a day school for children, and was so visible in his care for the sick that he was appointed health officer of the settlement.

A strong advocate of the rights of the settlers, Cary was elected vice-agent of the Liberian group in 1826. When health problems caused the white governor to return to the United States two years later, Cary assumed the duties. In response to another threat from African natives, he summoned the militia and made preparations for defense of the colony. But on November 8, 1828, he and six others were killed by an explosion in the process of making gunpowder. In honor of his many contributions to the colony, a Lott Carey (sic) Baptist Foreign Missionary Convention was formed in his honor.

Further Reading

Garrity, John A., and Mark C. Carnes, eds. *American National Biography*. Vol. 4. New York: Oxford University Press, 2002.

"Lott Cary: Slave, Missionary, and Colonial Leader," Christian History Institute. Available online. URL: http://www.gospelcom.net. Downloaded February 17, 2003.

Poe, William. "Lott Cary: Man of Purchased Freedom." *Church History* (March 1970): 49–61.

Chavis, Ben
(Benjamin Franklin Chavis, Jr.)
(1948–   ) *United Church of Christ clergy, civil rights executive*

Ben Chavis, Jr., has taken part in the Civil Rights movement from virtually every angle possible: from rebellious youth to international hero, from dynamic national leader to scandalous figure.

Benjamin Franklin Chavis, Jr., was born on January 22, 1948, in Oxford, North Carolina, near the Virginia border. He came from a long and distinguished line of African-American clergy that began with his great-great-great-grandfather JOHN CHAVIS. As a small boy, he heard the story of John Chavis attending what later became Princeton University and returning to North Carolina to teach the children of slave owners. At the same time, John Chavis secretly taught slave children, which led to his murder when whites discovered it.

Ben was raised along with three sisters in Oxford, where his father, a college-educated man, worked as a bricklayer and his mother as a teacher. He exhibited the courageous defiance of his forebears, joining the National Association for the Advancement of Colored People (NAACP) at the age of 12. A year later, he walked into the town's segregated library and demanded to know why he could not use the facilities. The authorities' only response was to call his parents, but the incident led to the integration of the library shortly thereafter. Nonetheless, his parents, concerned that Ben's militancy was attracting too much attention among whites, sent him to live with a sister in Lenoir, North Carolina.

Chavis attended St. Augustine College in Raleigh, North Carolina, for a brief time before transferring to the University of North Carolina at Charlotte. He majored in chemistry, with intentions of going on to medical school. But while in school, he became involved in the Southern Christian Leadership Conference, and when MARTIN LUTHER KING, JR., was assassinated

From his early days as a member of the famed Wilmington Ten to a career as a civil rights activist, Ben Chavis has been surrounded by controversy. He is seen here sitting with Louis Farrakhan (left). *(Corbis)*

in 1968, he became passionately committed to the cause of civil rights. In 1969, he made an unsuccessful run for city council in Charlotte and was ordained in the Detroit-based Black Christian Nationalist Church.

Chavis was recruited as an organizer for racial justice issues by Reverend Len White of the United Church of Christ (UCC) in 1970. One of Chavis's assignments was to travel to Wilmington, North Carolina, to help high school students in their fight against racial discrimination in the schools. On February 6, 1971, Mike's Grocery, a white-owned business, was firebombed. Chavis and nine others were arrested and convicted of arson and conspiracy. Despite

protests from clergy on the lack of evidence, Chavis was sentenced to 34 years in prison.

Taking a cue from King, who insisted that jail time could be spent profitably, Chavis continued his education while in prison. Confined by leg irons and handcuffs, he attended Duke University on study release and circumvented the prison's inflexible 10 P.M. lights-out rule by reading late at night in the bathroom, which was lit all night. The result of his efforts was a divinity degree in 1979.

Meanwhile, the case of the Wilmington Ten, as Chavis and his companions were called, drew international attention. Citing the dubious nature of the prosecution's case, Amnesty International declared them to be political prisoners and launched a major international effort to get them released. Finally, when three witnesses confessed that they had fabricated their testimony under pressure from authorities, Governor James Hunt reduced Chavis's sentence. After four and a half years in prison, Chavis was released in 1979. A Justice Department investigation then led to the overturning of the Wilmington Ten's convictions in 1980. "Our case was a victory for the whole movement," declared Chavis. "It showed people what is possible."

Chavis was ordained in the UCC in 1980 and began working for the denomination's Commission on Racial Justice. In 1983, he became involved in a protest against the dumping of thousands of tons of polluted soil in Warren County, North Carolina, the county with the largest percentage of black residents in the state. The protest failed, but during his involvement Chavis discovered a widespread national practice of using poor, powerless communities with large minority populations, such as Warren County, as waste sites for contaminated materials. He documented this reality and publicized it by coining the phrase "environmental racism." Chavis's work on this subject was so insightful that he later was named an adviser on environmental justice issues to the administration of President Bill Clinton.

Chavis was promoted to director of the UCC's Commission for Racial Justice in 1986. In the meantime, he bolstered his leadership credentials by earning a doctorate of divinity from Howard University. When the directorship of the NAACP became vacant in 1993, Chavis actively campaigned for the job and won the appointment. His selection as the youngest director ever of the organization was viewed with suspicion by a strong minority of the board, who worried that Chavis's views were not in tune with the traditionally moderate stance of the NAACP. Chavis did little to alleviate their fears with his rhetoric and actions. Integration

was no longer a priority for him. "The new mandate of the civil rights movement as we move into the 21st century is economic empowerment," he declared. He saw the NAACP's role as that of a champion of self-help and a builder of black institutions and businesses. Noting the group's dwindling membership, he vowed to energize it by appealing to younger blacks and broadening the appeal to include some of the more militant elements.

Chavis's strategy appeared to be working brilliantly during his first year as president. With his ability to speak the language of the younger generation, he was able to bring in 160,000 new members, most of whom were young. His high-profile leadership also helped the NAACP regain status as a meaningful force in race relations.

Chavis's aggressive style, however, presented problems that escalated quickly. His attempts to broaden the NAACP's base by engaging in dialogue with gang leaders and inviting radicals such as LOUIS FARRAKHAN to a conference of national black leaders rankled the conservative NAACP leadership. When he was discovered to have secretly spent $332,000 of the organization's money to settle a sexual harassment claim, the board quickly fired him. Chavis, however, continued to be active on his own. Building on relationships he had established over the years, he joined Farrakhan in organizing the Million Man March of black men on Washington, D.C., in 1984.

Further Reading

Bigelow, Barbara Carlisle. *Contemporary Black Biography.* Vol. 6. Detroit, Mich.: Gale Research, 1994.

Kotlowitz, Alex. "Ben Chavis' Gamble." *The New York Times Magazine,* June 12, 1994, pp. 40–48.

Melton, J. Gordon. *Religious Leaders of America.* 2d ed. Detroit, Mich.: Gale Research, 1999.

Thomas, Larry Reni. *The True Story behind the Wilmington Ten.* Hampton, Va.: U.B. and U.S. Communications, 1993.

Chavis, John

(ca. 1763–1838) *Presbyterian minister*

John Chavis was the first black graduate of what eventually became Princeton University and was one of the first African-American ministers in the Presbyterian church.

Chavis was born in about 1763, although historians disagree over whether he was born in the West Indies or in the Granville County region near Oxford, North Carolina, where he was raised. He maintained that he had been born free. His mother was Lottie Chavis, but his father's name has never been recorded.

He enlisted in the Continental army in 1778, and fought alongside his brother under General George Washington through much of the Revolutionary War, from White Plains and Brandywine to Yorktown. Sometime between the end of the war and the late 1790s he began studying theology at Washington Academy in Virginia. He then enrolled at what became Princeton University, where he studied under the school's president, Dr. John Witherspoon.

In 1801, the Presbyterian Church's General Assembly commissioned him to serve as a missionary to slaves in the South, which appears to be the first case of a black person trained by the denomination for Christian leadership. He spent time at Lexington and Hanover, Virginia, in the next several years, before settling in Orange County, North Carolina, in 1809. He obtained a preaching license that year and traveled through North Carolina, Virginia, and Maryland, conducting services in churches and homes of both blacks and whites. Whites were impressed with his orthodox Presbyterian theology, his clear and concise sermons, his understanding of Latin and Greek, and his speech, which was described in a 19th-century article as "remarkably pure" and free of black dialect and accent.

While continuing to preach, he opened a school in Fayetteville, North Carolina, and served as the principal. Such was his reputation that he attracted students from the most promi-nent white families in the area. Among his many students were Willie Mangum, later a U.S. senator, and Charles Manly, who became a North Carolina governor.

Chavis became involved in politics during the 1820s and 1830s, although his convictions ran counter to the mainstream of blacks. As a supporter of the aristocracy, he vehemently opposed Andrew Jackson, whom he considered an ill-bred backwoodsman. Chavis also spoke against the abolitionists, claiming that the sudden end of slavery would make life even worse for blacks. "All that can be done is to make the best of a bad bargain," he declared. He was upset by the violent aborted slave uprising led by NAT TURNER, for which he personally paid a price. Spurred by panic over the incident, the North Carolina legislature passed a law in 1832 banning blacks from preaching. In the summer of 1835, the legislature further degraded Chavis by stripping all blacks of the right to vote. In view of his close relationship with many prominent white former students, such acts were particularly galling to him.

The Presbyterian Church did little to oppose the prevailing hostility toward black preachers, choosing only to provide for Chavis's financial support. Chavis kept busy writing pamphlets such as the 6,000-word "Letter Upon the Atonement of Christ," published in 1837. Early biographical sources agree that he died in 1838. However, none of them makes mention of the story passed down through the generations by the Chavis family that he was murdered after whites discovered that he was secretly teaching slave children.

Chavis was almost entirely forgotten until the turn of the 20th century. Since then, a recreational park and a federal housing project in Raleigh, North Carolina, have been named in his honor.

Further Reading

Garrity, John A., and Mark C. Carnes, eds. *American National Biography.* Vol. 4. New York: Oxford University Press, 2002.

Knight, Edgar. "Notes on John Chavis." In *Black Apostles at Home and Abroad*. Boston: G. K. Hall, 1982.

Murphy, Larry G., ed. *Encyclopedia of African American Religious Biography*. New York: Garland Publishing, 1993.

Clements, George
(1932–   ) *Roman Catholic priest*

Father George Clements, one of the few African-American Roman Catholic priests, made a national impact while serving his parish on the South Side of Chicago with a combination of courage and tough love. The *Chicago Tribune* once wrote of him, "His methods may be excessive, but it's easy to appreciate and admire his outrage. . . . Father Clements is unrepentant."

Clements was born on January 26, 1932, in Chicago, Illinois, to Samuel and Aldonia Clements, a stockyard worker and homemaker, respectively. Raised in Chicago, he remembers wanting to be a priest since at least the age of 12, although he briefly considered the legal profession. Clements enrolled at Quigley Theological Seminary in Chicago and became the school's first black graduate. He obtained a bachelor's degree in philosophy and a master's degree in theology from Quigley, and then continued his education at St. Mary of the Lake Seminary in Mundelein, Illinois.

Clements stayed close to home after his ordination into the Roman Catholic Church in 1957, serving as an associate pastor at two Chicago churches. During this time, he was active in the Civil Rights movement and traveled to Selma, Alabama, to march with demonstrators. Upon learning that MARTIN LUTHER KING, JR., had been assassinated, he removed a statue of St. Anthony from his church and replaced it with one of King. Later in his ministry he served as a spiritual adviser to local Black Panther members and allowed them to use his church facilities for meetings.

In 1969, Clements was installed at pastor of Holy Angels Church, a large South Side Chicago church with its own school, and he immediately infused it with his own uncompromising, high-principled philosophy. A firm believer in self-help, he told his congregation that they would not depend on charity from anyone. This was their church, and they would take responsibility for it. Clements's attitude struck a chord with the congregation and the community. In little more than a decade, the church membership swelled from 1,500 to more than 4,000, and the church's annual giving jumped from $300,000 to more than $1 million.

Clements administered his school, which came to be the largest black Catholic elementary school in the nation, in the same way. He implemented a rule that parents of all students at the school must regularly attend Sunday mass with their families. Many resisted the policy at first or refused to take him seriously until Clements suspended 200 students when their parents failed to meet the requirement. Tuition was kept low at Holy Angels School, but Clements insisted that each family contribute to the school's fund-raising efforts. The school was in session all year, and any child falling behind in class was expected to come in on Saturday to work on his or her studies. Under Clements's direction, Holy Angels developed a national reputation for high academic achievement and strict discipline. "We are using the school as a tool for our real goal," Clements explained, "which is, of course, the moral uplifting of the people who come through here through their interaction with the Catholic Church."

Father Clements was fiercely protective of his parishioners and their community. In 1969, he organized a community boycott of grocery and drug stores that sold drug paraphernalia. When one wholesaler refused to allow him in the store to inspect his merchandise, Clements pounded on the glass door until it shattered, which resulted in his injury and arrest. He had more serious problems, however, with the drug dealers who resented his campaign against their livelihood. They made death threats against him, which prompted the city of Chicago to temporarily provide him with 24-hour-a-day bodyguards, and shot out a window at his rectory and vandalized his car. Clements never backed down. "I'm not going to stand by and watch my people die," he declared. U.S. drug policy director William Bennett praised him as one of 20 people in the nation on the front line in the fight against drugs. In 1991, Clements took an equally tough stand against a brewing company for introducing a malt liquor with twice the normal alcohol content of beer and, he alleged, targeting sales at black youth. The publicity he generated helped influence the company to abandon the product.

Such single-minded commitment often made Clements simultaneously a saint and a criminal in the public eye. One day, after being arrested while protesting the closing of a boys' club, he was hailed as a hero for persuading an armed man holed up in a building to surrender to police.

During his ministry, Clements became increasingly concerned about the numbers of parentless black children in society. As usual, he believed it was incumbent upon the black community to take care of the problem, and he encouraged his parishioners to adopt these children. But when he invited people from the state's Department of Child and Family Services to his parish to provide information on the subject, he was stunned by the poor response. Convinced that the problem was lack of awareness rather than rejection, he brought the issue to national attention in 1981 by declaring he would adopt a child himself. He then carried through on his promise by adopting a 14-year-old boy named Joey. The story was made into a 1987 network television movie entitled *The Father Clements Story*.

At first, his superior frowned on Clements's action. But the adoption (which Clements fol-

lowed by adopting two other boys) created a flurry of international publicity that achieved exactly what he wanted. The news coverage gave a boost to a new adoption program he created within the church called "One Church, One Child." The program led to 3,000 adoptions in the state of Illinois and expanded to 90 chapters in 30 states.

One of the bleakest moments in his ministry came in 1986, when Holy Angels Church burned to the ground. Defiantly, Clements announced that the church would rebuild without help from anyone, and he asked the congregation to dig deep into their pockets. But despite his words, thousands of dollars of financial gifts and in-kind labor poured in from people outside the congregation who were inspired by Clements's work. The new solar-powered church building was completed in 1991. Two weeks later, Clements retired; he spent his time on mission and counseling work and as a priest in the Bahamas. One of his fellow priests gave tribute to Clements's legacy, saying, "George, more than any person in the country, has given credibility to the Catholic Church for African Americans."

Further Reading

Bigelow, Barbara Carlisle. *Contemporary Black Biography.* Vol. 2. Detroit, Mich.: Gale Research, 1992.

Marshall, Marilyn. "Adopt a Child," *Ebony,* June 1981, pp. 28–38.

Mitchell-Powell, Brenda. *African American Biography.* Vol. 1. Detroit, Mich.: Gale, 1994.

Cleveland, James
(1931–1991) *Baptist clergy, gospel singer, musician*

James Cleveland was an acclaimed gospel singer and minister who organized the Gospel Music Workshop of America and also founded a thriving church in Los Angeles. According to his famous protégée, Aretha Franklin, "Anyone who heard him, you were touched by him. He was a motivator and an innovator."

Cleveland was born on December 3, 1931, in Chicago, Illinois, where his father worked for the Works Project Administration. As a child, he met gospel legend THOMAS DORSEY while attending Pilgrim Baptist Church, where his grandmother was a devout member and where Dorsey directed a choir. Dorsey was so impressed with the boy that he asked him to sing a solo. Cleveland was also inspired by singer MAHALIA JACKSON, who was on his newspaper route.

Cleveland performed frequently as a singer in his teens, to the point where he damaged his vocal cords. He began to concentrate on piano, and started writing music. His composition "Grace Is Sufficient" was presented at the 1948 National Baptist Convention. A year later, he joined a performing group known as the Gospelaires, primarily as an accompanist, and recorded his first song, "Oh, What a Time." Singer Roberta Martin liked his work so much that in the 1950s she bought compositions from him for a flat rate of $40 per song.

In 1953, Cleveland toured with Mahalia Jackson and then joined a group called the Caravans as a pianist and arranger. Eventually, he took part in the group's vocals and found that his voice, which had evolved into a raspy baritone, was compelling. The group had some success with such songs as "The Solid Rock." But Cleveland eventually left to form his own group, called the Gospel Chimes, in 1959.

He then moved to Detroit where he took a job as music director of New Bethel Baptist Church. The church's minister was the father of Aretha Franklin, with whom Cleveland worked to develop her singing talent. In later years, the two would collaborate and win a Grammy Award for their record "Amazing Grace." While in Detroit, Cleveland recorded "The Love of God" with a local choir. This attracted the attention of executives at the Savoy music company and they signed him to a contract in 1960.

In 1963, he recorded "Peace Be Still," one of the best-selling gospel albums of all time. On the strength of that effort, Savoy paid him a lucrative annual salary to do four albums a year.

That same year, Cleveland, who had become a licensed minister while in Detroit, moved to Los Angeles to lead the New Greater Harvest Baptist Church and also formed the James Cleveland Singers. In 1970, he started his own church, Cornerstone Institutional Baptist Church, which by the time of his death from respiratory failure on February 9, 1991, had grown to more than 7,000 members. Cleveland put out more than 100 albums in his career and was the first gospel singer to be given a star on Hollywood's Walk of Fame. But his greatest legacy is the organization of the Gospel Music Workshop of America in 1968, a national convention that provides instruction and inspiration for as many as 50,000 gospel singers annually.

Further Reading

Broughton, Viv. *Black Gospel: An Illustrated History of the Gospel Sound.* Poole, Dorset, England: Blandford Press, 1985.

Melton, J. Gordon. *Religious Leaders of America.* 2d ed. Detroit, Mich.: Gale Research, 1999.

Moritz, Charles, ed. *Current Biography, 1985.* New York: H. W. Wilson, 1985.

Phelps, Shirelle. *Contemporary Black Biography.* Vol. 19, Detroit, Mich.: Gale Research, 1998.

Coker, Daniel
(1780–1846) *African Methodist Episcopal clergy*

Daniel Coker holds the double distinction of being one of the founding organizers of the African Methodist Episcopal Church (AME Church) and the founder of the West Africa Methodist Church.

He was born Isaac Wright in 1780 in Baltimore County, Maryland, to Susan Coker, a white

English indentured servant, and Edward Wright, a slave. The scandalous situation was covered up by listing a mulatto on a neighboring plantation as the boy's mother and classifying the boy as a slave. Wright was raised along with several older white half-brothers from Susan Coker's previous marriage. They apparently got along well. The older boys took Isaac to school as their valet, which exposed him to learning that otherwise would have been denied him. There is also speculation that they may have helped him escape the plantation some time in his early teens. With his very light complexion, and going under the name Daniel Coker, he was able to avoid detection while living in New York.

He came under the influence of some Methodists when studying on his own in New York. Coker took so enthusiastically to the religion that he became a preacher. In 1801, Coker wanted to return to Baltimore to visit his family. He cleared the way for this reunion by first making arrangements to purchase his freedom.

Coker settled in Baltimore, and began teaching at the African Academy, the first school for blacks in Baltimore that employed black teachers. Both the school and the Black Methodist Society of Baltimore, a black congregation of which Coker eventually assumed leadership, were affiliated with the Sharp Street Methodist Church.

In 1808, Coker was ordained a deacon by progressive Methodist bishop Francis Asbury. While continuing to work at the school, he became a leader in the black community and was known for his strong abolitionist views. In 1810, he published his best-known writing, "A Dialogue between a Virginian and an African Minister," in which he answered the standard arguments against emancipation of slaves.

In the meantime, Coker and other blacks were becoming exasperated with the Methodist Church. For while the Black Methodist Society had become an independent black congregation, it was dependent upon white ordained ministers

for sacraments and was subject to white church authorities. After repeated failures to get their concerns addressed, Coker led several hundred black Methodists in Baltimore to declare their separation from the white church and form the African Methodist Society in 1815.

The following year he traveled to Philadelphia to meet with RICHARD ALLEN and others who were interested in forming a national black denomination. Coker served as vice chair of the conference and on April 9, 1816, was elected the first bishop of an independent black church in the United States. Historians have advanced widely varying reasons why he resigned the next day—from Coker's lack of interest to dissatisfaction with the light color of Coker's skin. Whatever the reason, he bowed out and Allen took on the historic role as leader of the church. Coker returned to Baltimore and guided his rapidly growing church to a membership of more than 1,000.

In 1820, Coker traveled to Africa, preceding LOTT CARY by a year as the first black missionary to that continent. All three agents of the Maryland Colonizing Society, the sponsor of the journey, died en route, leaving Coker in charge. He took the party to Sierra Leone to regroup, and when new agents arrived to lead the relocation to Liberia, he stayed behind and organized the West Africa Methodist Church.

Further Reading
Coan, Josephus. "Daniel Coker: 19th Century Black Church Organizer, Educator, and Missionary." *Journal of the Interdenominational Theology Center* (fall 1975): 17–31.

Coker, Daniel. "A Dialogue Between a Virginian and an African Minister (1810)." In *Pamphlets of Protest: An Anthology of Early African American Protest Literature, 1790–1860.* Edited by Richard Newman et al. New York: Routledge, 2001, 52–65.

Murphy, Larry G., ed. *Encyclopedia of African American Religious Biography.* New York: Garland Publishing, 1993.

Coleman, Mattie E.
(Mattie Eliza Howard)

(1870–1942) *Colored Methodist Episcopal missionary*

Mattie Coleman was far ahead of her time in blazing a trail through the medical profession for black women and was a driving force for women's empowerment both in the church and in society.

She was born Mattie Eliza Howard on July 3, 1870, in Sumner County, Tennessee, near Nashville. There is no mention of her mother in her biographical records, but her father was a minister in the African Methodist Episcopal Church (AME Church). Mattie was raised in a parsonage along with three younger siblings, and experienced a religious awakening at age 12. Her family believed in the value of education and after her graduation from high school at the age of 15 she was enrolled at Central Tennessee College in Nashville (renamed Walden University in 1900).

Little is known of her career following college until the turn of the 20th century, when she entered Nashville's Meharry Medical College. In 1902, she married P. J. Coleman, an aspiring minister of the Colored Methodist Episcopal Church (CME Church), established in 1870. Despite her father and her upbringing, Mattie switched to her husband's denomination.

She graduated from Meharry in 1906, and became one of the nation's first black female physicians. That year, her husband accepted a call to Wesley Chapel in Clarksville, Tennessee. Mattie Coleman joined him and set up her own medical practice in the community. She combined her medical training with her Christian beliefs by focusing much of her practice on the needy. At the same time, she began taking a more active role in spreading the gospel, evidenced by her leadership role as president of the Clarksville District Missionary Society. In 1909, she explained her involvement by saying, "There are many homes that are in the dark and polluted that may be lighted and pure by letting the sunshine of God's word in by a loving word and a kind deed."

Having blazed her own path through the male-dominated medical world, Coleman took on another male bastion in the CME Church. For many years she agitated for the establishment of a national CME women's organization in a denomination that had little use for women's leadership. Finally, in 1918, the group's convention allowed for the establishment of the Woman's Connectional Missionary Society (WCMS). Coleman was elected its first president, a post that she held for more than 20 years, and made it into an active force for mission in Tennessee. Historian Othal Hawthorne Lakey went so far as to state, "The WCMS evolved into the strongest and most viable organization of the CME church."

Keeping active in her professional world, Coleman was named first dean of women and medical adviser at Lane College in Jackson, Tennessee, in 1909. She worked for 20 years as a medical examiner and conquered yet another challenge by becoming the first graduate of Meharry's dentistry program. On the social front, she joined white women in the area of women's suffrage. She was largely responsible for a campaign that registered 2,500 new black women voters in Nashville in 1919. Coleman was also active in the temperance movement. Again combining her professional expertise with her Christian witness, she assumed leadership of the Tennessee State Vocational School for Girls from 1939 until her death in 1942.

Further Reading

"Dr. Mattie E. Coleman," *Christian Index* (March 1, 1994): 6.

Murphy, Larry G., ed. *Encyclopedia of African American Religious Biography.* New York: Garland Publishing, 1993.

Smith, Jesse Carney, ed. *Notable Black American Women.* Vol. 2. Detroit, Mich.: Gale Research, 1996.

Colemon, Johnnie
(Johnnie Haley)

(1921–) *founder of Christ Unity Temple*

Johnnie Colemon is the flamboyant founder and leader of one of Chicago's largest churches, the nondenominational Christ Unity Temple, based on her brand of New Thought Unity philosophy of practical Christianity.

She was born Johnnie Haley in Centerville, Alabama, to John and Lula Haley in 1921, and raised in Columbus, Mississippi. Through childhood, she felt unhappy with her masculine first name, the result of her father's desire for a boy, and what she considered an unattractive physical appearance. "I used to ask God why he sent me here looking like this," she remembers. Her sense of inferiority was reinforced at Wiley College, a traditionally black school, in Marshall, Texas, when she was denied admission to the sorority of her choice.

Upon graduation in 1943, she taught school in Canton, Mississippi, and then Chicago, Illinois. Eventually, she left teaching for business, working as a price analyst at the Chicago Market Center. She married Richard Colemon and kept his last name after she was widowed and even after she remarried.

Johnnie Colemon's life changed dramatically in the 1950s when, by her account, she was diagnosed with an undisclosed fatal illness and given six months to live. Shortly thereafter, she came across a pamphlet entitled "God Is Your Health; You Can't Be Sick," put out by the Unity Church. Although raised in the Methodist faith, Colemon had never been religious. But desperate and curious about the pamphlet's claim, she traveled to the Unity School of Practical Christianity near Kansas City, Missouri. Within a short time, Colemon found her health restored, and she responded by converting to the Unity philosophy. She enrolled in the school, was ordained into the denomination in 1956, and opened her

first church, the Christ Unity Center, in a YMCA building in Chicago.

At first, Colemon attracted only a few dozen members. When she expanded into a new building, the Christ Unity Temple, in 1963, her congregation still numbered only 200. But in the following years, her New Thought philosophy, which church historians Hans Baer and Marrill Singer described as a mixture of "holy materialism, positive thinking and practical Christianity," began attracting members. Colemon taught that religion was concerned with the present, not some future judgment and reward, and that the job of religion was to improve people's situations on Earth by helping them call forth the Christ that is within everyone. She broke with traditional Christianity on such matters as the existence of heaven and hell, and her avoidance of water in baptism. Her message became so popular that a new addition to the church, designed to accommodate more than 1,000 people, proved too small from the day it opened in 1973.

For a time, Colemon was an enthusiastic member of the Unity Church. In 1968 she became the first African-American president of the Association of Unity Churches. But lingering resentments over the organization's racial attitudes and other matters caused her to withdraw her congregation from the association and go independent in 1975.

Colemon's church was renamed Christ Universal Temple. She expanded her ministry by founding the Johnnie Colemon Institute to train teachers in the faith, and the Universal Foundation for Better Living. In 1985, aided by an anonymous donor, the church built a 4,000-seat facility on 32 acres on Chicago's South Side.

Colemon, who received a doctor of divinity degree from Wiley College in 1977, has been criticized for promoting materialism and ignoring biblical teachings that oppose it. She responds by saying, "God is money in action. God supplies my every need . . . anything I need when I need it; all I need do is name it." Her influence was recognized by Chicago's Mayor Harold Washington, who proclaimed August 18, 1985, to be "Reverend Dr. Johnnie Colemon Day."

Further Reading

Colemon, Johnnie. *Open Your Mind and Be Healed.* Marina del Rey, Calif.: DeVorss and Company, 2000.

Mabunda, L. Mpho. *Contemporary Black Biography.* Vol. 11. Detroit, Mich.: Gale Research, 1996.

Melton, J. Gordon. *Religious Leaders of America.* 2d ed. Detroit, Mich.: Gale Research, 1999.

Cone, James Hal
(1938–) *theologian*

James Cone is widely regarded as the most influential black theologian of the 20th century. It was he who found a way to reconcile the message of Western Christianity with the militancy of the Black Power movement and who forced religious academia to take the insights of African-American theologians seriously.

Cone was born on August 5, 1938, in Fordyce, Arkansas. He and one brother grew up in Bearden, Arkansas, a rural community of 1,200, where their father, Charlie, made a meager living as a woodcutter. James's childhood was a time of segregated schools, drinking fountains, and movie houses. Cone said that, as a child, he avoided white people "as if they were poisonous snakes."

Upset at the vastly inferior educational facilities afforded blacks in the segregated school system, Charlie Cone took the courageous step of filing suit against the Bearden school board to desegregate the schools. The action impressed his son, who later said, "No person has influenced me more than my father in his courage, sense of self, and the clarity of his commitment to end racial injustice."

The other large influence in James's life was Macedonia African Methodist Episcopal Church,

where his mother, Lucille, served as an orator. Cone attended church every Sunday as well as many evenings during the week. At these services, Cone first began to wrestle with the contradictions between the Christian message of love and unity and the blatant segregation of churches in the South.

Cone went on to attend Shorter College for two years, then transferred to Philander Smith College in Little Rock, Arkansas, from which he graduated in 1958. He became attracted to the study of theology because, in his words, "it opened the door to exploring faith's meaning for the current time and situation in which I was living." This interest led him to enroll at Garrett Theological Seminary in Evanston, Illinois. Cone loved the intellectual atmosphere of the school—the chance to research and debate and open himself to new ideas. There he wrestled with the problem of trying to locate the African-American experience in the context of Christianity. He was bothered by his perception that blacks tended to not only accept anti-intellectualism in their religion but actually seemed to promote it in favor of more emotion-based religion. Convinced that Jesus did not advocate ignorance, he set out to pursue a more reasoned approach to his faith.

At the same time, he found it increasingly difficult to reconcile traditional European Christian theology with his experience as an African American. Even at the seminary, he discovered a polarized environment and chafed at a system in which blacks were second-class citizens. Cone was profoundly influenced by the Civil Rights movement in the turbulent 1960s. As blacks began to assert their own identity in the culture, Cone began to ask new questions of the theological community. He wanted to know why none of the curricula at colleges and seminaries reflected any concern with an African-American perspective.

Cone earned his bachelor of divinity degree from Garrett in 1961, and then went on to earn a master's degree and a doctorate from Northwestern University. He returned to Philander Smith as a teacher in 1964, where, as a newly ordained minister, he served as pastor of Woodlawn African Methodist Episcopal Church. In 1966, he moved to Michigan to accept a teaching position at Adrian College.

The more Cone immersed himself in his studies of the history and culture of African Americans as it related to theology, and read works by such influential figures as MARTIN LUTHER KING, JR., and MALCOLM X, in which he was aided greatly by his wife, the former Rose Hampton, he became angered at the invisibility of blacks in theological circles. He noted that prior to the Civil Rights movement of the 1950s and 1960s, mainstream churches in the United States regarded segregated congregations as the acceptable norm. In the wake of the movement, none of them defended the existence of segregated churches. "It could be argued that Martin Luther Kings's contribution to the identity of Christianity in America and the world was as far-reaching as Augustine in the fifth century and Luther's influence in the 16th," he asserted.

Cone was particularly drawn to the work of Gayraud Wilmore and others, who urged religious leaders to take more seriously the Black Power philosophy that was scaring much of the white establishment. He believed that rather than fearing black assertion of identity, theologians should welcome it as evidence of God's presence. Cone was so brimming with ideas on where Black Power rhetoric meshed with theology that he wrote the book *Black Theology and Black Power* in a single month in the summer of 1968. The book was published the following year. Reminding his readers that "theology is always done for particular times and places and addressed to a specific audience," he staked out the position that Black Power was the central message of Christianity to the United States in the 20th century. Cone's revolutionary viewpoint attracted the attention of the academic

world, and his persuasive arguments forced them to take him seriously. Cone was immediately hailed as a brilliant, innovative theologian, and was rewarded with a faculty position at Union Theological Seminary in New York City.

He solidified his reputation with the publication of *A Black Theology of Liberation* in 1970. In this book, he gave a theological foundation for the recurring African-American emphasis on God as the champion of the oppressed. He saw the crux of Christian theology being God's liberating activity on behalf of the poor and powerless, as expressed throughout the Scriptures. "The form of Black religion that is expressed is the style of story," he wrote, "and its content is liberation." Therefore, he argued that Christianity, by its nature, demands participation in the goal of liberation. He pointed to African Americans as providing the eyes through which this truth is expressed to 20th-century America.

Some religious leaders have criticized Cone for reducing Christianity to a simplistic black-versus-white conflict. Others feel that he opened up a new perspective with such organized thought and elegance that he should be regarded as the most important black theologian of his time. Since his first two books, he has gone on to write two dozen more books, including *Risks of Faith: The Emergence of a Black Theology of Liberation* in 1999.

Further Reading

Cone, James H. *A Black Theology of Liberation.* Philadelphia: Lippincott, 1970.

———. *For My People: Black Theology and the Black Church.* Maryknoll, N.Y.: Orbis Books, 1984.

———. *Martin and Malcolm: Dream or Nightmare?* Maryknoll, N.Y.: Orbis Books, 1991.

———. *Risks of Faith: The Emergence of a Black Theology of Liberation: 1968–1998.* Boston: Beacon Press, 1999.

———. *Speaking the Truth: Ecumenism, Liberation, and Black Theology.* Grand Rapids, Mich.: Eerdmans, 1986.

Crouch, Andrae
(Andrae Edward Crouch)

(1942–) *gospel singer, composer, Church of God in Christ clergy*

Andrae Crouch has been a master at broadening the audience for gospel music by infusing his compositions with rhythm and blues, rock, and even country and western music. Music forms the main aspect of a ministry that includes pastoral duties at the church that his father served prior to his death.

He was born Andrae Edward Crouch on July 1, 1942, in Los Angeles, California, along with his twin sister, Sandra. The family was well-steeped in Christian ministry in the Church of God in Christ. Along with Andrae's father, Benjamin, who served as a preacher in addition to operating his dry-cleaning business, his uncle Samuel Crouch became a distinguished bishop in the church.

Both Sandra and Andrae's older brother Benjamin were musically talented at an early age, and Andrae joined them, singing in a trio in church on his father's radio program. The story of Andrae's beginnings as a music prodigy at the age of 11 contains an element of the divine presence. Apparently, his father was invited to preach at a church in Val Verde, California, that had a poor music program. At a loss how to solve the problem, he called Andrae to him and prayed that God would give him the gift of music. Two weeks later, according to Andrae, his father called on him to accompany the church choir on the piano in a rendition of the hymn "What a Friend We Have in Jesus," and despite having never played the piano before, Andrae was able to do a creditable job. Before long, Andrae was playing regularly in church and even directing the choir.

His musical abilities helped Crouch overcome shyness and a stuttering problem when he attended junior high school in Pacoima, California. He began to compose music at the age of 14.

In high school, he formed a musical group called the Cogics (an acronym for his denomination, the Church of God in Christ). Among its members were Billy Preston, who eventually became a well-known crossover musician in his own right.

Following high school, Crouch attended Valley Junior College in San Fernando and Life Bible College in Los Angeles. His father had high hopes of his becoming a pastor, and Crouch dabbled in ministry to drug addicts. But his heart lay in musical composition and performance. While working as an associate of David Wilkerson, an Assembly of God pastor who was nationally famous for his mission work to inner-city street gangs, Crouch found a way to combine the two interests. In 1968, he formed a musical group made of former drug addicts, and went on a brief tour with them.

The following year, he formed another group, the Disciples, that played pop-influenced Christian gospel music. The group put out its first album, *Take the Message Everywhere*, that year. After a couple more albums in subsequent years, Crouch branched out into solo work with the album *Just Andrae*. While the albums sold reasonably well for the limited gospel market, Crouch and the Disciples scored a breakthrough in 1972 with *One Touch of His Hand*. In this album, the blend of powerful lyrics with rhythms and arrangements from other popular music genres appealed to a broad spectrum of listeners. Quickly, Crouch and the Disciples became one of the most popular musical acts in the world. In 1974, he published an autobiography entitled *Through It All*. He and his group toured nationally and in 1975 and 1979 played before sold-out crowds at Carnegie Hall, went on world tours, and had their songs translated into more than 20 languages. Crouch won Grammy Awards in the gospel music category four years in a row, from 1978 to 1981. He expanded the boundaries of gospel music even further by making an appearance on the racy comedy show *Saturday Night Live* in 1980.

Such a willingness to speak to the secular market brought a barrage of criticism of Crouch as someone who was selling out to the fame and fortune of the worldly market rather than adhering to his beliefs and values. Crouch responded that there was nothing wrong with bringing his message to a wider audience. In defiance of the critics, he put out *Don't Give Up,* an album aimed directly at the secular market, in 1981.

Crouch's career was brought to earth in 1982 when he was arrested for cocaine possession. Crouch maintained that the powder police found in his car was merely chicken soup powder, and no charges were ever brought. But the incident and the negative publicity helped him to realize that his life was spinning out of control. He stopped touring and began spending more time with his family and his church. It was during this period in his life that he composed and arranged the music for the motion picture *The Color Purple,* for which he earned an Academy Award nomination in 1985.

Crouch's life reached a major crisis in 1993–94, when his father, mother, and older brother Benjamin all died within a few months. His dying father urged him to take over Christ Memorial Church of God in Christ in Pacoima, which he had spent most of his adult life building. But Crouch balked at the prospect of giving up his music to become a pastor. "I thought that if I took up the mantle of pastor I wouldn't be able to make music my first priority," he said. "But God just pointed out to me that He had given me everything and He wasn't about to take anything away." According to Crouch, his new direction was revealed to him when a mysterious force hurled him to the floor while he was listening to a sermon. Crouch has found since that his ministry work has helped to inspire new songs.

Crouch's influence on the Christian music scene has extended well past the 15 albums he has released. Songs such as "My Tribute" and "Soon and Very Soon" have entered the worship services and hymnbooks of mainstream U.S.

churches. In 1996, he was honored by the release of *Tribute: The Songs of Andrae Crouch,* a collection of his songs performed by many of the top Christian vocal artists in the nation. At the turn of the 21st century, he had earned nine Grammy Awards.

Further Reading

Broughton, Viv. *Black Gospel: An Illustrated History of the Gospel Sound.* Poole, Dorset, England: Blandford Press, 1985.
Burgess, Stanley M., et al., eds. *Dictionary of Pentecostal and Charismatic Movements.* Grand Rapids, Mich.: Zondervan, 1988.
Henderson, Ashyia N. *Contemporary Black Biography.* Vol. 27. Detroit, Mich.: Gale Research, 2001.
Murphy, Larry G., ed. *Encyclopedia of African American Religious Biography.* New York: Garland Publishing, 1993.

Crummell, Alexander
(1819–1898) *Episcopal clergy*

W. E. B. DuBois once said, "The more I met of Alexander Crummell, the more I felt how much that world was losing which knew so little of him." One of the most influential black clergymen of the late 19th century, Crummell saw it as his duty to guide blacks spiritually to reclaim the dignity of their character and their regard for humanity.

Crummell was born in New York City on March 3, 1819, the first son of Boston Crummell and Charity Hicks. His father had experienced the heights and depths of social standing as an African prince and then a slave. By the time of Alexander's birth, he was free again and establishing himself as a prosperous grocer in New York City. Determined to see his children educated, he hired white tutors in addition to sending all five children to the African Free School.

The Crummells were active members of St. Philip's Episcopal Church, pastored by Peter Williams. The ransacking of the church in the antiabolition riots of 1833 moved Alexander to devote himself to the antislavery cause, and he spent much of his free time working in the American Anti-Slavery Society offices.

High school opportunities for blacks were almost nonexistent at the time, but the Crummells learned of the Noyes Academy, an experimental school established by radical abolitionists in Canaan, New Hampshire. In 1835, Alexander enrolled at the school along with 13 other blacks and 28 whites. The townspeople, however, reacted violently to the school and in August 1835 brought in oxen to drag the school into a swamp a half-mile away.

Crummell had to settle for the Oneida Institute, a training school for manual labor, in Whitesboro, New York. Around that time, he was swept up in a religious fervor that changed his life. With the backing of his bishop, he applied for admission to the General Theological Seminary of the Episcopal Church. Although the seminary had no official policy of discrimination, he was refused admission without being given a reason. Encouraged by John Jay, grandson of the first chief justice of the U.S. Supreme Court, he agitated for admission but only fell further out of favor. He later commented, "Hardly a churchman, clerical or lay, would touch such a presumptuous Negro, such a disturber of the peace as myself."

Upon Jay's advice, he then applied for and was admitted to the Yale Theological Seminary in the Episcopal Church's Eastern Diocese. However, although he was allowed to attend classes, his name never appeared on the official college register. Crummell proved his mettle at that school, prompting one professor to report that no student had "given him more satisfaction" than Crummell.

Crummell was ordained a deacon at St. Paul's Cathedral in Boston on May 1, 1842, and assigned to a congregation in Providence, Rhode Island. He became so preoccupied with politics at that time, however, that he neglected his du-

ties and this, along with an abrasive personality, forced his resignation. He then organized a small congregation in Philadelphia, Pennsylvania, St. Bartholomew's, where he was ordained a priest in 1844. There, also, he married Sarah Elston, daughter of a leading black family in New York. The couple would have five children together.

Professionally, Crummell continued to struggle. After a brief stay in Philadelphia, he moved to New Haven, Connecticut, and then to St. Matthew's Episcopal Church in New York, where the pay was so meager that his family faced constant hunger.

Episcopal minister Alexander Crummell performed valuable church work in Africa and the United States and served as a spiritual mentor to many African-American clergy. *(Fisk University)*

During his early career, Crummell advocated working cooperatively with whites to improve the status of blacks in the United States. But in 1846, his efforts to abolish a law requiring property qualification for black voters failed. Discouraged, Crummell began to think more in terms of black self-reliance. "We appear to be unconscious that we are men," he once complained, and he made it part of his mission to change that.

In 1847, he traveled to England, a country he admired for its stand in abolishing the slave trade, in hopes of raising money for his ministry in the United States. While there, he received an opportunity to study at Cambridge University. Crummell was impressed by the lack of racism he found in England. He ended up staying for six years, obtaining his degree in 1853.

Rather than return to the United States, Crummell set out to implement his philosophy of enlightened black beneficence toward Africa. He had written an influential paper entitled "The Relations and Duties of Free Colored Men in America to Africa," which assumed a link between Christianity and civilization. He viewed blacks' problems as the result of moral weakness, which could be alleviated through Christian faith; self-hatred, which could countered by installation of pride in heritage; and industrial primitiveness, which American enterprise could solve. He saw Liberia as a haven for persecuted American blacks and urged their emigration there.

Putting his words into action, Crummell moved to Liberia, where he served as a professor at the College of Liberia. The experience, however, proved to be a disappointment. The college became ensnarled in political fights between blacks and mulattos that hindered any real progress. Discouraged, Crummell resigned in 1866, and headed back to the United States, now persuaded that African Americans were better off investing in the United States. The Episcopal Church appointed him "Missionary-at-Large to the Colored People of Washington, D.C." There he founded and presided over St. Luke's Church. Meanwhile, his Christian philosophy greatly influenced a generation of blacks. In *The Souls of Black Folk,* DuBois hailed him as a spiritual father figure who represented the world of ideals, intellect, character, and racial integration, which DuBois placed in stark contrast to what he saw as Booker T. Washington's crass materialism. A contemporary Presbyterian clergyman summed up Crummell's influence when he wrote, "No man understood more thoroughly the whole of thought, the caste of mind, the aspirations and the inward longings than did he, and no man had greater love and admiration for his people, or greater confidence in their future than he." Crummell died on September 10, 1898.

Further Reading

Litwack, Leon, and August Meier, ed. *Black Leaders of the Nineteenth Century.* Urbana: University of Illinois Press, 1988.

Newman, Richard, et al, ed. *Pamphlets of Protest: An Anthology of Early African American Protest Literature, 1790–1860.* New York: Routledge, 2001.

Oldfield, J. R. *Alexander Crummell and the Creation of an African-American Church in Liberia.* Lewiston, N.Y.: E. Mellen Press, 1990.

Shattuck, Gardiner H., Jr. *Episcopalians and Race.* Lexington: University Press of Kentucky, 2000.

Young, Henry J. *Major Black Religious Leaders, 1755–1940.* Nashville, Tenn.: Abingdon, 1977.

D

Daddy Grace
(Charles Manuel Grace, Sweet Daddy Grace, Marcelino Manoel da Graca)
(1881–1960) *founder of the House of Prayer*

Daddy Grace was the charismatic and controversial leader of a religious group that was reputed to have as many as 3 million members at its peak. By some estimates, the House of Prayer that he founded in the 1920s remains one of the largest independent Christian communities in the United States.

He was born Marcelino Manoel da Graca in 1881 in the Cape Verde Islands, a Portuguese possession off the coast of West Africa. He was one of 10 children of Emmanuel da Graca, a Portuguese stonecutter, and his wife, Delomba. The family apparently immigrated to the United States between 1900 and 1903, probably settling in the Portuguese community in New Bedford, Massachusetts. As he came of age, Marcelino, who Anglicized his name to Charles Manuel Grace, supported himself by various jobs such as cook on a railroad, grocer, and sewing machine salesman. There is evidence that in 1909 he married Jennie Lombard, with whom he had two children. But when he embarked on a religious career several years later, she wanted nothing to do with it. The couple soon divorced.

Calling himself Sweet Daddy Grace, he began preaching a brand of Holiness Christianity that evolved into a movement he called the United House of Prayer for All People on the Rock of the Apostolic Faith, commonly known as the House of Prayer. The name was based on a Bible verse, Isaiah 56:7, and Grace always insisted on using the term *house of prayer* instead of *church*.

He founded his first House of Prayer in West Wareham, Massachusetts, in the early 1920s. A few years later he traveled to the Middle East and founded a House of Prayer in Egypt. Returning to the United States, he began preaching in the Southeast, setting up tents in the poorest slums as a base for his operations, and using a fire hose for baptisms. His work in the ghettos led to the remark by one contemporary pastor that Grace "took a rock no one else would use and made it into the cornerstone of his church." Eventually, he established Houses of Prayer all the way from western New York to Florida. His greatest success came in Charlotte, North Carolina, which he visited in 1926. His following in that community grew so large that even as late as the 1960s, the House of Prayer was the largest black church in the city.

The House of Prayer was basically a one-man operation. Despite the fact that he was not regarded as a particularly captivating speaker, Grace had an aura about him that attracted attention. He wore his hair in a long, flowing style and was known for his long fingernails colored red, white, and blue.

Critics have noted that Grace did not have any specific theology or social program. He tended to speak in riddles and relied heavily on wordplay between his last name and the doctrine of grace to the point where virtually every Scriptural reference could be interpreted as referring specifically to him. Typical of his statements was, "If you sin against God, Grace can save you, but if you sin against Grace, God cannot save you."

Grace's greatest strength was in establishing new churches and raising funds. He urged members in the 100 to 300 Houses of Prayer that he founded to give generously to the organization. As his organization operated no programs, social or religious, and as all decisions in the spending of the funds were made entirely by Grace, many critics charged that the church's primary function was simply to get bigger and wealthier. Harshest of all was the critique of analyst Joseph Washington, who declared, "The movement was a profit-making venture by a black entrepreneur who succeeded by manipulating spiritual hunger into a system of self-aggrandizement."

Grace did use the funds to live a lavish lifestyle in a large mansion in Montclair, New Jersey, and owned various other properties, but he put most of the offerings back into the church. His popularity rested on the twin supports of inclusivity and assertion of healing power. The House of Prayer appealed directly to some of the poorest and most downtrodden of society and attracted most of its early members from that group. It showed no partiality as far as race. Grace himself did not especially identify with African Americans and was even accused of being condescending toward blacks.

Grace's reputation for miraculous powers was at the heart of his movement's growth. New converts were easy to recruit when hundreds of new followers told stories of personal healing that he conducted. Grace capitalized on this facet of his ministry to raise money by selling products such as toothpaste, soup, and coffee with his name on them that were reputed to have healing powers.

Stories of Sweet Daddy Grace's supernatural powers abounded. One common anecdote told by his supporters was that while Grace was being put on trial for some offense, he predicted that a sign from heaven would soon prove to all that he was a man of God. This was quickly followed by a giant fireball from the sky that knocked a huge branch from a tree in the courtyard outside of the trial room. While Grace never made any claims to divinity, he referred to himself as "God's Intermediary" and as "The Last Prophet."

Grace was in constant trouble with the law, yet never had a conviction against him sustained. When the Internal Revenue Service sued him for nonpayment of income taxes, he successfully argued that voluntary donations to his church were not taxable income. In 1934, he was prosecuted under a law known as the Mann Act for transporting a woman (one of his church workers) across state lines for immoral purposes. He was convicted and sentenced to a year in jail, but the conviction was overturned on appeal. The legal battles had no apparent effect on his popularity.

Grace died on January 12, 1960. Since the House of Prayer was so heavily dependent on him for leadership, the movement has had difficulty sustaining itself in the years since, but remains strong in several enclaves.

Further Reading

Davis, Lenwood G., ed. *Daddy Grace: An Annotated Bibliography.* New York: Greenwood Press, 1992.

Lincoln, C. Eric, and Lawrence H. Mayima. *The Black Church in the African American Experience.* Durham, N.C.: Duke University Press, 1990.

Lippy, Charles, ed. *Twentieth Century Shapers of American Popular Religion.* New York: Greenwood, 1989.

Delille, Henrietta

(1813–1862) *founder of Sisters of the Holy Family*

Henrietta Delille was the founder of one of the first African-American Catholic orders, the Sisters of the Holy Family, which continues its charitable services a century and a half after her death.

Delille was born in New Orleans in 1813, the youngest of three children of Jean-Baptiste Delille-Sarpy and Marie Dias. Delille-Sarpy was a white Creole, a French-speaking Roman Catholic descendant of the French colonists of Louisiana, and Dias was a free black who lived as his mistress. Creoles, both black and white, held unique advantages in the New Orleans area—many owned large expanses of property.

Henrietta was raised to follow her mother in the commonly accepted practice of well-bred black women acting as concubines to wealthy white Creole men. As such, she was educated in the fine arts and in social etiquette. At the age of 11, however, she met Sister Sainte-Marthe Frontier, who had just opened a school for young black women. Delille attended the school from 1824 until it closed in 1827. During that time, the free black students were encouraged to teach religion to slaves where it was permitted. Her experience at the school prompted Delille to become devoutly religious, and she alienated many relatives with her condemnation of extramarital cohabitation.

Worried about how her daughter would support herself, Marie Dias urged her to travel to France to become a nun. Delille, however, was interested in serving in New Orleans and refused to leave. Dias suffered a nervous breakdown in 1832, and her daughter was ruled a ward of the court until 1835. The following year, Delille and a white friend, Juliette Gaudin, attempted to form an interracial religious community. Neither the New Orleans nor the Roman Catholic authorities approved of the idea, however, and their plan had to be dropped.

Delille realized that she could accomplish her dream without white male backing. When Father Etienne J. F. Rousselon arrived in New Orleans from France in 1837, she and her friends prevailed upon him to sponsor their

Henrietta Delille organized the Sisters of the Holy Family, one of the first Catholic orders for African-American women. *(Friends of Henrietta Delille Commission)*

group. Rousselon agreed, although he, too, steered them away from an interracial organization. He requested that the church authorities allow him to found a Catholic society of free black women, with Delille as the leader. His request was granted in 1842, even as New Orleans was closing down other black religious groups, probably because of the special status of black Creoles, Delille's exceptionally light skin, and the fact that they were under the supervision of a white man. The black Sisters of the Holy Family, however, were not allowed to wear nun's habits in public.

Rousselon apparently envisioned the order as contemplative in nature, but Delille had other ideas. With the aid of wealthy supporters, the order opened a hospice in 1849 and a convent and school the following year. Delille completed her vows in 1852 after attending the all-white St. Michael's School. Under her leadership, the group grew and prospered. They were of immense aid to the city during various plagues that swept New Orleans in the 1850s. The sisters cared for so many sick and orphaned of both races that they had to open a new hospital annex in 1860.

Upon Delille's death on November 16, 1862, the order declined and most people thought it would disappear. But the Sisters of the Holy Family revived and remains active today.

Further Reading

Estes-Hicks, Onita. "Henrietta Delille: Free Woman of Color, Candidate for Roman Catholic Sainthood, Early Feminist." *Journal of the Interdenominational Theological Center* (spring 1995): 4–54.

Henderson, Ashyia N. *Contemporary Black Biography.* Vol. 27. Detroit, Mich.: Gale Research, 2002.

Hine, Darlene Clarke. *Black Women in America, A–L.* Brooklyn, N.Y.: Carlson Publishing, 1993.

Murphy, Larry G., ed. *Encyclopedia of African American Religious Biography.* New York: Garland Publishing, 1993.

Delk, Yvonne V.
(1939–   ) *United Church of Christ clergy*

Yvonne Delk was the first black woman ordained by the United Church of Christ (UCC) and the first woman to be nominated as president of a major denomination.

Delk was born in 1939 in Norfolk, Virginia, to working-class parents. Her father, Marcus Delk, Sr., worked in the city's naval yard during World War II, and then earned a living digging graves at Calvary Cemetery. Her mother, Cora, never got past the sixth grade in school. Yvonne grew up embarrassed about her humble origins, which were exacerbated by the city's social climate. Speaking of Norfolk's more affluent neighborhoods, she recalled, "We were not able to come anywhere in the area without folk assuming you were a maid."

The source of the family's dignity was religion, which stemmed from Yvonne's grandmother, Julia Delk, a Holiness minister who traveled across the country and even overseas in the 1920s and 1930s. Yvonne's mother was also extremely religious. "My mama was a praying woman, a spiritual guardian," she remembers. "We got prayed for every day we left out of that house." The family attended Macedonia African Christian Church, where Delk heard the preaching of a theology of liberation. She understood this liberating power of God to be not some distant utopian hope but a force ready to break loose in the present, even in the most segregated areas of the country, and she felt called by God to be part of that movement.

Following high school, Delk attended Norfolk State University, from which she graduated in 1961. Seeking a seminary to continue her training, she heeded the advice of her mentor, Reverend Percel Austin, to expand her horizons by attending Andover Newton Theological Seminary in Boston. At first, the culture shock of living in the all-white environment, combined with the pressure she felt to succeed, pushed her to the edge of a nervous breakdown. However, she recovered her balance and, after taking part in the Freedom Ride campaign for civil rights in the South in 1962, attained her degree in 1963.

Despite her upbringing in more traditionally black churches, Delk moved into the UCC and accepted her first assignment as a nonordained church worker at First Congregational Church in Atlanta. In 1965, she moved to a struggling church in a declining neighborhood in Cincinnati, where she worked as Christian education coordinator. Her work attracted the attention of church officials, who offered her an administrative position with the UCC's Board of Homeland Ministries. In the spring of 1970, she spent four months in Africa and found it so compelling that she considered staying. Instead, she returned to the United States and pursued her studies. In 1974, she became the first black woman ordained into the UCC.

During her career, her grandmother's influence has been evident in Delk's ability to connect emotionally with her listeners and in her leadership in forming the First United Holiness Women's Missionary Society. She also became the first woman and the first African-American director in the 114-year existence of the Community Renewal Society, an urban mission agency in Chicago. Delk has been active in many controversial debates with the church. In 1989, she took a key role in the National Dialogue on Abortion Perspectives. "As an African American, choice is essential to my understanding of what it means to function with dignity and respect," she wrote.

After 36 years in the ministry, she returned home to Norfolk in 1999. There she continues to espouse her view of inclusive Christian ministry, summed up in her words: "The gospel of Jesus Christ says the community is never complete until all of us are there at the table."

Further Reading

Berger, Rose Marie. "The World as God Intends." *Sojourners* (May 1999): 18–23.

Delk, Yvonne. "A Time For Action," *Sojourners* (March 1998): 25.

Divine, Father See FATHER DIVINE.

Dorsey, Thomas Andrew
(1899–1993) *gospel music founder*

Thomas Dorsey is often described as the father of gospel music. Although he did not create the genre, his influence in bringing blues into gospel music and his establishment of the gospel chorus in churches significantly altered the style of worship for many African-American communities.

Thomas Andrew Dorsey was born in 1899 in Villa Rica, Georgia, the oldest child of Etta and Thomas Madison Dorsey. His childhood was steeped in both organized religion and music. His father, a graduate of Atlanta Baptist College, farmed while he served two small country churches as a preacher, and his mother played organ for church services. One of his uncles, Corrie Hindsman, was a professional musician and hymn writer.

Unable to make a living preaching and farming, his parents moved to Atlanta in 1908, where his father worked as a laborer and his mother took in wash. Young Dorsey was humiliated by the move when he was demoted from third grade to first. He quit school altogether after completing fourth grade at the age of 13. By that time, he had shown great promise as a musician and was playing piano at parties and dances. He taught himself to read music and learned piano techniques by watching performers at the local vaudeville theater.

In 1916, Dorsey stopped in Chicago to visit an uncle while on his way to Philadelphia to look for work in the naval yards. He liked the city and decided to stay to pursue his musical career. He worked at menial jobs while seeking gigs at parties, and he enrolled at the Chicago

School of Composition and Arrangement. On October 9, 1920, he copyrighted his first piece of music, a blues song called "If You Don't Believe I'm Leaving You Can Count the Days I'm Gone." That same year, however, he suffered a nervous breakdown and returned to Atlanta to be under his mother's care for nearly a year.

When he returned to Chicago, he was talked into attending the 1921 National Baptist Convention. There he heard Reverend A. W. Nix, who was known for his recordings of his sermons, sing "I Do, Don't You?" Dorsey had fallen away from religion over the years, but the song struck such a deep chord in him that he became convinced that his calling in life was to spread the gospel through music. In 1922, he accepted a post as music director at Chicago New Hope Baptist Church and began writing his first sacred songs, including "If I Don't Get There" and "We Will Meet Him in the Sweet By and By."

These songs were not successful, however, and Dorsey returned to the secular music world to earn a living. He joined a group called The Whispering Syncopators for whom he began writing blues music. In 1923, King Oliver's Creole Jazz Band recorded his composition "Riverside Blues." This helped Dorsey establish a reputation as a composer and arranger. In 1924, he signed on as pianist and director of Ma Rainey's Wildcat Jazz Band. After two years of touring with this group, he suffered his second nervous breakdown, which left him unable to work for nearly two years.

Dorsey credited a sermon of H. H. Haley with helping him emerge from his depression. Again, he tried to channel his creative efforts into religious work, with songs such as "If You See My Savior, Tell Him That You Saw Me," and again found that his mixture of blues, jazz, and spiritual music found few buyers. While still composing gospel music on the side, he joined guitarist Hudson Whitaker and the two went on tour as Georgia Tom and Tampa Red. They gained such widespread popularity with their brand of "hokum blues" that they were able to cut 60 records between 1928 and 1932. In the meantime, Dorsey finally got the break he needed in gospel music when popular singer Willie Mae Fisher sang "If You See My Savior" at the August 1930 National Baptist Convention. The exposure enabled him to sell 4,000 copies of his music during the convention.

For a time, Dorsey continued to play in both the secular and sacred worlds, a position that was increasingly tenuous due to the sexually suggestive nature of his partner Whitaker's lyrics.

Thomas Dorsey changed the landscape of black religious music in the United States with his introduction and development of the gospel choir. *(Fisk University)*

But his growing popularity in the Baptist Church helped him slowly wean himself from the secular world. He began to make more of an effort to sell sheet music of his compositions, and he became involved in a worship innovation—the gospel chorus. Dorsey accompanied the African-American churches' first gospel chorus at Ebenezer Baptist Church in Chicago in 1931. Breaking with the staid tradition of church choirs, the chorus marched down the aisle and took up their position behind the pulpit. They swayed to the blues-based beat as they sang with emotional fervor. The experiment was so successful that Dorsey was asked to form a chorus at another Chicago church, Pilgrim Baptist.

Although he had never written choral music, Dorsey became the leader in the development of the gospel chorus. In August 1932, he traveled to St. Louis to help a church in that city organize a chorus. While there, he learned that his wife, Nettie, had died in childbirth. Rushing back home, he found the baby alive, only to see it die the following day.

In his grief, Dorsey turned to the piano for consolation and composed his most beloved song, "Precious Lord, Take My Hand." From that point he abandoned the secular music world and devoted his life to gospel music. In 1932, he founded the Dorsey House of Music, the first music company specializing in the work of black gospel music composers. In 1933, he founded the National Convention of Gospel Choirs and Choruses.

From 1933 to 1939, he toured with singer Sallie Martin, and then joined with MAHALIA JACKSON in the early 1940s. This combo ushered in the golden age of gospel music. Dorsey published more than 500 songs in his career; many a gospel music artist launched a career by singing a Dorsey composition. He continued to promote gospel music as president of the National Convention of Gospel Choirs and Choruses into the 1970s while also serving as assistant pastor of Pilgrim Baptist Church until

slowed by Alzheimer's disease. He died on January 23, 1993.

Further Reading

Broughton, Viv. *Black Gospel: An Illustrated History of the Gospel Sound.* Poole, Dorset, England: Blandford Press, 1985.

Harris, Michael. *The Rise of Gospel Blues: The Music of Thomas Andrew Dorsey in the Urban Church.* New York: Oxford University Press, 1992.

Dyson, Michael Eric
(1958–   ) *educator, writer, Baptist clergy*

An outspoken advocate of intellectualism, Michael Dyson has been a key voice in fusing religion, intellect, and inner-city street culture into a coherent whole. He has taken a celebrity approach to exercises of the mind, saying, "I want young people to look at me and go, 'Damn, I want to be like that brother. He sharp, he be on point. I want to make the life of the mind sexy.'"

Dyson was born on October 23, 1958, to Addie Mae Leonard, a teacher's aide in the Detroit ghetto. When he was two, his mother married Everett Dyson, an auto worker who adopted Michael and his older brother. A strong family work ethic and Dyson's academic talent helped negate the effects of a harsh environment. He read the dictionary to increase his vocabulary, pored over classic literature, skipped school to visit the library, and at the age of 12, won a speech contest.

During his junior year of high school, Dyson won a scholarship to attend a prestigious prep school in the suburbs. As one of only 10 blacks on campus, however, he was traumatized by racism and isolation. His grades suffered so badly that he was expelled and had to attend night school to complete his high school degree.

Dyson then became involved with a dancer/model whom he married when she became pregnant. He was fired from his job before the child was born, which forced the family to rely on welfare for survival. The couple were soon divorced, and Dyson supported his son by working in the same factory as his father.

In 1978, he finally got back on the academic track, enrolling at Knoxville College in Tennessee. Intrigued by the status of pastors as the "public intellectuals" of the black community, Dyson obtained a preaching license in the Baptist tradition in 1979 and was ordained in 1981. He served as pastor at three churches and worked at a factory to put himself through school. Dyson transferred to Carson-Newman College, in Jefferson City, Tennessee, only to be expelled for a year for boycotting chapel to protest the lack of black pastors on campus.

Dyson hit his academic stride at Princeton University, graduating with honors in the study of religion in 1985. He went on to earn a master's degree in 1991 while teaching at the Chicago Theological Seminary and a Ph.D. from Princeton in religious ethics and politics in 1993, while teaching at Brown University. After serving as director of the Institute of African-American Research at the University of North Carolina, he joined the faculty of Columbia University.

Dyson has been a prolific and controversial writer on religious topics, and has battled with the male-dominated African-American religious world by urging a greater role for women in the church. He is regularly consulted by the media for his insights into modern culture from the perspective of a black intellectual. Among his works are *Making Malcolm: The Myth and Meaning of Malcolm X, Reflecting Black: African American Culture,* and *Between God and Gangsta Rap: Bearing Witness to Black Culture.* While the last book criticized the excesses of popular rap music, Dyson urged its acceptance as a legitimate art form. His many articles providing insights into modern urban black culture as it relates to Christianity led to his nickname as the "Hip Hop Intellectual."

Further Reading

Dyson, Michael Eric. *Between God and Gangsta Rap: Bearing Witness to Black Culture.* New York: Oxford University Press, 1996.

Graham, Judith, ed. *Current Biography, 1997.* New York: H. W. Wilson, 1997.

E

Elaw, Zilpha

(ca. 1790–unknown) *Methodist spiritual autobiographer*

The name of Zilpha Elaw would never have been recorded in history had she not left detailed memoirs. Her writings provide a unique insight into the life of one of the first black woman missionaries.

Zilpha was born sometime around 1790 in the vicinity of Philadelphia to free black parents who brought her up in a pious fashion. Her mother died giving birth to her 22nd child when Zilpha was 12, at which time her father hired her out to a Quaker family. Her father died within two years, but she stayed with the Quakers until she was 18.

Zilpha had little interest in religion while living with the Quakers, who were fairly inactive in their faith. But she was captivated by the words of traveling Methodist preachers. After Jesus Christ appeared to her in a vision, she converted to the Methodist faith.

Two years later, she married Joseph Elaw, a fuller by trade. In 1811, they moved from the Philadelphia area to Burlington, New Jersey, where job opportunities were more plentiful, and had a daughter the next year. In 1817, Zilpha attended a revival meeting during which she fell into an ecstatic trance. The experience

left her convinced that her soul had been sanctified by God, and she began speaking out at revival meetings. At one such occasion in 1819, her words were so inspiring that many listeners told her that she was divinely inspired to preach.

Her renewed zeal increased the strain between Zilpha and her husband, who was uncomfortable with her religious fervor and feared public ridicule for allowing his wife to take on the "man's business" of preaching. But, encouraged mostly by whites, she began to feel that God wanted her to take on a preaching career. As long as Joe was around, that would not happen. But in 1923 he died of consumption. This did not immediately free Zilpha to preach, since she now had to support herself and her child. She worked for a time as a domestic and then opened a school for black children in Burlington. But she could not shake the call she felt. Despite a lack of support from any denomination or supervisory board, she left her daughter in the care of relatives and began to preach.

Elaw began her work in Philadelphia. In 1828, she showed unprecedented courage by carrying her message to slave states. For nearly two years she preached in Maryland and Virginia, running the constant risk of being arrested or kidnapped and sold into slavery. She then returned to New England and the Middle Atlantic states until 1840, when she became convinced she needed to take her mission to England.

Elaw spent the next five years in central England, preaching more than 1,000 sermons. She wrote of "thousands of privations, hardships, target fires, vexatious anxiety and deep affliction, to which my previous life was an utter stranger." Most discouraging was the prejudice she encountered, not because of race but because of gender. Yet she thanked God for a successful ministry, which she described in her book, *Memoirs of the Life, Religious Experience, Ministry, Travels and Labors of Mrs. Zilpha Elaw, An American Female of Colour,* published in London in 1846. Having left this valuable record of life as a religious pioneer, she apparently returned to the United States, but no further information about her exists.

Further Reading

Andrews, William L., ed. *Sisters of the Spirit.* Bloomington: Indiana University Press, 1986.

Murphy, Larry G., ed. *Encyclopedia of African American Religious Biography.* New York: Garland Publishing, 1993.

Elmore, Ronn
(1957–) *clergy, author, therapist*

Ronn Elmore, advertised as the Relationship Doctor, has found a niche as a Christian therapist and counselor who is often consulted by the media on such issues as marriage, family, and friendship.

Elmore was born on April 27, 1957, in Louisville, Kentucky. Although his father, grandfather, and great-grandfather were all ministers, Elmore broke out of the mold with his dream of becoming an actor and a dancer. At the age of 16 he left home to pursue the dream in New York City, where he studied at the Dance The-

atre of Harlem. He traveled to Europe and found a steady stream of acting and dancing jobs, including a stint at the famed Moulin Rouge in Paris. When business was slow, he supplemented his income by modeling.

In a couple of years, Elmore grew tired of the constant travel and returned to the United States. Still in love with show business, he thought he could stay involved in the entertainment field yet have a more stable life if he found work as a publicist. With that goal in mind, he attended Antioch University, from which he graduated in 1981 with a degree in public relations and journalism.

While waiting for job offers, he began volunteering at a local church. He quickly found the work and the relationships so fulfilling that he scrapped his former plans and decided to enter the ministry. Elmore enrolled at Fuller Theological Seminary in Los Angeles, where he focused on psychology and family counseling, while serving as an assistant pastor at Faithful Central Church. Upon graduation in May 1989, he persuaded his church to let him develop a counseling ministry. Elmore started the Relationship Center and the Relationship Enrichment Programs to help people, particularly African Americans, work through relationship issues from a Christian perspective. One of his emphases was on learning to give and accept forgiveness, which, he said, "is something that came straight from God—it's his invention." Elmore believed that he could best help couples come together in a spiritual commitment anchored in Jesus Christ.

Early in his work, most of his clients were women, and they expressed similar needs in dealing with the opposite sex. Elmore decided to hold a seminar called "How to Love a Black Man," figuring that this would allow him to help perhaps two dozen people at once. When nearly 200 showed up, he realized he had stumbled on a huge area of need. He began traveling throughout the United States holding seminars and attracting large audiences with his blend of psychology, Christianity, and humor.

In the early 1990s, Elmore began his own radio show in Los Angeles. He became a frequent guest on television talk shows and was often interviewed by the media on the topics of love, marriage, and family. In 1996, he published *How to Love a Black Man;* its success prompted him to follow it with *How to Love a Black Woman* in 1998. His celebrity status, however, did not distract him from ministry in the inner city of Los Angeles. He is the founder of Kingdom Shelter, which provides transition housing for homeless men, and a popular lay counseling program known as the Encouragers.

Further Reading

Elmore, Ronn. *An Outrageous Commitment: The 48 Vows of an Indestructive Marriage.* New York: Harper, 2003.

———. *How to Love a Black Man.* New York: Warner Books, 2001.

———. *How to Love a Black Woman.* New York: Warner Books, 1999.

Phelps, Shirelle. *Contemporary Black Biography.* Vol. 21. Detroit, Mich.: Gale Research, 1999.

el Shabazz, el-Hajj Malik See MALCOLM X.

Evans, Henry
(unknown–1810) *Methodist preacher*

Henry Evans was such a powerful preacher that he won over both whites and blacks, forming a remarkable interracial Methodist congregation in a southern city at the beginning of the 19th century and earning celebrity status throughout the region.

Evans is believed to have been born in the mid-18th century in Charles County, Virginia, of free parents. On his way to Charleston to set up shop as a shoemaker, he stopped in Fayetteville, North Carolina, sometime in the 1780s. He was so appalled by what he saw as the moral laxity of the slaves and the absence of any Methodist church, black or white, in town, that he felt it his duty to stay and preach to them, while plying his trade as a cobbler.

His efforts were not appreciated by the white townspeople, who suspected him of fomenting sedition, and who put him in jail for a time. Evans did not give up, however. He continued meeting secretly with slaves in the sand hills outside of town. Over the course of several years, his preaching and example made such an impact on the slaves' behavior that the townspeople had to admit that Evans was doing good work. In 1802, the city passed an ordinance authorizing black preachers to hold services on Sunday only, between sunrise and sundown, provided they had a license. Evans obtained a license and was able to preach openly.

As there was still no Methodist church in town, Evans began directing his message to all listeners and encouraged whites as well as blacks to attend his services. At first, the white community ignored him. But beginning in about 1807, his message began attracting them in large numbers. Despite the fact that he was barely literate, Evans's preaching, according to a Methodist bishop, was "so remarkable as to have become the greatest curiosity of the town, insomuch that distinguished visitors hardly felt that they might pass a Sunday in Fayetteville without hearing him preach." Ironically, so many whites attended services that there was no room for blacks, who had to make way for them, until extensions were added to each wing of the building. The general minutes for an 1810 meeting show that whites outnumbered blacks 110 to 87 in the congregation at that time. According to one source, the notion of a semiliterate black man presiding over whites in a congregation was too much for Methodist authorities to handle, and they sent a white minister to take charge. Evans, however, was allowed to remain, and in fact a room for him was built at the church.

Evans was known for his sincerity and unyielding faith. Shortly before his death, he came before the congregation and declared, "I have come to say my last word to you and it is this: None but Christ."

Following Evans's death in 1810, the mixed-race congregation thrived for several years, gaining such a reputation that in 1814 it was the host congregation for a large regional Methodist conference. But racial attitudes soon hardened. Whites withdrew and formed their own congregation. Evans's original black congregation was incorporated into the African Methodist Episcopal Zion Church in 1866.

Further Reading

"Divine Appointment." Historic Evans Metropolitan A. M. E. Zion Church web site. Available online. URL: http://www.nvo.com/evansmetropolitan/divineappointmenthenryevans/htm. Downloaded February 18, 2003.

Garrity, John A., and Mark C. Carnes, eds. *American National Biography.* Vol. 7. New York: Oxford University Press, 2002.

Murphy, Larry G., ed. *Encyclopedia of African American Religious Biography.* New York: Garland Publishing, 1993.

Satterwhite, John H. "An Interpretation of History: Henry Evans, Bishop James W. Hood." *AMEZ Quarterly Review* (October 1984): 28–31.

Fard, W. D.
(Wallace Fard Muhammad, Mahdi, Walli Farrad, Fred Dodd, Wallace Ford)
(ca. 1879 or ca. 1891–unknown) *founder of the Nation of Islam*

The man who went by the name W. D. Fard and a dozen other aliases was one of the most mysterious and bizarre religious figures of all time. He was the founder of the Nation of Islam, commonly known as the Black Muslims, which provided an alternative vision for blacks upset with the pace of civil rights progress in the United States, and achieved a national presence far out of balance with their numbers.

There are two versions of Fard's life history prior to 1930, each with several variations. By his own account, he was born in 1879 in Mecca, Saudi Arabia, the son of a wealthy member of the Koreeish tribe, to which the Islamic prophet Muhammad belonged. He was educated in England before coming to the United States to carry out his mission of revealing the truth to African Americans. According to different versions of this story, he either attended the University of California at an unspecified location or simply arrived in the United States on July 4, 1930.

According to Federal Bureau of Investigation (FBI) records, however, he was born on February 26, 1891, in New Zealand. Although Fard identified himself as black, FBI records list his mother as Polynesian and his father as British. He immigrated to the United States in 1913 and spent some time in Portland, where he married and had a son. He then abandoned them, lived briefly in Seattle under the name Fred Dodd, and then moved to Los Angeles, where he opened a café.

Police records show that Wallace Fard (or Ford) was arrested three times in that city. The first was for assault with a deadly weapon in 1918, a charge that was dropped. In January 1926, he was picked up for bootlegging and fined. A month later he was arrested on a felony narcotics charge and convicted. This brush with the law resulted in nearly three years in San Quentin State Prison before his release on May 27, 1929. His followers have disputed the entire FBI biography, accusing the organization of falsifying Fard's files and changing his fingerprints.

There is no dispute that Fard arrived in Detroit at the beginning of the Great Depression, supporting himself by selling silks, primarily to black customers. There he began proclaiming his novel ideas about the origins of the human race. Influenced by the claim of recently-deceased NOBLE DREW ALI that American blacks were descendants of the Moors, Fard declared that *Negroes* was a term invented by whites to put down the black race. In fact, "black men" were the original race of human beings, created by Allah. White people were recent mutations created on the island of Patmos by an evil black scientist through a process of grafting that took 600 years. Whites were therefore devils, an inferior race that Allah would destroy. Christianity, he said, was a religion created by whites to enslave blacks. Blacks should instead adopt Islam as their authentic religion. Although Fard's views on racial matters strayed far from established Islamic teachings, he followed the Islamic code on matters of prayer and diet. He told his followers to reject their last names—the slave names of their white masters—and instead use the letter X to signify their unknown ancestors.

According to his most devoted recruit, Elijah Poole, Fard introduced himself by saying, "My name is Mahdi; I am God, I came to guide you into the right path that you may be successful and see the hereafter." Recognizing Poole's leadership potential, he renamed him ELIJAH MUHAMMAD, made him his second in command, and went to his house every day to instruct him in the faith.

Fard's message came at a time when the first wave of the Great Depression had hit blacks particularly hard. They were the first employees let go and now, unable to find work, felt frustrated and powerless to improve their lot. Fard's message promoting black pride and focusing blame on the white power structure resonated particularly well at this time.

Fard started out by meeting with small groups of followers in their homes. Before long, however, his fame spread, bringing in hundreds of potential followers. Fard began holding meetings in various halls, which were soon overflowing with recruits. At one time, his followers, calling themselves the Nation of Islam, were reputed to number 5,000 in Detroit.

Fard created a temple in Detroit, then a second temple in Chicago; organized a semimilitary group called the Fruit of Islam; established the Muslim Girls Training Corps Class; and started a school. The school, called the University of Islam (although it was more of an ele-mentary school and high school), and Fard's views on military conscription led to trouble with the government. The Detroit School Board refused to recognize the school and attempted to force the Nation of Islam to return their children to the public schools. Fearful of inducing a violent backlash, however, the school board eventually backed off. The FBI became concerned when Fard preached that his followers were citizens of the Nation of Islam, not of the United States, and that therefore they were not to take part in any military matters, including the draft. Agents began monitoring the group, seeking to shut it down for seditious activity.

A bizarre murder committed by a man with a vague connection to the Nation of Islam provided the FBI with an excuse to arrest Fard on May 23, 1933. According to FBI records of an interview, Fard "admitted his teaching was strictly a racket," and that he was "getting all the money out of it he could." Although they were unable to pin any crime on him, the Detroit police labeled Fard an undesirable and ordered him to leave the city.

Fard went into hiding instead, preparing Elijah Muhammad to take over the organization. According to an article published in the *San Francisco Examiner* in 1963, reporter Ed Montgomery spoke with the woman who claimed to be his former wife. She told him that Fard worked for a while as a traveling suit salesman before arriving in Los Angeles in the spring of 1934. Failing in an attempt to reconcile with his wife, he sold his car and sailed to New Zealand. No one else has been able to account for Fard's disappearance.

Elijah Muhammad, who took over the Nation of Islam, declared Fard to have been Allah incarnate and initiated the observance of Savior's Day in his honor. Eventually, Muhammad built the group, which had been declining in number before Fard's disappearance, into a significant religious and political organization.

Further Reading

Kyle, Richard. *The Religious Fringe*. Downers Grove, Ill.: Intervarsity Press, 1993.

Moses, Wilson Jeremiah. *Black Messiahs and Uncle Toms: The Social and Literary Manipulations of a Religious Myth*. University Park: Pennsylvania State University Press, 1982.

Muhammad, Elijah. *The True History of Master Fard Muhammad*. Decatur, Ga.: Secretarius Publishing, 1997.

Farrakhan, Louis
(Louis Eugene Walcott)
(1933–   ) *Nation of Islam minister*

As the most outspoken member of the Nation of Islam, Louis Farrakhan has been one of the most polarizing figures in recent U.S. history. Praised by supporters as "the most eloquent rhetorician of black liberation of his time," and condemned by critics as a fascist, sexist, and a "hysterical preacher of hate," Farrakhan remains something of an uncomfortable enigma to the U.S. public. In a recent poll, more than half the respondents could not decide whether he had been a good or bad influence on the black community.

He was born Louis Eugene Walcott in 1933 in the Bronx, New York, under unusual circumstances. His mother, West Indian immigrant Mae Manning, named him after the man she loved rather than his father, Percival Clark, who had little to do with his son. He grew up in Roxbury, Massachusetts, a Boston enclave of West Indian culture, where his mother worked as a domestic.

Walcott was in many ways a model child—a choirboy at St. Cyprian Episcopal Church and a gifted musician who began playing violin at five and later performed on a national amateur talent show. He was academically gifted enough to earn acceptance at the prestigious Boston Latin High School (although he transferred out after one year due to discomfort among a predomi-

nantly white student body), and earned a track scholarship to Winston-Salem Teachers College in North Carolina. While there he married his high school sweetheart, Betsy. Later, he left school and returned to Boston.

During the 1950s, he worked as a calypso singer with the stage name "the Charmer," accompanying himself on the guitar and ukulele. Walcott enjoyed moderate success traveling the nightclub circuit. On a 1955 tour in Chicago, he heard a speech by MALCOLM X extolling the views of ELIJAH MUHAMMAD, leader of the Nation of Islam. This religion preached a black separatist, self-reliance philosophy similar to that of MARCUS GARVEY, maintaining that whites would never accept blacks as equal. But the Black Muslims, as the adherents were called, added strict dietary rules and moral behavior, and bristled with resentment of whites. This put them in opposition to some of the mainstream civil rights leaders who strove for integration and cooperation with whites. Walcott was so impressed that he abandoned his "slave" name and returned home to Boston as Louis X. He later adopted the name Farrakhan.

Farrakhan served as Malcolm X's protégé in Boston for a time. He applied his musical and artistic talents to the cause, writing two plays and several songs based on Nation of Islam teachings. He recorded one of these songs, "A White Man's Heaven Is a Black Man's Hell," which became a favorite Black Muslim anthem.

Farrakhan eventually took over leadership of the Boston mosque when Malcolm X moved on to Harlem, and he became utterly devoted to Elijah Muhammad. "I am wedded to this man whom I believe is the Messiah," he later declared, and he took to wearing a large gold ring covered with 40 diamonds that formed Muhammad's silhouette. Therefore, when Malcolm X became disillusioned with what he saw as Muhammad's hypocritical lifestyle and came to denounce the Nation of Islam as racist, Farrakhan reacted with venom. He accused Malcolm of spreading false

As the organizer of such events as the Million Man March, the Nation of Islam's Louis Farrakhan has been a polarizing figure for both black and white Americans. *(Schomburg Center for Research in Black Culture)*

rumors, and in December 1965, he wrote of Malcolm X, "such a man is worthy of death." When Malcolm X was assassinated two months later, suspicion fell on Farrakhan, who denied involvement but admitted he had created the climate that had produced the assassination. Farrakhan was rewarded for his faithfulness with leadership of the Harlem mosque that year.

When Elijah Muhammad died in 1975, his son WALLACE (WARITH) MUHAMMAD took over as leader of the Nation of Islam. He deviated from many of his father's positions, especially regarding antagonism toward whites, and at-

tempted to steer the Black Muslims into the fold of international orthodox Islam. Farrakhan, who disapproved of this policy, decided to take time off to travel in 1975 and 1976. But when Muhammad opened membership to whites in 1977, Farrakhan decided to break with him completely. He published a newspaper called *The Final Call* in which he asked true believers in the Nation of Islam to reject Warith Muhammad's leadership, return to the pure teachings of Elijah Muhammad, and revive the Nation of Islam as an exclusive enclave of the chosen people of God. He saw integration efforts as inherently harmful to blacks. "White supremacy produces in its wake black inferiority," he explained. "And black-inferiority thinking always measures success by how close we get to that which is superior."

Farrakhan's call to arms resonated with many poor young African-American males who saw little improvement in their economic status despite the work of the mainstream Civil Rights movement. They especially admired that he refused to modify his view to court the acceptance of the white establishment. He traveled nationwide on speaking tours in his trademark bow tie, telling large audiences, "All the progress we made has been lost. The brothers are back on the street shooting dope and dying."

But while Farrakhan built up an enthusiastic core of support, others viewed him as a racist hate monger. This proved problematic for blacks who were looking to share in the nation's power structure. During JESSE JACKSON's 1984 presidential campaign, Farrakhan backed him. But his backing proved a handicap that Jackson could not afford, particularly when Farrakhan was quoted as referring to Judaism as a "gutter religion." Reaction to Farrakhan was an almost universally swift and furious condemnation, and Jackson was put in the uncomfortable position of having to distance himself from his supporter. Farrakhan insisted that the media distorted his words and took them out of context in an attempt to sabotage Jackson's campaign, yet many of his later comments on Jews were far from conciliatory. Farrakhan dove further into controversy with claims of a federal conspiracy to flood black ghettos with crack cocaine.

Farrakhan's presence on the national stage reached its zenith with the Million Man March on Washington in 1995—an attempt to instill a sense of unity and purpose in black men and boys. The march reportedly drew close to 1 million participants and earned Farrakhan recognition as a national presence. Hugh Price, president of the Urban League, called it "the largest family values rally in the history of America." However, even many supporters of the march took care to repudiate Farrakhan's philosophy, and his influence within the black community remains mixed.

Further Reading

Farrakhan, Louis. *A Torchlight for America.* Chicago, Ill.: FCN, 1993.

Gardell, Mattias. *In the Name of Elijah Muhammad: Louis Farrakhan and the Nation of Islam.* Durham, N.C.: Duke University Press, 1996.

Graham, Judith, ed. *Current Biography Yearbook, 1992.* New York: H. W. Wilson, 1992.

Singh, Robert. *The Farrakhan Phenomenon: Race, Reaction, and Paranoid Style in American Politics.* Washington, D.C.: Georgetown University Press, 1997.

White, Vibert. *Inside the Nation of Islam: A Historical and Personal Testimony by a Black Muslim.* Gainesville: University of Florida Press, 2001.

Father Divine
(M. J. Divine, George Baker, Jr.)
(ca. 1880–1965) *founder and leader of Peace Mission*

One of the more mysterious religious figures of the 20th century, Father Divine offered hope, inspiration, and a helping hand to thousands of followers during the Great Depression. His was the best-known and most influential of the Holiness churches of that era.

Father Divine's origins are shrouded in obscurity. Some researchers claim he was born and raised in the Deep South, most likely South Carolina. Others say he was born in Providence, Rhode Island, before going south. Some claim his original name was George Baker, others say it was Major Jealous Devine, and birth dates range from 1879 to 1882. In any case, he grew up in the South, perhaps as the son of a sharecropper. Although Father Divine apparently had no formal education and was never ordained by any denomination, he became an itinerant preacher, traveling through the South, preaching with passion a message of hope and the equality of all people before God. The message was not well-received in the Jim Crow South; by his own estimation, he was nearly lynched 32 times.

Father Divine's career came into historical focus in 1919, when he purchased some property in Sayville, Long Island, New York. His intent was to work quietly for his vision of equality and service and to put the Christian philosophy into simple acts of everyday life. "I do not want anything out here in Sayville but my own Unadulterated Muse, My Own Spirit, and My own Life and my own unadulterated Love," he said.

He attracted little attention throughout the early 1920s as he set up his Peace Mission and provided food and work for a small group of followers. He opened his house to those who needed shelter, and by 1924 had 20 to 30 people working for him there. Father Divine preached a simple message of faith and equality; he was emphatic in his refusal to sanction any color or racial barrier. Any function of the Peace Mission was open to anyone. The worship services of the Peace Mission tended to be enthusiastic, in the Holiness tradition, and he took a hard line against what he viewed as sinful behavior. But it was Father Divine's magnetic personality that attracted and inspired his followers to such an unusual degree. He explained his charisma as

God's way of reaching people who needed to hear God but could not be reached by ordinary means. Kind and considerate to all, he encouraged his followers to approach him personally with any question or request. Father Divine came to represent security and protection from a hostile world, particularly when the nation fell into the grip of a grinding economic depression at the end of the decade. Just as important, he provided hope and a positive identity to people who were floundering in uncertain times.

Gradually, word spread about Father Divine's generosity and his ability to heal those who were sick. The Peace Mission eventually counted thousands of enthusiastic followers. By 1931, his fame had spread so far that busloads of worshippers and even tourists drove into Sayville to witness his activity. Father Divine was able to provide not just food but extravagant feasts for as many as 800 destitute people per day. The source of the funds that financed such charity has always been a mystery. Throughout his ministry, Father Divine never passed a collection plate and refused to accept contributions from anyone, yet he continually was able to provide for people's needs. He implied that it was all a result of faith. He taught that if a follower continued in poverty, it was not the fault of either God or the government, but of the follower for lack of faith in Father Divine. As a result, even the poorest of his disciples refused any kind of public assistance.

The mystery of Father Divine's deep material resources contributed to the growing notion that the leader of this group was divine in spirit as well as in name. Many of his followers began to address him as "God" and "Jesus Christ." Divine did little to discourage such talk. As time went on, his claims for himself grew grander. Father Divine had a large group of young women follow him around, taking notes on whatever he said. His sayings and deeds were compiled into a periodical called *New Day*. Excerpts from *New Day* were read at all Peace Mission meetings.

They came to be viewed as the sect's ultimate authority, replacing the Bible, whose reading Father Divine discouraged. He declared that true followers would abandon all other interests except for himself and his teachings. "Read my messages with an open heart and you will learn of Me and reserve Truth, such as man has never given," he wrote. "You are not dealing with man, but God."

One of the Peace Mission's most aggressive moves was a surreptitious attempt at housing integration. Using his white followers as buyers,

Father Divine and his Peace Mission inspired tremendous loyalty from a large urban following in the eastern United States. *(Corbis)*

Divine managed to acquire 2,000 acres of prime land in Ulster County, New York, on which he began to establish a rural cooperative.

Eventually, the neighbors back in Sayville objected to the bustle of activity surrounding Father Divine's home. In 1932, he and 80 followers were arrested and charged with disturbing the peace. Claiming that the arrests were racially motivated, Father Divine put up a spirited defense that attracted national attention. At one point, after several white followers testified that they believed Father Divine to be God, Judge Lewis Smith challenged their sanity. On May 25, 1932, Father Divine was found guilty and sentenced to a year in jail and a $500 fine. Two days later, Judge Smith died suddenly of a heart attack. This was viewed as the result of Father Divine's wrath and greatly enhanced his reputation, particularly when Smith's ruling was reversed by a higher court and the case was never retried. Father Divine began to claim great powers of retribution, including the carnage of World War II, as punishment for past behaviors.

In the early 1940s, Father Divine became entangled in a series of legal disputes. He fled from New York to Philadelphia to avoid lawsuits on the matters. His influence rapidly diminished during those years, and he ministered quietly to a group of a few hundred followers. Ironically, Father Divine, one of the most energetic proponents of racial equality, fell from favor just about the time the Civil Rights movement began to pick up steam. Social commentator Wendell King notes, "In the person of Father Divine is found as close to a resemblance to the charismatic type as most mortals could aspire to." But by the time of MARTIN LUTHER KING, JR., Divine had largely faded from memory, although small groups of followers remain in Philadelphia, and in several eastern states. Upon his death in 1965, his body was placed in a $300,000 shrine on his estate in an affluent Philadelphia suburb.

Further Reading

Birmingham, William. "God, Harlem, USA: The Father Divine Story." *Cross Currents* (spring 1993): 136–140.

Burkett, Randall, K., and Richard Newman. *Black Apostles: Afro-American Clergy Confront the Twentieth Century.* Boston: G. K. Hall and Company, 1978.

Burnham, Kenneth E. *God Comes to America: Father Divine and the Peace Mission Movement.* Boston: Lambeth Press, 1979.

Lincoln, C. Eric, and Lawrence H. Mayima. *The Black Church in the African American Experience.* Durham, N.C.: Duke University Press, 1990.

Moses, Wilson Jeremiah. *Black Messiahs and Uncle Toms: The Social and Literary Manipulations of a Religious Myth.* University Park: Pennsylvania State University Press, 1982.

Weisbrot, Robert. *Father Divine and the Struggle for Racial Equality.* Urbana: University of Illinois Press, 1983.

Fauntroy, Walter Edward
(1933–) *Baptist clergy, politician*

While not as widely known as some of his contemporaries, Walter Fauntroy played a key role in the civil rights struggle of the 1960s and won election as Washington, D.C.'s first representative in Congress.

Fauntroy was born on February 6, 1933, in Washington, D.C., the fourth of seven children of a patent office clerk and a part-time seamstress. He grew up during the Great Depression in a poor neighborhood on the city's northwest side, which he described as being surrounded by "the dope, the bootleg liquor, the payoffs to the cops, the general fear of the white man." He considered the New Bethel Baptist Church a "light in the wilderness," and spent many hours helping out at the church.

In his junior year at Dunbar High School, he experienced a call to the ministry. Congregation members helped him take the first step by raising funds for him to attend Virginia Union University in Richmond. Fauntroy graduated with honors in 1955, and then went on to Yale Divinity School. He enlisted in the Civil Rights movement and became close friends with MARTIN LUTHER KING, JR. Yale's president was so impressed with him that, upon Fauntroy's graduation in 1958, he offered him a position as dean. Fauntroy, however, felt he was needed at his home church and accepted a call to New Bethel.

In the 1960s, Fauntroy threw himself into the thick of the Civil Rights movement. In 1960, he was named director of the Southern Christian Leadership Conference's (SCLC) Washington chapter. In 1961, he helped coordinate the efforts of the Freedom Riders working for civil rights in the South, and two years later he played a major role in organizing the famous civil rights march on Washington, D.C. Fauntroy rose to the position of chairman of the board of the SCLC, from which he orchestrated the 1965 march from Selma to Montgomery in Alabama and the Poor People's Campaign in 1968, which sought to raise consciousness of poverty in the United States.

Throughout the decade he used his familiarity with Washington to serve as a lobbyist for civil rights legislation. In that role, he worked hard to facilitate passage of the historic Civil Rights Act of 1964 and the Voting Rights Act of 1965. He served as a civil rights adviser to President Johnson, who in 1967 appointed him vice-chair of the Washington City Council. Fauntroy took a leadership role in implementing the Model Inner City Community Organization, the largest inner-city renewal project in the nation and the first to be planned and administered solely by local residents.

When Congress voted to allow the District of Columbia to become a nonvoting member of Congress in 1970, Fauntroy ran for the office. With the support of the black religious commu-

nity, he won easily. In Congress, he provided the main impetus for legislation that granted the city self-governance. He held a high profile at the 1972 Democratic National Convention when he seconded the nomination of presidential candidate George McGovern. Fauntroy represented Washington until 1990, when he decided to run for city mayor instead. He lost that election, and since then he has formed a lobbying consulting firm and maintained his ministry at New Bethel.

Married to Dorothy Sims, Fauntroy has two children. He has explained his mixture of religion and politics by saying, "It is good news when his [Jesus's] followers of today act in the living present to feed the hungry, clothe the naked, and set at liberty those that are captive."

Further Reading

Haskins, Jim. *Distinguished African-American Political and Government Leaders.* Phoenix, Ariz.: Oryx Press, 1999.

Mabunda, L. Mpho. *Contemporary Black Biography.* Vol. 11. Detroit, Mich.: Gale Research, 1996.

Moritz, Charles, ed. *Current Biography, 1979.* New York: H. W. Wilson, 1979.

Ferguson, Catherine Williams
(Katy Ferguson)
(ca. 1779–1854) *Sunday school pioneer*

Katy Ferguson surmounted the tragedy of losing her husband and children before she was 20 to organize the first Sunday school in New York City.

She was born Catherine Williams in about 1779 in a schooner while her mother was en route from Virginia to New York City. Her mother was a slave who was being delivered to her new master, a Presbyterian elder. When Katy was seven, her mother was sold to another master. Williams recalled that "before we were torn asunder, she knelt down, laid her hand on my head, and gave me to God." That memory, as well as the Bible verses she had learned from her mother, helped to shape her life.

At the age of 14, Williams approached Reverend John Mason of the Murray Street Presbyterian Church in her Lower Manhattan neighborhood, concerned about the state of her soul. She emerged from the meeting fiercely committed to the church. Because of her race, she was not welcomed by many of the congregation members. Only when Mason personally escorted her to the altar was she able to receive communion for the first time.

In 1795, an abolitionist gave her half the $200 she needed to obtain her freedom in exchange for a year's work, and a generous merchant raised the other $100. At the age of 18, she marred a man whose name is recorded only as Ferguson. They had two children, but both father and children died within two years.

Katie Ferguson supported herself by baking and cleaning. She had a reputation as an expert in cleaning fine laces and other delicate material. But most of her income came from baking large cakes for weddings and other celebrations. When business was slow, she baked smaller cakes, which she brought to her customers. In so doing, she noticed a great number of homeless children and orphans wandering the streets. She began bringing them into her home on Sundays to give them religious instruction. Eventually, she took in many of the children and fed, clothed, and prayed for them until more permanent homes were found for them. In 40 years of providing this service, she took in 48 children, both white and black, including many unwed mothers, and children from poorhouses.

Word of Ferguson's Sunday school reached Reverend Mason, who visited her in 1814 and invited her to transfer her school to his church's basement. Since Ferguson's master had never allowed her to learn to read or write, her lessons had come entirely from her memory of the Scriptures taught to her by her mother. Mason provided her with congregation members to do much of the actual teaching.

Although the Sunday school movement had spread to the United States from its British origins in the early 1800s, Ferguson was unaware of the movement and began her Sunday school completely independent of it. She gave away all that she earned and died of cholera on July 11, 1854, as one of the city's most admired women. In 1920, the city of New York opened the Katy Ferguson Home for Unwed Mothers in her honor.

Further Reading

Arnett, Benjamin. "A History of the Negro Sunday School." The African American Journey web site. Available online. URL: http:www2.worldbook.com/features/aajourney/html/bh//8a.html. Downloaded March 25, 2003.

Hine, Darlene Clarke. *Black Women in America, A–L.* Brooklyn, N.Y.: Carlson Publishing, 1993.

Smith, Jesse Carney, ed. *Notable Black American Women.* Vol. 1. Detroit, Mich.: Gale Research, 1992.

Fisher, Elijah John
(1858–1915) *Baptist educator, administrator*

Elijah John Fisher was a constructive force for the National Baptist Convention in the late 19th and early 20th centuries. Among his greatest successes was transforming a squabbling, 600-member Chicago church into the largest Protestant congregation in the midwestern United States.

Fisher was born on August 2, 1858, in La Grange, Georgia, one of 17 children of Miles and Charlotte Fisher. All were slaves on a plantation owned by a Dr. Ridley until they were freed by the Union army in the summer of 1863. The family then took the last name of a kind former master, and stayed on the plantation another year until they could afford a down payment on a farm.

Miles Fisher frequently served as a lay preacher for First Baptist Church in La Grange, where black worshipers met after the whites' service was finished. When he died in 1875, the family was forced to sell the farm to meet outstanding debts. Elijah Fisher took a job as a miner in Anniston, Alabama, and then found better work as a butler. He married Florida Neely in 1877, with whom he had five children.

Fisher obtained a license to preach in 1879, and began teaching in a country school. Recognizing the limits of his own sporadic education, he attended Atlanta Baptist College for a year before accepting a new teaching position in Long Cane, Georgia. While running to catch the train that would take him to his new job, he was severely injured when his coat became caught under the train. He was pulled under, lost a leg, and nearly died. After a period of recovery, he worked as head teacher and principal of the newly organized La Grange Baptist Seminary.

Fisher left teaching after his ordination in 1882 and worked briefly at various small churches in Georgia before accepting a call to a church in Anniston, Alabama. Under his leadership, the church erased a large debt and built a new church. In 1885, he began a two-year term as assistant secretary of the Missionary Baptist Convention of Georgia. That was followed by two years as pastor of his childhood parish in La Grange, and a call to Mount Olive Baptist in one of Atlanta's worst neighborhoods. During Fisher's time at Mount Olive, the congregation eliminated its debt and more than doubled its membership. While serving the church, Fisher attended Atlanta Baptist and obtained his degree in 1890. He also edited the *Atlanta Tribune,* beginning in 1897.

In 1901, Fisher moved to Nashville, where he presided over construction of Spruce Street Baptist's new sanctuary. A year later he took a call to Olivet Baptist in Chicago, a congregation

that was imploding under internal strife. Working under his motto "be somebody, do something, have something," Fisher guided a congregation bogged down by two years of lawsuits and bickering into a new vision of ministry. By 1905, the congregation had more than tripled its membership, built a new sanctuary, and initiated an active social ministry. Five years later, Olivet Baptist boasted more than 3,100 members.

Fisher's long list of accomplishments included founding the Chicago Religious Training Seminary in 1912 and serving as national vice president of the National Baptist Convention for 10 years. His mediating influence was credited with staving off a schism in that denomination in 1913. Illness prevented him from performing a similar service when the National Baptist Convention split in 1915, and he died on July 31, 1915.

Further Reading

Fisher, Miles Mark. *The Master's Slave: Elijah John Fisher, A Biography.* Philadelphia: Judson Press, 1972.

Murphy, Larry G., ed. *Encyclopedia of African American Religious Biography.* New York: Garland Publishing, 1993.

Flake, Floyd
(1945–   ) *African Methodist Episcopal clergy, congressman*

Floyd Flake is a charismatic preacher at New York City's second-largest black church who served six terms in the U.S. House of Representatives in the 1980s and 1990s. During that time, he never relinquished his pulpit and regarded his elective post as merely an extension of his community-revitalizing ministry.

Flake was born on January 30, 1945, in Los Angeles, California, one of 13 children of Robert and Rosie Lee Flake. The family relocated to

Houston when Floyd was an infant; there Robert found work as a janitor. Neither parent had an education beyond elementary school. Floyd had little inclination to pursue academics himself until a teacher took a special interest in him and inspired him to take his studies seriously. Flake went on to attend the traditionally black Wilberforce College in Ohio, where he earned a B.A. degree in psychology in 1967. Ordained into the African Methodist Episcopal Church (AME Church) shortly thereafter, he spent the next several years moving between jobs in the sacred and the secular world. He alternated terms as associate pastor at two churches with a year as a social worker and two years as a marketing analyst for the Xerox Corporation.

While working as an assistant dean at Lincoln University in Pennsylvania, Flake began seriously considering the state of affairs for the nation's black students. In his view, students were coming to college unprepared. He discovered a similar problem at Boston University, where he worked as dean of students, chaplain, and director of the school's MARTIN LUTHER KING, JR., African-American Center. When he was asked twice to give up a comfortable, secure job in 1976 to take over the struggling Allen AME Church in Queens, New York, Flake turned it down. But when asked a third time, he felt the Lord was calling him to accept the challenge of making a difference in the community.

More than a century old, Allen AME Church had been in serious decline for years, along with its neighborhood. Flake applied his personal philosophy to the problem: "Complaining has never solved any problem. What's really important is for people to take their destiny in their own hands." Part of his strategy for getting rid of drug dealers and other negative elements was to buy up decaying commercial buildings in the area. The church then refused to extend leases to anyone except those who wanted to run legitimate businesses. The church eventually built 166 two-family houses for area resi-

dents, as well as a senior citizen center located on the site of a former junkyard.

Flake then confronted the issue of caring for the young by opening the Allen Christian School in 1982. The school, covering preschool through third grade, expected about 75 students but was swamped with 230 eager applicants. It eventually expanded to classes through grade eight and admitted 480 students; Flake considers it his greatest accomplishment in ministry.

Flake's work in the community combined with his pulpit eloquence to bring about a period of tremendous renewal in the church. Within a decade, Allen AME Church's membership rose from little more than 1,000 to more than 5,000. Flake's combination of emphasis on tithing 10 percent of income and his entrepreneurial dealings in the neighborhood boosted income considerably. Allen AME Church's annual giving rose from $250,000 to $1.5 million, one-third of which the church gave back in the form of community programs.

In 1986, the congressional district in which the church was located was engulfed in turmoil. The death of 13-term congressman Joseph Addabbo, combined with a local political scandal, left a void in the community. Several leaders in the community urged Flake to run for the vacant seat. After considerable soul-searching, Flake agreed, although he insisted that he would not be a career politician. He was a pastor first, and if he won election, his service in the U.S. House of Representatives would be part of that ministry. "I concluded I could use the position to extend what we had started at the church into the larger community." Flake lost that special election but, helped by the support of New York City mayor Ed Koch, won the regular election in 1986.

True to his word, Flake was a very unorthodox congressman. He refused to move from his community to Washington, choosing instead to commute to sessions. Politically, he was a maverick whose votes followed his convictions rather than any political line. Although a Democrat and a strong supporter of gun control, minimum-wage hikes, and cuts in defense spending, he joined the Republicans on such issues as tax cuts and welfare reform. He created the greatest controversy in his district with his support of a conservative buzz issue: school vouchers and school choice. His work in Congress, which focused primarily on inner-city issues, was hindered by rumors of a federal tax evasion and embezzlement investigation against him in 1991. The charges, however, were never substantiated, and the matter eventually was dropped.

Flake attributed his ability to maintain his balancing act between full-time pastor and congressman to the traditional role of the church in African-American lives. "For us the distance between the sacred and the profane is shorter than that distance is in white America," he said, "because most of the leadership in the black community has come from the church." Eventually, however, he longed to return full time to the church. In 1997, he stunned his constituents by suddenly announcing his retirement from politics.

By this time, Allen AME Church had grown to a formidable force in Queens. Under his leadership, the church was able to construct a new 2,500-seat sanctuary to serve a membership that had grown to more than 12,000 people. The neighborhood rebounded and is now home to many thriving enterprises. In addition to his work as pastor, Flake continues to be active on a broader scale, as a popular lecturer and public affairs columnist for the *New York Post*.

Further Reading

Flake, Floyd, and Donna Marie Williams. *The Way of the Bootstrapper: Nine Action Steps for Achieving Your Dreams.* San Francisco: Harper San Francisco, 2000.

Haskins, Jim. *Distinguished African-American Political and Government Leaders.* Phoenix, Ariz.: Oryx Press, 1999.

Lincoln, C. Eric, and Lawrence H. Mayima. *The Black Church in the African American Experience.* Durham, N.C.: Duke University Press, 1990.

Rees, Matthew. "King of Queens," *Reader's Digest,* (February 2001): 35–38.

Forbes, James
(James Alexander Forbes, Jr.)
(1935–   ) *Original United Holy Church International and Baptist clergy*

James Forbes is widely considered one of the top preachers in the United States, a man who provides an unusual blend of Pentecostalism, mainstream Baptist theology, and higher academic learning. For more than a decade he has been the lead pastor of Riverside Church in New York City, one of the most storied churches in the nation. In the words of a contemporary critic, "He brings to his preaching the wedding of classical Pentecostal warmth with concentration on the Holy Spirit and the incisive mind of the academic."

He was born James Alexander Forbes, Jr., on September 6, 1935, in Burgaw, North Carolina, one of eight children of James and Mable Forbes. The elder Forbes was a preacher and bishop in the Original United Holy Church, a Pentecostal group. Many of James, Jr.'s older relatives were preachers, including a grandmother and grandfather. He was expected to undertake the same vocation. He started down that path at an early age; as a preschool child he often stood on the coffee table in their home and imitated his father's thunderous preaching style. But as he grew older, Forbes resisted pressure to go into the ministry. When he attended Howard University, he was intent on a career in chemistry, until he experienced an irresistible call during his junior year.

Upon graduation from Howard in 1957, he enrolled at Union Theological Seminary in New York City. There he became a student of the art of preaching. Although he was not totally committed to the Pentecostal denomination of his father, Forbes found ways to blend elements of the fiery Pentecostal preaching style with a Baptist concern for progressive social action. Forbes received his bachelor of divinity degree from Union in 1962 and was ordained into both the Original United Holy Church International and the American Baptist Church.

In 1962, Forbes was assigned to spend the summer as an assistant pastor at the white Olin Binkly Memorial Baptist Church in Chapel Hill, North Carolina. It was a bold move at a time of civil rights unrest. Although subject to some racial taunts and incidents, Forbes succeeded in winning the trust of the parishioners and opening their eyes to a broader vision of the church's ministry. Showing a rare comfort in both of the distinctly different denominations, Forbes went on to serve St. John's United Holy Church in Richmond, Virginia, Holy Trinity Baptist Church in Wilmington, North Carolina, and St. Paul Holy Church in Roxboro, North Carolina.

Forbes continued to pursue higher education, and in the 1970s he earned doctorate degrees from Colgate University in Hamilton, New York, and Dickinson College in Carlisle, Pennsylvania. In 1976, he was named associate professor of preaching at Union Theological Seminary. While serving in that capacity, he again crossed over into Pentecostal ministry by serving as a pastor at Forbes Temple United Holy Church in Jamaica (Queens) New York.

By the early 1980s, Forbes was recognized as a master of his craft. In 1984, *Ebony* magazine declared him to be one of the top 15 black preachers in the nation. That same year, Union Theological Seminary promoted him to full professor of preaching. In 1989, Forbes published a book entitled *The Holy Spirit and Preaching*. In it he argued that much preaching in the United States neglected the power of the Holy Spirit in favor of an overly rational approach. According to Forbes, preaching involved the use of the

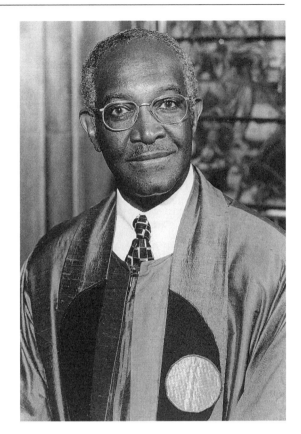

James Forbes's powerful preaching led members of New York City's prestigious Riverside Church to call him as senior pastor in 1989. *(Photo by LaMoitte Teunissen)*

heart and the head together. He believed that preachers who ignored the power of the Holy Spirit in their preaching were ignoring a powerful resource for personal and social transformation. "Preachers must master techniques of their art. They must know when to turn loose, let it go, and trust that the life-giving Spirit, who stands with us through all of this, can complete the 'bringing forth,'" he wrote.

At the same time, Forbes insisted that preaching could not be overly spiritual, off-the-cuff exhorting based on what was currently popular. "I do not begin a sermon from the headlines of *The New York Times,*" he declared. "My emphasis is on Biblical preaching that has social relevance."

In 1989, the famous Riverside Church, a church endowed by the Rockefeller family with a long tradition of prominent pastors dating back to Harry Emerson Fosdick in the 19th century, was searching for a new lead pastor. The 2,500-member church, which was associated with both the American Baptist Church and the United Church of Christ, was reeling from controversy created by its most recent pastor, the antiwar activist William Sloane Coffin. The search committee sifted through nearly 500 suggested candidates for the position. Two hundred of those applied. Each candidate was asked to name some of the preachers that they most admired. The name that came up most often was that of Forbes, who was teaching across the street from the church at Union Seminary. The search committee decided to take a close look at him and, believing he would be a good choice to heal the rifts created in the multiethnic church, ended up calling him to the position. On June 1, 1989, Forbes took over the pastorship. Recalling that he had marched down that same aisle to receive his degree in 1962, Forbes said, "I never would have thought that this pulpit was in the realm of possibility."

While at Riverside, Forbes drew attention for being in the forefront of the church's response to the AIDS epidemic. He experienced a storm of criticism in 1992 when he tried to dismiss an associate pastor, David Dyson, and ruffled feathers with what some characterized as an overly autocratic style. Other vocal critics accused him of raiding the church's endowment to pay for current programs and chastised him as being outside the mainstream tradition with such actions as ending a sermon with an altar call. Forbes weathered the storm, however, and continues to be held in high esteem throughout the country for what supporters call a "deft blend of prophetic criticism and priestly patience."

Further Reading

"Books on the Theme of the Holy Spirit." *Living Pulpit* (January 1996): 34–37.

Dyson, Michael Eric. "New Days, Great Traditions: James Forbes at Riverside." *Christianity and Crisis* (March 3, 1989): 52.

Forbes, James. *The Holy Spirit and Preaching.* Nashville, Tenn.: Abingdon Press, 1989.

Murphy, Larry G., ed. *Encyclopedia of African American Religious Biography.* New York: Garland Publishing, 1993.

Ford, Louis H.
(Louis Henry Ford)
(1914–1995) *Church of God in Christ bishop*

Louis Ford was a pastor and presiding bishop of the Church of God in Christ who made such an impact on the people of the South Side of Chicago during his ministry that the city named a major freeway in his honor.

He was born Louis Henry Ford on May 23, 1914, in Clarksville, Mississippi. He was called to the ministry in the Church of God in Christ at the age of 12. In contrast to most pastors, Ford's parish ministry was focused almost entirely on one congregation. In the mid-1930s, he began preaching on the street corners of the South Side until, in 1936, he had attracted enough interest to begin a new congregation, St. Paul Church of God in Christ.

Ford first came to national prominence due to his pastoral care in a horrendous racial incident. Emmett Till, a 14-year old Chicago youth, was visiting relatives in Money, Mississippi, in August 1955, when an incident occurred in which he was accused of making a smart comment to a white woman in a grocery store. That night Till was kidnapped, beaten, and slain. His killers were never convicted. The brutality of the murder brought it national prominence, and it was Louis Ford who presided at Till's funeral. Despite such close contact with the vicious face of racism, Ford preached a message of restraint and determination. "Don't let your anger be your weakness," he counseled young blacks. "You don't have to stop what you're doing and fight every racist who comes along to bother you. Outsmart him by finishing what you're doing and then pick the right moment to deal with the situation." Among the young people he profoundly influenced was ROBERT M. FRANKLIN, who went on to became a nationally renowned educator. In his own ministry, he worked tirelessly to advance the cause of civil rights.

Ford was one of the pioneers who brought the Church of God in Christ from its southern roots into the Midwest. During the 1950s, he founded the denomination's Illinois Jurisdiction. These efforts, and his abilities as a pastor, gained him recognition by his national denomination, and he was elected the Church of God in Christ's assistant bishop in 1972. Ford held that position for 18 years, all the while continuing his ministry at St. Paul. In 1990, he was elected international presiding bishop and chief apostle of the Church of God in Christ, which had become the nation's fastest-growing African-American church, with a membership of nearly 7 million. During his tenure, he was known for his work with the elderly, young, disabled, hungry, homeless, and chemically dependent, and he became a personal adviser of President Bill Clinton.

Ford died in Harvey, Illinois, on March 31, 1995, after 60 consecutive years of service to the St. Paul congregation. One of his denominational elders commented, "Bishop Ford has done more than erect buildings in Lexington, Memphis, and Chicago, he has built and rebuilt the spirits of people." In honor of his lifetime of influence on the South Side, the Calumet Expressway in Illinois was renamed Bishop Henry Ford Memorial Freeway shortly after his death.

Further Reading

"Bishop Ford." Church of God in Christ web site. Available online. URL: http://www.fjicogic.com/bishopfordbackground.htm. Downloaded February 28, 2003.

"Louis H. Ford, 1914–95." *Christian Century* (April 26, 1995): 452.

Foreman, George
(1949–   ) *minister, boxer*

George Foreman underwent a remarkable transformation during his life from vicious young hood to intimidating world champion boxer to lovable symbol of middle-aged Americans.

He was born on January 10, 1949, in Marshall, Texas, to J. D. and Nancy Foreman. "Almost from the time I was born, anger and hunger shaped my youth," he recalls. Foreman grew up in a tough neighborhood in Houston. Although a good student, he ran with criminals while his mother worked hard to support her seven children. When he was 16, his sister told him about the Job Corps, a government program to teach skills to low-income youth. Eager for a new life, Foreman signed up for a program in Oregon. He took his hot temper with him, however, and was quick to use his fists. While listening to a Cassius Clay (Muhammad Ali) fight on the radio, a coworker suggested he make use of his size and prickly disposition to become a boxer. Foreman took the advice and moved to a Job Corps center in California that had a boxing program.

Brute strength and uncanny quickness enabled Foreman to make the U.S. Olympic team in 1968 after only 18 amateur fights. At the Summer Olympics in Mexico City, he pounded Soviet champion Ionis Chepulis into submission in the second round and won the gold medal in the super-heavyweight division.

Foreman then turned professional and displayed his frightening strength against a variety of foes. In 1969–70, he won all 25 of his fights, 22 of them by knockout. On January 22, 1973, he took on the rugged Joe Frazier and knocked Frazier to the mat six times in two rounds to score a quick victory. Many boxing experts consider Foreman to be the most powerful puncher of all time. He was not exaggerating when he said, "My opponents didn't worry about losing to me. They worried about getting hurt."

Most boxing fans feared for Muhammad Ali's health when the veteran boxer—then 32 to Foreman's 25—entered the ring against Foreman in Zaire, on October 30, 1974. But by employing a clever strategy of covering up while allowing Foreman to punch himself into exhaustion, Ali neutralized the big champion and knocked him out in the eighth round.

The unexpected loss shattered Foreman's confidence and knocked his life off balance. He retreated to his ranch in Marshall, where he became prone to fits of violence and went on a huge spending spree. He attempted to get himself back together in the ring, but on March 17, 1977, suffered another upset loss to Jimmy Young and was hospitalized for mental exhaustion.

Realizing his life was out of control, Foreman abandoned the ring and turned to religion. He started the Church of the Lord Jesus Christ in a rundown building in Houston, and founded the George Foreman Youth and Community Center. Needing an influx of funds for his projects, Foreman shocked boxing fans by returning to the ring at the age of 38, after a 10-year retirement. Most fans ridiculed his efforts as a publicity gag. Foreman went along with the ribbing but was serious about his boxing. From 1987 to 1990, he recorded a string of 19 straight knockouts. In 1991, he took champion Evander Holyfield to the limit in their fight before losing. Three years later, the 45-year-old Foreman beat the much younger British title-holder Michael Moorer. Foreman has been married five times and is the father of five sons, all of whom are named George, and five daughters. Foreman continues to serve his church and his foundation in Houston, although he is best known as a media pitchman for products such as a barbecue grill.

Further Reading

Berger, P. "Body and Soul," *New York Times Biographical Service* (March 1991).

Foreman, George, with Joel Engel. *By George: The Autobiography of George Foreman.* New York: Villard, 1995.

Goldberg, Jonah. "Politics and Pugilists." *Commentary* (June 1997): 51–55.

Franklin, Robert M. (Robert Michael Franklin)
(1954–   ) *educator*

Robert M. Franklin arose from an inner-city environment to become one of the nation's foremost religious scholars and preachers.

He was born Robert Michael Franklin on February 2, 1954, in Chicago, Illinois, to Robert Lee Franklin and Ethel Franklin. He and his three younger siblings were raised amid a large extended family that had migrated from rural Mississippi to Chicago during the Great Depression.

Robert thought of his home as a safe compound amid a sea of violence. Many of his friends were intimidated into joining gangs, but Franklin's family stood firmly for Pentecostal values and the value of education. He remembers his grandmother once defusing a volatile situation by stepping between two street gangs and speaking to them about the love of Jesus. Franklin was also influenced by Bishop Louis Ford, a nationally known figure in the Church of God in Christ, who was pastor of his home congregation.

Franklin's efforts to stay on the straight and narrow took a devastating blow when he was expelled from school and fired from his job as a food store clerk on the same day. The expulsion was in punishment for his participation in a walkout protesting the slaying of Black Panther leader Fred Hampton. His family reacted supportively, however, and, in Franklin's words, "I returned to school with the determination of a bull." His teachers at Morgan Park High School were stunned by the change in Franklin, formerly an indifferent student, who soon rose to the top of the honors classes.

Franklin went on to study at Morehouse College in Atlanta, obtaining a degree in political science and religion in 1975. He then went to England to study, and there encountered the writings of contemporary religious writer C. S. Lewis. While there, Franklin reported having an emotional encounter with the Holy Spirit. After that, Franklin traveled to Spain, Morocco, and the Soviet Union, and returned to the United States ready to dig even more deeply into religious thought.

He enrolled at Harvard Divinity School, where he obtained a master's degree in 1979, writing his thesis on why men leave the church. Franklin then served for six years as assistant pastor of his childhood church, St. Paul, while studying further at the University of Chicago. During this time, Franklin also worked as a hospital chaplain and served as an instructor and associate director of ministerial studies at Prairie State College, in Chicago Heights, Illinois.

Franklin earned his doctorate from the University of Chicago in 1985, whereupon he was hired as a professor, dean, and assistant director of black church studies at Colgate Rochester Divinity School in New York. In 1989, he became assistant professor of ethics and society and director of black church studies at Candler School of Theology, Emory University, in Atlanta, Georgia.

While at Emory, he wrote *Liberating Visions: Human Fulfillment and Social Justice in African American Thought*, examining the intellectual and political influence of Booker T. Washington, W. E. B. DuBois, MALCOLM X and MARTIN LUTHER KING, JR. He concluded that "as long as we are engaged in the process, we are God's agents for doing the work of reconciliation in the world." In 1995, he became the Ford Foundation project officer for Rights and Social Justice, and shortly thereafter accepted the presidency of Interdenomination Theological Seminary, the nation's largest black seminary. He is married to Dr. Cheryl Goffney, an obstetrician, with whom he made a pact that each would support the other fully both professionally and personally.

Further Reading

Franklin, Robert M. *Another Day's Journey: Black Churches Confronting the American Crisis.* Minneapolis, Minn.: Fortress, 1997.

"Interview with Robert M. Franklin." Emory University's Center for the Interdisciplinary Study of Religion web site. Available online. URL: http://www.law.emory.edu/cisr/seniorfellows_Franklin.htm. Posted Summer 2001.

Phelps, Shirelle. *Contemporary Black Biography.* Vol. 13. Detroit, Mich.: Gale Research, 1997.

G

Gardner, Eliza Ann
(1831–1922) *abolitionist, African Methodist Episcopal Zion Church leader*

Eliza Ann Gardner is regarded as the "mother" of the African Methodist Episcopal Zion (AMEZ) Missionary Society and was one of New England's most tenacious defenders of women's equality in religious matters.

She was born in New York City on May 28, 1831, the daughter of James and Eliza Gardner. When she was young, the family moved to the predominantly black West End section of Boston, where her father enjoyed a profitable career as a contractor for sailing vessels. His work made it possible for Gardner to enjoy a comfortable childhood, but she quickly learned that many others of her race were less fortunate, and was taught that she had an obligation to help them. Her family was active in the local African Methodist Episcopal Church, and their home served as a station for the Underground Railroad, which smuggled runaway slaves from the South to freedom.

Gardner's interest in the slavery issue intensified because of her education at the only public school for black children in the city, which was taught by abolitionist teachers. As a result, she became acquainted with many nationally famous abolitionist leaders. An excellent student,

Gardner earned a number of scholarships. However, as few black women at the time were able to pursue higher education or professional careers, she learned the art of dressmaking to support herself once she finished school.

While working at that trade, Gardner actively participated in church and political issues. In 1865, she began teaching Sunday school, a task she continued for the rest of her life. Her abilities in this area were recognized when she was named the Sunday school superintendent for the black churches in Boston in 1888.

Gardner's most lasting contribution was the organization of the Zion Missionary Society in New England, which later became known as the Ladies Home and Foreign Mission Society. This group played a large role in the support of black missionaries to Liberia. In 1884, the male-dominated AMEZ Church questioned the appropriateness of the women's missionary society, as it appeared to be taking a role in what they considered the male domain of religious leadership. Gardner met the arguments in favor of disbanding the group head on, saying

> If you commence to talk about the superiority of men . . . if you persist in telling us that after the fall of man we were put under your feet and that we are intended to be subject to your will, we cannot help you in New England one bit.

Gardner's defense helped turn the tide and win support for the renewal of the women's mission society.

Among Gardner's other contributions were finding work for young black women in homes of wealthy whites; being a founding member, in 1893, of the Woman's Era Club of Boston, the first black women's club in the area; serving as chaplain for the National Federation of Afro-American Women convention in 1895; and helping lay the groundwork for the formation of the National Association of Coloured Women at the end of the century.

Gardner, who never married, lived into her 90s as a matriarch of the AMEZ Church. She died in Boston on January 4, 1922.

Further Reading

Kalisa, Beryl Graham. "Let the Women Keep Silent in the AME Zion Church: Eliza Ann Gardner," *AMEZ Quarterly Review* (October 1996): 31–36.

Smith, Jesse Carney, ed. *Notable Black American Women.* Vol. 2. Detroit, Mich.: Gale Research, 1996.

Garnet, Henry Highland
(Henry Trusty)
(1815–1882) *Presbyterian clergy, writer, abolitionist*

Few American abolitionists of the mid-19th century spoke with the passion and authority of the Presbyterian minister Henry Highland Garnet, a former slave. Although viewed in many circles as a voice of black radicalism, Garnet believed strongly in the destiny of the United States as a land of racial harmony.

Garnet was born on a slave plantation in Kent County, Maryland, on December 23, 1815, the grandson of a West African Mandingo Empire tribal ruler who was captured by slave traders. His parents, George and Henrietta Trusty, worked for Colonel William Spencer

until Spencer's death in 1824. At that time, fearful that their family would be split up, they made a desperate dash for freedom with their two children and seven other friends. They settled in New Hope, Pennsylvania, where his father set up shop as a shoemaker, and Henry was able to enroll in public school.

In 1826, Henry went to New York City and enrolled in the African Free School, run by Peter Williams. At that time, he changed his last name to Garnet to disguise himself from slave hunters who were still looking for him. He eventually found work as a cabin boy on a ship that sailed the Caribbean and as a cook on a ship that logged a regular route between New York City and Washington, D.C., until a severe leg infection forced his return to New York.

Garnet showed promise as a student and was allowed to take classes at the Curtis Episcopal Collegiate School in 1831, where he and the two other African-American boys sat in a separate area and listened in on the class activities. In 1834, he and ALEXANDER CRUMMELL and a few other blacks entered an experiment in integrated education at the Noyes Academy in New Hampshire. The townspeople, however, did not share the views of the school. During the summer they destroyed the school and surrounded a house where the black students were living before Garnet dispersed them with a musket shot.

Garnet had only recently taken an interest in organized religion, being baptized at the First Colored Shiloh Presbyterian Church the year before. He now pursued that interest and enrolled at the Oneida Theological Institute in New York in 1836. Upon completing his studies in 1839, he lived in Troy, New York, where he taught school and followed DANIEL PAYNE to Liberty Street Presbyterian Church, the only black Presbyterian church in the region. That same year, he led a successful petition drive to gain formal recognition for the church from the national Presbyterian denomination. Garnet advanced his education under the tutelage of a white pastor from 1839 to 1843. By 1843, he had obtained his license to preach and was ordained as minister of Liberty Street Church.

During that time, Garnet stepped forward as a leading figure in the abolitionist movement, preaching a form of racially conscious Christianity in which he called for a repentance on the part of America and a renewal of its Christian heritage. In 1840, he withdrew from the American Anti-Slavery Society over philosophical disagreements with the leaders, and formed his own American and Foreign Anti-Slavery Society. He also became an active behind-the-scenes leader in the Underground Railroad, which facilitated escapes of black slaves.

By 1843, his reputation was such that he was invited to be the keynote speaker at the

Few Americans were as effective in their denunciation of the institution of slavery as the 19th-century Presbyterian preacher Henry Garnet. *(Library of Congress)*

National Negro Convention in Buffalo, New York. It was there that Garnet delivered his "Address to the Slaves of the United States of America." In it, he called on slaves to resist their bondage in the name of God on the grounds that freedom of spirit is necessary in order for people to worship God properly. He urged slaves to take their plight to the court of world opinion and appeal to the universal laws of human decency. The most radical and publicized part of his speech was his call for slaves to use force in their cause if necessary. This controversial speech shocked many of its listeners, but it was so persuasive that it failed to be adopted as the convention's official position by only one vote. Four years later, the National Negro Convention endorsed his views.

Garnet grew frustrated with white Christianity's indifference to the abolitionist cause. In 1848, he led his church out of the Presbyterian denomination and renamed it the Church on Liberty Street. This triggered a period of itinerant evangelical and abolitionist preaching. He ministered for a time to unchurched blacks in Buffalo, and then in 1850 sailed for Europe. Fluent in French and English, Garnet made a tremendous impression before various European antislavery groups and reconciled with his former denomination. The United Presbyterian Church of Scotland was so impressed with Garnet that they sponsored him on a mission to Jamaica.

Returning to New York in 1855 because of poor health, Garnet took on responsibilities as pastor of the First Colored Shiloh Presbyterian Church in New York City. In 1858, he was elected president of the African Civilization Society. But despite his interest in African roots, he was lukewarm at best about the emigration of African Americans back to Africa. He remained certain that the United States would soon extend all rights of society to blacks. "The Western world is destined to be filled with a mixed race," he wrote prophetically. Citing the biblical loyalty of Ruth, he urged blacks not to abandon the United States but to plan their future in that land.

When the Civil War broke out, Garnet was an early advocate of allowing blacks to serve in the Union army. In 1862, he volunteered to serve as chaplain of some of the first black units training at Riker's Island. In doing so, he incurred the wrath of racist New Yorkers. An angry mob chased him during a race riot in 1863, and likely would have killed him were it not for the compassion of an Irishman who hid him.

As the war turned in favor of the Union, Garnet grew in influence and reputation. In 1864, he was called to a prestigious pastorate at Fifteenth Street Presbyterian Church in Washington, D.C. On February 12, 1865, the chaplain of the U.S. Senate invited him to be the first black person to speak before Congress, on the issue of the proposed 13th amendment to the Constitution. Garnet used the occasion to praise the United States for obeying God by taking the pains to eliminate slavery, thus "saving the succeeding generation from the guilt of oppression and from the wrath of God."

Garnet resigned his pastorate in 1866 to take on new duties as president of Avery College in Pennsylvania. After four years in that capacity, he returned to Shiloh Presbyterian in New York. He remained there until 1881, when President Garfield appointed him ambassador to the republic of Liberia. Garnet died a month after his arrival in Liberia, on February 13, 1882.

Further Reading

Litwack, Leon, and August Meier, eds. *Black Leaders of the Nineteenth Century.* Urbana: University of Illinois Press, 1988.

Newman, Richard, et al., eds. *Pamphlets of Protest: An Anthology of Early African American Protest Literature, 1790–1860.* New York: Routledge, 2001.

Swift, David E. *Black Prophets of Justice: Activist Clergy before the Civil War.* Baton Rouge: Louisiana State University Press, 1989.

Young, Henry J. *Major Black Religious Leaders, 1755–1940.* Nashville, Tenn.: Abingdon, 1977.

Garvey, Marcus Mosiah
(1887–1940) *social revolutionary*

Marcus Garvey's Universal Negro Improvement Association of the 1920s is commonly regarded as the largest black social movement of the 20th century. However, black historians such as E. Franklin Frazier regard Garvey's organization, which operated under the slogan "One Aim! One God! One Destiny," as more religious in character than political.

Marcus Mosiah Garvey was born in 1887 in St. Ann's Bay, Jamaica. He was the 11th child of Marcus and Sarah Garvey. Nine of his siblings died in childhood. As Garvey was growing up, his best friends were white. But at adolescence the racial gulf between them suddenly opened, leaving him hurt and confused. "Then I realized I had to fight for a place in the world," he later remarked.

His father was a master stonemason, a stern man whose stubborn streak led to his financial ruin when Marcus was 14. At that time, Marcus was forced to leave school to work as a printer's assistant. There he came in contact with a huge library that provided him with a wealth of information on various subjects. Two years later, he went to work for his uncle at a print shop in Kingston. Attracted by the power of oratory, he constantly studied the dictionary to improve his vocabulary.

Eventually, Garvey became a foreman at one of Jamaica's largest printing companies. In 1907, he took the side of the workers in a strike. This resulted in his being blacklisted by employers, which triggered a lifelong interest in politics. Garvey then left Jamaica to work at a banana plantation in Costa Rica. He was so sickened by the harsh treatment of the workers by the British companies that he traveled to London to protest. There he used his knowledge of the printing business to found a short-lived newspaper in support of his views.

Having failed to prick the British conscience, Garvey returned to Central America. Wherever he went—Panama, Ecuador, Honduras, Nicaragua, Colombia, Venezuela, back to Jamaica and to England again—he found the same appalling exploitation of common laborers, particularly blacks. In each case he started a newspaper that advocated for change, only to fail.

Garvey's experience showed him that blacks throughout the world had no political voice. A strong, forceful character, Garvey decided to be that voice. Upon returning to Jamaica in 1914, he organized the Universal Negro Improvement and Conservation Association and African Communities League, later shortened to UNIA. Its goals were to improve local economic and educational opportunities and to promote a new spirit of racial pride in blacks. "The world has made being black a crime," he declared. "I hope to make it a virtue." From the start, however, Garvey's work met with fierce opposition from affluent blacks who viewed it as a threat to their status.

In 1916, Garvey traveled to the United States to observe the situation of blacks in that country. His arrival coincided with growing tension between the races. African Americans were incensed that their brothers were dying for the Allied cause in World War I, yet were treated so abysmally at home. During the next few years, deadly race riots would sweep the northern cities, prompting blacks to withdraw into their own communities for support and protection.

In this climate, Garvey preached that blacks were not an inferior race, but a group with an illustrious history who had fallen on hard times due to their own moral indifference and sloth. He believed that under the proper guidance, and with a strong combined effort, the black people of the world could rise up and be great again.

This view was greatly influenced by his upbringing in the Wesleyan Church and by the African heritage that made no distinction between religious and secular life. The result was a merging of Christian concepts with black-identity rhetoric. Quoting Psalm 68—"A prince shall come forth from Egypt; Ethiopia shall soon stretch forth her hand to God"—Garvey saw himself as a black Moses who would lead his people from oppression to freedom and glory. He taught that God had created all people as equals and that his wrath was kindled against those who caused suffering among his children. In Garvey's view, God had no color. But since it was natural for people to conceive of a God like them, he urged them to think of God as black as a means of solidifying the black peoples of the world. Pessimistic about the possibility of whites and blacks living together in peace, he advocated the purchase of African land as preparation for a mass return to Africa as the "Promised Land."

By this time, Garvey had developed his oratory and publishing skills to a high level. He was able to spread his ideas in such a clear and inspirational form that even blacks in faraway lands, such as Kenya's future president Jomo Kenyatta, came under his influence. Garvey's periodical, *Negro Word,* which began publication in 1918, reached a weekly circulation of 200,000 by the early 1920s. The UNIA established more than 700 branches in 38 states as well as several hundred branches outside the country.

Convinced of the importance of religion to his cause, Garvey worked hard to recruit clergy of all denominations to UNIA. The weekly branch meetings were held on Sunday evenings and were indistinguishable in many ways from a church service.

The UNIA worked hard to create and support black enterprises. Its most ambitious project was the Black Star Line of steamships, which employed more than 1,000 African Americans. This

Marcus Garvey led the most popular black nationalist movement of his time, which was built on a strong foundation of religious overtones. *(Library of Congress)*

undertaking, however, led to Garvey's demise. His increasingly radical views, his inability to work with other leaders, and the ceremonial pomp that included appearing in military uniform with a plumed hat offended many American blacks. This led to vicious quarrels in the press, including an occasion when W. E. B. DuBois denounced Garvey as "a lunatic or a traitor." These harsh public criticisms eroded Garvey's leadership among blacks, which then fell apart altogether when Garvey was found guilty of violating financial laws relating to Black Star stock in June 1923 and sentenced to five years in prison. President Coolidge commuted

his sentence on November 10, 1927, and Garvey was then deported as an undesirable alien. While his movement fizzled in his absence in the United States, Garvey spent the rest of his life in Jamaica and England, seeking financial support and publishing newspapers. He died poor and in isolation on June 10, 1940.

Further Reading

Burkett, Randall K. *Garveyism as a Religious Movement.* Metuchen, N.J.: Scarecrow Press, 1978.

Cronon, Edmund David. *Black Moses: The Story of Marcus Garvey and the UNIA.* Madison: University of Wisconsin Press, 1955.

Franklin, John Hope, and August Meier, eds. *Black Leaders of the Twentieth Century.* Urbana: University of Illinois Press, 1982.

Garvey, Amy Jacques, ed. *The Philosophy and Opinions of Marcus Garvey.* London: Frank Cass, 1967.

Moses, Wilson Jeremiah. *Black Messiahs and Uncle Toms: The Social and Literary Manipulations of a Religious Myth.* University Park: Pennsylvania State University Press, 1982.

Watson, Edward. "Marcus Garvey's Garveyism: Message from a Forefather." *Journal of Religious Thought* (winter–spring 1994–95): 77–94.

Gloucester, John
(1776–1822) *pioneer Presbyterian clergy*

John Gloucester founded the first black Presbyterian church in the United States and, despite obstacles thrown in his way by society and the ecclesiastical authorities, was well on his way to establishing the Presbyterian Church as a legitimate option for blacks before his untimely death.

Little is known of Gloucester's early life, but he is believed to have been born into slavery around 1776. Notice of him first appeared in 1807 when he arrived in Philadelphia with his master, Gideon Blackburn, who was a Presbyterian minister. By that time, Gloucester was married, with four children. Blackburn converted Gloucester to the Presbyterian faith and provided him with a religious education. Impressed with his slave's learning and commitment, Blackburn sponsored him as a pastoral candidate before the Tennessee Synod of the Presbyterian Church. In 1807, the church's general assembly approved his commission as a missionary in the employ of the Philadelphia Evangelical Society. In order to facilitate Gloucester's ministry, Blackburn granted him his freedom. But in failing to free Gloucester's wife and children, he placed a tremendous burden on the new missionary that would consume much of his efforts for many years.

Gloucester began his ministry by preaching in private houses in Philadelphia. He was so successful that he quickly outgrew these small confines and took to preaching in the street. Blessed with a powerful singing voice, he attracted crowds often as early as 6 A.M., and then began giving his message. On rainy days, he retreated to the shelter of a schoolhouse.

Early in his first summer of preaching, Gloucester had gathered 23 devoted followers whom he organized into the First African Presbyterian Church. From 1807 to 1810, he split his time between his mission work and studying for ordination. Gloucester was ordained into the Tennessee Synod on April 30, 1810, and transferred into the Philadelphia presbytery the following year. By that time, Gloucester and his congregants had grown tired of begging white churches for the use of their facilities in odd hours when the sanctuaries were not in use. He began raising funds and organizing a building campaign for a new church building. Showing tremendous optimism about its work, the congregation completed its brick structure in 1811, with a seating capacity of 650.

Gloucester served the congregation well through the years, but because he was still employed as a missionary by the Philadelphia Evangelical Society, he was never called to be its official pastor. He spent many years balancing his missionary/ministry duties with efforts to free his family. In pursuit of that objective, he traveled to most of the larger cities in both the South and North and attempted to raise funds. Still short of his goal, he traveled to England, where he was finally able to raise the needed money.

Gloucester was so capable in his duties that several denominations offered him better wages to join them. But he remained committed to his church despite the difficulties of trying to make inroads in a population that had no Presbyterian tradition. In June 1820, deteriorating health caused by tuberculosis forced him to retire from the ministry. His early death, on May 2, 1822, at the age of 46, severely stunted Presbyterian efforts to cultivate black membership. Gloucester had three sons who became Presbyterian pastors, but none wielded his influence. His home church declined in the years following Gloucester's recommendation that his son Jeremiah replace him. The church called another pastor instead, under whose leadership the congregation stagnated.

Further Reading

Catto, William T. A Semi-Centenary Discourse, Delivered in the First African Presbyterian Church, Philadelphia, May 1857. Freeport, N.Y.: Books for Libraries, 1971.

Murphy, Larry G., ed. Encyclopedia of African American Religious Biography. New York: Garland Publishing, 1993.

Gomes, Peter John
(1942–) Baptist clergy, theologian

Peter Gomes is regarded as one of the nation's foremost theologians and preachers. His open declaration of his homosexuality has made him a lightning rod for one of the church's most controversial issues.

Peter John Gomes was born on May 22, 1942, in Boston, Massachusetts, the son of Orissa and Peter Lobo Gomes. He was raised in nearby Plymouth, where his father, an immigrant from the Cape Verde Islands, worked for a cranberry producer, and his mother was the first black woman to clerk in the Massachusetts State House.

Gomes acknowledges that he enjoyed a privileged childhood and, as an only child, was somewhat pampered. His mother read him classical literature before bed every night. "It would be very fashionable to say that I overcame tremendous odds and huge obstacles and clawed my way to wherever I am, but I disappoint many people when I say I can't say that." Gomes was active in the local Baptist church, and was president of his class at Plymouth High School. Upon graduating in 1961, he attended Bates College in Lewiston, Maine, supporting his education by working as a choirmaster and organist. He obtained his degree in history in 1965.

Although intrigued by religion, Gomes believed that the subject was beneath the level of intellectualism to which he aspired. Only reluctantly was he persuaded by friends to try a year at Harvard Divinity School. He found it surprisingly to his liking and stayed to earn his bachelor of divinity degree in 1968. Gomes was ordained into the American Baptist Churches in the U.S.A. Among his accomplishments was winning a prize as the seminary's top student preacher.

However, Gomes returned to his history focus and accepted a job as a history teacher and director of freshman studies at Tuskegee Institute in Alabama. Living among a black population in the South was something of a culture shock for Gomes, an easterner for whom race had never previously been an issue. Nevertheless, he insists he would have been content to continue in that position had he not been called in 1970 to be an assistant minister at Harvard's Memorial Church.

Once he arrived on campus, Gomes's obvious ability catapulted him quickly to higher positions. By 1974, he was both pastor of the Memorial Church and Harvard's Plummer Professor of Christian Morals. An additional feather in his cap was *Time* magazine's ranking him as one of the seven best preachers in the United States.

While Gomes preferred to be known simply as a Christian and not as a member of any racial or sexual orientation, he became increasingly concerned over what he saw as abuse of Scripture regarding homosexuality. He came to be-

Peter Gomes of Harvard University has become one of the most widely sought religious speakers in the 21st century. *(Jon Chase/Harvard News Office)*

Grier, Rosey
(Roosevelt Grier)
(1932–   ) *clergy, community activist, football player*

Rosey Grier is a gentle giant who has wandered in and out of the national spotlight during a diverse career as a football player, singer, actor, community activist, and clergyman.

Roosevelt Grier was born on July 14, 1930, on a small peanut farm near Cuthbert, Georgia, the seventh of 11 children of farmers Joseph and Ruth Grier. To help the family in difficult economic times, he began working in cotton fields at the age of nine. A year later, the family relocated to Roselle, New Jersey. It was there that Grier, exceptionally large and strong for his age, discovered football. His prowess as a lineman earned him a scholarship to Pennsylvania State University, where Grier not only made All-America in football but set a national shot put record.

In 1955, he signed with the New York Giants and enjoyed a stellar career that included a National Football League title and two All-Pro selections. One of football's largest players at more than 300 pounds, he was traded to the Los Angeles Rams in 1963, where he became a member of that team's legendary Fearsome Foursome defensive line until his retirement in 1968. The move to Los Angeles put him in prime position to enhance his burgeoning entertainment career. He cut several albums as a singer and appeared as an actor on several television shows, including a recurring role on *Daniel Boone.*

A kind and gentle man, Grier had always taken an interest in community service. He found a political outlet for his interest in the presidential campaign of Robert Kennedy in 1968. Grier became a close associate of Kennedy and was with him the day he was assassinated in June of that year. Grier left the nation with an indelible image when he tackled the assassin, Sirhan Sirhan, and shielded him with his body from the irate crowd while crying for the loss of his friend.

The incident "left a big hole in my dreams," Grier remembered, "and I didn't see how I could fill it." He dropped out of political activism and struggled to find a renewed sense of purpose. In the 1970s, he found a brief diversion as the writer and promoter of a book on needlepoint for men.

However, Grier gradually slipped into depression until a friend insisted that he accompany him to Crenshaw Christian Center, a nondenominational church led by FREDERICK K. C. PRICE. There, Grier found a sense of peace and calling that prompted a drastic change in his life. He became an ordained minister in 1983 and went from liberal Democratic activism to ardent support of the Republican Christian right. Grier worked quietly in campus ministry and in 1984 founded a resource center for teens in inner-city Los Angeles.

While following the O. J. Simpson murder case, Grier was struck by the fact that no one appeared to be ministering to Simpson in jail. Grier took it upon himself to offer Christian counseling, visiting twice weekly with Simpson. The visits turned controversial when an inmate claimed to have overheard Simpson confessing his guilt to Grier. But although he was subpoenaed on the matter, Grier declined to reveal the content of their discussions, citing clergy privilege. Since then, he has returned to work in the inner city. His unusual recurring appearances on the public stage were explained by a *Sports Illustrated* reporter who commented, "He acts out of his own innocence, his own need to do good, and then is surprised (and maybe a little pleased) to find himself a public figure."

Further Reading
Grier, Rosey, and Dennis Baker. *Rosey: An Autobiography: The Gentle Giant.* Tulsa, Okla.: Honor Books, 1986.

Phelps, Shirelle. *Contemporary Black Biography*. Vol.
13. Detroit, Mich.: Gale Research, 1997.

Grimké, Francis
(1850–1937) *Presbyterian pastor*

Francis Grimké, kin to a distinguished family of
white southern aristocrats, was one of the more
influential and militant black religious leaders of
the early 20th century.

Grimké was born in 1850 on the Charleston,
South Carolina, plantation of his father, Henry
Grimké, an aristocratic farmer and lawyer. His
mother, Nancy Weston, was a slave on the plantation. She became nurse to Henry Grimké's
children upon his wife's death, and eventually
rose to a position as the mistress of the plantation. When Henry died of yellow fever in 1852,
ownership of Weston and her three children
passed to Henry's son Montague. For a time,
Montague let them live as virtually free blacks.
But when he tried to sell them in 1860, Francis
ran off and joined the Confederate army as an officer's valet. When he returned to Charleston
two years later, Montague had him thrown in
prison, where he nearly died, then sold him to
another Confederate officer.

At the war's end, the freed Grimké attended
school briefly in Charleston before sponsorship
by an abolitionist allowed him to attend a school
in Stoneham, Massachusetts. Two white aunts
then financed his education at Lincoln University in Pennsylvania, from which he graduated in
1870 at the top of his class. Racial barriers prevented Grimké from achieving his goal of becoming a physician, and he turned to law
instead. He enrolled at Howard University and
earned his law degree in 1874.

By that time, however, he had changed his
focus to the ministry, which required another
three years of education at Princeton Theological Seminary. In 1878, Grimké was finally ready
to embark on his career, accepting a call to the

15th Street Presbyterian Church in Washington,
D.C. There he married Charlotte Forten of
Philadelphia. The couple had only one child,
who died in infancy. Ten years into his ministry,
he was called to Laura Street Presbyterian in
Jacksonville, Florida. He stayed there until
1889, when he returned to the 15th Street
church in Washington and remained there for
the rest of his life.

Over the years, Grimké became increasingly
impatient with lack of progress and the church's
hypocrisy on racial issues in the United States.
His sermons could be shockingly blunt; he referred to the U.S. version of Christianity as "the

A Presbyterian minister working largely in the
Washington, D.C., area, Francis Grimké was a powerful
advocate for blacks' rights in the late 19th century.
(Fisk University)

miserable apology that now goes under that name." His frustration over the lack of response to racial concerns from the Presbyterian Church led him to form the Afro-Presbyterian Council in 1893.

For a long time, he confined his comments to an ecclesiastical context. But a series of lynchings and race riots, and the United States's poor treatment of black soldiers returning from World War I, pushed him to take a more politically active stance. At one point he urged African Americans "to be prepared to defend themselves against such organization and murderous assaults as were made upon them in Atlanta" during the 1906 race riot.

Grimké was an influential force at the 1906 meeting of the Afro-American council that widened the split between radical and conservative blacks, and pushed for the 1908 conference from which the National Association for the Advancement of Colored People emerged. A man of strict morals, sometimes referred to as "the Negro Puritan," he was convinced to the end of his days that God was "getting ready to shake himself loose from this miserable semblance of Christianity that exists to set up in the earth a type of religion that will truly represent the spirituality and teachings of Jesus Christ."

Further Reading

Bowden, Henry Warden. *Dictionary of American Religious Biography*. Westport, Conn.: Greenwood Press, 1993.

Grimké, Francis J. *The Works of Francis J. Grimké: Addresses, Sermons, Thoughts and Meditations, Letters*. Washington, D.C.: Associated Publishers, 1942.

Montgomery, William E. *Under Their Own Vine and Fig Tree: The African-American Church in the South, 1865–1900*. Baton Rouge: Louisiana State University Press, 1993.

H

Harris, Barbara Clementine
(1930–) *Episcopal bishop*

In one of the most dramatic and controversial church conventions of the 20th century, Barbara Harris won election as the first female bishop in the history of the Episcopal Church.

Harris was born on June 12, 1930, in Philadelphia, Pennsylvania, one of three children of Walter and Beatrice Harris. She was extremely active as a youth at St. Barnabas Episcopal Church, playing piano for the church choir and founding a youth group that grew into one of the city's largest. But since the Episcopal Church did not ordain women, she never considered a ministerial career.

After completing high school, she took some training in advertising and then went into public relations in the business world. She worked her way up to an executive position with Joseph Baker Associates in the late 1950s and early 1960s. In 1960, she married Raymond Rollins, but the marriage quickly disintegrated, ending in divorce in 1963. In 1966, she took a job as public relations executive with the Sun Oil Company. In the meantime, she kept active in religious and social causes. She traveled south to take part in civil rights demonstrations and voter registration drives. In 1965, she joined MARTIN LUTHER KING, JR.'s Selma-to-Mont-

gomery march. When she was back home in Philadelphia, she became involved in prison ministry. Along with spending countless hours in the prisons, she served on the board of the Pennsylvania Prison Society for 15 years.

In 1968, St. Barnabas, which she continued to attend, merged with the predominantly white St. Luke's congregation. Uncomfortable with the establishment mentality that resulted, she transferred to the more liberal Episcopal Church of the Advocate. There she became involved in pushing for ordination of women in the church. In July 1974, Harris cut short a business trip to lead a procession of 11 women at the church who were ordained by retired bishops without the approval of the church authorities. The Episcopal bishops of the United States declared the ordinations invalid, but a 1976 convention voted to accept the ordinations and open the Episcopal ministries to women.

At about this time, Harris became interested in entering the ministry herself. She confided this to her rector, who advised her to pray about the matter for a year. When Harris did so and found her desire remained as strong as ever, the rector supported her candidacy. Harris, who had never attended college, took classes at the Metropolitan Collegiate Center and Villanova University from 1977 to 1979. She was ordained a deacon in September 1979 and a priest in

Barbara Harris prevailed in a hotly contested election to become the nation's first female Episcopal priest. *(Mr. David Zadig)*

October 1980. At the same time, she continued her education via correspondence courses from the Urban Training Unit of Sheffield, England, which she completed in 1981.

Harris began her ministry in a familiar setting, the Philadelphia prisons, as well as at a small parish in Morristown, New Jersey. She quickly gained a reputation as an outstanding speaker with strong liberal views which, combined with her public relations expertise, landed her a position as executive director of the Episcopal Church Publication Company in 1984. In this capacity, she was charged with administration of some social justice programs and production of *The Witness*, a magazine with a strong social justice focus. Through her impassioned articulation in a regular column in *The Witness* of liberal viewpoints on issues ranging from apartheid in South Africa to acceptance of homosexuals in the church, Harris gained wide exposure within the church. She also served as interim rector at the Church of the Advocate during this time.

At the September 1988 convention of the Episcopal Church, the stage was set for an epic battle between activists determined to make a statement by electing a female bishop to a vacancy at the Massachusetts Diocese, and conservatives who strongly opposed women in the clergy. Harris was advanced as a top candidate for bishop, along with Denise Haines, archdeacon for Missions and Urban Ministry in the Diocese of Newark. Election required a majority of both the clerical and lay voters. Because of her wide exposure as a columnist, Harris was better known, and after the first ballot, it was apparent that the choice was between her and Marshall Hunt of Lowell, Massachusetts.

After three ballots, Harris appeared to have lost the race. Hunt won a majority of the lay votes and was only five votes short among clerics. On the fourth ballot, Hunt increased his majority among the lay and came within two votes of capturing the majority among clerics, who continued to lean slightly to Harris. Intense lobbying ensued as they prepared for the next round of voting. Harris's candidacy was hindered by three factors: continued opposition to women clergy, conservative dislike of her liberal viewpoints on social issues, and dissatisfaction with her limited and irregular theological education. On the other hand, many Episcopalians had been striving for years to break through the church's gender barriers and refused to let this chance slip away. *Christian Century* magazine reported that the contest for bishop "was fought in the trenches, with words spoken in love but also spoken directly, painfully, and in some cases with a cost of friendship." Finally, on the seventh ballot, the clergy support of Harris swayed the lay voters, who elected her. Harris was consecrated on February 11, 1989, in Boston.

Since that time, Harris has worked to strengthen the women's cause in the church by moderating her statements and forging amicable relationships with all elements of the Episcopal Church.

Further Reading

Harris, Barbara. "In That Great Gettin' Up Morning: An Anniversary Interview with Barbara Harris." *Witness* (January 1999): 24–26.

Melton, J. Gordon. *Religious Leaders of America.* 2d ed. Detroit, Mich.: Gale Research, 1999.

Mitchell-Powell, Brenda. *African American Biography.* Vol. 2. Detroit, Mich.: Gale, 1994.

Moritz, Charles, ed. *Current Biography, 1989.* New York: H. W. Wilson, 1989.

Phelps, Shirelle. *Contemporary Black Biography.* Vol. 12. Detroit, Mich.: Gale Research, 1996.

Smith, Jesse Carney, ed. *Notable Black American Women.* Vol. 1. Detroit, Mich.: Gale Research, 1992.

Haynes, Lemuel

(1753–1833) *pioneer Congregationalist pastor*

Lemuel Haynes was far ahead of his time as a black man gaining religious authority in white society. He was the first African American to receive an advanced college degree, the first ordained in North America, and the first of any denomination to minister to a white congregation.

Haynes was born on July 18, 1753, in West Hartford, Connecticut. He never knew his parents, a white mother and a black father, who abandoned him in infancy. He was given the surname of the owner of the house in which he was born and, at five months, was taken to Middle Granville, Connecticut, to be the indentured servant of a farmer, David Rose. The Rose family came to consider him as their own child.

Haynes spent most of his youth working on the farm but he also attended school when it was available, a few months a year. An eager pupil, he later recalled, "I made it my rule to know something more every night than I knew in the morning."

A strict Congregationalist, Rose had the family gather to read a sermon by a well-known pastor every Saturday evening, and Haynes was often assigned the task of reading. One evening he read a sermon that was markedly different from the usual. When Rose inquired as to who the author was, Haynes reluctantly admitted that it was his own composition. The family was so impressed that they predicted a fine career for him in the ministry, despite the fact that such a profession had never been open to blacks in America.

Haynes's term of indenture with the Roses ended in 1774, and shortly thereafter he enlisted in the revolutionary minutemen of Massachusetts. At the outbreak of the fighting at Lexington, he signed up for duty as a soldier, one of more than 5,000 black soldiers who fought in the Revolutionary War. He was among Ethan Allen's Green Mountain Boys who captured Fort Ticonderoga. During the war, he wrote a daring pamphlet condemning slavery on moral grounds. "By the cruel hands of oppressors they have been forced to view themselves as a rank of beings far below others," he wrote, of the condition of slaves. The work, which was not published until 1783, is one of the earliest open denunciations of slavery in U.S. history.

After his war experience, in the late 1770s Haynes returned to Middle Granville to farm and study. He turned down an offer to attend Dartmouth College, and instead studied Latin and Greek in his spare time under a pair of local pastors. Haynes was licensed to preach in 1780 and ordained by the Congregational Church later in the same year. He began his ministry at a new Congregational church in his home town. It was there that he met a white parish schoolteacher, Elizabeth Babbit, whom he married on September 22, 1783.

In 1785, Haynes moved on to a congregation in Torrington, Connecticut. A number of white parishioners initially opposed his ministry because of his race but soon came to accept him. Among those in his congregation were the parents of John Brown, the radical antislavery activist. In 1788, Haynes accepted a position as pastor of a church in West Rutland, Vermont. He was regarded as a powerful preacher and proved so adept at organizing revivals that the Connecticut and Vermont Missionary Societies recruited him to take charge of backwoods revivals.

In 1804, Haynes was awarded an honorary master of arts degree from Vermont's Middlebury College, making him the nation's first black to receive such an honor. The following year he achieved prominence with a sermon he delivered in response to remarks by Hosea Ballou, a well-known Universalist minister. In it, Haynes defended traditional New England Calvinist piety, urged his listeners to focus on right living and preparation for eternal life, and attacked the Universalist view with a mixture of satiric wit and strong condemnation. In his most impassioned passage, he compared Universalists to the serpent who tempted humans to turn against God in the first chapter of Genesis. The sermon was published and reprinted for several decades. In addition, a collection of Haynes's sermons was so popular that it went through 70 editions and was reputed to be the most reprinted work since Bunyan's *Pilgrim's Progress*.

Haynes's staunch Federalist views brought him into conflict with many of his parishioners during the War of 1812. When he spoke strongly against the secessionist current that ran through New England because of its opposition to the war, the hostile reaction caused him to resign his position at West Rutland and accept a new call

to a church in Manchester, Vermont, at the age of 65.

In Manchester, he gained more notoriety by championing the cause of two brothers who were accused and convicted of killing a mentally challenged brother-in-law who had disappeared without a trace. Widely criticized for protesting their innocence, Haynes was vindicated when the missing man finally appeared just days before the brothers' scheduled execution.

In 1822, the 69-year-old Haynes returned to Granville and served there until his death

Lemuel Haynes served as a pastor of white congregations in the 18th century, long before such practices were accepted in most parts of the country. *(Schomburg Center for Research in Black Culture)*

on September 28, 1833. His life had demonstrated that it was possible for a black man to achieve great success in an entirely white world. His exemplary ministry is credited with influencing a generation of Vermont citizens regarding race and slavery. One of his friends, Stephen Bradley, went on to introduce a bill in the Senate that abolished the slave trade in the United States. While the effort failed, it helped create an awareness of the situation among New Englanders.

Yet despite his accomplishments and influence, Haynes took no credit as either a pioneer or role model. Calvinistic to the end, he had the words, "Here lies the dust of a poor hell-deserving sinner, who ventured into eternity trusting wholly on the merits of Christ for salvation," engraved on his tombstone.

Further Reading

Jelks, Randal. "The Character and Work of a Spiritual Watchman Described: The Preaching of Lemuel Haynes and the Quest for Personal Freedom." *Fides et Historia* (winter 1994): 126–33.

Newman, Richard. *Black Power and Black Religion.* West Cornwall, Conn.: Locust Hill Press, 1987.

Sernett, Milton, ed. *African-American Religious History: A Documentary Witness.* Durham, N.C.: Duke University Press, 1999.

Sidwell, Mark. "The Fruit of Freedom: When Given a Limited Opportunity to Grow, These African-American Christians Blossomed." *Christian History* (1999): 38–41.

Healy, Eliza
(Sister Mary Magdalene)
(1846–1919) *Roman Catholic nun, educator*

Eliza Healy embarked on her religious career late in life, joining her brothers, JAMES and PATRICK HEALY, in overcoming racial barriers to show remarkable leadership in the Roman Catholic Church.

Healy was born on December 23, 1846, in Macon, Georgia, one of 10 children of Irish immigrant Michael Healy and his former slave Mary Elizabeth Smith. Healy, a prosperous farmer who had acquired 1,300 acres of farmland and 40 slaves, circumvented Georgia law against interracial marriage by secretly taking Mary Elizabeth Smith as his wife.

Since state law prohibited the emancipation of the children of slaves, he made plans to relocate to the North in 1850, where six of the couple's children were already attending school. Before that could happen, Mary Elizabeth Smith died suddenly in May, and Michael Healy died three months later. Eliza and her two youngest siblings were sent to New York to live with their brother Hugh. Her older siblings, in attending Catholic schools, had converted to the faith, and Eliza joined them by being baptized on June 13, 1851. Later that year, her family sent her to begin her education under the auspices of the Notre Dame Sisters of St. John's in Quebec. Healy continued her education at Villa Maria in Montreal, from which she graduated in 1861.

At that point, she rejoined her family, first living with brother Eugene in Boston, and then moving to a home in West Newton, Massachusetts, that brother JAMES AUGUSTINE HEALY, now a priest, had bought for the family's use. Eliza enjoyed the fruits of James's prosperity, joining him on an extensive trip to Europe and the Middle East in 1868. She lived at the West Newton house for 12 years, apparently content to be without significant responsibilities in life.

Her serene existence was jolted when the Panic of 1873 nearly wiped out all of James's investments. She decided to pursue her own career as a nun and a teacher, and in 1874 entered the novitiate of the Congregation of Notre Dame in Montreal. After a long and rigorous program of education, she took her final vows in 1882, and assumed the name Mary Magdalene.

Her first teaching assignment was at St. Patrick's School in Montreal, followed by stints at several other schools in Ontario and Quebec. While teaching at Huntington, Quebec, she was appointed superior of a debt-ridden order of nuns. Demonstrating for the first time her administrative skills, she helped the order achieve solvency.

Following an assignment as director of English studies at Mother House in Montreal in 1898, and another job as teacher in 1900, she was transferred to Villa Barlow at St. Albans, Vermont. The school had been hopelessly in debt when she arrived, and even a community attempt to assume control of it to save it was floundering. During her 15 years at the school, Sister Mary Magdalene restored the once-prestigious school back to its former glory and beyond. According to the school's historical records, "She had the talent to administer with wisdom, tact, and kindness without violating the laws of her instinctively demanding nature."

Having worked such a miracle, she was asked to repeat her success at the College of Notre Dame in Staten Island, New York, in 1918. However, after only one year, she died of causes reported variously as heart failure, cancer, and an infection resulting from a laundry accident on September 13, 1919.

Further Reading

Garrity, John A., and Mark C. Carnes, eds. *American National Biography.* Vol. 11. New York: Oxford University Press, 2002.

Smith, Jesse Carney, ed. *Notable Black American Women.* Vol. 1. Detroit, Mich.: Gale Research, 1992.

Healy, James Augustine
(1830–1900) *Roman Catholic priest, bishop*

Along with several of his brothers and a sister, ELIZA HEALY, James Healy advanced into uncharted territory for blacks by seeking a professional career in the Roman Catholic Church.

He overcame a large measure of prejudice against his mixed-race background to become the first African American to attain the rank of bishop in the world's largest church body.

James was born on April 6, 1830, near Macon, Georgia. He was the oldest of 10 children born to Michael Healy, an Irish immigrant who operated a prosperous plantation, and his former slave Mary Elizabeth Smith. Defying both convention and Georgia law against interracial marriages, the two lived as husband and wife.

Concerned about the status of his children in Georgia, Michael Healy sent them to Quaker schools in the North. In the fall of 1837, James led the exodus of the Healy children, enrolling first at a school on Long Island, New York, and later at one in Burlington, New Jersey. The schools were unpleasant for Healy, as the Quaker philosophy of tolerance was not practiced by all the students. Healy resented the constant racial comments that attacked both his Irish and African-American heritage.

He had a much better experience at the Jesuits' newly founded College of the Holy Cross in Worcester, Massachusetts, where he and three of his brothers enrolled in 1844. The Healy family was not religious; none of the children had ever been baptized. They enrolled in the school strictly for the academics. But once there, the Healy boys were captivated by the Roman Catholic faith and requested to be baptized.

By the end of his second year at Holy Cross, James Healy had decided to seek a religious vocation. He did not join the Jesuits, apparently because of some concern as to how he would be accepted because of his race, although his lighter-skinned brother, Patrick, eventually joined the order. Instead, he planned to get an advanced degree and become a professor of theology.

Healy certainly had the academic credentials for the career; in 1849 he graduated at the top of the first graduating class at Holy Cross. He then continued his studies at Sulpician Seminary in

Montreal. Shortly after he enrolled there, his parents both died. Although his parents had left him ample financial support, supplemented by the generosity of family friends, the deaths put Healy in an awkward spot. In preparation to receive orders into the Roman Catholic Church, he was required to produce documents attesting to his baptism and his parents' marriage. Due to Georgia's prohibition on interracial marriages, there were no official documents relating to their marriage. Eventually, however, the Catholic Church recognized the unusual situation and accepted the marriage as valid.

Healy then continued his studies at St. Sulpice Seminary in Paris in 1852. While he was there, one of his younger brothers died after his boat swamped while he was watching yet another brother depart across the Atlantic. The incident moved Healy to abandon his pursuit of an academic career and instead go into parish ministry. He finished his schooling and was ordained on June 10, 1854.

Healy then returned to the United States, where he was assigned to serve as an assistant to his friend Bishop John Fitzpatrick. He proved so valuable in this role that he moved up from administrative secretary to the position of chancellor in 1855. During his decade of service in this administrative post, he spent much of his time fighting discrimination directed not at African Americans but at Roman Catholics. It was the era of the anti-Catholic Know-Nothing Party, which gained strength throughout New England, and Healy was a visible presence in combating its oppressive legislative agenda.

After Bishop Fitzpatrick's death in 1865, Healy took on duties as a priest at St. James Catholic Church in Boston, located in a largely working-class Irish community in southeast Boston. The congregation expressed strong misgivings about a priest with African-American ancestry. Their attitude changed, however, after a series of deadly epidemics of typhoid, influenza, and tuberculosis swept through the area. Despite the highly contagious nature of the diseases, Healy never hesitated to go out and administer the sacraments to those afflicted. This courage and compassion quickly earned him not only acceptance but admiration among his parishioners. A decisive and assertive leader, he led the congregation through the building of a new church sanctuary.

For a time, James Healy's career was eclipsed by that of his younger brother PATRICK HEALY, who became the first African American to obtain a doctorate degree and then, in 1872, was named president of the prestigious Georgetown University in Washington, D.C. But James Healy's popularity as a priest and his reputation within the church as an effective administrative leader grew, and on February 12, 1875, he was named bishop of Portland, Maine, the first African-American bishop in the Roman Catholic Church.

During his early years as bishop, Healy ran into some unwelcome controversy when he felt compelled to dismiss a priest from his diocese. The priest, skilled in church law, fought the dismissal, accusing Healy of violating canon law, and won. The case prompted Healy to undertake painstaking attention to detail ever after.

During his 25 years as bishop in Maine and New Hampshire, Healy had to put up with recurring rumors about his parentage and fought against continuing anti-Catholic sentiment in the region. He enjoyed excellent relations with his fellow bishops, and presided over a period of sustained growth in his diocese. A man of intense dedication, he frequently drove himself into exhaustion, which required periods of recovery. A stroke in 1893 left him unable to speak, but he gradually recovered. Healy died on August 5, 1900, of a heart attack.

Some black historians criticize Healy and his brothers because, while stalwart in their defense of Catholics against societal bias, they displayed an apparent indifference, if not rejection, of their black heritage. In the words of Cyprian Black, "They never used their position to champion the cause of their fellow blacks." On the other hand, they are widely praised for their tenacity in overcoming professional barriers against African Americans within the church.

Further Reading

Adams, Russell L. *Great Negroes Past and Present*. Chicago: Afro-American Publishing Company, 1969.

Garrity, John A., and Mark C. Carnes, eds. *American National Biography*. Vol. 11. New York: Oxford University Press, 2002.

Henderson, Ashyia N. *Contemporary Black Biography*. Vol. 30. Detroit, Mich.: Gale Research, 2002.

"The Life and Times of Fr. John Healy." Chapters of Dublin History web site. Available online. URL: http://www.andego.ie/~kfindly/General/healy. Updated February 24, 2003.

Raboteau, Albert J. *A Fire in the Bones*. Boston: Beacon Press, 1995.

Healy, Patrick

(1834–1910) *Jesuit, university president*

Patrick Healy was one of the illustrious Healy family who achieved fame in the late 19th century. (See HEALY, ELIZA and HEALY JAMES.) He was the first African American admitted to the Society of Jesus (Jesuits), the first to obtain a doctorate, and the first to achieve the position of president of a Roman Catholic university.

Healy was born on February 27, 1834, in Jones County, South Carolina. He was one of 10 children born to Michael Healy, an Irish immigrant who operated a prosperous plantation near Macon, Georgia, and his former slave, Mary Elizabeth Smith. Defying both convention and Georgia law against interracial marriages, the two lived as husband and wife.

Michael Healy also circumvented Georgia's law against teaching reading and writing to slave children by instructing his children at home and then sending them to Quaker schools in the North. After attending a school in Flushing, New York, Patrick Healy joined his brothers at the College of the Holy Cross in Worcester, Massachusetts, in 1844. There he enthusiastically adopted the faith of this Roman Catholic institution. There is evidence that the racial prejudice his brothers encountered in school was somewhat muted for Patrick because of his lighter complexion.

After completing his course work in 1850, Healy decided to become a Jesuit. He spent two years training for entry into the order at Frederick, Maryland. He began teaching at Jesuit institutions in 1852, first at St. Joseph's College in Philadelphia, and then at Holy Cross. In 1858, he sailed to Rome to continue his studies. He soon transferred to Louvain, Belgium, where he was ordained in 1864 and completed his doctoral degree the following year, making history as the first African American with a doctorate.

Healy then spent a year on introspective retreat at Lyons, France, before returning to the United States in 1866 to begin his duties as professor of philosophy at Georgetown University in Washington, D.C. He rose quickly through the administrative ranks, becoming dean of the college in 1868, vice president the following year, and vice rector in 1873. In 1874, church authorities in Rome approved his selection as the university's president. In that position, Healy presided over a major remodeling of the school, which he patterned after the Gothic architecture he had seen in Belgium, and initiated a modernization of the curriculum.

Poor health forced him to resign from the post in 1882, but the contacts he had made and the respect he had earned as college president in the nation's capital gave him considerable influence in the community. He was an adviser to three U.S. presidents. His work on the Catholic Commission on Indian Affairs made him partic-

One of several influential Healy siblings, Patrick Healy served as president of Georgetown University. *(Georgetown University Special Collectors Division)*

ularly knowledgeable regarding Native American concerns.

When Healy finally recovered his health in 1891, he was assigned to St. Joseph's Church in Providence, Rhode Island, as an assistant pastor. He then assumed the pastorate at St. Lawrence Church in New York City in 1895. After a decade of service, he undertook his final call as spiritual director of St. Joseph College in Philadelphia in 1906. He died on January 10, 1910, in Washington, D.C.

Further Reading

Foley, Albert S. *Dream of an Outcast: Patrick Healy.* New Orleans: Portals Press, 1989.

Garrity, John A., and Mark C. Carnes, eds. *American National Biography.* Vol. 11. New York: Oxford University Press, 2002.

Hood, James Walker
(1831–1918) *African Methodist Episcopal Zion clergy and bishop*

James Walker Hood had virtually no formal education yet learned so much on his own that he became an author, historian, educator, and one of the longest-serving and most successful bishops of the African Methodist Episcopal Zion Church (AMEZ Church).

Hood was born on May 30, 1831, in Kennett Township, Pennsylvania. His parents were poor tenant farmers who moved around so often that Hood spent only a few months of his life in any formal school. Fortunately for him, his grandmother spent time teaching him to read, write, and orate. His first public speech as a youth was a reaction to the 1857 Dred Scott Supreme Court decision, in which he predicted the end of slavery in the near future. Hood was raised in a devout Methodist household—his father was a preacher and a farmer—yet he experienced a long period of religious doubt in his teen years. This was resolved in 1848 when he made a strong commitment to the church.

Hood married Hannah Ralph in 1852, but she died three years later. Shortly after her death, Hood experienced a call to preach and began preparing himself for the ministry. In 1859, the Northeast Conference of the AMEZ Church accepted the unschooled Hood as a candidate for ministry on trial. He made a good impression and was ordained in 1860.

Hood spent much of the Civil War as a missionary to Nova Scotia. But in 1864 he was one of five ministers recruited by the AMEZ Church to preach to the newly emancipated slaves in Union-occupied territory in the South. Hood was by far the most successful of the five. Although he spent some time in Florida and Kentucky, he made his greatest impact in North Carolina. Arriving ahead of the rival African Methodist Episcopal church, he established the AMEZ Church as the region's major denomination by bringing churches in Beaufort, Fayette, New Bern, and Wilmington into the AMEZ fold.

Hood stayed in North Carolina for the rest of his life, establishing and strengthening new AMEZ churches. At the end of the Civil War, he served as a delegate to the writing of a new state constitution. In 1872, he was elected bishop. Ironically, the man with no formal education also played a key role in education in his community, first as an assistant superintendent of public instruction for the state and later as the major force behind the creation of Zion Wesley Institute, the AMEZ's first college. Hood served as chairman of the board at the college, soon renamed Livingstone College, for 30 years.

Hood developed a talent for communicating both orally and in writing. In 1884, he published a collection of sermons that were so well received that he added a second volume in 1908. He also wrote two books dealing with the AMEZ Church's history. A progressive force in both church and community, he was the first black bishop of any denomination to ordain a woman (Julia Foote, in 1894), and his advice on racial matters was prized by the administration of President Theodore Roosevelt. He was by far the longest-serving bishop of his time. Shortly before his retirement in 1916 at the age of 85, the AMEZ Church named its new seminary on the Livingstone campus in his honor. He died in 1918.

Further Reading

Martin, Sandy Dwayne. *For God and Race: The Religion and Political Leadership of AMEZ Bishop James Walker Hood.* Columbia: University of South Carolina Press, 1999.

Melton, J. Gordon. *Religious Leaders of America.* 2d ed. Detroit, Mich.: Gale Research, 1999.

Montgomery, William E. *Under Their Own Vine and Fig Tree: The African-American Church in the South, 1865–1900.* Baton Rouge: Louisiana State University Press, 1993.

Hooks, Benjamin Lawson
(1925–   ) *Baptist clergy, NAACP leader*

Benjamin Hooks has gone through a wide variety of careers in his lifetime. In the process he has studied and influenced the Civil Rights movement from many angles: as a lawyer, judge, minister, businessman, administrator, and director of the National Association for the Advancement of Colored People (NAACP).

Benjamin Lawson Hooks was born on January 31, 1925, in Memphis, Tennessee, the fifth of seven children of Robert, Jr., and Bessie Hooks. He enjoyed a more comfortable lifestyle than many of his black contemporaries due to the success of his father's photography business. The family also had a keen interest in education, dating from the days when his paternal grandmother was one of the first black women to graduate from college. (She also helped establish an NAACP chapter in Memphis.)

Hooks attended Porter Elementary School and Booker T. Washington High School in Memphis. Upon his graduation in 1941, he enrolled at LeMoyne College and later at Howard University. He saw action in World War II as a staff sergeant in the all-black 92nd Infantry combat unit. The bitter irony of guarding Italian prisoners who were allowed to eat in restaurants that were off-limits to him strengthened his resolve to work for racial justice.

Hooks felt that he could best accomplish this by going into the ministry. However, his father, who had become disenchanted with organized religion, strongly discouraged this, and Hooks pursued a career in law instead. Since no

Tennessee law school would admit a black student, he enrolled at DePaul University in Chicago, and he obtained his law degree in 1948. Returning to Memphis, he began practicing law. While judges treated him fairly in court, white attorneys routinely addressed him as "boy."

In 1951, Hooks married Frances Dancy, a schoolteacher, with whom he would have one daughter. Three years later, he made a bid for public office, running for state legislator. He lost that race, however, as well as subsequent runs for a judgeship in 1959 and 1963. Hooks began

Benjamin Hooks broke new ground for African Americans as a Tennessee lawyer, judge, and head of the Federal Communications Commission. *(Schomburg Center for Research in Black Culture)*

to involve himself in demonstrations for civil rights during this period. Despite his successful legal career, Hooks continued to feel the call to the ministry, and he finally became an ordained Baptist minister in 1956. That year he began serving as a pastor at Middle Baptist Church in Memphis while continuing his legal work.

In 1961, Hooks was hired as assistant public defender in Shelby County. There he found himself in the front lines of the civil rights battle. During a civil rights case in Somerville, Tennessee, he and several other lawyers were escorted from town by a group of sheriffs whose shotguns were in plain sight. Hooks thought they would be killed, especially when a shot was fired, but the sheriffs went no further than intimidation.

Hooks took on a hectic schedule in the mid-1960s when he added pastoral responsibilities at Greater New Mount Moriah Baptist Church in Detroit to his duties. For eight years he alternated Sundays preaching at his Memphis and Detroit congregations. His duties only increased when, in 1965, Tennessee governor Frank Clement appointed him to fill a vacancy in the Shelby County criminal court system. That made Hooks the first black judge in criminal court in Tennessee and the first anywhere in the South since Reconstruction. The following year he won election to a full term as judge. In desperate need of an assistant and secretary during these busy years, he recruited his wife, Frances, who selflessly gave up her teaching career to support him.

In 1968, Hooks struck out on a new path, resigning as judge to take a job as president of the MAHALIA JACKSON Fried Chicken franchises. The company, however, failed to make much of a dent in the market share of its larger competitor, Kentucky Fried Chicken, and folded by 1972.

That same year, President Nixon was looking to fulfill a campaign pledge to put an African American on the seven-member Federal Communications Commission. Hooks's combination of legal expertise, experience as producer and host of a local television show *Cornerstones in Black and White* in Memphis, and his Republican credentials made him the ideal choice. When criticized for arriving late at his first press conference, he made no apologies. "It has taken 38 years for us to get a Black commissioner, so I decided . . . to take all the time I wanted," he said. The new position took him to Washington, D.C., and forced him to finally give up his dual parishes. Believing that access to the airwaves was crucial to the efforts of blacks to get their story in front of the public, he worked hard to have blacks accepted into the federal communications system. During his term, minority ownership of media outlets increased fivefold.

On November 6, 1976, the NAACP board of directors unanimously chose Hooks to be executive director of their organization, to succeed retiring Roy Wilkins. The group's membership had declined in recent years and it had taken on a staggering debt. Declaring that the Civil Rights movement was far from dead, Hooks accepted the job with a vow to pursue the same goals of inclusivity for blacks in society, only with new style and energy. "If anyone thinks that we are not going to demonstrate and protest . . . they had better roll up the sidewalks," he said.

Although he frequently clashed with the NAACP board chair, Hooks accomplished what he set out to do. Within three years he cut the organization's $1 million debt in half, and he eliminated it completely by the end of his administration. He expanded membership by more than 100,000 members with initiatives such as establishing more NAACP chapters on college campuses. He also kept alive the NAACP tradition of effective community programs and active campaigning on behalf of civil rights. While he was in office, several of his major goals, such as the establishment of a federal MARTIN LUTHER KING, JR., holiday, an extension to voting rights legislation, and tough sanctions against the apartheid regime of South Africa were all enacted. He made certain that minority viewpoints were heard on such controversial issues as welfare reform, the environment, national health insurance, and urban renewal. Despite his Republican background, Hooks took a leading role in opposing many of the cuts to social programs made by Presidents Reagan and Bush. Yet at the same time, he urged blacks to take responsibility for improving their own situations. "I'm calling for a moratorium on excuses," he declared.

Hooks retired as executive director of the NAACP in January 1993. He remained active as senior vice president of a black investment firm and as president of the National Civil Rights Museum in Memphis until slowed by a heart attack and quadruple bypass surgery in 1994.

Further Reading

Bigelow, Barbara Carlisle. *Contemporary Black Biography.* Vol. 2. Detroit, Mich.: Gale Research, 1992.

Hooks, Benjamin. "The First Liberty Summit," *Journal of Law and Religion* (1990): 189–211.

Mitchell-Powell, Brenda. *African American Biography.* Vol. 2. Detroit, Mich.: Gale, 1994.

Moritz, Charles, ed. *Current Biography, 1978.* New York: H. W. Wilson, 1978.

Hosier, Harry
(Black Harry)
(ca. 1750–1806) *pioneer Methodist preacher*

Black preachers are generally acknowledged to be among the most dynamic pulpit orators in the United States. The tradition started with Harry Hosier who, although illiterate and never ordained, was considered a peerless spiritual orator by the most learned men of his time.

Hosier was born around 1750, near Fayetteville, North Carolina, but little else is known of his life until he surfaced in the Baltimore area as a free man around 1780. He was converted by preachers of the newly forming Methodist

Church in America and in a short time became a startlingly effective lay exhorter for the faith. His work came to the attention of Francis Asbury, soon to be the first Methodist bishop in the United States, who was one of the few major religious leaders actively interested in bringing blacks into the church. In one of his diaries, Asbury wrote, "I have thought if I had two horses, and Harry (a coloured man) to go with me, and drive one, and meet the black people, and to spend about six months in Virginia and the Carolinas, it would be attended with a blessing."

Hosier became Asbury's servant and accompanied him on many of his circuit-riding missions. He may have been the first black person licensed to preach in the United States. In any case, on May 13, 1781, he preached along with Asbury at Fairfax Chapel in Falls Church, Virginia, which is the first recorded instance of a black person preaching in a white church. As Hosier's fame grew, Asbury took to announcing well in advance that "Black Harry," as he was known, would be preaching, thereby insuring a large crowd. The compliments Hosier received on his sermon were so profuse that Asbury worried conceit would ruin him. Apparently, however, Hosier retained a sense of humility throughout his ministry.

In the early 1780s, John Wesley of England, founder of the Methodist Church, sent a representative, John Coke, to observe the organizational efforts of Methodist adherents in the United States. Hosier was assigned to be his guide, and during their travels occasionally took to the pulpit himself. Coke reported, "I really believe he is one of the best Preachers in the world, there is such an amazing power that attends to his preaching."

Hosier could not read or write, but relied on a brilliant memory to prepare his sermons. In fact, he was afforded opportunities to become literate, but chose not to for fear it would adversely affect his preaching. When the Methodists declared themselves a separate denomination in

1784, Hosier was one of a number of Methodists who traveled from New England to the Carolinas, preaching the word.

Despite his obvious talents and commitment, Hosier was never ordained in the Methodist Church, even though black contemporaries such as RICHARD ALLEN were. The reasons for this are not clear. It was rumored that he became an alcoholic who was addicted to wine, but if true, he apparently was able to control the problem. He suffered periods of depression during his later years. Historians speculate that both of these problems may have been a result of disappointment over the lack of respect accorded to him as a lay exhorter (rather than an ordained minister).

Hosier traveled almost constantly in carrying out his mission, spending his final years on the Maryland and Pennsylvania circuit. He died in Philadelphia in May 1806. Despite his lack of recognition, his efforts were crucial in helping to make the fledgling Methodist church far more inclusive than most of the other denominations of its time.

Further Reading

Bowden, Henry Warden. *Dictionary of American Religious Biography*. Westport, Conn.: Greenwood Press, 1993.

Smith, Warren T. *Harry Hosier: Circuit Rider*. Nashville, Tenn.: Abdingdon Press, 1994.

Howard, M. William, Jr. (Moses William Howard, Jr.)
(1946–)   *Baptist clergy, administrator*

Howard has enjoyed a distinguished career as a pastor, administrator, and head of the largest ecumenical church organization in the United States.

He was born Moses William Howard, Jr., on March 3, 1946, in Americus, Georgia, the son of Moses W. Howard and Laura Howard. His entire childhood was spent in this small town, where he regularly experienced the sting of segregation. "If I were to say that picking cotton in the hot sun in southwestern Georgia and having grandmothers being referred to as 'girl' by teenage white men has not informed my ministry, I would be telling you a lie," he has said.

After graduation from Sumter High School in Americus, he attended Morehouse College in Atlanta and became active in the Civil Rights movement. While in school, he also served as a researcher on the autobiography of African-American educator BENJAMIN MAYS. He obtained a B.A. degree from Morehouse in 1968 and moved on to Princeton Theological Seminary. In 1970, he married Barbara Jean Wright, with whom he later had three children. While studying at Princeton, Howard began serving as an associate pastor at First Baptist Church in 1970 and added chaplaincy duties with the United Campus Ministries at Rutgers University a year later. He received his master of divinity degree from Princeton in 1972 and took a job as director of the African American Council of the Reformed Church in America, a position that he would hold for 20 years. He was also ordained into the American Baptist Church in 1974.

During his long term of service with the African American Council, Howard immersed himself in civil rights, social justice, and ecumenical issues. In 1974, he became active in the National Council of Churches (NCC), the largest ecumenical religious organization in the nation, with membership that would surpass 50 million by the year 2000. He chaired numerous committees and served as moderator for panels and discussions. The NCC recognized his leadership ability by voting him the organization's president in 1979.

Howard focused his administrative efforts on strengthening the NCC's existing racial, social, and Christian education programs. Howard took on an even higher profile in 1979 when he was allowed to conduct Christmas Eve services for employees of the U.S. Embassy in Teheran, Iran, who were being held hostage by anti-American protesters. Howard's ecumenical bent also led him to involvement with the World Council of Churches. He traveled around the world exercising leadership at conferences and seminars, and was particularly active in garnering opposition to South Africa's racist apartheid policies.

When his term as NCC president was over, Howard took a political stance by serving as JESSE JACKSON'S floor leader in the latter's bid for president at the Democratic National Convention in 1984. Eight years later, he moved into the academic realm, accepting a position as president of New York Theological Seminary, the largest Christian seminary in the state. Ever in search of new and varied challenges, Howard returned to parish ministry in 2000 as pastor of Bethany Baptist Church in Newark, New Jersey.

Further Reading

"Howard: From Picking Cotton to Pushing Racial Justice," Christianity Today, December 1, 1978, p. 48.

Murphy, Larry G., ed. Encyclopedia of African American Religious Biography. New York: Garland Publishing, 1993.

Oblander, David G. Contemporary Black Biography. Vol. 25. Detroit, Mich.: Gale Research, 2001.

J

Jackson, Jesse Louis
(1941–) *Baptist clergy, political activist*

Jesse Jackson has been the most visible African-American leader since MARTIN LUTHER KING, JR. An ordained Baptist minister, Jackson was the first black to make a serious run for the U.S. presidency, and his work in such areas as voter registration, equal opportunity hiring, and education have touched the lives of millions of Americans.

Jesse Louis Jackson was born on October 8, 1941, in Greenville, South Carolina, to a 16-year old girl, Helen Burns. The father was Noah Robinson, Burns's married next-door neighbor, who worked as a cotton grader. For nearly three years, Burns struggled to support herself and her child, giving up ambitions of a singing career. In 1944, she married Charles Jackson, who soon went off to fight in World War II. Upon his return, he worked as a janitor, while Helen took in laundry for nearby Furman University. Together they worked hard to move into a better neighborhood. Jesse looked upon Charles Jackson as his father and was formally adopted by him when he was a teen.

Despite the poverty in which they lived, young Jackson was taught to care for others. His mother regularly transported groceries for illiterate elderly neighbors and, at the age of nine,

Jesse volunteered to read newspapers to the same people. He worked hard to earn his keep in the family, with jobs as a caddie, delivery boy, and waiter. Not only was he a top student in school, but he excelled in football, baseball, and basketball. Football was his favorite sport, and he quarterbacked his Sterling High School team to the state championship. The Chicago White Sox offered him a professional baseball contract, but Jackson turned it down in favor of a football scholarship at the University of Illinois.

He quickly discovered the almost universal bias of football coaches against black athletes playing quarterback. Unwilling to switch positions, and miserable at the school, he transferred after one year to North Carolina A & T in Greensboro. There, the urgency of civil rights activism lured him away from sports. He joined a campaign to integrate Greensboro's restaurants, theaters, and hotels and soon found himself one of the leaders of the demonstrations, sit-ins, and picket lines. The 10-month campaign's effectiveness in opening up white businesses to African Americans earned Jackson a statewide reputation. He became student body president at the school as well as president of the North Carolina Intercollegiate Council on Human Rights. By his senior year, Jackson had signed on as director of Southeast operations for the Congress of Racial Equality (CORE). That same year he met

Jacqueline Brown. In 1964, Jackson married Brown, graduated from North Carolina A & T with a degree in sociology, and began working for Governor Terry Sanford as a political organizer of young Democrats in the state.

Jackson, however, felt moved toward religious studies. In 1965, he was awarded a Rockefeller grant to attend Chicago Theological Seminary. There he became involved in both local and national civil rights campaigns. He traveled to Selma, Alabama, to take part in the 1965 voting rights campaign, and there met MARTIN LUTHER KING, JR. When King decided to take his Southern Christian Leadership Conference (SCLC) campaign for integration to

Jesse Jackson established himself as a political and social ombudsman and was the first African American to make a serious run for the U.S. presidency. *(Schomburg Center for Research in Black Culture)*

Chicago, he selected Jackson to take charge of a black economic empowerment program in the city that became known as Operation Breadbasket. Jackson directed a 1967 boycott against the national A & P grocery store chain for failing to live up to pledges to hire more black workers. The 14-week boycott ended with an agreement by A & P to hire 264 more African Americans and to open up their distribution system to black suppliers.

King rewarded Jackson by naming him national director of Operation Breadbasket, which had expanded into 16 cities. This full-time job necessitated Jackson's dropping out of the seminary, although he was ordained in the Baptist Church on June 30, 1968, and served as an associate minister at Fellowship Baptist Church in Chicago.

As one of the SCLC's most promising young leaders, Jackson was often called upon when a pressing civil rights concern emerged. In April 1968, he was asked to join King and other SCLC leaders in Memphis to help black sanitation workers who were striking for equal pay and advancement opportunities. On April 4, 1968, King was shot to death on a balcony at a Memphis hotel with Jackson close by. Jackson, who referred to King as "my father figure, my brother figure and my teacher," returned to Chicago the following day, still dressed in a sweater spattered with King's blood, and passionately spoke to the city council, urging it to adopt King's goals.

In Chicago in 1969, Jackson organized the Black Exposition, which honored African-American achievements in business and culture. He continued to direct Operation Breadbasket until 1971, when a disagreement with SCLC head RALPH ABERNATHY over control of Operation Breadbasket funds prompted him to leave the organization. On December 25, 1971, Jackson announced the formation of a new social justice group, People United to Save Humanity (Operation PUSH). It was Jackson's dream to expand the Civil Rights movement on two fronts: combatting specific social issues in the black community such as drug abuse, teen pregnancy, truancy, and violence; and building a worldwide campaign to eliminate poverty and oppression and work for the rights of the powerless. One of Operation PUSH's programs was a project called Excel, funded by a Ford Foundation grant, which focused on helping disadvantaged teens to stay in school and achieve academically. In one of the more dramatic instances of Excel's success, Central High School in Kansas City saw its absentee figures fall from 500 to 200 a day.

In 1972, Jackson ventured back into the political arena. He challenged Chicago mayor Richard Daley's slate of candidates to the national Democratic convention, charging that it violated the party's new rules requiring proper representation of the young, minorities, and women. Jackson's challenge was upheld. Throughout the 1970s, Jackson worked hard to make Operation PUSH a viable force. He made skilled use of the mass media to publicize the group's efforts and thereby became one of the nation's most recognizable public figures. President Jimmy Carter responded to Jackson's growing international prestige by sending him on unofficial diplomatic errands to further the cause of peace in areas such as South Africa and the Middle East.

With the election of Ronald Reagan to the presidency in 1980, federal support of civil rights and social programs eroded. Jackson was one of the few public figures who had the standing and the political courage to challenge Reagan's handling of such issues. An inspiring speaker, Jackson became the leading critic of the Reagan administration policies, which he believed were rolling back the hard-earned progress of the Civil Rights movement.

In November 1983, Jackson formally announced his candidacy for the Democratic Party nomination for president. Jackson's campaign, however, was doomed from the start. Many important black leaders feared that Jackson's candidacy would divide the party so that it could present no serious challenge to the Republicans, and they backed Vice President Walter Mondale. Jackson had few wealthy supporters and little money with which to run a campaign. His troubles multiplied when a reporter cited an off-the-record reference by Jackson to New York as "Hymietown," which was considered a slur against Jews. The inflammatory statements by one of his supporters, Black Muslim leader LOUIS FARRAKHAN, in Jackson's defense only exacerbated the situation. As a result, Jackson was not a major factor at the convention.

Jackson continued with his international campaign for justice and freedom over the next several years. In 1986 he formed the Rainbow Coalition, an alliance of the poor and marginalized of all races, as a political arm of PUSH and made another run for the presidency. This time Jackson struck a chord with millions of voters, black and white. Never before had an African American made a serious challenge for the presidential nomination of a major party. He gathered the support of three times as many whites as he had in 1984, doubled his total votes, and won 14 primary elections. In the process he registered 2 million new voters. Jackson's efforts put him a close second to the Democratic Party's nominee, Michael Dukakis, and provided him with considerable influence at the national convention. Among the concessions Jackson won was the appointment of his campaign aide, Ron Brown, as Democratic national chairman.

In 1990, Jackson was elected shadow senator from Washington, D.C. While he had no vote in the Senate, the position allowed him a platform from which to address his concerns, particularly that of statehood for the District of Columbia. That same year, Jackson traveled to Iraq and negotiated the release of Western prisoners captured by Saddam Hussein's army in their invasion of Kuwait. In 1992, Jackson continued his political empowerment program by traveling to 27 states to register black voters. He overcame some initial divisiveness between his camp and that of Bill Clinton to play a major role in Clinton's capturing the White House in 1992. For the rest of the decade he remained a visible figure as a champion of the underdog in society. He was particularly active in 1996 when he led a protest of the film industry for under-representation of black actors in Academy Award nominations, and of Texaco and Mit-subishi for what he and others saw as their racist hiring practices. The same year, he merged Op-eration PUSH and the Rainbow Coalition into the Rainbow Push Action Network, which es-tablished operations as far away as China, Japan, and Indonesia.

Jackson's effectiveness was somewhat com-promised at the end of the 20th century by reports of his infidelity. However, his legacy lives on in his son, Jesse, Jr., who was elected to Congress by his Chicago district in 1995.

Further Reading

Frady, Marshall. *Jesse: The Life and Pilgrimage of Jesse Jackson.* New York: Random House, 1996.

Jackson, Jesse L. *Straight from the Heart.* Philadelphia: Fortress, 1987.

Moritz, Charles, ed. *Current Biography, 1986.* New York: H. W. Wilson, 1986.

Reed, Adolph L., Jr. *The Jesse Jackson Phenomenon.* New Haven, Conn.: Yale University Press, 1986.

Timmerman, Kenneth R. *Shakedown: Exposing the Real Jesse Jackson.* Washington, D.C.: Regnery, 2002.

Jackson, Joseph Harrison

(1900–1990) *Baptist clergy, denominational president*

Joseph Jackson represented the conservative ranks of African Americans during the turbulent years of the 1950s and 1960s. While he agreed with the goals of civil rights activists, he disagreed strongly with them on tactics. That he spoke for a sizable segment of the black religious population is evidenced by his many terms as head of the National Baptist Convention (NBC), one of the largest black Protestant church bodies in the United States.

Joseph Harrison Jackson was born on September 11, 1900, in Rudyard, Mississippi, the son of Emily and Henry Jackson. Raised in rural Mississippi, he pursued a calling in the ministry from an early age. Jackson was ordained in the Baptist Church in 1922, then attended Jackson College while serving as pastor in Macomb,

Joseph Jackson broke with Martin Luther King, Jr., in the 1960s and advocated a more conservative approach to civil rights issues. *(Corbis)*

Mississippi. He earned his B.A. degree from Jackson College in 1926, the same year in which he married Maude Alexander. In 1927, he relocated to Omaha, Nebraska, to take over the pastoral duties at Bethel Baptist Church. While doing so, he continued his studies in town at Creighton University, from which he obtained an M.A. degree. In 1934, Jackson moved on to Monumental Baptist Church in Philadelphia, and began his foray into denominational leadership by serving as secretary for the NBC's Foreign Missions Board. After traveling to Africa that same year, he displayed his writing talent and his lifelong concern for foreign missions by writing a book called A Voyage to West Africa and Some Reflections of Modern Missions.

Jackson's accomplishments and preaching ability attracted the attention of the huge, historic Olivet Baptist Church on Chicago's South Side, which called him as head pastor in 1941. He would remain as pastor of the church for the rest of his ministerial career. In 1950, Jackson, who liked to describe himself as a preacher and not a theologian, published another book of his religious reflections, Stars in the Night. His prestige grew steadily within the NBC, and in 1953 he was elected president of that church body. Just before his election, the denomination's constitution had been amended to limit a person to four one-year terms as president. However, in 1957, Jackson ran for a fifth consecutive term, declaring the amendment to be in violation of the group's constitution. His reelection on such terms firmly established him in control of the NBC.

Jackson initially was supportive of the black clergy leadership of the Civil Rights movement. He had worked closely with MARTIN LUTHER KING, SR., a key member of the NBC's board of directors, for many years and was impressed with the efforts of his son. At the 1956 NBC convention, Jackson called upon "every leader of our denominational work across the nation to support the [civil rights] movement to the full ex-

tent of their ability." The following year he fully endorsed the Southern Christian Leadership Conference's (SCLC) bus boycott in Montgomery, Alabama, and efforts to integrate the Little Rock, Arkansas, school system. He went so far as to call for a national holiday to celebrate May 17, the anniversary of the 1954 Brown v. Board of Education Supreme Court ruling that ended government-sanctioned discrimination.

Late in 1957, however, he began to have concerns over MARTIN LUTHER KING, JR.'s, leadership of the civil rights campaign. He was critical of the strategy of nonviolent civil disobedience, believing that it would foster lawlessness in the black community, would polarize relations between blacks and whites, was contrary to the gospel of Jesus, and was unpatriotic. Instead, Jackson urged blacks to prepare the way toward peaceful integration, using the courts as the most radical instrument of change. The disagreements between Jackson and King simmered under the surface for several years before breaking out in 1960. That year, Jackson faced the first serious challenge to his presidency in the form of GARDNER C. TAYLOR, a man with impressive credentials as pastor of Concord Baptist Church in Brooklyn, president of the Protestant Church Council of New York City, and the only black member of New York City's board of education. Backed by King's supporters at the annual convention, Gardner ran such a close race that both sides believed they had won. The issues of due process and constitutionality had to be decided in the courts and, after two years of wrangling, Jackson was declared the winner.

By that time, the King faction had lost faith in the process. After seeking the backing of the convention for their efforts in the Civil Rights movement and receiving none at the 1961 convention, King and his supporters broke off and formed their own denomination, the Progressive National Baptist Convention. The friction between Jackson and King grew progressively worse. Jackson refused to endorse King's march on Washington in 1963, at which the latter delivered his historic "I Have a Dream" speech. When King organized a march in Chicago to demonstrate for equal rights, Jackson would have nothing to do with it.

He distanced himself further from more aggressive African Americans. When James Forman wrote the *Black Manifesto* as a demand to society to give African Americans their due, Jackson criticized the National Council of Churches for taking the document seriously. He took issue with JAMES CONE'S theology of liberation, saying, "If the Negro church accepts [Cone's] point of view . . . then black people will become the outstanding proponents of racial segregation." Jackson presented his view of civil rights issues in a book called *Unholy Shadows and Freedom's Holy Light*, which was strongly critical of King, although it did not mention him by name.

Jackson's arguments resonated with many conservative blacks, who kept him firmly at the helm of his 8-million-member denomination. His views were also taken out of context and used by right-wing groups to attack King and the concept of equality. In 1969, a political organization called We The People named Jackson its Patriot of the Year.

In 1980, Jackson presented his definitive, retrospective view of his long term of leadership at the head of his church in a 790-page book called *A Story of Christian Activism: The 100-Year History of the National Baptist Convention*. He held the presidency for three solid decades until finally defeated in 1982 by Theodore Jemison of Louisiana. Jackson died on August 18, 1990.

Further Reading

Hamilton, Charles V. *The Black Preacher in America.* New York: William Morrow, 1972.

Jackson, Joseph. *Eternal Flame: The Story of a Preaching Mission in Russia.* Philadelphia: Christian Education Press, 1956.

———. *Many but One: The Ecumenics of Charity.* New York: Sheed & Wallace, 1964.

Paris, Peter J. *Black Religious Leaders: Conflict in Unity.* Louisville, Ky.: John Knox Press, 1991.

Jackson, Mahalia
(1911–1972) *gospel singer*

Mahalia Jackson's powerful singing voice and fervent religious emotion combined to make her one of the United States's best-known singers despite her refusal to cross over into popular music. She was the celebrity personality who helped bring gospel music into the mainstream of black religious culture.

Jackson was born on October 26, 1911, in New Orleans, Louisiana. Her father, John Jackson, worked as a longshoreman by day, a barber by night, and as a preacher at a small church on Sunday. When her mother, Charity, died, five-year old Mahalia went to live with her Aunt Duke. There she experienced an austere Christian upbringing, absent of outward signs of affection. Singing Christian songs was one of the few diversions that met with acceptance, and Jackson took to it with gusto. "In our house, we shut down from Friday night until Monday," she once said. "I was singing almost as soon as I was walking and talking." From the beginning, she had a powerful voice, which she displayed singing in the choir at her father's church. Her musical taste was influenced by various factors, including the driving rhythms of a Sanctified Church next door to her home, the jazz and blues being played on the streets of New Orleans, and her own personal fascination with the Book of Psalms.

Few career options were available for an African-American girl in New Orleans at the time, and Jackson left public school in the eighth grade to earn money as a laundress and maid. At 16, she decide to move to Chicago to pursue a dream of becoming a beautician or a nurse. With the help of two aunts, she found a place to live and did laundry for white customers, worked as a motel maid, and found employment at a date factory while seeking opportunities in her preferred fields.

In the meantime, she found an anchor at the Greater Salem Baptist Church, where she joined the choir. In a short time, her singing voice attracted notice and she was called on to sing solos. At first, Jackson's singing was strictly an avocation as she moved ahead with her career plans, studying at a beauty school and then opening first a small beauty shop and then a flower shop in Chicago.

Mahalia Jackson's soulful renditions of spiritual music made her one of the nation's first nationally recognized religious recording artists. *(Library of Congress)*

But in 1930 she was invited to join with four others to form the Johnson Gospel Singers, who toured black churches in the area. The more they traveled, the more their reputation grew, particularly that of Jackson, and eventually they traveled throughout the United States. Their repertoire was almost exclusively gospel tunes, which had begun to replace spirituals and traditional hymns as the favorite form of expression in the religious music of American blacks.

Jackson so outshone the rest of her quintet that she moved toward solo performances. At these performances, Jackson fused disparate elements of black religious music. Although in the mainstream of the contemporary gospel music, she paid close attention to black traditions in music. But at the same time, she bucked the movement of black churches that were trying to discourage the emotional enthusiasm of their members in favor of a more solemn dignity. Jackson performed in a startlingly uninhibited manner, rocking back on her heels and breaking into shouts of joy during her performances. When criticized for such displays, she responded, "If it was undignified, it was what the Bible told me to do . . . I want my whole body to say all that is in me."

At first, Jackson's insistence on expressing the full range of her emotions closed many doors to her, and she had to be content with performing in small churches. But her genuine expression and thundering voice gradually won converts. In 1934, she cut her first record, "God Gonna Separate the Wheat from the Tares," which gained widespread popularity in the South.

However, Jackson's husband, Isaac Hockenhull, whom she married in 1936, had little interest in his wife's career. He belittled her talent and ambitions and refused to let her accept many offers to travel and perform. After Jackson divorced him in 1943, her career finally took off. She went on a highly publicized tour with gospel legend THOMAS ANDREW DORSEY, and then in

1945 her recording of "Move On Up a Little Higher" won favor with jazz and blues fans as well as traditional gospel fans. Despite the influence of blues on her music, Jackson insisted that she was not a blues singer. "Blues are songs of despair," she noted, "but gospel songs are songs of hope." However her music was described, "Move On Up a Little Higher" sold more than a million copies. More than any other performer, Jackson had created a large and devoted audience for gospel music.

Jackson reached the zenith of her influence in the 1950s. During that decade she regularly performed at and sold out Carnegie Hall. With a world tour in 1952, her fame spread to Europe and Asia. She even achieved a national radio show, which ran on CBS from September 1954 to February 1955, and made appearances on national television. In *Musical America*, a writer explained her popularity: "Here was a woman unafraid to express her faith without restraint and in her own individual manner."

At this point, Jackson could easily have rocketed into megastar status by crossing into the secular mainstream. But she steadfastly refused to sing anything but religious music, and she refused to perform in nightclubs. Although she continued to put out records, in the late 1950s she began to devote more of her time to the Civil Rights movement. She was a vocal supporter of the Montgomery, Alabama, bus boycott, and she sang for hundreds of thousands of civil rights supporters at the march on Washington in 1963, just before MARTIN LUTHER KING, JR., delivered his legendary "I Have a Dream" speech.

In her later years, Jackson suffered from poor health due to a heart condition. She died on January 27, 1972, in Evergreen Park, Illinois.

Further Reading

Broughton, Viv. *Black Gospel: An Illustrated History of the Gospel Sound.* Poole, Dorset, England: Blandford Press, 1985.

Hinson, Glenn. *Fire in My Bones: Transcendence and the Holy Spirit in African American Gospel.* Philadelphia: University of Pennsylvania Press, 2000.

Jackson, Mahalia, with Evan McLeod Wylie. *Movin' On Up.* New York: Hawthorn Books, 1966.

Sicherman, Barbara, et al., eds. *Notable American Women: The Modern Period.* Cambridge, Mass.: Harvard University Press, 1980.

Jackson, Rebecca Cox
(1795–1871) *Shaker visionary*

Rebecca Cox Jackson experienced a midlife conversion that moved her to take a leading role in the Shaker religious movement of the 19th century. Her autobiographical writing ranks as one of the most vivid records of the spiritual thought among mystical religious groups of that century.

She was born in 1795, near Philadelphia. Her father, who is unknown, died around the time of her birth. Her mother, Jane, was unable to care for her, so Rebecca lived with her maternal grandmother for the first several years of her life. She rejoined her mother at age six and spent most of her time caring for younger siblings while her mother worked.

Virtually nothing is known of Rebecca's life from the age of 13, when her mother died, until she began writing her autobiography 22 years later. At that time, she was married and working as a seamstress in Philadelphia. She was terrified of thunderstorms until July 1830, when, in the middle of a storm, she suddenly became overwhelmed by the merciful nature of God. As she knelt in prayer she felt a deep "love for God and all mankind," and her storm phobia disappeared.

Neither her husband, Samuel Jackson, nor her brother Joseph, a pillar of the local African Methodist Episcopal Church (AME Church), approved of Jackson's resulting new career as a preacher. In fact, when her work led her to separate from Samuel, he responded violently. "Samuel sought my life day and night," she wrote, but through "obedience to the light that was revealed in my soul . . . I was able to know what he was agoing to do."

Following an inner voice of God, she began preaching across Pennsylvania, New York, and New England. Opposition from the male-dominated AME Church only increased her fervor as she sparked public revivals among people of both races.

Eventually her views on celibacy as the only way to faithfully follow Christ led her to investigate the Shaker movement. During her first visit to a Shaker community near Albany, New York, in 1843, she recalled, "the power of God came upon me like the waves of the sea." Part of the appeal was the Shakers' pioneering stand on integration and equality of the races. The Shakers, in turn, recognized this mystical visionary as a prophet. She joined the Shaker community, contributing to its welfare by sewing and frequent preaching.

In the 1850s, she came to see the Shakers as too self-absorbed to contribute to the social advancement of blacks. She split with the group for a time when it refused to approve her plan to establish a Shaker mission to blacks in Philadelphia. Eventually, they reconciled and Jackson became a Shaker eldress in April 1859. She went on to establish a community of black Shakers in Philadelphia that survived for 40 years after her death in 1871.

In addition to her 40 years of preaching, Jackson's most noteworthy contribution to the world was her spiritual autobiography, an amazingly detailed and compelling account for a woman with no education. Although regarded as an eccentric by many, she received the endorsement of AME Church leader MORRIS BROWN, who reported after seeing her at work, "If ever the Holy Ghost was in any place, it was in that meeting."

Further Reading

Garrity, John A., and Mark C. Carnes, eds. *American National Biography*. Vol. 11. New York: Oxford University Press, 2002.

Jackson, Rebecca Cox. *Gifts of Power: The Writings of Rebecca Jackson, Black Visionary, Shaker Eldress.* Amherst: University of Massachusetts Press, 1981.

Walker, Alice. "Gifts of Power: The Writings of Rebecca Jackson." In *In Search of Our Mother's Gardens.* New York: Harcourt Brace, Jovanovich, 1984.

Jakes, T. D.
(Thomas Dexter Jakes)
(1957–) *Higher Ground Always Abounding bishop, author*

At the turn of the 21st century, T. D. Jakes had established himself as one of the United States's most influential, dynamic, innovative, and celebrated pastors. The congregation he founded in Dallas, Texas, has grown at an unprecedented rate and has been hailed as a prototype of the megachurch of the future.

Thomas Dexter Jakes was born on June 9, 1957, in South Charleston, West Virginia. His parents, Odith and Ernest, were accomplished, middle-class African-Americans. Odith worked as a home economics teacher and Ernest built a successful janitorial service.

Thomas knew from an early age that he wanted to preach. As a youth, he was nicknamed "Bible Boy" for his penchant for wandering in the hills, preaching to an imaginary audience. The strongest influence in his ministry came when he was 10 and his father developed a kidney disease. For the next five years, Thomas mopped blood from a dialysis machine and comforted his grieving mother while watching his father slowly die. The experience left Jakes with a profound empathy for the suffering of fellow humans.

Jakes inherited his father's business acumen and succeeded at various sales enterprises with products from newspapers to vegetables to cosmetics. He began his church career when he was hired as musical director at a local Baptist church. Jakes then began preaching while taking psychology courses at West Virginia State College and digging ditches to supplement his income.

In 1980, at the age of 23, he founded the Greater Emmanuel Temple of Faith in Montgomery, West Virginia. Beginning services in a storefront with only 10 members, he gradually began to attract members with his combination of Pentecostal-style worship and social action. A year later, he married Serita Ann Johnson and procured a steady job at a Union Carbide plant. The plant shut down in 1982, and Jakes lost his job. But at the same time, his church began a rapid expansion. Eventually, it became Jakes's full-time job as the congregation moved to new facilities in Charleston, West Virginia. He formed a special Sunday school group for abused and troubled women and began a popular local radio program. The core of his message was an offer of support in trying times and inspiration for people to surmount their difficulties through positive Christian action. According to Lee Grady of *Charisma* magazine, "He taps into the core of human weakness and need and then proclaims Christ as an answer to that, in a way that causes people to stand up and shout." The appeal of his message cut across racial lines; more than 40 percent of his congregation was white. While building his ministry, Jakes continued his education via International Christian University, a correspondence school based in Merced, California, from which he achieved a bachelor's, master's, and doctoral degree.

Jakes grew from a local phenomenon to a national figure in 1993 with the publication of his book, *Woman, Thou Art Loosed!*, based on a sermon he had delivered the previous year. The book, which offered comfort and inspiration to abused women, sold more than 2 million copies. Jakes later created a musical based on the book, which earned him a Grammy nomination in the gospel music category. In 1993, Jakes also launched a television show, *Get Ready with T. D. Jakes*. He continually expanded his television presence, until he was regularly preaching to millions on the Black Entertainment Television network and the Trinity Broadcasting Network. He also created the T. D. Jakes Ministries Annual Conference, which attracted as many as 50,000 people. Jakes became famous for his long, spellbinding, hard-hitting sermons on a wide variety of subjects dealing with contemporary society. "I have a need to impact my generation's economic truths and relational truths as well as biblical truths," he explained.

In 1996, Jakes relocated to Dallas to create a new church from scratch. Such was his influence on his parishioners that 50 families followed him from West Virginia to Texas. Jakes purchased a 28-acre parcel of land, previously owned by a televangelist sentenced to jail for tax evasion, in the economically struggling Oak Cliff section of South Dallas. There he constructed the Potter's House, a palatial sanctuary with a seating capacity of 8,200.

It was an audacious show of optimism, but Jakes quickly began filling seats. In the congregation's first year of existence, Jakes attracted 7,000 members. By the end of the second year the membership rolls had swelled to 17,000. Jakes's church reached 26,000 a couple of years later, making it the fastest-growing and one of the largest congregations in the nation. His movement created a network of churches called the Higher Ground Always Abounding, for which Jakes serves as bishop.

Jakes's indefatigable energy and creativity have led him to initiate a vast array of programs and innovative outreach techniques. "I have an urgency about life that is abnormal," he observes. "I seize life like a person coming out of drowning seizes air." The Potter's House initiated nearly 50 programs to improve the quality of life of those in its depressed neighborhood, including efforts aimed at the homeless, substance abusers, and prostitutes. Always attuned to technological resources, Jakes added a state-of-the-art sound system and laptop computers for parishioners in the sanctuary. The church donated satellite dishes to 260 prisons so it could beam its telecasts to inmates around the United States.

In addition to his expanding televised ministry, Jakes has written more than 20 books. In 2001, he embarked upon a joint effort with the Hallmark company to market a line of greeting cards based on his sermons and writings.

All this activity has brought fame and wealth to Jakes. Two presidential candidates in 2001, George W. Bush and Al Gore, declared themselves admirers of him. Jakes baptized football star Deion Sanders. Royalties from his works allowed him to move into a $1.7-million mansion on White Rock Lake in Dallas. Although fellow clergy have criticized him for promoting consumerism over biblical justice, Jakes defends his actions as providing a model for the poor of how a person can rise to prosperity within the law and within the framework of a religious life. He has vowed to continue his high-energy course of ministry. "My definition of success," he says, "is to be able to birth out every creative thought God has breathed into me before I die."

Further Reading

Phelps, Shirelle. *Contemporary Black Biography*. Vol. 17. Detroit, Mich.: Gale Research, 1998.

Thompson, Clifford, ed. *Current Biography, 2001*. New York: H. W. Wilson, 2001.

Van Biema, David. "Bishop Unbound," *Time*, December 11, 2000, p. 88.

———. "Spirit Raiser." *Time*, September 17, 2001, pp. 52–55.

Johnson, Mordecai Wyatt

(1890–1976) *Baptist clergy, college president*

The 1926 selection of Mordecai Johnson, a 36-year-old Baptist minister, to be president of Howard University was greeted with suspicion in the academic world. However, Johnson justified the choice by turning the Washington, D.C., school into one of the most respected academic institutions in the country.

Mordecai Wyatt Johnson was born on December 12, 1890, in Paris, Kentucky, the son of former slaves. Wyatt Johnson married Carolyn Freeman after his first wife's death, and Mordecai was their only child. Carolyn worked as a domestic and Wyatt as a mill worker and part-time preacher.

Johnson attended Roger Williams University in Nashville, Tennessee (universities at that time often included curricula as low as elementary school), Howe Institute in Memphis, and Atlanta Baptist College (later Morehouse College), where he completed his secondary schooling and undergraduate degrees. Raised under the strict discipline of his father, Mordecai Johnson developed into a serious, hardworking young man. Although his skin was so light that he could easily pass for white, Johnson always identified himself as black, accepting the hardships that that entailed. Not only did he excel academically, but he was also the star quarterback on the football team. He made such an impression on the staff at Atlanta Baptist that they offered him a job as English teacher and acting dean right out of college.

Johnson accepted the challenge for one year, but then left to pursue his interest in a theological education. He attended the University of Chicago and then went to Rochester Theological Seminary, where he became fascinated by the social gospel theology of Walter Rauschenbusch. After obtaining his divinity degree in 1917, he accepted a call as pastor of

First Baptist Church in Charleston, West Virginia. There he put his social activism message to work by founding a chapter of the National Association for the Advancement of Colored People (NAACP). In 1921, he was granted a leave of absence to study at Harvard Divinity School, where he earned a master's degree in sacred theology. He returned to Charleston and served his parish until 1926. At that time he received a surprising call to take over the presidency of Howard University in Washington, D.C., a black school whose previous 10 presidents had all been white. The selection of a black president was greeted with elation by most of the black community, although many academics thought that Johnson's background as a Baptist minister with limited teaching experience and unimpressive academic credentials put him in over his head.

Administrating with an iron hand, however, Johnson eased the school's chronic money shortage by obtaining funding from the government. He improved the medical school, one of two in the nation that admitted students without regard to race. But his most important accomplishment was building up the law school. Recognizing the importance of legal persuasion for the Civil Rights movement, Johnson strengthened the program from one that offered only night classes to a top-flight law school. Its most prominent student, Thurgood Marshall, used knowledge gained at the school to win 25 of the 32 civil rights cases he argued before the Supreme Court. (Marshall later became a Supreme Court justice.) Johnson oversaw the attraction of the best African-American scholars in the world to the faculty, including theology professor HOWARD THURMAN. He was a popular speaker for civil rights—with his excellent memory he often spoke for 45 minutes without referring to notes.

During Johnson's 34 years as president, the school's enrollment swelled from 2,000 to 10,000. He retired in 1960 and died on September 10, 1976.

Mordecai Johnson orchestrated an educational environment at Howard University that allowed it to produce several generations of outstanding black leaders. *(Schomburg Center for Research in Black Culture)*

Further Reading

Garrity, John A., and Mark C. Carnes, eds. *American National Biography.* Vol. 12. New York: Oxford University Press, 2002.

McKinney, Richard J. *Mordecai: The Man and His Message.* Washington, D.C.: Howard University Press, 1998.

Murphy, Larry G., ed. *Encyclopedia of African American Religious Biography.* New York: Garland Publishing, 1993.

Smith, Jesse Carney, ed. *Notable Black American Men.* Vol. 1. Detroit, Mich.: Gale Research, 1999.

Jones, Absalom

(1746–1818) *Methodist Episcopal priest*

Absalom Jones was the first African-American priest of the Methodist Episcopal Church. Together with RICHARD ALLEN, he founded the Free African Society, initiated the separation of blacks from white-dominated churches into congregations of their own, and was an influential force in Philadelphia's social and political structure.

Jones was born into slavery in Sussex, Delaware, on a date variously recorded as August 6 or November 6, 1746. While working as a house slave, he picked up the rudiments of reading by begging moments of instruction from anyone who knew how. He saved the pennies given him for good service until he could purchase a speller and a Bible. In 1762, his mother and six siblings were sold; Jones was taken to Philadelphia, where he worked as a handyman in his master's store. He was allowed to attend night school for a brief period to learn practical mathematics for use in business.

In 1770, Jones married a slave for whom he was able to purchase freedom with borrowed funds. He worked tirelessly to repay the loan. Jones remained a slave himself until October 1, 1784. At that time, he continued to live with his former master and worked as his employee. Jones became committed to the Christian religion through the efforts of the Methodist Episcopal Church and was licensed as a lay preacher in 1786.

His interest in religion brought him into fellowship with Richard Allen, a Methodist who had been recruited to preach to black members of St. George's Episcopal Church in Philadelphia. Although St. George's had mixed membership, it was far from integrated. Blacks were not allowed to be buried in the church's cemetery, and they had to worship at 5 A.M. on Sunday so as not to interfere with the white services. Concerned about this second-class status, Allen proposed forming a separate black church. Since few of his supporters backed a separate church, Allen set aside the idea for a time.

Jones and Allen, however, began serious discussion about the needs of African-American churchgoers. In April 1787, the two joined a group of ex-slaves and Quaker philanthropists to form the Free African Society. The first nondenominational Christian society in the United States, the Free African Society offered Christian fellowship and advocated Christian doctrine in opposition to social ills such as drinking and gambling, provided medical and economic support to free blacks, and advocated for the cause of abolition.

Through industriousness and thrift, Jones was able to purchase a lot and a house in 1788. The more societal freedom he enjoyed, however, the more the hypocritically oppressive atmosphere of St. George's Church bothered him. When the rapid increase in African-American members made the white church membership uncomfortable, they ended the practice of black services and undertook a major remodeling that included a new gallery with separate seating for blacks.

This led to a famous incident that occurred in 1787, according to most sources. Following the completion of the remodeling, Jones, Allen, and several other blacks entered St. George's for services. They climbed the stairs to the balcony and sat in the seats they had formerly been assigned. However, changes had been made during remodeling, and blacks had been moved to a different section. While they were kneeling in prayer, an agitated white sexton approached them and began berating them.

According to Allen's account, "I raised my head and saw one of the trustees . . . have hold of the Rev. Absalom Jones, pulling him off his knees and saying, 'You must get up; you must not kneel here.'"

Together with his friend Richard Allen, Absalom Jones helped establish a powerful black religious presence in Philadelphia in the late 18th century. *(Schomburg Center for Research in Black Culture)*

Shocked at being disturbed at a sacred moment, Jones replied, "Wait until the prayer is over and I will trouble you no more."

"No," replied the sexton, "You must go now or I will call for aid and force you away."

This was the last straw for Allen and Jones, both of whom were determined to create a religious setting where they could worship with dignity. The Free African Society led the fund-raising for the proposed African Church of Philadelphia. Allen, however, broke with the society over several issues, including the denominational affiliation of the new church. Most of the black churchgoers in Philadelphia, like Jones, had grown up in the Episcopalian community, which had been active among blacks in Philadelphia since the 1740s. They voted to retain their affiliation with this church, with only Jones joining his Methodist friend, Allen, in dissenting.

While Allen decided to go his own way and founded the African Methodist Episcopal Church (AME Church), Jones stayed with the society and its decision to affiliate with the Episcopal Church. They purchased a lot and began building the African Church of St. Thomas. The work was interrupted by a devastating plague of yellow fever, during which Jones earned the admiration of thousands for his courageous work in caring for victims and providing decent burial for the dead. Finally, on July 17, 1794, the new church was ready for services. When it was dedicated into the Episcopal Church in December of that year, it boasted a roster of 246 members. Ever gracious to his friend, Jones influenced the church to call Allen as its minister; however, Allen declined.

A major problem for the new black churches was lack of qualified clergy. The denomination's rules required ordained clergy, all of whom were white, to administer sacraments. Lay people, however, could be recruited to lead services, and, because of his reading ability and the leadership he had shown, Jones was designated the lay reader for St. Thomas. Recognizing that stopgap measures were needed to provide black leadership, the church waived its normal requirements of knowledge of Greek and Latin for ordained clergy, and on August 6, 1795, made Jones the first black deacon in the denomination. However, the church refused to allow St. Thomas any participation at church conventions.

Jones remained active both in the church and in community work for the rest of his life. His most notable accomplishment late in life was the organization of the Black Legion, a group of 3,000 black soldiers formed to fight in the War of 1812. He died on February 13, 1818.

Further Reading

Garrity, John A., and Mark C. Carnes, eds. *American National Biography*. Vol. 12. New York: Oxford University Press, 2002.

Lapsansky, Phil, ed. "In Memoriam: Absalom Jones and the African Slave Trade," *Anglican and Episcopal History* (September 1996): 276–277.

Lincoln, C. Eric, and Lawrence H. Mayima. *The Black Church in the African American Experience*. Durham, N.C.: Duke University Press, 1990.

Newman, Richard, et al., eds. *Pamphlets of Protest: An Anthology of Early African American Protest Literature, 1790–1860*. New York: Routledge, 2001.

Jones, Charles Price
(1865–1949) *cofounder of Church of God (Holiness)*

Along with CHARLES HARRISON MASON, Charles Price Jones laid the foundation of the Church of God, the fastest-growing religious denomination in the United States in the 20th century. A later split between him and Mason resulted in Jones leading a group that became known as the Church of God (Holiness).

Jones was born on December 9, 1865, in Texas Valley, Georgia. He was raised in a strong Baptist family in rural Georgia but left home after his mother died in the early 1880s. He ended up in Crittenden County, Arkansas, where he was converted by Baptists and joined Locust Grove Baptist Church. Jones began preaching at the church in 1885, although he did not get his official preaching license until 1887.

During the next couple of years he earned a living by teaching school before enrolling at Arkansas Baptist College. He supported his studies by serving as a pastor to Pope Creek Baptist Church in 1888, and then at St. Paul Baptist Church in Little Rock, where he was ordained in October 1888.

Jones graduated in 1891 and then assumed the pastorship of Bethlehem Baptist Church in Searcy, Arkansas. After a year, he moved on to Tabernacle Baptist in Selma, Alabama. There he came in contact with the Holiness movement, which taught that faithful Christians could experience a direct work of the Holy Spirit that sanctified them, or made them holy.

When Jones accepted a call as pastor of Mount Helm Baptist Church in Jackson, Mississippi, in 1895, he took his newly adopted Holiness teaching with him. Some of his congregation responded enthusiastically, while others were strongly opposed to what they considered heretical teaching. Jones and a friend, Charles Harrison Mason, convened a group of Holiness-inspired Baptist preachers who formed a new denomination called the Church of God, soon renamed the Church of God in Christ. Jones's greatest contributions to the cause were a booklet entitled "The Work of the Holy Spirit in the Churches," published in 1896; a Holiness magazine called *The Truth*; and numerous spiritual songs and hymns.

At first, Jones attempted to keep his movement within the Baptist Church. But in 1900, he withdrew completely from the Baptist denomination and even tried to remove the name *Baptist* from his Mount Helm congregation. A power struggle ensued, which Jones lost. He and his supporters formed Christ Temple Church in Jackson, which joined the loose confederation of Church of God in Christ congregations that Jones and Mason had started. Jones served as president of this rapidly growing organization's annual convention until 1907, when he split with Mason over a disagreement about the necessity of speaking in tongues. Jones and his followers formed their own denomination called the Church of God USA, or Church of God (Holiness), whose growth, while steady, has not kept pace with Mason's Church of God in Christ.

In 1915, Jones was invited to visit the Church of God (Holiness) in Los Angeles by its pastor, William Washington, to preside over a revival series. He liked the area so much that he stayed and founded a new church, Christ Temple, in 1917. Jones served as the church's pastor as well as the president of the Church of God (Holiness) until 1927. He then retired but continued to write songs and poetry for the church. Jones died on January 19, 1949, in Los Angeles.

Further Reading

Blumhofer, Edith. "Jesus Only: The Ministry of Charles Price Jones." *Assemblies of God Heritage* 7 (spring 1987): pp. 9–14.

Melton, J. Gordon, ed. *Biographical Dictionary of American Cult and Sect Leaders.* New York: Garland, 1986.

Spencer, Jon Michael. "The Hymnody of Charles Price Jones and the Church of Christ (Holiness) USA," *Black Sacred Music* (fall 1990): 14–29.

Jones, James Francis Marion   See PROPHET JONES.

Jones, Jehu, Jr.

(1786–1852) *pioneer Lutheran minister*

Jehu Jones, Jr., initiated a bold ministry to establish African-American Lutheran churches in the 1830s, a project which, if supported, might have changed the face of Lutheranism in the United States.

Jones was born into slavery in Charleston, South Carolina, in 1786. His father, Jehu Jones, Sr., learned his trade from his master, a tailor. This skill enabled the elder Jones to acquire enough money to purchase his freedom in 1798, buy a house, and open a hotel in Charleston. The Jones family were members of St. Philip's Episcopal Church. But shortly after the Lutheran Church of German Protestants began welcoming blacks in 1816, Jehu, Jr., and his wife, Eliza, began attending.

Jones followed his father into tailoring and lived a quiet life until 1830, when he became interested in joining a group of Charleston blacks who were emigrating to Liberia. Believing he could accomplish great work in this new land, he sought an appointment as a missionary to the colony. His pastor, John Bachman, supported his quest and sent him to American Lutheran headquarters in New York with an endorsement for his ordination in 1832. Since the group was preparing to leave soon, the normal process was abbreviated and Jones was ordained on October 24, 1832, at the age of 46.

However, when he returned to Charleston to embark with the group, he was arrested under a law banning free blacks from entering South Carolina. Jones was forced to leave the state and so was unable to join the Liberian emigrants. He returned to New York where he tried, but failed, to raise funds to make the journey himself.

Rejoined by his family in 1833, Jones decided that God intended him to be a missionary to northern free blacks for the Lutheran faith. Friends tried to persuade him to join a church with more ties to the black community, but Jones stayed loyal to the denomination in which his nine children were baptized. He began preaching in Philadelphia in January 1834. A tireless worker, Jones visited more than 2,780 families in a single year. By February, he had attracted enough interest in Philadelphia to plan the building of a black Lutheran church. In June, he bought two lots and began construction on St. Paul Lutheran Church. That same year, Jones started black congregations in Gettysburg and Chambersburg, Pennsylvania.

Those who heeded his call, however, were the poorest of the poor in society, with little money to contribute to the enterprise. By June 1835, Jones was already fighting off creditors. For the next couple of years, Jones fought feverishly to keep the church afloat. He appealed to the Lutheran Church's Pennsylvania synod for a loan, but was denied. Similar appeals to non-Lutheran charities such as the American Colonizing Society were similarly rebuffed. The final straw came in 1838, when the congregation's fund-raising fair had to be canceled due to an outbreak of rioting against Philadelphia's African Americans. The church building was then repossessed and sold.

Jones later requested permission to establish a black Lutheran church in New York City. Not only was his request turned down, but the officials issued a report criticizing his efforts in Philadelphia and denying his legitimacy as a Lutheran pastor. Despite this, Jones remained loyal to the church, resumed his mission work in Philadelphia, and somehow managed to keep his congregation together. As late as 1851, he was able to write, "I continue to preach to the colored congregation of St. Paul Lutheran." He died on September 28, 1852, in Centreville, New Jersey.

Further Reading

Johnson, Jeff G. *Black Christians: The Untold Lutheran Story.* St. Louis, Mo.: Concordia Publishing House, 1991.

Johnson, Jr., Karl E., and Joseph A. Romero. "First African American Lutheran Minister." *Lutheran Quarterly* (winter 1996): 425–441.

Jones, Robert Elijah
(1872–1960) *Methodist Episcopal bishop*

Robert Jones was the first African-American bishop in the predominantly white Methodist Episcopal Church who was entrusted with supervision of congregations in the United States—the previous black bishops had all been assigned to Africa.

Jones was born on February 19, 1872, in Greensboro, North Carolina, the son of Sidney and Mary Jane Jones. He experienced his conversion to the Methodist Episcopal faith when he was 16. After attending high school, he stayed in Greensboro to pursue his education at Bennett College. Shortly after entering the school, he took on pastorates of small, black Methodist Episcopal parishes in the area, beginning with Leaksville in 1891, moving on to Lexington and Thomasville in 1892, and on to Reidsville the following year. He was ordained a deacon in 1893 and obtained his college degree in 1895. Jones then enrolled at Gammons Theological Seminary, where he was named an elder of the church in 1896, and earned his divinity degree in 1897.

That same year, Jones accepted a position as an assistant editor of the *Southwest Christian Advocate,* the primary publication of the Methodist Episcopal Church serving its black conferences. He also renewed his studies at Bennett College, from which he earned his master of divinity degree in 1898. After four years at the *Southwest Christian Advocate,* he married Velana MacArthur and took on new responsibilities as field secretary of his denomination's Sunday School Board.

In 1901, Jones was invited back to the *Southwest Christian Advocate,* this time to take over as the publication's chief editor. Over the next two decades, he used that forum to influence the direction and content of debate over key church issues, and was regularly selected as a delegate to the denomination's annual general assembly. One of the issues on which he wrote concerned the desirability of electing a black bishop. After more than a decade of sometimes heated debate on the subject, the issue was resolved with the election of Jones and Matthew Wesley Clair, Sr., as Methodist Episcopal bishops in 1920. While Clair was assigned to oversee work in Africa, Jones was assigned to head the church's black conference in the United States.

While serving as bishop, Jones lived in New Orleans, from where he helped establish the Gulf-side Assembly in Waveland, Mississippi, a network resource center for black Methodists. He was active in the community, serving as president of the black YMCA, as a member of company boards, a press association, and a business league.

Jones's most important service to his church was in many ways his most frustrating leadership experience. He served on every committee charged with facilitating the merger of the Methodist Episcopal Church with the Methodist Episcopal Church South and the Methodist Protestant Church. Jones strongly opposed the organizational scheme created by the Joint Commission on Unification that segregated all black congregations within the church into a separate, nongeographic conference, on the grounds that this amounted to the establishment of segregation as official church policy. Jones was unable to sway the rest of the committee, which approved the segregation plan that was put into effect with the consummation of the merger in 1939. Worse yet, he came under heavy criticism from black church members for the actions of the committee, despite his own opposition.

Jones retired from active service in 1944 and died in 1960.

Further Reading

Melton, J. Gordon. *Religious Leaders of America.* 2d ed. Detroit, Mich.: Gale Research, 1999.

Kelly, Leontine Turpeau
(1920–) *Methodist bishop*

Leontine Kelly was the first African-American woman to achieve the rank of bishop in a mainstream Christian denomination. She accomplished this although she did not begin her preparation for a ministerial career until she was 50.

She was born Leontine Turpeau on March 5, 1920, in Washington, D.C., the seventh of 10 children of Reverend David and Ila Turpeau. The family was widely spaced in age; Leontine was 17 years younger than her oldest sister. Her upbringing was steeped in religion. Reverend Turpeau was pastor of Mount Zion Methodist Episcopal church, a black church of that predominantly white denomination in the District of Columbia. Teenie, as her family called her, was active in the congregation. Inspired by the life of MARY MCLEOD BETHUNE, she wrote and directed her own religious drama. Segregation was a fact of life for the Turpeaus. Among the humiliations Leontine remembered from her youth was the fact that blacks were allowed to use the high school swimming pool only on Fridays before it was drained for the weekend.

Believing that African Americans must prepare themselves to struggle for acceptance in society, her father insisted that all his children have an opportunity for a college education, even when the Great Depression made funds tight. Leontine Turpeau enrolled at the University of Cincinnati in 1937 but transferred to West Virginia State College the following year. While in school, she met Gloster Bryant Currant, an up-and-coming young leader in the National Association for the Advancement of Colored People (NAACP). The two were married in September 1941 and moved to Detroit. There Gloster Currant built an NAACP branch with a membership of 25,000, the largest in the nation. This accomplishment helped him win appointment as the organization's national youth director in 1946, which required a move to headquarters in New York City. His work became so all-consuming that Leontine found herself parenting their three children alone, with few friends as support. The marriage deteriorated over the years, with the crisis coming to a head upon Gloster's ordination as a deacon in 1953. Leontine, who suffered through months of illness and depression at that time, did not go back to New York with him but stayed with her family in Cincinnati. The couple could not reconcile and were divorced in 1955.

Suddenly, Leontine found herself in need of income, with no employment experience and little training. She eventually found employment as director of the children's activity at Fellowship House, an establishment dedicated to improving race relations. But within a short time she met and married Reverend James David Kelly and relocated to Knoxville, Tennessee, where he was pastor of a Methodist church. The couple then moved to Edwardsville, Virginia, where James Kelly established a thriving congregation, Galilee Methodist Church. Leontine Kelly was content in her role as homemaker, caretaker for their four children, and partner in her husband's ministry. But that life ended when David developed cancer and died in 1968.

Pushed into the ministry by a family tragedy, Leontine Kelly became a pioneer clergywoman in the United Methodist Church. *(United Methodist News Service)*

Again, Kelly found herself in a precarious existence. The leadership of Galilee church requested that she stay on as interim pastor, even though she had no theological training. Kelly did so while also working as the first black schoolteacher at Northumberland County High School, and rearing her children single-handedly. Her work at the church convinced her, as well as many others, that she would make a fine minister. In fact, her bishop once reported of her, "The black minister in Virginia who had done by far the most outstanding work and whom I wanted to appoint a district supervisor in the conference unfortunately did not satisfy the technical requirements of the office."

While Kelly was pondering whether to pursue a career in ministry, she felt the strong presence of the Holy Spirit in the summer of 1969, which decided the issue for her. She began her theological studies in 1970, largely through correspondence courses, while continuing to work. She was made a deacon in 1972 and, after obtaining a scholarship, enrolled full time at Union Theological Seminary in Richmond, Virginia. She completed her master of divinity degree in 1976 and was ordained an elder the following year.

Kelly then accepted a position as associate program council director for the Virginia Annual Conference Council on Ministries. When the time and travel commitments for the job began encroaching too heavily on her family time, she resigned and accepted a call to Asbury United Methodist Church in Richmond. As a preacher, she showed an exceptional ability to interpret Bible readings in a way that made the message personal to the listener. At the same time, she stayed active within the denomination, exercising leadership on national boards and councils. As with many women who broke gender barriers in religious leadership, she experienced considerable resistance from established denominational leaders, many of whom quoted words from the apostle Paul that appeared to reject female leadership in the church. "I know what Paul said," Kelly responded, "but Paul didn't call me—God did."

After six years of successful ministry at Asbury, Kelly moved into church administration. Her effectiveness as an organizer and the speaking abilities that made her a popular guest at conferences and services throughout the East Coast prompted her consideration for the office of bishop. On July 20, 1984, the 64-year old Kelly was consecrated as the first African-American woman bishop of a prominent Christian denomination, overseeing the states of California and Nevada.

Kelly did not serve long in this position, retiring in 1988. But in her short term of ministry she made such an impact that she was awarded a dozen honorary doctorates. Nobel Peace Prize winner Desmond Tutu playfully said of her, "She really made men understand why women say that when God created man she was experimenting." In October 2000, Kelly was elected to the National Women's Hall of Fame in Seneca Falls, New York.

Further Reading

Current, Angella. *Breaking Barriers: An African American Family and the Methodist Story.* Nashville, Tenn.: Abingdon, 2001.

Henderson, Ashyia N. *Contemporary Black Biography.* Vol. 33. Detroit, Mich.: Gale Research, 2002.

Hine, Darlene Clarke. *Black Women in America, A–L.* Brooklyn, N.Y.: Carlson Publishing, 1993.

King, Barbara Lewis

(1930–   ) *nondenominational clergy*

Reverend Barbara Lewis King is the founder of one of the largest and most active nondenominational churches in Atlanta, Georgia. One contemporary clergyman said of her, "She has earned a place in Atlanta's black power structure whether no one else wanted her to have it or not."

She was born Barbara Lewis in Houston, Texas, in 1930, to parents who were divorced shortly after her birth. Her father, Lee Andrew Lewis, was the first black motion picture operator in Texas. Barbara was primarily raised by her grandmother, Ida Bates Lewis, who personified for her the power of the Holy Spirit. During her childhood, Barbara was actively involved at Antioch Baptist Church. She expressed a desire to be a preacher at age six, and began teaching Sunday school at 13. Although she felt called to preach, male pastors discouraged her from pursuing a ministerial career.

Lewis enrolled at Texas State University in 1948, only to be stricken with tuberculosis. She then spent four years convalescing in a sanatorium, where she was introduced to the Unity School of Christianity. This group taught that since humans are created in God's image, all can experience divine personal power. Lewis claimed that she was cured of her disease after heeding a radio evangelist's call to put her hands on the radio and pray. She returned to Texas State in 1951 and graduated in 1955 with a B.A. degree in social work. Moving on to Atlanta University, she completed her master's degree in social work and there met the first of her three husbands, Moses King, whose name she has kept.

Barbara King relocated to Chicago, where she was employed as a social worker with the city housing administration. There, in 1961, she met a vivacious pastor, JOHNNIE COLEMON, and signed on as her director of administration. After Colemon encouraged her to begin a ministry of her own, King studied at the Baptist Training School of Chicago and the Unity Institute of Continuing Education in Missouri. Upon being ordained into the ministry in 1971, King returned to her sociology career as a professor of social work at Atlanta University. But in her spare time, she began a small Bible study group for women in her living room. By the time she accepted a job as dean of students at Spelman

College in Atlanta, the group had grown into a congregation that King called the Hillside Chapel and International Truth Center. In 1977 she started a new project, the Barbara King School of Ministry.

Although her work was dismissed by some as a women's cult, King's nondenominational, unaffiliated church continued to grow. By 1985, it had outgrown its building. King took advantage of this opportunity to build a new church-in-the-round that eliminated the function of a pulpit, which she saw as a barrier to communication. The church, completed in 1991, now claims nearly 5,000 members.

King has continued to add pieces to her ministry on a regular basis. In the 1990s, she created a television show, *A New Thought . . . A New Life,* and founded a holistic health center and a downtown meditation center. In addition, the six-foot, five-inch King started Tall Is Beautiful, a clothing store for tall women. Regularly lauded by the city of Atlanta for her community contributions, she cites as the goal of her ministry "to touch someone's life and help them to see their very special talent to be given to the world as only they can do."

Further Reading

King, Barbara L., *Transform Your Life: Revised and Expanded.* New York: Perigee, 1995.

Phelps, Shirelle. *Contemporary Black Biography.* Vol. 22. Detroit, Mich.: Gale Research, 1999.

King, Martin Luther, Jr.

(1929–1968) *Baptist clergy, civil rights leader*

Martin Luther King, Jr., is credited with being the major force behind the Civil Rights movement of the 1950s and 1960s that brought about the dismantling of legal segregation in the United States. King's accomplishments were such that black writer MICHAEL ERIC DYSON,

among others, called King "arguably the greatest American ever produced on our native soil." King's intellectual prowess and dynamic speaking ability allowed him to present an effective civil rights strategy that combined his personal faith in the power of Christian love, the black religious tradition of social activism, and Gandhi's philosophy of nonviolent civil disobedience.

King was born on January 15, 1929, in Atlanta, Georgia, to Alberta and MARTIN LUTHER KING, SR. When Martin, Jr., was a toddler, his father took over the pastorate of the influential Ebenezer Baptist Church in Atlanta. Determined that his children would not suffer the extreme poverty of his youth, Martin, Sr., provided them with a comfortable life. He was a devout, determined man, who required his children to recite memorized Bible verses at the dinner table.

Martin, Jr., was a sensitive boy who instinctively despised violence. Twice before the age of 13, he attempted to commit suicide. Racial discrimination disturbed him deeply. While eating on a railroad car, King saw a curtain drawn to separate white diners from black. "I felt just as if a curtain had come down across my whole life," he recalled. He was never more angry in his life than when he was forced to give up his seat and stand for 90 miles on a bus ride from Macon to Atlanta.

King was such an exceptional student that he skipped several grades in school and entered Morehouse College at the age of 15. Although his father wanted his son to follow him into the ministry, King balked. He had doubts about religion and found the black Christian's emotional style of worship embarrassing. It seemed to him that the legal profession offered a better opportunity for affecting society.

However, under the influence of such people as Morehouse president BENJAMIN ELIJAH MAYS, King came to see his calling as a pastor. He was ordained in 1947 and, after graduating from Morehouse in 1948, enrolled at Crozier

Theological Seminary in Chester, Pennsylvania, where he was one of only six blacks among 100 students. At Crozier he was voted president of the student body, completed his divinity degree at the top of his class in 1951, and was awarded a fellowship to study for his doctorate at Boston University. At Boston, he met Coretta Scott, who gave up her dream of a singing career to marry him in 1953.

After obtaining his Ph.D. in systematic theology, King was wooed by three colleges as a professor, and offered pastorates of two northern churches. But believing he had a duty to serve in the South, he instead accepted a call to Dexter Avenue Baptist Church in Montgomery, Alabama, in September 1954. He had been on the job less than three months when Rosa Parks was arrested for violating the city's segregated busing laws on December 1. The black community rose up in protest. On December 5, they formed the Montgomery Improvement Association to organize a bus boycott. Despite being a newcomer, King had already impressed the city with his education and inspirational oratory and he was chosen to lead the group.

For King, taking on oppression in society was not a political issue but a moral one. "It has always been the responsibility of the church to broaden horizons, challenge the status quo and the mores when necessary," he declared. While in college he had become intrigued with the nonviolent resistance philosophy of Mohandas Gandhi. In the bus boycott, King found a chance to employ Gandhian tactics alongside the Christian message of love and forgiveness. Under King's leadership, Montgomery blacks established a car pool system of 300 vehicles as alternate transportation, formed a communications structure, and raised money to support the boycott.

The white community retaliated with violence. King and many other blacks were threatened and harassed. At one point, King wanted to quit the effort. But after fervent

Martin Luther King, Jr., pastor of a small church in Montgomery, Alabama, became the driving force behind the Civil Rights movement of the 1950s and 1960s. *(Library of Congress)*

prayer, he came to understand his position as a call from God and from that point, refused to give in to fear. On January 30, King's home was firebombed. Angry blacks were on the verge of rioting in retaliation, but King defused the situation. Offering concrete evidence of the type of movement he wished to lead, he urged his followers to practice love and forgiveness. While they would not obey unjust laws, neither would they strike back, pass judgment, or hate.

On February 21, 1956, King and nearly 100 others were indicted on charges of conspiring to organize an illegal boycott. A month later, King was found guilty and fined $500. The car pool was ruled illegal. King refused to back down, and African Americans began walking instead. Finally, on December 20, 1956, the Supreme Court ordered the desegregation of Montgomery's buses.

This tremendous breakthrough, achieved through nonviolent protest, earned King immediate national recognition. Southern church leaders decided to follow up on this success with an ongoing campaign for racial justice. On January 10, 1957, King and nearly 60 other clergy from 10 states formed the Southern Christian Leadership Conference (SCLC), and again King was chosen to head the group. King spent much of the next two years organizing, planning strategies for nonviolent confrontation, and writing a book called *Stride Toward Freedom,* which told the story of the Montgomery boycott. Having achieved celebrity status, he traveled to a Harlem bookstore to sign autographed copies. There, on September 20, 1958, a mentally ill woman stabbed him with a letter opener, nearly killing him.

King recovered and resumed work, but discovered that his duties with the SCLC took him from home far too often. In January 1960, he left Dexter Baptist and moved to Atlanta, where the SCLC headquarters was located. In October of that year he was harassed by Georgia police on petty traffic violations that threatened to put him in jail. His treatment provoked outrage across the nation. Senator John F. Kennedy of Massachusetts used his influence to free King, which earned him valuable support among Southern blacks in the upcoming presidential election.

King set to work coordinating a desegregation campaign in Albany, Georgia. Nine months later, the campaign dissolved, having accomplished little. King concluded that he and his associates had made a mistake in attacking the entire Albany power structure rather than focusing on one area, such as the economy. He used the lessons learned from this defeat to prepare for a crucial campaign in Birmingham, Alabama. On April 3, 1963, the campaign began with demonstrations at restaurants, a downtown store boycott, and daily mass marches. King was arrested on April 12, and was widely criticized by black clergy for his civil disobedience. King responded with his "Letter from a Birmingham Jail," which laid out clearly the goals and philosophy of the Civil Rights movement.

In the view of many historians, the turning point of the Civil Rights movement came when Birmingham authorities attacked the peaceful marchers with dogs, nightsticks, and fire hoses. A shocked national television viewing audience was moved, in the words of historian August Meier, "to face the problem of Southern discrimination in a way it never had before."

After winning some concessions in Birmingham, King took part in the March on Washington in August 1963. There he gave his famed "I Have a Dream" speech, which further inspired a nation to reexamine its social policies. Congress responded to the new consensus by passing the 1964 Civil Rights Act, and the Jim Crow laws of the South began to crumble. King's efforts in this achievement were recognized when he was awarded the Nobel Peace Prize on December 10, 1964.

In 1965, King turned his attention to voting rights, focusing on Selma, Alabama, where only 1 percent of the county's blacks was registered.

A brutal assault on demonstrators, followed by King's decision to turn back rather than risk further confrontation, undercut King's status with younger, more militant blacks. Although the campaign culminated in an impressive 25,000-person march to the state capital in Montgomery and helped prompt passage of the Voting Rights Act in Congress, King found himself under assault from many quarters. Angry urban blacks scoffed at his nonviolent message and his refusal to endorse Black Power, which did not mesh with his Christian views. On the other extreme, conservative blacks led by JOSEPH HARRISON JACKSON of Chicago deplored his confrontational tactics.

Meanwhile, the Federal Bureau of Investigation (FBI), whose director, J. Edgar Hoover, called King "the most notorious liar in the country," stepped up its six-year campaign to discredit King. King encountered even more controversy when he began speaking against the Vietnam War in 1966.

That same year, he took his campaign for civil rights to northern cities. During summer of 1966, a series of tense marches took place in hostile white neighborhoods in Chicago. In 1967, King began organizing a huge rally in Washington for the dispossessed of all races, called the Poor People's Campaign. He took time off from that effort in March 1968 to support black sanitation workers who were striking for equality in their jobs. Following a march marred by violence on March 28, he prepared for a second march the next week. On April 4, he was standing on the balcony of the motel in which he was staying when he was assassinated by a man investigators identified as James Earl Ray.

His associate RALPH ABERNATHY defined what King meant to black Americans by saying, "He articulates the longings, the hopes, the aspirations of his people in a most earnest and profound way." King's many contributions to civil rights were memorialized when Congress in 1983 declared the third Monday of January, King's birthday month, a national holiday.

Further Reading

Baldwin, Lewis V. To Make the Wounded Whole: The Cultural Legacy of Martin Luther King, Jr. Minneapolis: Augsburg/Fortress, 1992.

Carson, Clayborn, and Kris Shepard. A Call to Conscience: The Landmark Speeches of Dr. Martin Luther King, Jr. New York: Warner Books, 2001.

Cone, James H. Martin and Malcolm: Dream or Nightmare? Maryknoll, N.Y.: Orbis Books, 1991.

Fairclough, Adam. To Redeem the Soul of America: The SCLC and Martin Luther King, Jr. Athens: University of Georgia Press, 1987.

King, Coretta Scott. My Life With Martin Luther King, Jr. New York: Holt, Rinehart and Winston, 1969.

King, Martin Luther, Jr. Chaos or Community. New York: Harper & Row, 1964.

———. Stride Toward Freedom: The Montgomery Story. New York: Harper & Row, 1958.

———. Why We Can't Wait. New York: Harper & Row, 1964.

Paris, Peter J. Black Religious Leaders: Conflict in Unity. Louisville, Ky.: John Knox Press, 1991.

Powledge, Fred. Free at Last? The Civil Rights Movement and the People Who Made It. Boston: Little, Brown, 1991.

Washington, James M. ed. A Testament of Hope: The Essential Writings of Martin Luther King, Jr. San Francisco: Harper & Row, 1986.

King, Martin Luther, Sr.
(Mike King, Daddy King)
(1899–1984) Baptist clergy

Although not nearly as famous as his son, Martin Luther King, Sr., provided a courageous model of Christian social activism that inspired MARTIN LUTHER KING, JR., and other civil rights activists in their fight for African American civil rights.

King was born on December 19, 1899, in Stockbridge, Georgia. There was a dispute over the given name of this second of nine children; his father, James Allen King, called him Martin Luther, while his mother, Delia, insisted that his name was Michael. His family called him Mike.

King grew up in the Jim Crow South, where he saw a black man beaten and lynched merely for smiling, and he himself was beaten badly by a white racist. Home life could be equally bleak. His father was a quarryman who lost a hand in an explosion and had to scrape out a living as a sharecropper in a town where, according to King, whites believed that "cheatin' a nigger ain't really doin' nothin' wrong." While his mother was religious in the Baptist tradition, his father was not.

James King often made life miserable with his alcoholism, violent temper, and reluctance to let his children off from farm work to attend school.

Mike King was blessed with a tremendous singing voice, which he used in church choir and then as an occasional preacher. At the age of 18 he realized that he needed an education in order to advance in the ministry. He moved to Atlanta and enrolled at a school where he was placed in the fifth grade, despite his age. Supporting himself by manual labor, he put in five years at the school and then attempted to enroll at Morehouse College. Although he failed the entrance tests, King was admitted on the strength of his impassioned pleas to the college president. King failed freshman English twice but, through sheer determination, graduated in 1930, with a B.A. degree in theology.

By this time he was married to Alberta Williams, daughter of the respected pastor of Ebenezer Baptist Church in Atlanta. While King was serving as minister at two small Georgia churches, his father-in-law died, and King was called to take his place. He spent the next 40 years as the minister at Ebenezer, building it into one of Atlanta's largest churches.

In addition to his stirring sermons, King was well ahead of his time in campaigning for equal rights for blacks and in calling attention to the plight of the poor. Ignoring those who warned him not to rock the boat, he led a march on city hall in 1936, demanding equal voting rights for African Americans, and an end to the poll tax and literacy requirements for voting. He also worked hard to raise the pay of black teachers to that of whites doing the same job.

It was King's dream to have his son, Martin Luther, Jr., join him as copastor at Ebenezer. But the younger King's heroic struggle for civil rights ended with his assassination in 1968. More tragedy was in store for King, Sr., as another son, A. D., drowned in 1969, and his beloved wife, Alberta, was shot and killed by a gunman while playing the organ in church in 1974.

Despite a life of violence at the hands of whites, King never strayed from his Christian ideals, his belief in nonviolence, and his advocacy for the disadvantaged. He played a major role in delivering the black vote for Jimmy Carter's presidential bid in 1976 and delivered the benediction at the Democratic National Convention in 1976 and 1980. King died from heart disease on November 11, 1984, in Atlanta, Georgia.

Further Reading

King, Martin Luther, Sr., with Clayton Riley. *Daddy King: An Autobiography.* New York: Morrow, 1980.
Raboteau, Albert J. *A Fire in the Bones.* Boston: Beacon Press, 1995.

Kofey, Laura Adorkor
(Laura Champion, Laura Adorkor Kofy, Laura Adorkor Kofi)
(ca. 1875–1928) *founder, African Universal Church*

Laura Adorkor Kofey (also spelled Kofy or Kofi) was a mysterious woman of great charisma who founded the African Universal Church in the 1920s. Like GEORGE ALEXANDER MCGUIRE, she provided a religious framework for the black nationalist ideology of MARCUS MOSIAH GARVEY during her brief ministry.

Much confusion obscures the details of Kofey's life prior to her emergence into the public eye in the 1920s. Dates given for her birth range from 1875 to 1893. Historian Richard Newman has determined that she was born in Ghana, outside the city of Accra, in 1875. Kofey claimed to be the daughter of King Knesipi, who sent her to the United States to encourage African Americans to move to Africa.

She arrived in the United States via Canada in the 1920s and settled in Detroit. There she became active in Garvey's Universal

Negro Improvement Association (UNIA). In 1926, Kofey moved to Florida, where she assumed a position of leadership in the local UNIA chapter. However, Kofey came into conflict with Garvey, who was mired in legal problems that resulted in his deportation in 1927. According to Garvey's supporters, Kofey acted without official authorization to collect funds in the UNIA name for the purchase of a sawmill in Africa and boat fare to that continent. Garvey's supporters suspected that she was taking advantage of Garvey's popularity among blacks to raise money for her own use. As a result, Garvey disassociated himself from her in 1927. His supporters accused Kofey of fraud, claiming her real name was Laura Champion and that she had been born in Athens, Georgia.

Kofey, however, denounced the UNIA and established her own movement in a religious context under the name African Universal Church, employing Garvey's themes of African identity and pride. "Go back to yourselves; that's back to Africa and that is back to God," she proclaimed. She stressed that it was necessary for blacks to work together to advance their community. A colorful personality who called herself the "Warrior Mother of Africa's Warriors of the Most High God," Kofey proved to be such a captivating speaker that she was able to attract many former Garvey backers to her cause.

Tension between Kofey and the UNIA strained to the breaking point in early 1928. As Kofey was addressing a large and enthusiastic crowd of her followers at Liberty Hall in Miami on March 8, 1928, an assailant forced a pistol through a crack in a door and shot her to death. The enraged crowd who witnessed the assassination beat to death a Garvey loyalist whom they believed to have pulled the trigger. Two other UNIA members were later arrested but were eventually released due to lack of evidence, and no one was officially charged with the crime.

Kofey had inspired such dedication in her followers that the African Universal Church continued to grow in the years following her death, establishing branches in New York, Georgia, and Alabama. In recent years, however, the group has declined to the point of near invisibility.

Further Reading

Newman, Richard. *Black Power and Black Religion.* West Cornwall, Conn.: Locust Hill Press, 1987.

Wiesenfield, Judith, and Richard Newman, eds. *This Far by Faith: Readings in African-American Women's Religious Biography.* New York: Routledge, 1995.

L

Laveau, Marie
(ca. 1794–1881) *cult leader, voodoo priestess*

Marie Laveau is regarded as one of the most powerful women in American religion during the 19th century due to the widespread belief in her mystical powers as the Voodoo Queen of New Orleans.

The date of her birth is listed by various sources as between 1790 and 1794. She was a free black born in New Orleans, the illegitimate daughter of Charles Laveau and Marguerite Carcantel. Little is known of her early life except that she was raised in the Roman Catholic faith.

In 1819, she married Jacques Paris, a free black carpenter, and was given a house as a dowry by her father. The marriage was unhappy. According to some, she left her husband and began referring to herself as a widow long before he died. Other stories say that Paris simply vanished under mysterious circumstances and was believed to have died. At any rate, Laveau found herself alone and began to support herself as a hairdresser and as a cook at the county jail. These occupations provided her with access to news and secrets that she was able to use to her advantage when she began claiming mystical powers.

Somehow she became involved with voodoo (also known as voudou or Vodun), a system of belief that incorporated magic that had been brought to New Orleans by African slaves in the late 18th century. Laveau combined this African-based religious tradition with her understanding of Catholicism to create a new form of spiritual belief. Using her beauty, dramatic talent, business sense, and intelligence-gathering ability, she projected an image of enormous power. Laveau had charms, amulets, and magic potions reputed to work for protection or to wreak havoc on an enemy. Before long, slaves hoping to run away sought her out for blessings, politicians came to her for good luck, and the curious came to her for her powers of divining the future. All of this was done in secret, as these practices were not considered acceptable in open society.

Belief in voodoo was rampant among various elements in New Orleans in the early 19th century, and Laveau had to surmount the challenges of numerous rivals. By 1830, however, she had become the most powerful voodoo practitioner in New Orleans, using as a base of operations a house given to her by a woman whom she had helped acquit of a crime. A shrewd business operator, she made a fortune selling charms and potions (known as gris-gris) and charging whites admission to attend secret rituals. For several decades, she maintained a position of power, influence, and intimidation that was unheard of for a woman of her time.

Laveau began living with Louis Duminy de Glompion, a free black with whom she was reported to have had 15 children. She was elected "Queen for Life" by her supporters and participated in secret nighttime ceremonies and celebrations. Laveau exhibited a strong sense of social justice. She regularly visited prisons and cared for the poor and homeless. Eventually, she returned to her Catholic roots and in 1875 renounced voodoo. Her work, however, was carried on by her daughter, also named Marie, who bore such a resemblance to her mother that she perpetuated a myth of eternal youth, posing as her mother long after the original Marie had died on June 16, 1881. Although the daughter achieved fame as the high priestess of voodoo for a time, the movement faded to insignificance by the end of the century.

Further Reading

Hine, Darlene Clarke. *Black Women in America, A–L.* Brooklyn, N.Y.: Carlson Publishing, 1993.

Mulina, Jesse Gaston. "The Case of Voodoo in New Orleans." In *Africanism in American Culture.* Bloomington: Indiana University Press, 1990.

Lee, George

(1903–1955) *Baptist clergy, civil rights martyr*

George Lee, the courageous but largely unheralded hero of voting rights for minorities, was the first activist to give his life for the cause in the modern Civil Rights movement.

Lee was born and raised on a plantation in Mississippi. The only education he received was during a brief time at a segregated plantation school. Yet he had taught himself a great deal about the legal rights of Americans before coming to the town of Belzoni in western Mississippi. He served as pastor of the local Baptist church,

ran a small grocery store in town, and also operated his own printing press. Lee was convinced that the key to African Americans gaining equality under the law was to exercise their legal right to vote. This was a novel concept in Humphrey County, Mississippi, where blacks, despite outnumbering whites nearly two to one, had been denied the vote so long that none of them even thought about the issue.

Along with his friend Gus Courts, Lee organized a local chapter of the National Association for the Advancement of Colored People (NAACP). From his pulpit, he urged his parishioners to register to vote and to pay the poll tax levied on voters. He held meetings on the subject to educate potential voters and used his printing press to put out leaflets arguing for voter registration.

In the words of civil rights leader Roy Wilkins, "Reverend Lee did not just tell the people what they ought to do. He gave them an example." Lee was the first black person to go to the polls, where the sheriff refused to accept his poll tax payment and turned him away. After Lee reported the incident to federal authorities, local authorities tried another tack. Lee and his wife would be allowed to vote on the condition that he cease his efforts to enlist other black voters. Lee refused. In the end, the local authorities had to allow him to vote, but the anger he stirred up was palpable. Nevertheless, Lee continued his campaign to register black voters.

A white citizens' council then organized in town to stop the black voting drive. They obtained the names of all registered black voters and used this list to get those people fired from their jobs and denied credit. Registered voters' rents were also raised. Nonetheless, in less than a year, Lee was able to recruit 92 black voters. Despite all the harassment, he maintained a conciliatory tone. He simply called attention to the law and noted that blacks in neighboring counties were voting with no problems. "We respectfully ask that you will at this time endorse and support our efforts to become full-fledged citizens of this county," he said.

However, the efforts to stop him grew increasingly violent. Car windshields were broken, a black club was destroyed, and Lee began to receive death threats. His wife, Rosebud, urged him to quiet his efforts but, as she reported later, "He said somebody had to lead."

On May 7, 1955, Lee received a visit from some menacing whites at his grocery store. That evening, as he was driving home, he was killed by a shotgun blast from a passing car. The sheriff declared the death to be due to a traffic accident and refused to acknowledge the convincing evidence that Lee had been shot. The case was never pursued, and Lee is now honored by civil rights organizations as a martyr for the cause of voting rights.

Further Reading

Carson, Clayborn, et al., eds, *Eyes on the Prize: Documents, Speeches and First-Hand Accounts from the Black Freedom Struggle, 1954–1990.* New York: Penguin Books, 1991.

Morris, Aldon. "Strategy of the Crusade for Citizenship Progress." In Aldon Morris, *The Origins of the Civil Rights Movement,* New York: Free Press, 1984, pp. 104–105.

Lee, Jarena
(1783–unknown) *African Methodist Episcopal evangelist*

Jarena Lee is the first known African-American female to petition for the right to preach in an established church denomination.

Few details of her life are known outside of what she wrote in two autobiographies. She was born on February 11, 1783, in Cape May, New Jersey. She wrote that her parents, whose names she does not mention, were "wholly ignorant of the knowledge of God." At the age of seven, she was separated from her parents and sent to work as a servant some 60 miles from her home. There in the early 1800s, she was converted to Christianity at a religious meeting. After struggling through four years of doubt and contemplating suicide, she emerged with a strong urge to evangelize. She organized a predominantly female prayer-and-song band in Philadelphia and in 1809 petitioned Rev. RICHARD ALLEN, pastor of Bethel African Methodist Episcopal Church, for permission to preach. Allen denied her on account of her sex. For Lee, a feminist who continually reminded people that Jesus died for women as well as men, "It was as if a fire shut up in my bones."

In 1811, she married Rev. Joseph Lee, pastor of a small black church in Snow Hill, New Jersey, near Philadelphia. She was so lonely in this isolated setting, away from her friends, that she begged her husband to move back to Philadelphia. She had a dream, however, that persuaded her that her husband had to lead his flock, and left him alone thereafter.

Lee lost five of her family members over the next several years, culminating with her husband's death in 1817. She then returned to Philadelphia with her two remaining children and renewed her effort to evangelize, petitioning "to be permitted the liberty of holding prayer meetings in my own hired house and of exhorting as I found liberty." Allen, who was the African Methodist Episcopal (AME) Church's bishop by this time, had no problem with a woman leading prayer meetings and granted the request. Some time later, she was in church listening to Rev. Richard Williams expound on a passage from Jonah when, in Lee's words, Williams "lost the spirit." Impulsively, Lee jumped to her feet and picked up the thread that Williams had left dangling. When she finished the sermon, she sat down trembling with fear that she had overstepped her bounds and would be expelled from the church. But Bishop Allen, who was among the congregation, rose and gave her effort a ringing endorsement. Allen was so impressed with her preaching that in 1823 he attempted to get her a staff position at Bethel, but the congregational leadership refused to consider it.

Billing herself as the first female preacher of the AME Church, Lee became an itinerant evangelizer, primarily in New England. According to her autobiography, she preached to whites and Indians as well as blacks in churches, schools, camp meetings, homes, and marketplaces. In one year alone, she traveled 2,325 miles, much of it by foot, and delivered 178 sermons. "My health was much destroyed by speaking so often and laboring so very hard, having a heavy fever preying on my system," she wrote.

Despite no formal education, she kept a journal of her work. With some editorial help, she published these at her own expense in two volumes. The first, *The Life and Religious Experience of Jarena Lee*, appeared in 1835, and *Religious Experiences of Jarena Lee* followed a dozen years later. No record exists of Lee's life after her journal entries.

Further Reading

Andrews, William L., ed. *Sisters of the Spirit*. Bloomington: Indiana University Press, 1986.

Lincoln, C. Eric, and Lawrence H. Mayima. *The Black Church in the African American Experience*. Durham, N.C.: Duke University Press, 1990.

Sidwell, Mark. "The Fruit of Freedom: When Given a Limited Opportunity to Grow, These African Americans Blossomed." *Christian History* (1999): 38–41.

Liele, George

(ca. 1750–1820) *pioneer Baptist preacher*

George Liele is widely regarded as the first licensed and ordained African-American Baptist preacher as well as the founder of the first African-American congregation to organize a foreign mission.

Liele was born around 1750 to slaves known only as Liele and Nancy, on the Virginia plantation of Henry Sharp. A few years prior to the American Revolution, Sharp moved to Burke County, Georgia, taking George Liele with him. It was there that Liele was converted after hearing a sermon by Rev. Matthew Moore, a local white Baptist preacher. Shortly thereafter, Liele experienced his own call to preach. His master, a devout Baptist deacon, gave him his freedom so that Liele could travel to plantations along the Savannah River and preach the gospel. Most of his audiences were slaves on plantations, but he also preached to congregations of mixed membership. He was ordained for this purpose on May 20, 1775.

The Revolutionary War divided the loyalties of South Carolina residents, many of whom supported the British Crown. Among these was Sharp, who served as a Tory officer, and Liele. When Sharp died in 1778, Liele's freedom and his pro-British stance drew the wrath of whites. Some reports say that Liele was protected from these people by British officers occupying Savannah; others say that he was forced to borrow $700 to prevent him and his family from being sold into slavery. Either way, his activities and movements were severely limited for the duration of the war.

In 1783 a British colonel left Savannah to live in Jamaica, and he agreed to take on Liele as an indentured servant. While waiting for favorable sailing weather in July, Liele embarked on one last mission up the Savannah, and it was on this trip that he converted ANDREW BRYAN to the faith.

Liele was able to work off his debt to the colonel sometime before 1785. He then resumed his ministerial career, supplementing his income by farming and hauling goods. It was Liele who founded the first black Baptist church in Jamaica. By 1795 this congregation, worshiping in an outdoor meeting place, numbered 350 people, most of them slaves. In 1893, he was able to raise enough money and provide enough labor to build a sanctuary. Shortly thereafter, he founded a school for the children of his parishioners.

Liele took great care not to offend the authorities. He welcomed examination of his ministry from whites and unfailingly asked permission from owners for their slaves to join his congregation. Nonetheless, his efforts were not welcomed on an island whose religious life was dominated by the Episcopal Church, and whose power brokers were fearful of slave revolts. Liele's services were repeatedly interrupted, and he lived under constant suspicion of fomenting insurrection. In 1801, he and several companions were arrested on charges of sedition. One of the group was convicted and hanged; Liele barely escaped with his life. He also spent time in debtors' prison when the church fell behind in its loan payments. In 1805, his work was further targeted by the enactment of a law banning preaching to slaves.

This law, however, was never strictly enforced. Liele's church continued to grow to a membership of more than 500. Twenty years after Liele's death in 1820, that congregation became the first black church in the Americas to send a group of missionaries to Africa.

Further Reading

Hamilton, Charles V. *The Black Preacher in America.* New York: William Morrow, 1972.
Sernett, Milton. "The Expatriot Option: Some Blacks, Like George Liele, Had to Immigrate to Live and Minister Freely." *Christian History* (1999): 32–33.
Sernett, Milton, ed. *African-American Religious History: A Documentary Witness.* Durham, N.C.: Duke University Press, 1999.
Wagner, Clarence M. *Profiles of Black Georgia Baptists.* Gainesville, Ga.: privately published, 1980.

Little, Malcolm See MALCOLM X.

Lowery, Joseph Echols
(1924–) *Methodist clergy, civil rights organization administrator*

Joseph Lowery is a Methodist pastor who was one of the organizers of the Southern Christian Leadership Conference (SCLC) and served as its president from 1977 to 1997. Associates have called him "the consummate voice of biblical-social relevancy, a focused prophetic voice—speaking truth to power."

He was born Joseph Echols Lowery on October 6, 1924, in Huntsville, Alabama, where his

Methodist pastor Joseph Lowery was a key figure in the organization of the Southern Christian Leadership Conference. *(Birmingham Public Library Department of Archives and Manuscripts)*

father was a small businessman who operated a mortuary and a poolroom. Lowery has provided scant information about his younger days in Huntsville or the specifics of a wandering college career that included undergraduate stints at Knoxville College, Alabama A & M, and Paine College, in Augusta, Georgia, where he obtained his B.A. degree. Upon choosing a career in ministry, he earned a bachelor of divinity degree from Paine Theological Seminary, and went on to do postgraduate work at Garrett Theological Seminary in Evanston, Illinois.

Lowery was ordained a Methodist and admitted to the predominantly black Central Alabama Conference of the Methodist Church in 1950. That same year he married Evelyn Gibson, with whom he would have three children. For a brief time, he worked as the editor of the *Birmingham Inquirer,* a small black-owned newspaper. In 1952 he accepted a call to be pastor of the Warren Street Methodist Church in Mobile, Alabama.

His intense interest in social justice led Lowery to support the Montgomery bus boycott sparked by the arrest of Rosa Parks and led by the Montgomery Improvement Association and MARTIN LUTHER KING, JR., in 1955 and 1956. The success of that effort in obtaining a federal injunction desegregating the Montgomery bus system led King, Lowery, and other black preachers from 10 southern states to form a regional version of the Montgomery Improvement Association. All of them believed that civil rights were a moral issue and that it was part of their Christian calling to lead the battle against discrimination, using the tactics of nonviolent civil disobedience. After some debate, they called their organization the Southern Christian Leadership Conference (SCLC). King was chosen as president, Lowery as vice president, and RALPH ABERNATHY as secretary-treasurer. The group rapidly became a major force in organizing desegregation and voters' rights campaigns around the South.

In 1961, Lowery left Warren Street to accept a position as administrative assistant to Charles Golden, the Methodist bishop in Nashville. While in Nashville, Lowery took an active part in a movement to desegregate the city's hotels and restaurants. In 1964, Lowery returned to parish ministry and Alabama, accepting a call to St. Paul's Methodist Church in Birmingham, the site of the SCLC's most publicized desegregation effort. During this time, the Methodist Church was undergoing a merger with the Evangelical United Brethren to form the United Methodist Church. At the church's 1966 convention, Lowery led a demonstration of black delegates expressing opposition to the traditional segregated administrative church structures, which were then dismantled.

Lowery was a dynamic preacher and speaker who refused to mince words in the service of his cause, yet was also regarded as a voice of reason. Typical of his style was a meeting in which the SCLC heads met with Alabama's segregationist governor George Wallace in an attempt to defuse racial violence. Lowery attempted to ease the hostility, yet held his ground by telling Wallace, whom he knew to be a Methodist, "I am speaking to you as a Methodist preacher to a Methodist layman."

Respect for Lowery grew so high that in 1967 he was named chairman of the board of the SCLC. A year later, he took over as head pastor of Central United Methodist Church in Atlanta, the oldest and largest Methodist congregation in the city. Under his leadership, the congregation put social concerns at the forefront of its ministry as sponsor of a 240-unit low-income housing development. During Lowery's tenure, the church added 2,000 members.

In the meantime, Lowery stayed active in civil rights efforts throughout the nation. Despite being repeatedly jailed, he persisted in organizing successful voter registration drives, one of which was a key factor in the election of a black mayor in Birmingham, which only a decade earlier had been called the most segregated city in the South. He fought against police brutality, and worked to reclaim land that had been illegally and unethically taken from blacks over the past several generations.

Gradually, however, in the decade following King's assassination in 1968, the SCLC began to lose influence, media coverage, and support. In 1977, when the organization was riddled with debt and its membership had dropped drastically, it called on Lowery to take over as president. The initial transition was made even more difficult due to conflict between moderates and militant members. But Lowery established control and redirected the SCLC toward goals of financial stability, while maintaining its traditional presence as a mainstream advocate of economic, political, and social equality for all. In the late 1970s, Lowery led demonstrations in support of such justice issues as the Wilmington Ten, who had been questionably convicted of arson and conspiracy in a racially charged trial. In 1979, he took the SCLC into uncharted waters by moving into the international scene, and created controversy by expressing support for Palestinian homeland rights and pushing for peace in the Middle East. In response to critics, Lowery noted that the Bible commissioned Christians to preach to all the world. He criticized congressional spending proposals that took money away from social causes in favor of the military.

In the 1980s, Lowery led a march in Wrightsville, Georgia, to protest employment discrimination. Two years later, he took to the streets in Carrollton, Georgia, to protest the conviction of two black voter registration workers on charges of vote fraud.

In 1986, Lowery accepted a call to lead the 2,500-member Cascade Methodist Church in Atlanta. He continued to lead the SCLC, urging people to avoid complacency on issues of civil rights. "We fought too long, we prayed too hard, we wept too bitterly, we bled too profusely, we died too young to let anybody ever turn back the clock on racial justice," he thundered to a crowd celebrating the 25th anniversary of the 1964 Civil Rights Act. "We ain't going back."

Lowery remained active in the 1990s, providing leadership in investigating a rash of burnings of black churches and in advocating for the retention of affirmative action, before finally retiring from the SCLC presidency in 1997.

Further Reading

Bigelow, Barbara Carlisle. *Contemporary Black Biography.* Vol. 2. Detroit, Mich.: Gale Research, 1992.

Moritz, Charles, ed. *Current Biography, 1982.* New York: H. W. Wilson, 1982.

Smith, Alice. "Civil Rights Leader Retiring Again," *Christian Social Action,* (December 7, 1999): 32–33.

Smith, Jesse Carney, ed. *Notable Black American Men.* Vol. 1. Detroit, Mich.: Gale Research, 1999.

Lyons, Henry
(1942–   ) *Baptist clergy, denominational president*

Few religious figures have risen as quickly to the heights of denominational power and then crashed as abruptly as Henry Lyons. Within months he went from being the leader of the nation's largest black denomination to a prison inmate convicted of grand theft and fraud.

Lyons was born on January 17, 1942, in Gainesville, Florida, to a 17-year-old woman who chose not to marry the father, and he was raised by his maternal grandparents. When he was 12, a pastor at his Baptist church predicted he would one day lead the Baptists. The claim puzzled him at first, but later fueled his ambition for church leadership. Lyons attended Bethune-Cookman College in Daytona Beach, Florida, and graduated from the Morehouse School of Religion in Atlanta in 1968. While at school, he pastored Abyssinian Baptist Church in Brunswick,

Georgia, and then moved on to Macedonia Baptist in Atlanta in the late 1960s.

In 1971, Lyons took a position as dean at Cincinnati Baptist Bible College. After one year, he accepted a call to Bethel Metropolitan Baptist Church in St. Petersburg, Florida. During his many years of service there, he achieved a reputation as a fine preacher, a social activist, and a denominational leader. Lyons was named president of the Florida General Baptist Convention in 1982 and distinguished himself by spearheading construction of low-income housing.

After serving as vice president on the national church level, Lyons campaigned for the presidency of the National Baptist Convention USA (NBC-USA) following the retirement of Theodore Jemison in 1994. Ironically, in view of later events, he ran on a reform platform calling for more accountability in budget matters. Lyons won a narrow victory under such controversial circumstances that the election was challenged in court by the loser. The case, however, was eventually decided in Lyons's favor. "I have received a clear mandate, orders, from God himself," he declared.

Lyons's presidency started on a positive note. He made great strides in reducing the organization's debt, often at the expense of his own comfort. Under his direction, the NBC-USA made a major contribution in the relief of war-torn Rwanda, and Lyons stood out as a champion of affirmative rights.

The trouble started in July 1997, when his wife of 25 years, Deborah, discovered that he shared ownership of a $700,000 house with an NBC-USA employee named Bernice Edwards. Incensed at what she believed was an affair, she found the house, set fire to it, and was eventually convicted of arson. The incident wakened authorities to irregularities in Lyons's business dealings and triggered an investigation that uncovered a widespread web of corruption. Various organizations had given the church $244,000 to help rebuild black churches burned down by arsonists, yet only $30,000 of that made its way to the churches. Lyons collected $1 million for using his influence to aid a Canadian funeral home chain. He sold what was purported to be an 8.5-million-member mailing list of the NBC for $4 million, yet provided fewer than 500,000 names, many of which proved to be bogus. He failed to disclose to church officials the fact of his two previous marriages in 1966 and 1969, and lavished church funds on his mistresses.

Despite the allegations, which led to criminal charges, the NBC-USA initially reaffirmed its confidence in Lyons, who pleaded for forgiveness from his followers. But many church members shared the anger of Rev. CALVIN OTIS BUTTS of New York, who accused Lyons of bringing "spiritual wickedness into high powers."

In March 1999, Lyons resigned his presidency. The criminal charges resulted in a sentence of five and a half years in prison for racketeering and grand theft.

Further Reading

Gilbreath, Edward. "Redeeming Fire." *Christianity Today* (December 6, 1999): 38–47.

Melton, J. Gordon. *Religious Leaders of America.* 2d ed. Detroit, Mich.: Gale Research, 1999.

"Pastor warns of Split in Black Denomination," *Christian Century* (December 10, 1997): 1150–51.

Phelps, Shirelle. *Contemporary Black Biography.* Vol. 12. Detroit, Mich.: Gale Research, 1996.

Wilson, Mike. "The Struggle for the Soul of Henry Lyons." St. Petersburg Times. Available online. URL: http://www.sptimes.com/lyons-special. Downloaded February 18, 2003.

Malcolm X
(Malcolm Little, el-Hajj Malik el-Shabazz)
(1925–1965) *Nation of Islam clergy, speaker, social activist*

Malcolm X once described himself as the "angriest black man in America." During the Civil Rights movement of the 1960s, this Nation of Islam minister provided frustrated blacks with an alternative to the nonviolent, Christian focus of MARTIN LUTHER KING, JR., an alternative that frightened and enraged much of white America. With his blazing intensity, deft organizational skills, and mastery of public debate, Malcolm X infused a spirit of independence that affected the African-American community long after his death.

He was born Malcolm Little on May 19, 1925, in Omaha, Nebraska, the son of Earl and Louise Little. Earl was an itinerant Baptist preacher, and both parents were active in MARCUS GARVEY's Universal Negro Improvement Association, a popular black nationalist organization. They were frequently harassed by whites for their views, and moved several times in Malcolm's early days before attempting to put down roots in East Lansing, Michigan, in 1929. One of Malcolm Little's earliest vivid memories was of a group of whites setting fire to their house. Earl Little was killed in 1931 by what was

officially called a streetcar accident, but the family was convinced he was murdered at the hands of the white supremacists who continually threatened him. Louise Little never recovered from the incident and eventually was committed to an insane asylum in 1939.

Malcolm Little managed to retain focus on school throughout the trauma. He was a fine student, popular among his predominantly white classmates, and was preparing to be a lawyer until one of his teachers—a kindly, well-meaning black person—told him that being a lawyer was not a realistic goal for an African American and that he should think of something like carpentry instead. After that, Little began withdrawing into a world of bitterness. With neither parent available to guide him, he fell into bad habits and bad company until he became incorrigible. After a series of run-ins with welfare officials and stints in reform school and foster homes, he traveled to Boston in 1941 to live with his half sister, Ella Collins. At first he found honest work on the railroads, but gradually he moved into illegal activity, such as hustling, dealing drugs, and other petty crimes. The man called Detroit Red by his criminal associates because of his reddish hair was arrested for larceny in early 1946. He was convicted and sentenced to 10 years in Massachusetts's Concord Reformatory.

Nation of Islam minister Malcolm X provided a fiery counterpoint to the nonviolent teachings of Martin Luther King, Jr. *(Library of Congress)*

While serving his sentence, Little displayed such a foul mouth and hatred of religion that fellow inmates gave him the nickname Satan. But he heeded his brother's suggestion that he take a look at the Temple of Islam's teachings, which he described to Malcolm as "the natural religion for a black man." Little was thunderstruck by the racial doctrine of the Black Muslims because it connected so closely with his own experience. He had lived in a world in which *black* was a synonym for *evil* and *white* a synonym for *good,* and in which the whites acted very much like the "devils" that the Black Muslim religion portrayed them to be. Little began reading everything he could find on the Temple

of Islam, and before long had become one of its most zealous proponents. Fellow inmates and guards were stunned by the change this brought in Little, who suddenly became extremely disciplined in his habits according to Temple of Islam (soon changed to Nation of Islam) law. He followed the group's philosophy of rejecting his given last name as a "slave name" and began calling himself Malcolm X, with the X standing for the unknown name of his African forebears.

Upon his parole from prison in 1952, Malcolm X became the Black Muslims' most dynamic and effective spokesman. He became a minister for the Nation of Islam in Detroit, Michigan, and then started temples in Boston, Massachusetts, and Philadelphia, Pennsylvania, before being named to lead the temple in New York City. In all these urban areas, he urged black people to shake off the chains imposed by the white devils. At a time when Martin Luther King, Jr., and others in the Southern Christian Leadership Conference (SCLC) were working for integration, Malcolm X rejected this philosophy as just another attempt to mollify blacks into accepting their inferior position in society. Instead, he argued for complete separation of blacks from the corrupt white society and urged them to take responsibility for their behavior by adhering to the Nation of Islam's codes of behavior, which included strict dietary and prayer laws.

Due largely to Malcolm X's influence, the Nation of Islam doubled in size from 1955 to 1960, from 15 temples to 30. Malcolm had firmly established himself as the number-two man within the organization and was becoming far more famous than his superior, ELIJAH MUHAMMAD. He further increased his exposure by founding a periodical called *Muhammad Speaks.*

Malcolm X and the Black Muslims made little impact, however, outside the inner city until 1959. In that year, television station WNTA-TV in New York produced a documentary entitled "The Hate That Hate Produced," which provided a sensational, negative image of the movement. The publicity concerning the group's racial teachings produced outrage among both whites and blacks, with such groups as the National Association for the Advancement of Colored People and the SCLC condemning them. But it also inspired young, angry blacks to join the cause. The Black Muslims strained racial tensions even more by making alliances with racist groups like the Ku Klux Klan and the American Nazi Party, who shared their views on the desirability of the separation of the races.

Malcolm X became a menacing figure to much of white America and to moderate blacks with his criticism of Martin Luther King, Jr.'s efforts at nonviolent protest. He believed that attempts at a peaceful solution would only favor the white oppressors. "Revolution is bloody," he proclaimed. "Revolution is hostile, revolution knows no compromise, revolution overturns and destroys everything that gets in its way."

While Malcolm X was making enemies among the white establishment, he was quietly making even more dangerous ones within the Nation of Islam. Some of Elijah Muhammad's lieutenants viewed him as overly ambitious and as a threat to the status of their leader. The more Malcolm X grabbed headlines, the more uncomfortable they became. Meanwhile, Malcolm X was becoming disillusioned with some of Elijah Muhammad's leadership. A family man with six daughters through his marriage in 1958 to Betty X, he was stunned to learn that Muhammad had ignored his own teachings of strict morality and had fathered at least 13 children through eight women. Furthermore, he grew increasingly frustrated at Muhammad's disinterest in organizing on a political front.

Tension between the two men reached a head when, in the immediate aftermath of President John F. Kennedy's assassination in November 1963, Muhammad ordered his followers to keep silent to avoid any possible backlash by angry whites. Malcolm X, however, let slip a comment to a reporter about the assassination being "chickens coming home to roost." Muhammad then suspended him from his post for 90 days.

Shortly thereafter, Malcolm X announced that he was breaking away from the Nation of Islam to form his own Muslim mosque. During a trip to Mecca in 1964, he was impressed by the lack of race consciousness among orthodox Muslims. He concluded that Muhammad was wrong in painting all whites as devils. He returned to the United States in 1964 determined to move more in the direction of orthodox Islam. Symbolic of this was another change of name from Malcolm X to el-Hajj Malik el-Shabazz. He also strove to form a more moderate and all-encompassing approach to uniting blacks, Muslim and non-Muslim alike, in the effort to end racial discrimination in the United States. "We have to keep in mind that we are not fighting for integration, nor are we fighting for separation, we are fighting for recognition as free humans in this society," he now claimed. To that end, he formed a new political group called the Organization of Afro-American Unity. This modified approach brought him a degree of reconciliation with King, of whom he said, "If white people realize what the alternative is, perhaps they will be more willing to hear Dr. King."

At this point, however, he found himself under relentless assault from the two extremes of his opponents. The Federal Bureau of Investigation (FBI) ran a continual campaign to undermine his credibility, while his former colleagues in the Black Muslims labeled him a traitor. On February 14, 1965, his home was firebombed by Nation of Islam members. Seven days later, while he was addressing an Organization for Afro-American Unity rally at the Audubon Ballroom in New York City, he was assassinated by Nation of Islam gunmen.

Death, however, did not silence Malcolm X. Later in 1965 his autobiography, written with the help of author Alex Haley, appeared on bookshelves. The book became one of the most influential and insightful works ever written on the inner city African-American view of the civil rights struggle in the United States. Malcolm X reached yet another generation of listeners when the book was made into a highly acclaimed motion picture in 1992, directed by Spike Lee, with Denzel Washington in the title role. Countless numbers of people who have disregarded Malcolm X's religious attitudes have nonetheless been inspired by his fierce struggle for liberty.

Further Reading

Breitman, George. *The Last Year of Malcolm X: The Evolution of a Revolutionary.* New York: Pathfinder Press, 1967.

Clarke, John Henrik. *Malcolm X: The Man and His Times.* New York: Macmillan, 1969.

Cone, James H. *Martin and Malcolm: Dream or Nightmare?* Maryknoll, N.Y.: Orbis Books, 1991.

Franklin, John Hope, and August Meier, eds. *Black Leaders of the Twentieth Century.* Urbana: University of Illinois Press: 1982.

Meyers, Walter Dean. *Malcolm X: By Any Means Necessary.* New York: Scholastic, 1994.

Malcolm X, with Alex Haley. *The Autobiography of Malcolm X.* New York: Grove Press, 1965.

Paris, Peter J. *Black Religious Leaders: Conflict in Unity.* Louisville, Ky.: John Knox Press, 1991.

———. *Malcolm X Speaks: Selected Speeches and Statements.* New York: Merit Publishers, 1965.

Marino, Eugene Antonio
(1934–2000) *Roman Catholic archbishop*

Eugene Marino was the first African American to attain the rank of archbishop in the Roman Catholic Church. His service in this capacity was cut short by a sensational incident of indiscretion, but he recovered to perform valuable service within the church.

He was born Eugene Antonio Marino on May 28, 1935, in Biloxi, Mississippi, the sixth of eight children of Lottie and Jesús Marino. Lottie was a native of Biloxi who worked as a maid.

Jesús, a Puerto Rican immigrant, worked as a baker. Eugene Marino was raised in the Roman Catholic faith and found it a comfortable and nurturing environment. "I took in my faith like my mother's milk," he once said.

While a teenager attending segregated schools in Biloxi, Marino decided on a career in the ministry. After graduation from high school, he attended Epiphany Episcopal College in Newburgh, New York. He joined the Josephite order, a Catholic group founded in the 19th century with a specific mission to blacks. Marino completed his novitiate in 1956 and moved on to St. Joseph's Major Seminary in Washington, D.C. He earned his bachelor of arts degree in 1962, and began teaching at Epiphany Apostolic College. Two years later he was ordained a priest. Marino continued at his teaching post until 1968 while he studied for his master's degree at Fordham University. He then returned to St. Joseph's, where he served as spiritual director. In 1971, he was chosen vicar general of the Josephites, putting him second in command in the organization.

The church hierarchy recognized his leadership skills, and on September 12, 1974, he was given the post of auxiliary bishop in the Washington, D.C., diocese. In that capacity, he was particularly effective in advocating for, recruiting, and providing spiritual support for blacks in this heavily African-American city. During the next decade there was considerable debate within the Catholic Church about the fact that the few African-American bishops in the church had been assigned only to auxiliary roles. Marino emerged as a serious candidate to break that barrier in 1985 when the American bishops elected him secretary of their national conference.

On May 5, 1988, Marino was named the first African-American archbishop. Significantly, he was assigned to the archdiocese of what had emerged as the most important city in the former Confederacy, Atlanta. Marino gratefully accepted the honor, saying, "It means that the church recognized the wealth within its ranks, that it is a church of significant minorities."

Marino acquired a reputation as an effective leader of the 156,000 Roman Catholics under his authority and was treated favorably by the press. In May 1990, however, Marino suddenly went on leave, reportedly due to stress and exhaustion. Two months later, he shocked the diocese by resigning. The news emerged and was given wide play in the press that Marino had been involved in an affair with a 27-year-old woman who had a history of romantic involvement with clergy. Ironically, Marino had been highly praised for establishing strict guidelines in his archdiocese dealing with sexual misconduct. There were conflicting reports about the involvement, some saying that the two had been married as early as December 1988.

Marino quietly disappeared into counseling before eventually emerging as a chaplain to the Sisters of Mercy in Alma, Michigan. In 1995, he was named spiritual director of an outpatient program for clergy at St. Vincent Hospital in Harrison, New York. His duties included counseling clergy on substance abuse and sexual misconduct. In the words of one associate, "He came in with such woundedness and out of that came such healing." Shortly after retiring, Marino died of a heart attack in Manhasset, New York, on November 12, 2000.

Further Reading

Henderson, Ashyia N. *Contemporary Black Biography.* Vol. 30. Detroit, Mich.: Gale Research, 2002.
Mitchell-Powell, Brenda. *African American Biography.* Vol. 3. Detroit, Mich.: Gale Research, 1994.
Sothers, Ronald. "Culture Blends as Atlanta Installs a Black as Catholics' Archbishop." *New York Times,* May 6, 1988, 7.

Mason, Charles Harrison
(1866–1961) *founder of the Church of God in Christ*

Prior to the work of Charles Harrison Mason, organized black Christianity in the United States was concentrated primarily in offshoots of the Methodist and Baptist traditions. Mason cofounded a new Pentecostal denomination, one that GAYRAUD WILMORE has called "one of the most powerful expressions of black religion in the world," and guided it through division and strife into the fastest-growing denomination in the United States.

Mason was born on September 8, 1866, on a farm outside Memphis, Tennessee. His parents, Jerry and Eliza Mason, were former slaves who eked out a living as tenant farmers. The family moved to Plummersville, Arkansas, when Charles was 12 to escape a yellow fever epidemic. The boy's help was needed on the farm and so he spent little time in school.

Mason, who was raised Baptist, was intensely religious as a boy. Upon moving to Plummersville, he professed his faith and was baptized by a Baptist minister. He heard the old folks' tales of the exuberant religion back in the slave days, before such demonstrative expression of faith was discouraged as uncivilized, and longed for a return of that kind of religion.

The move to Arkansas did not free the family from the specter of epidemics. Mason's father succumbed to plague in 1879, and Mason was near death the following year before he recovered miraculously. Little is known of his life during the following decade. In 1891, he was licensed to preach in the Baptist Church, but there is evidence that he did some part-time preaching before then.

In 1891, he married Alice Saxton, the daughter of his mother's best friend, but she was so opposed to his proposed career as a preacher that she divorced him within two years. Mason was heartbroken by the loss. He struggled to find himself in the following months and accepted a position as minister at Mount Gale Missionary Baptist Church in Preston, Arkansas. At about the same time, he read a newly published autobiography of the missionary AMANDA BERRY SMITH. The book inspired Mason to aim high in his ministry. Having decided that he needed a better education for his work, he entered Arkansas Baptist College in November 1893. The school, however, introduced him to methods of biblical criticism that he found worthless, if not offensive. He left school abruptly, after just a few months, and resumed his ministry at Mount Gale.

By this time Mason had become heavily involved in the Holiness movement, which seemed to recapture some of the vigor that he admired in the religion of slave days. The Holiness doctrine said that the Holy Spirit provided a second work in addition to proclamation of the word: that of sanctification, or making holy, and this was an important component of salvation. Mason came to believe that his successful oration at a Baptist convention was evidence of his strong faith, and later that year he claimed the gift of divine sanctification. His enthusiasm for this facet of religion was fueled by his friendship with another Arkansas Baptist minister, CHARLES PRICE JONES. Both Mason and Jones began preaching the doctrine of sanctification in their churches. "Get the experience, get saved, get a knowledge of it," proclaimed Mason. "Have the mind of Christ."

Parishioners generally responded favorably to exhortations, and attendance at his church increased dramatically. The Baptist Church, however, disagreed strenuously with Mason's sanctification theology. Before long, much of Arkansas was in an uproar over the dispute between Mason and the Baptists. When Mason persisted in promoting his view in his church, he was excluded from fellowship in the Baptist Association.

Undaunted, Mason called for a convention of Baptist ministers who agreed with his approach to organize and spread their message. In 1895, Mason and Jones organized a new denomination, the Church of God, at a meeting in Lexington, Mississippi. Mason had been praying for a new name for his church, and while walking the streets of Little Rock, Arkansas, he felt that God directed him to passages in the biblical book of Thessalonians that revealed this name to him. At this initial meeting of the Church of God, Mason sold copies of a booklet he had written entitled, "The Work of the Holy Spirit in the Church."

With Mason providing effective preaching and Jones contributing writings and songs, the new movement grew rapidly under the revised name Church of God in Christ. They started churches and recruited converts across much of the South. Nonetheless, over the years Mason came to feel that something was still missing in his ministry, that he still lacked the fullness of the

Charles H. Mason broke from his Baptist upbringings to organize the Church of God in Christ, presently the fastest-growing denomination in the United States. *(Flower Pentecostal Heritage Center)*

Holy Spirit. He became intrigued with reports coming out of Los Angeles of the Spirit-filled Azusa Street Mission led by WILLIAM JOSEPH SEYMOUR and decided to investigate in March 1907. The experience was everything he had hoped for. Mason received what he called the Baptism of the Holy Spirit through speaking in tongues. "There came a wave of glory into me, and all of my being was filled with the glory of the Lord," he exclaimed. After spending several weeks at the Azusa Street Church, he returned to the Church of God's headquarters in Memphis, bursting with excitement about this phenomenon that he now considered essential to Christian faith.

His efforts to bring the Church of God into the Pentecostal sphere, however, met with resistance from Jones and others. At the 1907 general assembly in Jackson, Mississippi, the denomination split. Mason and his followers formed the Church of God in Christ (COGIC), while Jones led a group that now called itself the Church of God (Holiness). Mason was chosen as general overseer of his group and was later honored as senior bishop and chief apostle. He was able to exercise almost complete authority within the church for the rest of his life.

Mason's church was largely rural and evenly split between blacks and whites during the early years. He had the advantage of shepherding the only legally incorporated church in the Pentecostal movement at the time. Therefore, many white Pentecostal ministers sought out Mason for ordination and the right to perform legally recognized functions and joined the COGIC. In the 1910s, however, the Pentecostal movement began following the path of other religious bodies and split into black and white camps. Although Mason enjoyed fine relations with white clergy, the COGIC evolved into an almost exclusively black movement. As large numbers of blacks began to move into the cities in search of employment, they brought their religion with them, and COGIC's emphasis became more urban beginning in the late 1930s.

By the time of Mason's death on November 17, 1961, the Church of God in Christ numbered more than 5,000 congregations and was well on its way to becoming one of the leading black denominations in the United States.

Further Reading

Burgess, Stanley M., et al., eds. *Dictionary of Pentecostal and Charismatic Movements.* Grand Rapids, Mich.: Zondervan, 1988.

Maxwell, Joe. "Building the Church (of God in Christ)." *Christianity Today* (April 8, 1996): 25–28.

Melton, J. Gordon. *Biographical Dictionary of American Cult and Sect Leaders.* New York: Garland Publishers, 1986.

Synan, Vinson. *The Holiness-Pentecostal Tradition.* Grand Rapids, Mich.: Eerdmans, 1997.

Tucker, David M. *Black Pastors and Leaders.* Memphis, Tenn.: Memphis State University Press, 1975.

Mason, Lena Doolin
(1864–unknown) *Methodist preacher, poet*

Lena Mason was one of the most highly regarded religious leaders and renaissance women of her time. Although little information on her exists today, her rise from humble beginnings and limited education to be a preacher, evangelist, artist, and poet was a stunning accomplishment for a woman of her day.

She was born Lena Doolin on May 8, 1864, in a soldier's barracks in Quincy, Illinois, where her mother, Relda (also listed as Reba) Doolin, had escaped from slavery in the South. Little is known of her father, Vaughn Doolin, except that he was away fighting in the Civil War at the time of her birth, and that he and his wife had five more children after Lena and moved with the family to Hannibal, Missouri.

Lena Doolin appears to have been religiously inclined from a very early age, a product of her parents' devout Christian beliefs. She reported receiving her first call to preach at the age of seven, at about the time she joined the African

Methodist Episcopal church in Hannibal. She attended Douglass High School in Hannibal and then went on to Knott's School in Chicago.

In 1883, she married George Mason, with whom she had six children, only one of whom survived to adulthood. At about age 23, she began to act on her perceived call to preach. Surprisingly, she was popular among white listeners and spent the first three years of her ministry in exclusively white congregations. From there she branched out and became affiliated with the Colored Conference of the Methodist Church. She is said to have traveled and preached in nearly every state of the union, with a five-month stay in Minneapolis, Minnesota, as perhaps her most notable success. According to a contemporary clergyman, "One only needs hear Mrs. Mason to understand how it is that one never tires of listening to her." She apparently kept close tabs on the fruit of her efforts and at the end of her life claimed to have brought 1,617 people into the faith.

Mason's poetry was considered to be of exceptional quality, although there were few outlets open to her for publication, and so only two poems have survived the years. She wrote of the condition of her people with a rare feeling and insight. In "The Negro in Education," she took a standard proslavery argument and stood it on its head. Verse after verse agreed with the sentiment that education makes a person unfit for slavery, and used that as encouragement for blacks to get education.

In "A Negro in It," Mason was far ahead of her time in arguing against the trivialization of African-American accomplishments and in uncovering the crucial roles of black people through history. Again, she provided a hard-hitting twist in her poem in the memorable lines:

> White man, stop lynching and burning
> This black race trying to thin it
> For if you go to heaven or hell
> You will find some Negroes in it.

The date and circumstances of Mason's death have not been recorded.

Further Reading

Curry, Ora Anderson. "Uncrowned Queen." African American Women: Community Builders of Western New York. Available online. URL: http://wings.buffalo.edu/uncrownedqueens/files/mason_lena.htm. Downloaded February 17, 2003.

Hine, Darlene Clarke. *Black Women in America, A–L.* Brooklyn, N.Y.: Carlson Publishing, 1993.

Smith, Jesse Carney, ed. *Notable Black American Women.* Vol. 1. Detroit, Mich.: Gale Research, 1992.

Mays, Benjamin Elijah
(1894–1984) *educator, Baptist clergy*

Benjamin Mays served as a mentor and inspirational leader to a generation of African-American leaders. A Baptist preacher and educator, Mays built up Morehouse University from a struggling school to one of the most respected academic institutions in the United States. A 1971 article in the *Harvard Theological Review* cited him as one of three outstanding black clergy who made a lasting impact on American life. A decade later, Atlanta mayor ANDREW YOUNG described him as "most certainly one of the key preachers, and probably most of the black officials owe where they are to Dr. Mays."

Benjamin Elijah Mays was born on August 1, 1894, in rural Epworth, South Carolina, the youngest of eight children of former slaves Hezekiah and Louvenia Mays. He grew up at a time when whites renewed their persecution of blacks in South Carolina with zeal. The year after his birth, the state constitution was amended to disenfranchise blacks, and when he was six, South Carolina senator Ben Tillman reacted to President Theodore Roosevelt's hosting of Booker T. Washington at a White House dinner by saying, "The action of President Roosevelt in entertaining that nigger will necessitate our killing a thousand niggers in the South before they learn their place again." Mays's first memory of whites involved a group of racists looking for an excuse to lynch a black man. They cursed his father and made him take off his hat and bow.

Hezekiah Mays had little interest in educating his children. Until he reached the age of 15, Ben never spent more than three months a year in school, as his chores on their farm took priority. Louvenia Mays was illiterate, yet she instilled in her son the conviction that he was inferior to no one. Benjamin Mays was further inspired by the people at their Baptist church who made him believe that he had value as a human being.

Despite his limited schooling, Mays developed a passion and an aptitude for learning. At the age of 15, recognizing the limits of the dilapidated local school, he left home to attend the Baptists' McCormick School, 24 miles away. He worked his way through school, performing menial jobs such as cleaning outhouses. During his junior year, Mays had to finally assert his independence from his father by refusing his order to come home in the spring and help with the planting.

Mays excelled at the school and then went on to Virginia Union for one year in 1916. But his competitive nature prompted him to seek a chance to measure himself against whites. He enrolled at Bates College in Maine, where he had his first close social contact with whites. In addition to attaining high honors as a student, Mays participated in debate and football. It was there that he met his first wife, Ellen Harvin.

After completing his degree, he attempted to enter the Newton Theological Seminary but was rejected because of his race. Instead, he went to the University of Chicago, where he spent three semesters before John Hope, the president of Morehouse University in Atlanta, recruited him as a teacher. Mays moved to Atlanta where he taught mathematics, psychology, and religion, in addition to serving as the pastor

Fueled by a passionate Christian commitment, Benjamin Mays attained a position of unparalleled respect among blacks in the field of education. *(Schomburg Center for Research in Black Culture)*

of Shiloh Baptist Church, a small black congregation. During this time, Ellen died, and after three years at Morehouse, Mays returned to school in Chicago. He obtained his master's degree there in 1925 and then accepted a position as an English teacher at South Carolina State University. While there, he met another teacher, Sadie Gray, whom he married. This presented a vocational problem in that the school did not allow couples to teach together. The Mayses then moved to Florida to work with the Tampa Urban League. At about that time, Benjamin Mays was inspired by the example of Eugene V. Debs, a socialist who relentlessly raised concerns about the poor. In his work, Mays advocated for the poor and those with legal problems, and attempted to challenge some segregation laws. But he stood squarely against the African separatist movement of MARCUS GARVEY. Mays believed that a commitment to Christian principles combined with the expansion and enforcement of existing democratic principles could create a just and equitable society. "I want to preach the gospel of peace, goodwill, justice, and brotherhood—not to Negroes and for Negroes, but to men and for men."

In 1928, Mays moved back to Atlanta to take on the position of student secretary for the national Young Men's Christian Association (YMCA) in the South. While in that position, he was recruited by the Institute of Social and Religious Research to direct a groundbreaking, comprehensive, scientific study of black churches in the United States. Along with Joseph Nicholson, Mays spent 14 months gathering data from 609 urban and 185 rural congregations. They then wrote up their findings in a book called *The Negro's Church* (1933), which has come to be regarded as a classic analytical work. Mays had harsh words for both white American religious institutions' failure in the area of race relations, and for the black church, which he characterized as "static and nonprogressive." Yet he also found that the black church had "the potential to become possibly the greatest spiritual force in the United States."

After completing the work, Mays returned to the University of Chicago to continue his education. This time he fought against the school's policies of discriminatory seating, housing, and service. Shortly before he completed his Ph.D. in 1935, he was offered the position of dean of Howard University's School of Religion. Under his guidance, the school recruited an impressive faculty and tightened its organizational structure so that it became the nation's second black seminary to receive official accreditation. During his years at Howard, Mays studied and traveled abroad where he met Mahatma Gandhi, whose philosophy he came to greatly admire.

Mays's work on the black church study, combined with his achievements at Howard, made him a prominent scholar and educator. On May 31, 1940, he was named president of Morehouse College, a traditionally black school in Atlanta. Mays observed that although the existence of schools for blacks signified a failure of American race relations, they were nonetheless necessary. Morehouse was in such desperate shape when Mays took over that it had become more or less a subsidiary of Atlanta University. But Mays approached the task with his usual mixture of passion and competence. "I will serve this institution as if God Almighty sent me into the world for the express purpose of being the Sixth President of Morehouse College," he declared.

He instituted immediate changes to create a more motivated and involved student body. It was he who came up with the innovation, which later became standard at institutions of higher learning, to appoint students to all major committees. He made himself accessible to students; he set aside a block of time every Tuesday to address students and answer their questions. His personal concern and keen insights helped him to inspire and motivate students to a rare degree. His most noted protégé was MARTIN LUTHER KING, JR., who regarded him as a model of what a pastor should be: highly rational, deeply moral, and socially involved.

While Mays shaped Morehouse College into one of the nation's finest academic institutions, he remained a dedicated servant of God. "The aim of education," he said, "should be to glorify God and serve mankind." He frequently gave sermons, rarely using a note when he spoke, and he combined intellectual stimulation with spiritual renewal. He was cited by *Ebony* magazine in 1954 as one of the top 10 black preachers in the United States.

Mays worked hard to be a positive force in bringing about racial equality. He was the first African American elevated to the rank of vice president of the Federal (later National) Council of Churches. It was he who made the famous indictment of organized religion: "Sunday morning at 11 o'clock is the most segregated hour in America." Mays's influence was so great that President John F. Kennedy nominated him to serve on his Civil Rights Commission. However, the Senate objected to his "bias" in favor of desegregation and accused him of being a communist, a charge that infuriated Mays. Rather than fight the battle, Kennedy withdrew the nomination. Mays provoked further controversy in the late 1960s by opposing U.S. involvement in Vietnam. He insisted that war, poverty, and racism were the three great failures of society that had to be eliminated.

Mays resigned as president of Morehouse in 1969 at the age of 75. Rather than retire, however, he ran for a spot on Atlanta's board of education. He not only won but was selected as its chairman, serving until 1981. During that time, he also served as an adviser to President Jimmy Carter. Mays wrote several important books in his later years, most notably *The Negro's God as Reflected in His Literature,* and two autobiographical works, *Lord, the People Have Driven Me On,* and *Born to Rebel.*

Long before his death on March 28, 1984, he had lived to see such a monumental change in the South that he was perhaps the most widely respected citizen in Atlanta, and Georgia congressman W. J. B. Dorn publicly hailed him as "the greatest man I have ever known."

Further Reading

Carter, Lawrence Edward, Sr. *Walking Integrity: Benjamin Elijah Mays, Mentor to Martin Luther King, Jr.* Macon, Ga.: Mercer University Press, 1998.

Lincoln, C. Eric, and Lawrence H. Mayima. *The Black Church in the African American Experience.* Durham, N.C.: Duke University Press, 1990.

Mays, Benjamin. *Born to Rebel: An Autobiography.* New York: Scribners, 1971.

———. *The Negro's God as Reflected in His Literature.* New York: Russell and Russell, 1938.

Mays, Benjamin, and Joseph Nicholson. *The Negro's Church.* New York: Institute of Social and Religious Research, 1933. Reprint, New York: Russell and Russell, 1968.

Rothe, Anna, ed. *Current Biography, 1942,* New York: H. W. Wilson, 1942.

McGuire, George Alexander
(1866–1934) *founder of the African Orthodox Church*

George Alexander McGuire tied into MARCUS MOSIAH GARVEY's vision of an international black nation in his creation of the African Orthodox Church. One of the earliest militant black religious leaders, he called for black pride and the rejection of the traditional Christian view of a white God.

McGuire was born on March 26, 1866, in British Antigua in the West Indies, the oldest son of prosperous farmers Edward and Mary Elizabeth McGuire. He was raised in the Episcopal Church of his father, but was strongly influenced by the Moravian faith of his mother. He had no lack of educational opportunities when he graduated from Mico College for Teachers in 1886 and the Nisky Theological Seminary (Moravian) in St. Thomas in 1888. McGuire was called to a Moravian congregation in Frederickstad, Saint Croix, Virgin Islands, which he served until 1893. At that time he immigrated to the United States, where he came in contact with the African Methodist Episcopal Church (AME Church). McGuire joined the church, was confirmed in 1895, was made a deacon in 1896, and became a priest the following year.

McGuire's career encompassed a wide range of positions and locations. He served briefly at congregations in Cincinnati, Richmond, and Philadelphia, and earned a reputation for administrative and preaching skill. After working in the Arkansas Diocese as Archdeacon for Colored Work in 1905, he moved to Cambridge, Massachusetts, to serve as priest to St. Bartholomew's Church, a fast-growing congregation of West Indian immigrants in 1911. He then took a position as secretary of the American Church Institute for Negroes in New York, followed by a five-year stint as rector of an Anglican church in his native land of Antigua.

He returned to the United States in 1919, where he attempted to organize his own independent Episcopal congregation. His calls for a new black militancy were answered by the rise of Marcus Garvey and his Universal Negro Improvement Association (UNIA). McGuire credited Garvey with "inculcating pride and nobility of race and pointing out to a downtrodden and discouraged people their star of destiny." He joined Garvey's movement, rising to a position of chaplain general while he laid plans for a new African church in the Episcopal tradition. He created the Universal Negro Catechism in an effort to reform black Christianity.

Despite his incorporation of religion into his philosophy, Garvey did not endorse McGuire's efforts. The relationship between the two was often volatile; in fact, McGuire was once suspended from the UNIA. On September 2, 1921, however, McGuire succeeded in organizing some black Episcopal churches into the African Orthodox Church, with himself as archbishop. He declared that such a church was necessary in order for blacks to "erase the white god from your hearts. We must go back to the native church, to our own true God." The African Orthodox Church grafted Episcopal formality on African roots. Carried along by the success of Garvey's black independence movement, it started strongly. McGuire was able to set up Endich, a seminary for teaching black theology. But then the effort began to stagnate. Its emphasis on the Anglican traditions of formal liturgy and apostolic succession of bishops held little appeal for the independent-minded blacks he was trying to reach. Nor was McGuire's revolutionary notion of a black God widely accepted. With the onslaught of the depression in the early 1930s, the church went into a decline that accelerated with McGuire's death in 1934.

Further Reading

Burkett, Randall, K., and Richard Newman. *Black Apostles: Afro-American Clergy Confront the Twentieth Century.* Boston: G. K. Hall and Company, 1978.

Shattuck, Gardiner H., Jr. *Episcopalians and Race.* Lexington: University Press of Kentucky, 2000.

McKenzie, Vashti Murphy
(1947–) *African Methodist Episcopal bishop*

Vashti McKenzie, a phenomenally successful second-career minister, was the first woman to break the gender barrier in the hierarchy of the traditionally male-dominated African Methodist Episcopal Church (AME Church).

She was born Vashti Murphy on May 30, 1947, in Baltimore, Maryland, to a middle-class family. Her great-grandfather, John Murphy, had been the founder of the *African American* newspapers, for which her mother, Ida, wrote. Her grandmother had been a founder of Delta Sigma sorority, a national Christian African-American service organization founded in 1913. Her father, Edward, worked for the federal government.

As a youngster, Vashti sang in the choirs at St. James Episcopal Church, where her family was actively involved. The family also strongly supported the Civil Rights movement. One of the highlights of Vashti's youth was when her parents took her out of a summer camp in August 1963 so that she could attend MARTIN LUTHER KING, JR.'s, famous "I Have a Dream" speech at the civil rights demonstration in Washington, D.C.

Murphy went on to attend Morgan State University in Baltimore. During her junior year there, she left school to marry Stan McKenzie, a professional basketball player with the Baltimore Bullets. Shortly thereafter, Stan was traded to the Phoenix Suns. Joining him in Arizona, Vashti found work as a reporter for the *Arizona Republic* newspaper. A strikingly beautiful woman, she also began a career as a professional model.

When Stan retired from basketball in 1974, the couple returned to Baltimore. There Vashti resumed her college studies at the University of Maryland—College Park, obtaining a degree in journalism. Over the next several years she began writing a column for the newspaper her family published, continued modeling, served as hostess of a local weekend television entertainment show, and gave birth to three children.

Eventually, she moved into the radio business, serving as a daytime disc jockey for a gospel music station, WYBC, in Washington, D.C. She performed well enough to be promoted to program director at the station. But while serving as hostess, she was often touched by the anxiety and despair of callers who were searching for some direction in their lives. She came to wonder if she had a calling that she had not answered. She joined the AME Church and after a period of fasting and praying, began to pursue a career in ministry.

McKenzie left her job at the radio station and worked out arrangements for day care so that she could attend Howard University School of Divinity. After obtaining her master of divinity degree, she moved on to Union Theological Seminary in Dayton, Ohio, where she earned her doctorate.

McKenzie was ordained a deacon in 1984 and was assigned to a tiny congregation in Chesapeake City, Maryland. The following year, she was ordained into full-time ministry and took over the pastorate at Oak Street African Methodist Episcopal Church in Baltimore.

In 1990, she accepted the position as minister of Payne Memorial AME Church, a historic, century-old congregation in Baltimore's inner city that had fallen on hard times. There she

earned a reputation as, in the words of the *San Francisco Bay View*, "a visionary in urban ministry." McKenzie was acclaimed both as an inspiring speaker and a solid organizer. *Ebony* magazine cited her as one of the top African-American preachers in the nation. Meanwhile, under her leadership Payne Memorial grew from 330 members to 1,700 in a decade. Its array of community services and programs ranged from a youth summer camp, an after-school program, scouts, mentoring, radio and television ministry, and a job service that worked with more than 1,000 clients. The church also took over the management and operation of a struggling public school in its neighborhood. In McKenzie's words, "We were able to move . . . to the concept of reshaping our spiritual and community service delivery needs from one of just coping and adapting to one of empowerment."

McKenzie's popularity spread far beyond the church's borders and she spent much time traveling to speaking engagements. She used her writing skills to chronicle her struggles to assume a leadership role in a church that had historically been a bastion of male domination despite its largely female membership. In 1996, her first book, *Not Without a Struggle: Leadership Development for African-American Women in Ministry*, was published.

That same year, McKenzie followed another calling, one that had come to her while in the midst of a sermon. She decided to take her leadership challenge another step and pursue the office of bishop. The 2.5-million member AME Church had never had a female bishop in its two centuries of existence, and McKenzie met with stiff resistance on many fronts. Many conservative AME members thought there was something wrong with a woman seeking such an office. But support surfaced in many other areas, both from individuals and from groups such as the Delta Sigma Theta sorority (for which she served as national chaplain), which contributed $50,000 to her campaign.

McKenzie's quest succeeded on July 11, 2000, when she was one of four people appointed to the post of bishop out of 42 candidates. While acknowledging the significance of breaking what she called "the stained-glass ceiling"—the gender barrier among bishops in the AME Church—she has been quick to downplay her own role in the process. "I stand on the shoulders of the unordained women who served without appointment or affirmation," she said in her acceptance speech.

As there were no open positions for AME bishops in the United States, McKenzie was assigned to Africa, where she presided over the church in Botswana, Lesotho, Mozambique, and Swaziland. Recognizing there was still work to be done in overcoming gender bias in the church, she wrote a second book, *Strength in the Struggle: Leadership Development for Women*, published in 2002.

Further Reading

McKenzie, Vashti Murphy. *Not Without a Struggle: Leadership Development for African-American Women in Ministry.* Cleveland, Ohio: United Church Press, 1996.

———. *Strength in the Struggle: Leadership Development for Women.* Cleveland, Ohio: Pilgrim Press, 2001.

Thompson, Clifford, ed. *Current Biography, 2000.* New York: H. W. Wilson, 2000.

Michaux, Lightfoot Solomon
(1884–1968) *Church of God (Holiness) clergy, radio minister*

Michaux, the founder of an offshoot of the Church of God (Holiness) denomination, was the first black minister to make effective use of the airwaves to spread his message.

Lightfoot Solomon Michaux was born on November 7, 1884, in Newport News, Virginia. His father was a former merchant marine who had settled into a profitable business as a supplier of poultry and seafood. As a teen, Michaux left school to work for his father. In 1904, he opened his own store as well as a dance studio. The businesses thrived, especially during World War I, and he moved to a comfortable house in Hopewell, Virginia.

Although raised in a devout Baptist family, Michaux became an active member of St. Timothy's Church of God (Holiness). In 1906, he married Mary Eliza Pauline, who became intensely religious. With some of his business profits he built her a Holiness church of her own to lead, called Everybody's Mission. Michaux himself felt the call to preach and became licensed and ordained in the Church of God (Holiness). When business declined at the end of the war, he returned to Newport News to work with his father, and established a new church there.

The continuing financial slump hindered Michaux's plans to expand his ministry at his Newport News church. He attacked the problem by forming the Gospel Spreading Tabernacle Building Association to raise funds. The venture proved a great success. This was noticed by Church of God (Holiness) leader CHARLES P. JONES, who thought Michaux's talents could be put to use in other locations and instructed him to move. Michaux rebelled at the outside control and in 1921 left the denomination to form his own branch of the Church of God. After founding a congregation in Hampton, Virginia, he moved up the coast, starting churches around Chesapeake Bay and finally ending up in Washington, D.C., in 1928.

At about that time, Michaux began to recognize the potential of radio to spread his spiritual message to a vast audience. In 1929, he gained approval to run a religious program on station WSJV in Washington. He had just begun to establish an audience when he received a huge break: the station was sold to the CBS radio network, which picked up his show and gave it a national audience.

Michaux featured his church's choir on his program along with his own sermons, which were a blend of Holiness theology and positive-thinking psychology. By 1934, his daily show aired on more than 50 stations. At its peak in the mid-1930s, his Saturday night program reached an estimated 25 million listeners as well as an international audience that picked it up on shortwave, altogether the largest regular audience ever achieved by a black religious personality to that time. Because of his popularity, he was the first black man allowed access to Madison Square Garden for one of his gatherings.

Michaux's philosophy was relentlessly upbeat. He became known as the "Happy Am I Evangelist," and began dispensing Christian goodwill through job programs and social services that were especially welcomed in the depression era. Although his audience declined with radio in the 1940s, he remained an influential figure in Washington with his friendships with first ladies Eleanor Roosevelt and Mamie Eisenhower. He undertook the creation of the largest privately owned black development program in the United States, which built the 596-unit Mayfair apartment complex in 1948. That same year, he was the first preacher to broadcast on television, on station WTTG in Washington, D.C.

In 1964, Michaux reorganized his ministries under the name Gospel Spreading Church. He died on October 10, 1968, in Washington, D.C.

Further Reading

Melton, J. Gordon, ed. *Biographical Dictionary of American Cult and Sect Leaders.* New York: Garland, 1986.
Newman, Richard. *Black Power and Black Religion.* West Cornwall, Conn.: Locust Hill Press, 1987.
Sernett, Milton. *Bound for the Promised Land.* Durham, N.C.: Duke University Press, 1997.
Webb, Lillian Ashcroft. *About My Father's Business: The Life of Elder Michaux.* Westport, Conn.: Greenwood Press, 1981.

Moore, John Jamison
(1814–1893) *African Methodist Episcopal Zion bishop*

John Moore, a bishop in the African Methodist Episcopal Zion Church (AMEZ Church), earned recognition for establishing his denomination on the West Coast and was a leading advocate of social and political action in that area.

Moore was born on October 14, 1814, in Martinsburg, Virginia, to Turner and Savannah Moore. His mother was a free black woman living in Maryland who was kidnapped into slavery in Virginia at the age of 15. She married and had six children; the family's name was established as Moore after they were sold to owners with that name. When Moore was six, the family attempted a daring escape with the aid of some Quakers. The four oldest children, however, were recaptured and sold into slavery further south. Moore and his parents and one sibling succeeded in reaching Bedford County, Pennsylvania. There Moore was hired out as an indentured servant to a farmer who taught him basic reading and writing. The farmer cheated him by keeping him for several years past his agreed commitment. Moore finally left and walked to Harrisburg, where he worked as a common laborer.

He experienced a religious conversion in 1833, and, after briefly working in Bedford County as a store porter, he returned to Harrisburg, determined to be a preacher. He obtained his preaching license in 1834 and spent the next several years working and trying to compensate for his lack of education by hiring private tutors. In 1839, Moore joined the AMEZ Church. He was ordained a deacon in 1842 and an elder the following year. Moore began his ministry by traveling throughout the Allegheny Mountains preaching to miners and fugitive slaves. In the late 1840s, he settled into a position as pastor of Big Wesley AMEZ Church in Philadelphia.

In 1852, Moore left on an ambitious quest to help in the expansion of the mission of the AMEZ Church into California. After founding small churches in the Napa Valley and San Jose, he established the first black church in San Francisco, which soon became the largest AMEZ Church on the West Coast. It was there that he also started the first school for black children in the new state. For several years, he taught groups of from 25 to 65 students, and eventually became the school's principal. He experienced a humiliating rebuff when he was the first African American to attend the state teacher's convention in 1855. The chair announced that, due to Moore's presence, anyone who wished to leave the convention was free to do so. Moore continued to advocate for blacks, however. He was most persistent in his efforts to persuade the state to abolish laws that disqualified blacks as witnesses against whites in criminal cases.

Moore left California in 1858 to follow a large migration of black miners seeking gold in British Columbia, supporting himself by cutting wood and manufacturing charcoal and investing in a mining company. His ministry was not well-received among the miners, however, and by the end of the Civil War, he had returned to San Francisco.

Moore was elected bishop in 1868 and assigned to the East Coast, where he solidified his reputation as an outstanding preacher, teacher, and social justice advocate. His last major accomplishment was authoring *The History of the African Methodist Episcopal Zion Church in America,* published in 1884. Moore died on December 9, 1893.

Further Reading

Murphy, Larry G., ed. *Encyclopedia of African American Religious Biography.* New York: Garland Publishing, 1993.

Mother Smith
(Willie Mae Ford Smith)

(1904–1994) *singer, African Methodist Episcopal Zion Church and Church of God Apostolic evangelist*

Willie Mae Smith, commonly known as Mother Smith, was widely regarded as the most talented, versatile, and innovative gospel singer of her era. She was ordained in both the African Methodist Episcopal Zion Church (AMEZ Church) and the Church of God Apostolic, and she popularized a method of concert evangelizing known as the song and sermonette.

She was born Willie Mae Ford on June 23, 1904, in Rolling Fork, Mississippi, the seventh of 14 children of Clarence and Mary Ford. Her father struggled to provide for his many children on an income as a railroad brakeman; the children often slept four in a bed for lack of space. The family moved to Memphis, Tennessee, when Willie Mae was a young child and then to St. Louis in 1917. Mary Ford opened a restaurant the following year, and Willie Mae was forced to drop out of the eighth grade to help her mother run it.

Both parents were strict Baptists with a gift for singing, and they often performed duets in local churches. The children inherited their vocal interest and talent. In 1922, Clarence Ford organized his daughters into a quartet known as the Ford Sisters. Willie Mae, who had the strongest voice, was the lead singer of the group, backed up by Mary, Emma, and Geneva. The Ford Sisters made a favorable impression with their lively rendition of gospel music and were invited to perform at the National Baptist Convention in 1924. Their performance was too lively for the staid Baptists, who were still fighting what they regarded as the primitive African influence of demonstrative worship, so their reception was cool.

Soon afterward, the quartet broke up as Ford's sisters began to marry. But the family agreed that Willie Mae should continue with her career and offered to support her efforts. Although she enjoyed listening to popular music such as blues, she initially intended to go into classical performance. But after hearing a gospel performance by Artelis Hutchins of Detroit at the 1926 National Baptist Convention, she made up her mind to commit to gospel music. She was determined, however, to put her own stamp on the emerging genre. "If I wasn't the first to sing free, as the spirit told me, I don't know who was," she once claimed. "I didn't hear anybody sing with a beat before me, either, not gospel solo."

Ford's career as a gospel singer appeared to be over when she married James Smith, a man nearly 20 years older than she, in 1929, and quickly became pregnant with the first of their two children. But the stock market crash of 1929 triggered an economic depression that severely curtailed James Smith's hauling business. Needing to make money, Willie Mae Smith went out on the road to perform.

By the early 1930s, her talent had attracted the attention of gospel music pioneer THOMAS DORSEY, who invited her to join him and Sallie Martin on tour. Her association with Dorsey led Smith to undertake various jobs in the gospel music establishment. She organized church gospel choirs in Saint Louis, and then in 1936 founded and presided over the Soloists Bureau of the National Convention of Gospel Choirs and Chorus, a group dedicated to developing young talent in the field. Smith also served many years as a director of the National Baptist Convention's education department.

Despite her many commitments, Smith spent an average of three weeks out of four on the road singing during the late 1930s and 1940s. In 1937, she came out with the song that would be her standard over her career, "If You Just Keep Still." Smith continued to spar with Baptist Church officials who complained that her style of gospel was closer to secular blues than to reverent church music. Eventually, in 1939, she left the Baptist Church for

the Church of God Apostolic, a Pentecostal/Holiness group that baptized in the name of Jesus only, not the Trinity. Previously she had made fun of Holiness groups, but now, as she explained to friends, "Honey, this child got soused good." The Church of God Apostolic, which allowed far more expression and emotion in worship than did the Baptist Church, gave her far greater freedom to perform as the spirit moved her.

At about this time, Smith cut back on her singing to emphasize her evangelizing. She was ordained in the Pentecostal Lively Stone Apostolic Church in St. Louis, as well as in the AMEZ Church. Her concerts evolved into revivals. Smith interspersed gospel songs with lengthy evangelistic homilies; in a two-hour performance she might sing only 10 songs. She frequently experienced gender discrimination from pastors looking to make use of her popularity and ability but who were not willing to surrender the pulpit to a woman. In most churches, Smith had to do her preaching and singing from the floor.

As a gospel soloist, Smith was applauded for her dramatic renditions that could range from a barely audible whisper to a wall-rattling crescendo in a single song. She inspired audiences by livening up traditional church hymns such as "What a Friend We Have in Jesus" and "Blessed Assurance" with gospel rhythms. Unfortunately, her music has been lost to posterity. Smith never signed with a record company or recorded music on her own, relying on the passing of a collection plate at her concerts and revivals, and on income from singing lessons. Many of her protégés, however, did record and they often used her arrangements.

Smith was featured in a 1982 film documentary on gospel music called *Say Amen, Somebody*. She died in St. Louis on February 2, 1994.

Further Reading

Broughton, Viv. *Black Gospel: An Illustrated History of the Gospel Sound*. Poole, Dorset, England: Blandford Press, 1985.

Hine, Darlene Clarke. *Black Women in America, M–Z.* Brooklyn, N.Y.: Carlson Publishing, 1993.

Smith, Jesse Carney, ed. *Notable Black American Women.* Vol. 1. Detroit, Mich.: Gale Research, 1992.

Weisenfield, Judith, and Richard Newman, eds. *This Far by Faith: Readings in African-American Women's Religious Biography.* New York: Routledge, 1995.

Mother Waddles See WADDLES, CHARLES-ZETTA.

Muhammad, Elijah
(Elijah Poole, Robert Poole, Elijah Karriem)
(1897–1975) *Nation of Islam prophet*

Elijah Muhammad took the philosophy and organization of W. D. FARD and built it into a significant social, political, and religious force—the Nation of Islam. Under his leadership, the Black Muslims created an outlet for blacks impatient with the direction of the Civil Rights movement and angry at the inequities of the white-dominated establishment.

He was born Robert Poole on October 10, 1897, in Sandersville, Georgia, the sixth of 13 children. His father, William Poole, was a Baptist minister, who gained his primary livelihood from sharecropping. His mother, Mariah, worked as a domestic. The family moved to Cordele, Georgia, in 1900, where Poole attended school through the fourth grade. During his early teen years, he helped with farm chores, and earned money chopping and selling firewood. On one occasion, while bringing a load of firewood to town, he came across the grisly remains of a lynching victim, an incident that profoundly affected him.

At the age of 16, Poole left home and moved to Macon, Georgia, where he supported himself with various hard-labor jobs. In 1919, he had just begun working on a section gang for the railroad when he married Clara Evans. He continued at the job until 1923, when he moved his young family to Detroit in search of better economic opportunities.

Even there, Poole's lack of marketable job skills left him unemployed for long stretches of time. The family, which came to include eight children, had to go on public assistance. The situation grew worse in late 1929 when the Great Depression shut down many businesses. Ashamed of his inability to support his family, Poole grew depressed and indulged in alcoholic binges that often left him lying unconscious in a gutter.

In this condition, he attended a meeting led by W. D. Fard, whose brand of racially charged religion was gaining popularity among frustrated, impoverished urban blacks. Poole became one of Fard's most devoted followers, and the leader rewarded him with special attention. According to Poole, "Fard came to my house almost daily and taught me about Islam." Insisting that his followers drop their "white slave names," he renamed his disciple Elijah Karriem. Within a year, Karriem had risen to the number two spot of leadership in the movement, and Fard renamed him Elijah Muhammad in honor of his position.

Fard taught that Christianity was a white religion designed to enslave blacks and that Islam was the true religion of blacks. He ordered his followers to consider themselves citizens of the nation of Allah, not the United States. This view aroused the suspicions of the Federal Bureau of Investigation (FBI), who viewed the group as seditious and began aggressive police action against it. Muhammad was given six months probation for contributing to the delinquency of a minor by refusing to place his children in public school.

Sometime in 1934 Fard broke off contact with the movement and never reappeared. Muhammad took over the group, proclaiming himself the "Messenger of Allah," and declaring that Fard had been Allah incarnate. The transition, however, did not go smoothly. Some Black Muslims, as they called themselves, suspected Muhammad of doing away with Fard. Others rebelled against Muhammad's declaration of Fard as divine and believed he had been merely a prophet. By 1935, a rival faction had gained control of most of the members, leaving Muhammad with only a dozen or so followers. He fled Chicago, fearing murder at the hands of his rivals, and began a seven-year period of virtual exile.

Muhammad eventually settled in Washington, D.C., where he founded a temple and began rebuilding his base. His teachings, however, again attracted the attention of the FBI. Muhammad's preaching that Black Muslims should not fight for the United States because they were citizens of Islam only, laid him open to charges of sedition. He was arrested on May 8, 1942, on charges of failing to comply with draft laws. After meeting bail he returned to Chicago to avoid further trouble. But the FBI was alert to the Black Muslims there as well. In November of the same year, they closed Temple #2 and arrested Muhammad and 38 others for inciting draft evasion. Muhammad was sentenced to prison, serving his sentence at federal facilities in Milan, Michigan, until his release on August 24, 1946.

His perceived persecution at the hands of the white authorities solidified Muhammad's standing. He emerged from jail as the undisputed leader of a group whose loyalty and dedication became unyielding. In the 1950s, the Nation of Islam began attracting larger numbers of followers, particularly with the emergence of MALCOLM X as one of his chief assistants. During that decade, Muhammad began the first steps in building a self-sufficient business enterprise within the Nation of Islam. The movement doubled in size from 1955 to 1960, from 15 temples to 30.

Beginning in 1959, the Nation of Islam became embroiled in one highly publicized contro-

versy after another. First, television station WNTA-TV in New York produced a documentary entitled "The Hate That Hate Produced," which provided a sensational, negative image of the movement. The publicity concerning the group's racial teachings produced outrage among both whites and blacks, but it also inspired young, angry blacks to join the cause. Muhammad strained racial tensions even more by making alliances with racist groups like the Ku Klux Klan and the American Nazi Party, who shared his views of the desirability of the separation of races.

In the aftermath of President John F. Kennedy's assassination in November 1963, Muhammad ordered his followers to keep silent to avoid any backlash by angry whites. Malcolm X, however, let slip a comment to a reporter about the assassination being "chickens coming

Building upon the teachings of W. D. Fard, Elijah Muhammad rose from desperately poor conditions to lead the Nation of Islam into the national spotlight. *(Library of Congress)*

home to roost." Muhammad suspended him for 90 days in what came to be a growing estrangement between the two major Black Muslim figures. Malcolm X became especially disillusioned when he learned that, in violation of the strict moral code that he preached, Muhammad had fathered at least 13 children with eight women. Malcolm X came to repudiate many of Muhammad's teachings, and he was assassinated on February 21, 1965.

In later years, Muhammad muted his more strident racial views. The Nation of Islam provided a model to many inner-city blacks who looked with pride upon their discipline, ability to clean up crime-ridden neighborhoods, rehabilitate criminals, and conduct profitable businesses.

Muhammad suffered from increasing health problems in his later years. After his death on February 25, 1975, in Chicago, leadership of the Nation of Islam passed to his son WALLACE MUHAMMAD, who attempted to bring the group more into the mainstream of Islamic religion.

Further Reading

Bigelow, Barbara Carlisle. *Contemporary Black Biography.* Vol. 4. Detroit, Mich.: Gale Research, 1993.

Evanzz, Karl. *The Messenger: The Rise and Fall of Elijah Muhammad.* New York: Pantheon, 1999.

Kyle, Richard. *The Religious Fringe.* Downers Grove, Ill.: Intervarsity Press, 1993.

Melton, J. Gordon, ed. *Biographical Dictionary of American Cult and Sect Leaders.* New York: Garland, 1986.

Muhammad, Elijah. *Message to the Black Man in America.* Decatur, Ga.: Secretarius Publishing, 1997.

Muhammad, Wallace D.
(Warith Deen Muhammad)
(1933–   ) *Nation of Islam minister*

After the death of his father, Warith Deen Muhammad took over the radical Nation of Islam (NOI) and initiated reforms that transformed it into a more orthodox Muslim group and eventually merged it into the international Islamic community.

He was born Wallace Muhammad on October 30, 1933, in Hamtramck, Michigan, the seventh of eight children of Clara and ELIJAH MUHAMMAD. His father lived in exile or in prison for much of his youth, and the family struggled through grave poverty. But Elijah Muhammad eventually emerged as the leader of the Nation of Islam, a group that preached black separatism under a greatly modified form of the Islamic religion. Wallace attended both elementary and secondary school at the group's Muhammad University of Islam in Chicago.

While in high school, Muhammad took courses in Arabic, through which he learned that the Nation of Islam's teachings deviated radically from the Koran (Qur'an), the authoritative writings of Islam. This apparently diminished his enthusiasm for his father's work. He married, began a family, and had dreams of pursuing a career as an electrical engineer. His father, however, disapproved of any career outside his organization, and his son did not challenge him. He began assuming various duties within the Nation of Islam, working his way up to a leadership position in the Fruit of Islam, a paramilitary security force. In 1958, he was appointed minister of the Nation of Islam's Philadelphia temple.

Soon afterward, he received a draft notice from the U.S. military and registered as a conscientious objector. The government assigned him to alternative duty at a state hospital. However, his father pressured him into refusing the assignment, which resulted in the son being sentenced to three years in jail. As with his father, the prison term enhanced Muhammad's standing among the Nation of Islam, and he emerged in January 1963 as a top leader. Muhammad, however, had grown close to MALCOLM X, and when Malcolm grew disenchanted with the Nation of Islam and left it in 1964, Muhammad turned away from the group as well. For a decade he supported himself as a painter, welder, and upholsterer.

In 1974, he reconciled with his father and rejoined the Nation of Islam. When Elijah Muhammad died the following year, Wallace Muhammad, going by the name Warith Muhammad, was the leader's surprise choice as his successor. The changes he induced were even more stunning. He renounced the Nation of Islam's ban against whites and disbanded the Fruit of Islam. He made dozens of changes to steer his group into the mainstream of Muslim thought, such as changing the name of their houses of worship from *temple* to *mosque*. He declared that previous Nation of Islam stories about whites being a failed experiment of a mad scientist were merely symbolic. In March 1976, he announced that the group no longer considered Fard to be Allah and that his father was not Allah's messenger, but rather one who was divinely inspired. He honored both founders for having inspired a worthy cause but declared, "We're trying to get away from a lot of the spiritual spookiness so we can deal with reality the way it is." The changes were challenged by LOUIS FARRAKHAN, who led his followers back to many of the original Nation of Islam stances.

In the late 1970s, Muhammad changed the name of his movement to the American Muslim Mission and resigned as head of the organization, passing governing power to a 17-member council. He encouraged his followers to dissolve their national structure and integrate themselves into the international Muslim community, which the group did in 1985.

Further Reading

Henderson, Ashyia N. *Contemporary Black Biography.* Vol. 27. Detroit, Mich.: Gale Research, 2001.

Kyle, Richard. *The Religious Fringe.* Downers Grove, Ill.: Intervarsity Press, 1993.

Muhammad, Wallace. "Self-government in the New World." In *African-American Religious History:*

A Documentary Witness. Edited by Milton C. Sernett. Durham, N.C.: Duke University Press, 1999, pp. 499–510.

Sernett, Milton, ed. *African-American Religious History: A Documentary Witness.* Durham, N.C.: Duke University Press, 1999.

Murray, Pauli
(1910–1985) *Episcopal priest, lawyer*

Pauli Murray battled many discriminatory roadblocks and overcame racial and gender barriers in her struggle to attend graduate school and seminary and to enjoy successful careers as a teacher, lawyer, author, and priest.

Murray was born on November 20, 1910, in Baltimore, Maryland. Her parents, William and Agnes Murray, were both a mixture of black, European, and Native American ancestry, and were highly educated. William, a graduate of Howard University, was a principal in the Baltimore public schools, and Agnes worked as a nurse. Unfortunately for Pauli, she had little contact with either parent. Her mother died of a cerebral hemorrhage in 1914, and her father suffered from the lingering effects of typhoid fever that made him too depressed and violent to care for his children. At her mother's request, Murray went to live with her Aunt Pauline Fitzgerald, separated from her five brothers and sisters because, as her mother said, "She is not like the other children and I'm afraid they will ruin her disposition." Fitzgerald took the girl to her home in Durham, North Carolina, raised her in the Episcopal faith, and eventually adopted her.

Murray was an exceptional student who graduated at the top of her class at Hillside High School, a black school in Durham. She had her heart set on attending Hunter College in New York City, but was denied entrance due to Hillside's substandard high school curriculum. Although disappointed, she refused to admit defeat. She spent one year as the only black student at a New York City high school, preparing for her entrance needs. She was accepted at Hunter in 1929, only to find herself financially strapped by the economic depression that followed the stock market crash. Undaunted, she returned to Durham for a year to work and earn money, and then returned to Hunter in 1931. She graduated from the school in 1933 with a bachelor's degree in English.

Once out of school, Murray began working as a remedial reading teacher in the New York City schools under a Works Project Administration (WPA) program. In 1938, she applied to graduate school at the University of North Carolina. Her rejection, and the blunt explanation that "members of your race are not admitted to the University," attracted national attention. Such incidents spurred Murray to became active politically. Following her arrest and incarceration in Virginia, in March 1940, for refusing to move further back on a bus to take a broken seat in deference to a white person, Murray resolved to study law.

She enrolled at the Howard University Law School in 1941, where she found work for both the National Association for the Advancement of Colored People (NAACP) and the Congress of Racial Equality (CORE), and was voted senior class president. When she graduated with honors in 1944, her promise was such that she was awarded a fellowship for graduate study in law, which she intended to use at Harvard University. Harvard, however, rejected her because women were not allowed in its law program. Instead, she enrolled at the University of California, Berkeley, where she attained her L.L.M. degree in 1945. After passing the bar exam, she was rewarded in 1946 with an appointment as California's first black deputy attorney general, an honor that helped her win recognition as the 1946 Woman of the Year by the National Council of Negro Women (NCNW). However, her own illness and the more serious illness of her Aunt Pauline forced her to resign and move

Pauli Murray broke formidable gender barriers in both law and religion. *(The Schlesinger Library, Radcliffe Institute, Harvard University)*

back east. She worked as a law clerk in New York before passing the New York bar exam and being hired by a law office. Still a political activist, in 1949 she made an unsuccessful run for New York City council.

At this time, she began work on her most important contribution to the law, a book called *States' Laws on Race and Color*, published in 1951. Famed civil rights lawyer and eventual Supreme Court justice Thurgood Marshall referred to that work as the bible for lawyers fighting segregation. Shortly thereafter, she put her law career on hold to devote herself full time to researching and writing a biography of her grandparents, Robert and Cornelia Fitzgerald. The book, originally meant for her family's benefit, was published commercially in 1956 under the title *Proud Shoes*. In that same year, Murray was hired as the only female lawyer at one of New York's most prestigious law firms.

In 1960, the ever-active Murray traveled to Ghana to spend 18 months teaching law in that country. She returned to Yale University in 1961 and began graduate study that culminated in a doctor's degree in juridical science in 1965, the first such degree ever awarded to an African American. During her studies, Murray was appointed to a federal committee on civil and political rights. A year later, she joined Betty Friedan and others in founding the National Organization for Women (NOW), a feminist group. Murray then undertook administrative duties as vice president of Benedict College in Columbia, South Carolina, in 1967. She returned to the classroom in 1968 as a professor of law and politics at Brandeis University. Throughout her varied careers, Murray had always been active in the church and felt some sense of call to the Episcopal Church. The door to ordination in that denomination, however,

had always been closed to women, even more so than the doors to law school. A shift in societal views began to open the possibility of ordination for women in the 1970s. Inspired by the death of a friend, Murray decided to answer the call to the ministry. She entered General Theological Seminary in New York in 1973 for yet another career change. Again she found herself the only female enrolled in her class. After completing her studies, Murray was ordained a priest on January 8, 1977, the first African-American woman to receive that commission.

She took up her duties that year at the Episcopal Church of the Atonement in Washington, D.C. Murray also served as a priest to hospitals and shut-ins in Alexandria, Virginia, and at the Church of the Holy Nativity in Baltimore, before retiring in 1984. She moved to Pittsburgh, where she was hard at work on her autobiography when she died of cancer on July 1, 1985. The work was published posthumously as *Song in a Weary Throat: An American Pilgrimage*.

Further Reading

Murray, Pauli. *Proud Shoes: The Story of an American Family.* New York: Harper & Row, 1978.

———. *Song in a Weary Throat.* New York: Harper & Row, 1987.

Shattuck, Gardiner H., Jr. *Episcopalians and Race.* Lexington: University Press of Kentucky, 2000.

P

Paul, Thomas
(1773–1831) *pioneer Baptist preacher, missionary*

Thomas Paul was one of the leaders of the movement for independent African-American churches, and was easily the most influential black person in Boston in the early 19th century.

Paul was born of free black parents on September 3, 1773, in Exeter, New Hampshire, the son of a laborer who fought in the Revolutionary War. Paul was educated in a Baptist school in Hollis, New Hampshire. He and three of his six brothers became strongly committed to the Baptist Church and became preachers. Paul began preaching in 1801 and was ordained into the ministry in West Nottingham, New Hampshire, on May 1, 1805. At about that time, he married Catherine Waterhouse, with whom he would have three children.

The Pauls moved to Boston after his ordination, and there he quickly assumed leadership among a group of African Americans who had grown upset with the white custom of delegating blacks to separate, inferior seating sections in houses of worship. Paul organized the group into a separate congregation on August 5, 1805. They built the African Meeting House, which Paul, despite his Baptist leanings, opened up as a place of worship for blacks of all faiths in late 1806. Although supported by funds from sympathetic whites, the African Meeting House was the only building constructed and owned by blacks in the city. Only people of color were allowed to engage in the common custom at the time of purchasing pews in the church which were theirs to use during services. Ironically, the custom of church segregation was so powerful that when Paul preached his initial sermon there, he reserved the first floor for whites and had blacks sit in the balcony.

Paul also served as chaplain of Prince Hall's black Masonic Lodge. When Hall died in 1807, Paul emerged as the undisputed leader of Boston's growing black community. He built the African Meeting House into a thriving house of worship, and established a school for black children on the building's first floor.

News of Paul's success in building a separate black congregation quickly reached New York City, where black Baptists asked Paul to help them establish such a church. Paul traveled to New York and stayed long enough to found Abyssinian Baptist Church on July 15, 1809. This church prospered through the 20th century as one of the largest and most famous churches in the nation.

Paul then returned to Boston where he formed the African Baptist Church, and worked for the betterment of the black community. In

1815, he traveled to England under the sponsorship of the English Baptist Missionary Society, and returned to the United States more fervently committed than ever to the abolitionist cause. In 1823, he succeeded in getting the society to send him as a missionary to Haiti. Upon his arrival, he pronounced that country "the best and most suitable place offered to emancipated people of color for the enjoyment of liberty and equality," and envisioned a large exodus of blacks to the land. But the staunch opposition of the Catholic population, exacerbated by Paul's inability to speak French, discouraged him, and he soon returned to Boston.

In his later years, Paul worked hard for the abolitionist cause. He opened his church doors for a meeting of William Lloyd Garrison's abolitionist society, the first such society in New England, and became a close friend of DAVID WALKER, whom he joined in creating *Freedom's Journal*, the first African-American newspaper in the United States. Poor health forced Paul's retirement in 1829, and he died two years later.

Further Reading

Adams, Russell L. *Great Negroes Past and Present.* Chicago: Afro-American Publishing Company, 1969.

Garrity, John A., and Mark C. Carnes, eds. *American National Biography.* Vol. 17. New York: Oxford University Press, 2002.

Payne, Daniel
(1811–1893) *African Methodist Episcopal bishop*

Daniel Payne, an early bishop in the African Methodist Episcopal Church (AME Church), was instrumental in raising the standards of education for clergy. He also became the first president of a black college.

Payne was born on February 24, 1811, in Charleston, South Carolina, the son of London and Martha Payne. London Payne's father was English, his mother black, and Martha's parents were black and Native American; both were born free and were devout Christians.

By the time Daniel was nine, both parents had died. He was raised by his great-aunt, who sent him to the Minors' Moralist Society School for two years and engaged a tutor for him in the classical languages. At 12 he became apprenticed to a carpenter, but by the age of 17 he was working for a tailor. Payne had a passion for learning, and continued his education on his own through reading textbooks.

In 1829, he had a religious conversion that set him on his vocational course. According to Payne, he felt a hand on his shoulder and heard a voice proclaim, "I have set thee apart to educate thyself in order that thou mayest educate thy people." He responded by opening a school for black students, teaching free children by day and slaves by night. At first he attracted only six students, not nearly enough to provide him with a living. But he persevered until the school became the most popular black school in Charleston.

Just when his career as an educator seemed to be going well, two misfortunes struck. In 1832, Payne suffered a permanent eye injury while watching a total eclipse of the sun, which affected his ability to read. Around the same time, South Carolina legislators, frightened by the NAT TURNER slave rebellion, began passing legislation outlawing the teaching of blacks. Payne had to close down the school and, on March 9, 1835, moved north with hopes of studying for the ministry.

Most white clergy advised him to prepare for missionary work in Africa, but a Lutheran named Daniel Strobel was looking for a young black man to train under him at Gettysburg Theological Seminary. Payne did so for two years, supporting himself as a waiter and shoeshine attendant, until his deteriorating eyesight made further study impossible.

The seminary president urged Payne to work in the AME Church, where he would be more readily accepted. But Payne was leery of that denomination's negative attitude toward education and so became licensed by the Lutheran Church and ordained in 1939. The church, however, never found any parish for him. Payne served briefly as pastor of a small black Presbyterian church in East Troy, New York. He then turned down an opportunity to be a traveling spokesman for the American Anti-slavery Society, believing it an inappropriate activity for a clergyman. In 1840, he returned to his original career plan by opening a school in Philadelphia. Within two years, he had 60 students enrolled.

By this time Payne had decided that, despite his misgivings about it, the AME Church afforded him his best chance for a meaningful ministry. He wrote a series of eight essays published in the official AME Church magazine in which he argued that ignorance made the oppression of blacks possible. After joining the denomination himself in 1841, he was assigned to Israel AME Church in Washington, D.C. There Payne became a leading advocate for religious education and a severe critic of traditional African religious influences. "The time is at hand," he said, "when the ministry of the AME Church must drive out this heathenish mode of worship or drive out all the intelligence, refinement, and practical Christians who may be in her bosom." Payne's proposals for educating the clergy met with overwhelming rejection at the 1844 AME General Conference until presiding bishop MORRIS BROWN supported them and got them passed.

Payne served at an AME church in Baltimore from 1845 to 1850. During that time he suffered tragedy when his wife, Julia Ferris, died within a year of their marriage. Payne would eventually marry a second time, to Eliza Clark, in 1853. Payne was a slight man, weighing barely 100 pounds, and was frequently ill with a host of

ailments, including cholera and malaria. Yet he worked tirelessly, helping to organize churches and schools around the country. In 1849 and 1850, he visited every church in the AME denomination to collect information for a book on its history. So highly regarded was his work that the AME Church rewarded him on May 7, 1852, by making him a bishop.

In this role, Payne continued to focus on education, setting up schools and literary organizations and training mothers to teach children in their homes. In 1855, he moved to Tawawa Springs, Ohio, where the predominantly white Episcopal Church was opening a new school for black children. Wilberforce University, as it was named despite being primarily an elementary school, opened in 1856, but financial troubles, at least partially attributable to the Civil War, forced it to close in 1863. The Episcopal Church then offered to sell the school to the AME Church for $10,000. Payne jumped at the chance, raised the funds, and reopened the school in July 1864 with himself as president. However, the school was burned down by arsonists on April 14, 1865.

At the time, Payne was beginning to supervise an organization of new black churches in South Carolina, North Carolina, and Georgia, which added 4,000 new members to the AME Church rolls. Yet he found time to again take on the task of raising funds for rebuilding. Under his leadership, Wilberforce University came back stronger than ever. Payne served as the school's president through 1876, by which time it had established a reputation as a solid, college-level institution.

Payne, an active abolitionist, compared the Confederate armies to the legions of the Pharaoh in the Bible. He believed slavery to be a huge barrier to the spread of Christianity because slaves found it hard to reconcile Christian doctrine with the attitudes of their white masters. When the Emancipation Proclamation was signed in 1863, beginning the freeing of the slaves in the United States, Payne exclaimed, "Thou, O Lord, and thou alone couldst have moved the heart of this needy Nation to have done so great a deed for this weak, despised, and needy people." A board member of the African Civilization Society, he firmly believed that it was in the best interest of blacks to eventually return to Africa.

In addition to the establishment of Wilberforce, Payne's most lasting contribution was his book *The History of the African Methodist Episcopal Church*, published in 1891. Payne died on November 29, 1893.

Further Reading

Kuennig, "Daniel A. Payne, First Black Lutheran Seminarian," *Lutheran Theological Seminary Bulletin* (fall 1987): 3–16.

Montgomery, William E. *Under Their Own Vine and Fig Tree: The African-American Church in the South, 1865–1900*. Baton Rouge: Louisiana State University Press, 1993.

Payne, Daniel. *History of the African Methodist Episcopal Church*. New York: Johnson Reprint, 1891.

———. *Recollections of Seventy Years*. New York: Arno Press, 1968.

Stuempfle, Herman G. "Daniel Payne As Hymn Writer," *Hymn*, January 1993, pp. 29–31.

Young, Henry J. *Major Black Religious Leaders, 1755–1940*. Nashville, Tenn.: Abingdon, 1977.

Pennington, James William Charles ("Fugitive Blacksmith")

(1808–1870) *Congregational, Presbyterian, and African Methodist Episcopal clergy, historian, theologian*

James Pennington, known as the "Fugitive Blacksmith," was a self-taught runaway slave who not only became a minister but was the first African American awarded a doctor of divinity degree from a European university.

He was given the name James at his birth in 1808 on the farm of a Colonel Gordon on Maryland's Eastern Shore. He received no education but acquired skills as a blacksmith, which made him valuable property to his master. After working as a slave for 21 years, Pennington ran away from the farm. At one point he was recaptured, but he escaped and, with the aid of some Quakers, made his way to Pennsylvania. Taking the name Pennington to throw off slave trackers, he moved to Brooklyn, New York, and there became a member of the Presbyterian Church.

Pennington spent five years educating himself, focusing especially on languages and theology. While doing so, he made a courageous stand at a convention in 1831, where he denounced the American Colonization Society, risking the wrath of his employer, who was president of the Brooklyn chapter of the society. But his arguments were so convincing that his employer dissolved the chapter.

Pennington formed a school for black children on Long Island, New York, in 1833. Soon afterward, he felt called to the ministry. In 1835, he accepted a teaching position in New Haven, Connecticut, and attempted to enroll at Yale University for theological training. He was not accepted at the school but was allowed to stand in the hall during lectures and given permission to use the library.

Guided by his motto, "What saith the Lord,—that will I do," he returned to Long Island in 1837 to teach at his old school and start a new church. A year later, Pennington was ordained by the Congregational Church. In 1840, he became the first African-American pastor of the Colored Congregational Church in Hartford, Connecticut, where he served until 1847. As evidence of the esteem in which he was held, the Hartford Central Association of Ministers, of which he was the only black member, twice voted him president of their group. In 1841, Pennington published *A Textbook of the Origin and History of the Colored People,* the first such history of blacks in America.

He made three trips to Europe in his lifetime, as a lecturer on abolitionism and biblical theology. The third trip occurred shortly after he took over the pastorship of First Shiloh Presbyterian Church, the largest black Presbyterian church in New York City, in 1848. While he was in England, he grew alarmed about the recently passed Fugitive Slave Law and decided to stay in Europe to avoid possible recapture. At that time, virtually no one, not even his wife, knew of his status as a fugitive slave. Pennington wrote a book entitled *The Fugitive Blacksmith,* published in 1849, which went through three editions in one year. He lectured for a time at the University of Heidelberg in Germany, where, on December 19, 1849, he was awarded an honorary doctor of divinity degree.

Pennington returned to the United States in the early 1850s after negotiating compensation with his former owner. Although ruined financially—from purchasing the freedom of a brother and from the legal expenses of a lawsuit against railroad discrimination—and battling alcoholism, he continued to serve churches in Connecticut and Long Island. In 1865, he was ordained by the African Methodist Episcopal Church and served parishes in New Orleans, Louisiana; Natchez, Mississippi; and Portland, Maine, before his death in Jacksonville, Florida, where he was attempting to establish yet another church, in October 1870.

Further Reading

Pennington, John. "The Fugitive Blacksmith." In *Great Slave Narrations.* Edited by Arna Bontemps. Boston: Beacon Press, 1969.

Swift, David E. *Black Prophets of Justice: Activist Clergy before the Civil War.* Baton Rouge: Louisiana State University Press, 1989.

Young, Henry J. *Major Black Religious Leaders, 1755–1940.* Nashville, Tenn.: Abingdon, 1977.

Perkins, John
(1930–) *author, lay organizer*

Despite little education and a blue-collar background, John Perkins is credited with articulating one of the most influential visions of Christianity in the 20th century. It was Perkins who synthesized a holistic vision of Christianity that bridged a growing gap between elements promoting evangelism and those advocating social activism, thus providing a rationale for many conservative evangelicals to reverse course and take up concerns of the social gospel in the 1980s.

Perkins was born in 1930 on a cotton plantation near New Hebron, Mississippi. He was the youngest of five children born to Maggie and Jap Perkins, both of whom died before he reached his first birthday. John was put in the care of his paternal grandmother and a large extended family who supplemented their meager income as sharecroppers by running a clandestine gambling operation and dealing in bootleg whiskey. Perkins completed only the third grade in school before dropping out. He experienced his share of prejudice, including an incident in which a white boy shot at him with a BB gun. In 1947, one of his brothers was killed by the New Hebron police under shady circumstances, which prompted Perkins to leave the area and relocate to California. He found employment on a foundry production line, where he demonstrated an engaging personality and leadership skills as a union organizer.

Shortly after marrying Vera MacBuckley in 1951, Perkins was drafted into the army and was stationed in Okinawa during the Korean War. In 1953, he returned to California, supporting his growing family by working first as a janitor and then as a welder. Prior to this time, Perkins showed little interest in religion, but in 1957 he experienced a powerful conversion, prompting him to begin his own ministry efforts at outreach in the community. He found that he had a particular affinity for reaching juveniles, and decided to concentrate his ministry in that area.

Against the wishes of his wife, he and his family returned to Mississippi so that John could minister to young people in the community where he had been reared. At that time, he had no particular theological bent other than a desire to teach Christianity to children. "I did not come back to Mississippi with a holistic concept of the Gospel," he has said. "I found it after I got there." Perkins began by teaching summer school and received permission to teach Bible classes to children at the black public school in nearby Mendenhall. According to Perkins, from 1960 to 1969, "I had my way in the public schools," separation of church and state issues notwithstanding. He also taught youth Sunday school and conducted special Lenten meetings.

The longer he taught in Mendenhall, the more he recognized that his students had many needs that could not be filled by spiritual teachings. He saw that factors such as poverty, racism, and teen pregnancy dragged them into a hopeless existence. He recalled, "The realities of daily life in rural Mississippi reminded us constantly of what God had taught us during the first crucial years: evangelism is not enough."

As a result, Perkins was drawn into the Civil Rights movement that had intensified in the South in the early 1960s. He read the story of Jackie Robinson, who broke the color barrier in major league baseball, to his children to inspire them to achieve. He advocated for the community to provide leisure facilities for teens, and he railed against the many liquor establishments, largely owned by church members, that he believed were enticing young people into trouble. Eventually, his outspoken views on these subjects drew the ire of Christians who thought such concerns detracted from the true mission of saving souls, and who got him removed from his local church.

Undaunted, Perkins began organizing social ministries with a strong evangelical Christian flavor. In 1965, he and his friend R. A. Buckley launched a new ministry called Voice of Calvary Bible Institute to advance their socially responsible Christian evangelism. The same year, he began organizing a campaign to register black voters. In quick succession, he helped form the Berean Bible Church and a child care center.

The fight for racial equality became personal for Perkins in 1967 when three of his children broke the color barrier at the previously all-white Mendenhall High School. On an economic front, Perkins initiated the Federation of

Despite limited education, John Perkins's writings greatly advanced the cause of social justice among conservative Christians. *(Billy Graham Center)*

Southern Cooperatives, which formed farming co-ops, stores and other businesses, and created jobs. He helped start affordable-housing projects and wholesome facilities for teens. He was arrested in 1969 for disturbing the peace with his civil rights agitation and, in February 1970, was arrested along with other picketers and beaten so severely by police that he was confined to a hospital for an extensive period of time.

Upon being released from the hospital in 1971, Perkins moved to Jackson, Mississippi, where he continued to head the far-flung social and evangelical ministries of the Voice of Calvary. As he continued to put his social evangelical theology into action, his organization became a model for community development and attracted a nationwide audience. He put his views and the life story that had shaped them into a cohesive package by publishing *With Justice for All* in 1982. Perkins's approach in his writing was honest and straightforward. "When I preach and teach they don't expect me to make no kind of spectacle," he once said. In simple language, he told how he rejected the supposed dichotomy between spiritual and social needs and instead focused his ministry on taking care of the whole person. His many concrete examples of how he put his views into action demonstrated that such an approach was far more than just a theory. Authors William J. Petersen and Randy Petersen cited Perkins's book as one of "100 Christian Books That Changed the Century" by showing that social compassion had a major influence on Christian ministry worldwide in both rural and urban areas. Despite his strong social activism, Perkins's credentials with the conservative element of the nation were confirmed when he was awarded an honorary doctor of law degree from Wheaton College in 1980 and was named to President Ronald Reagan's Task Force on Hunger in 1983. Perkins has spent his later years continuing his ministry in Pasadena, California.

Further Reading

Perkins, John. *With Justice for All.* Ventura, Calif.: Regal Books, 1982.

Petersen, William J., and Randy Petersen. *One Hundred Christian Books That Changed the Century.* Grand Rapids, Mich.: Fleming H. Revell, 2000.

Perry, Harold Robert
(1916–1991) *Roman Catholic priest*

Harold Perry was the first African-American bishop in the Roman Catholic church in the 20th century. A quiet, dignified leader, he provided a calming influence in the Deep South during a time of turmoil over civil rights.

He was born Harold Robert Perry on October 9, 1916, in Lake Charles, Louisiana, the oldest of six children of Frank and Josephine Perry. The Perrys were descendants of French Creoles and as such were devout Catholics. Neither Frank, a rice mill worker, nor Josephine, a domestic cook, were high school graduates, but they encouraged all of their children to advance as far as they could academically.

The family grew up in an integrated neighborhood across the street from Sacred Heart Church and a block from the church school. Perry, who served as an altar boy, knew from the age of 12 that he wanted to be a priest and never entertained a doubt thereafter. He applied to several seminaries; however, most U.S. Roman Catholic seminaries were not open to blacks at the time, and Perry found one door after another shut to him. "Until then," he later recalled, "it had not occurred to me that my race would be a handicap in anything I wanted to do."

Finally, Perry made contact with the Society of the Divine Word, a missionary order that actively recruited minorities. Just as he was accepted by the St. Augustine Seminary in Bay Saint Louis, Mississippi, in 1930, however, the Great Depression devastated the family's income, and Perry had no money to pay the tuition. His career advanced only through the grace of a priest who paid his tuition for the first four years of school. Perry responded by being the only member of his 26-person class to complete the high school and college curriculum at the school, finishing in 1937.

In 1937, he traveled to East Troy, Wisconsin, to make his novitiate in the society. He then began theological studies at Saint Mary's Seminary in Techny, Illinois, in 1938, and returned to Saint Augustine's the following year. He completed his studies in 1943 and was ordained a priest on January 6, 1944. After serving as an assistant priest in Lafayette and then Saint Martinsville, Louisiana, he moved on to a similar position at Pine Bluff, Arkansas, in 1948. In 1951, he became a priest at Saint Gabriel's Church in the all-black town of Mound Bayou, Mississippi, before undertaking the task of founding and leading the 1,000-member congregation in Broussard, Louisiana, in 1952. He served as rector of Saint Augustine from 1958 to 1963, and on July 8, 1963, he became the first African American to deliver the invocation at an opening session of Congress.

After promotion to supervisor of the Society of the Divine Word's southern province in 1964, he was surprised to be chosen as bishop in early 1966 and assigned to New Orleans. When confronted by skepticism that a black man could function effectively in such a post in the South, he responded simply, "I was effective as a priest. I expect to be effective as a bishop."

While emphasizing that he was not a Catholic version of MARTIN LUTHER KING, JR., Perry worked quietly for social justice as bishop, while also serving pastorates in the area. His tenure was one of little controversy due to his dignified, conciliatory nature. Perry retired in 1985, due to heart trouble, and died on July 17, 1991, in Marrero, Louisiana.

Further Reading

Murphy, Larry G., ed. *Encyclopedia of African American Religious Biography.* New York: Garland Publishing, 1993.

"Perry, Harold R., Bishop, 1917–89." *Christian Century,* September 4, 1991, p. 803.

Smith, Jesse Carney, ed. *Notable Black American Men.* Vol. 1. Detroit, Mich.: Gale Research, 1999.

Powell, Adam Clayton, Jr.
(1908–1972) *Baptist clergy, politician*

Adam Clayton Powell, Jr., gave African Americans the most powerful voice they had ever had on the national level. His popularity in the Harlem neighborhood of New York City, where he preached every Sunday, was so great that he was once endorsed for election by the Democratic Party, the Republican Party, and independent political parties. Powell chaired Congress's influential Education and Labor Committee in the 1960s. Although his flamboyance and careless lifestyle diluted his message and often embarrassed supporters, he was an effective advocate for minorities and the economically disadvantaged throughout much of his career.

Powell was born on November 29, 1908, in New Haven, Connecticut, at about the time that his father, ADAM CLAYTON POWELL, SR., was called to serve as head pastor of the 100-year-old Abyssinian Baptist Church in Midtown New York City. While Adam, Jr., was growing up, his father directed the relocation of the church to Harlem, where it became the largest black church in the world. Powell, Sr.'s success in real estate, together with his wife Mattie's status as heir to a considerable fortune, together combined to provide a comfortable life for young Adam.

Powell was a good student in high school but made a poor adjustment in his freshman year at City College of New York, where he flunked out of school. He recovered, however, after transferring to Colgate University. While at

Flamboyant pastor and congressman Adam Clayton Powell, Jr., enjoyed such popularity in his Harlem district that no political party dared oppose him. *(Corbis)*

Colgate, Powell attempted to join a whites-only fraternity and was denied when the fraternity conducted a background check that revealed his heritage. (Both he and his father were light-skinned and could have passed for white.) Such snubs served to cement his determination to work for racial equality.

In his senior year, Powell deferred to his father's wishes and gave up his goal of a medical career to become a minister. Upon graduation in 1929 he joined his father as assistant pastor and business manager of Abyssinian Baptist. At the same time, he attended Columbia University's graduate school, from which he earned a master's degree in 1932.

At Abyssinian Baptist, Powell discovered his effectiveness in leading the community in social justice issues. In 1931, he led a march of 6,000 demonstrators to City Hall to protest the firing of five African-American physicians from Harlem Hospital. This action led to all five being reinstated. In 1935, he attracted considerable media attention by writing a weekly column for one of the New York newspapers in which he criticized people such as the charismatic preacher FATHER DIVINE.

In 1937, at the age of 29, Powell succeeded his retiring father as head of Abyssinian Baptist. Powell was not shy about using the power of his pulpit to advance the message of racial equality. He organized a large soup kitchen to meet the needs of the depression-era unemployed. He became a powerful force on the community level as the cochairman of the Greater New York Unemployment Coordination Committee, fighting for black economic empowerment. One of his most significant accomplishments was using the threat of a boycott to extract a promise from city bus officials to hire more than 200 blacks for the previously whites-only positions of bus driver and mechanic.

Powell's popularity and effectiveness as a community organizer persuaded him to go into politics while remaining in his position at Abyssinian Baptist. He ran for city council and won election as New York's first black alderman in 1941. Powell focused his attention on issues of social justice, even if they did not pertain to city government. He was outspoken in his criticism of the federal government for imprisoning Japanese-American citizens during the war, pointing out that the policy was racially motivated. He also condemned the newspapers for what he considered to be a racially divisive policy of identifying people in news articles by race.

His work on the city council was not a particularly satisfying experience, as his fellow council members seldom cooperated with him. Powell looked to the people for support. In February 1942, he began editing a newspaper, *The People's Voice,* in which he advocated his views.

When the redistricting of New York City carved out a congressional district in Harlem, Powell decided to set his sights on higher political office. By this time, he was so popular in Harlem that all political parties endorsed him when he announced his candidacy for Congress in 1945, and he won a special election for the new seat without any real opposition. This made him one of only two African Americans in the U.S. House of Representatives at the time. Powell proudly referred to himself as the first black congressman "with an attitude." He refused to abide by the segregated rules of Washington, D.C.'s restrooms, baths, and barber shops. When Mississippi's segregationist representative John Rankin refused to sit next to him, Powell responded by saying he did not want to sit by Rankin either and called for an investigation of Rankin as a fascist.

Although Powell had not previously affiliated himself with a political party, he joined the majority Democrats and was rewarded with a seat on the Education and Labor Committee. Powell quickly distinguished himself as the leading spokesman in Congress for civil rights. In 1946, he tacked on an amendment to a federal school lunch program bill that assured that black children would be served as well as white children.

As Powell became more familiar with the operations of Congress, he went on the attack even more aggressively. In the early days of the Eisenhower administration, he criticized Secretary of the Navy Robert Anderson for dragging his feet on orders to desegregate military facilities. This led to stepped-up efforts to integrate bases. Powell was most famous for attaching what became known as the "Powell amendment," which banned distribution of federal moneys to any school that discriminated on the basis of race, to various pieces of legislation. Even liberals criticized him for the tactic, which jeopardized and even killed crucial projects such as school construction funds, but Powell insisted that racial justice had to be a cornerstone of the nation's policy. Powell also introduced legislation banning employers and unions from discriminating on the basis of race or religion. His bill, which was blocked in the U.S. Senate, did not become law until 1964. Well ahead of his colleagues on many justice issues, Powell was one of the first to decry the repressive actions of the House Un-American Activities Committee.

During the 1950s, Powell became enmeshed in a series of legal battles and political controversies that would continue for the rest of his life. The Internal Revenue Service charged him with tax fraud for filing a false income tax return in 1951. Powell fought the charge and finally won in 1960. In the 1956 election, he bucked the Democratic Party and endorsed Republican president Dwight Eisenhower. Democrats tried to punish him by running a candidate against him in his congressional primary, but that candidate lost badly. In 1960, Powell's offhand reference on a television news interview to a woman as a "bag woman" for the New York City police triggered a libel suit against him. Powell declined to appear at the trial and the jury awarded the woman $211,500. Powell refused to pay, pending all appeals of the process, which led to more trouble in the late 1960s.

Powell was often frustrated by the lack of respect accorded him on the Education and Labor Committee. But with the retirement of Senator Graham Barden in 1961, Powell's seniority earned him the chairmanship. The *New York Times* charged that Powell's "miserable record as a legislator and his extreme absenteeism all tend to disqualify him as a reasonable and effective chairman." Yet during his six years of leadership, the committee produced a remarkable amount of work, including 39 pieces of legislation in an 18-month period. Among its accomplishments were the establishment of a minimum wage and development of a federally sponsored student loan program. President Lyndon Johnson praised him lavishly for his record of accomplishment. Powell, however, took heavy criticism for endorsing the Black Power movement and voting against such legislation as the 1965 Voting Rights Act, which he felt was a sop to middle-class blacks.

At this point, Powell had become the most powerful black legislator in U.S. history. However, his penchant for controversy, cavalier lifestyle, three marriages, careless statements, and extravagant trips at government expense supplied his enemies with plentiful ammunition. When Powell refused to pay the 1960 libel judgment, he was charged with contempt of court and an arrest warrant was issued. For months Powell visited Harlem only on Sundays to preach at Abyssinian Baptist, a day when the warrant could not be served. He was then charged with criminal contempt, which meant that even Sundays were not safe, and he went into exile. On March 1, 1967, the House voted him unfit for office by a 307–166 margin, and refused to let him take his seat. A special election for the seat was held, which Powell won with a resounding 87 percent of the vote. His seat remained vacant for two years.

Powell was largely vindicated in the end. The libel suit was resolved in 1969, largely in his favor. That same year the Supreme Court ruled that the House of Representatives had violated the Constitution in denying him his seat. Powell returned to Congress, but by then the damage had been done, and he narrowly lost to Charles Rangel in the 1970 primary. He died of cancer in Miami, Florida, on April 4, 1972.

Further Reading

Franklin, John Hope, and August Meier, eds. *Black Leaders of the Twentieth Century.* Urbana: University of Illinois Press, 1982.

Gore, Bob, Robert L. Gore, Jesse Jackson, and Calvin O. Butts, *We've Come This Far: Abyssinian Baptist Church: A Photo Journal.* New York: Stewart, Tabori and Chang, 2001.

Hamilton, Charles V. *Adam Clayton Powell, Jr.: The Political Biography of an American Dilemma.* New York: Atheneum, 1991.

Paris, Peter J. *Black Religious Leaders: Conflict in Unity.* Louisville, Ky.: John Knox Press, 1991.

Powell, Adam Clayton, Jr. *Adam by Adam: The Autobiography of Adam Clayton Powell, Jr.*, New York: Dial, 1971.

Powell, Adam Clayton, Sr.

(1865–1953) *Baptist clergy*

Adam Clayton Powell, Sr., recognized the great potential for church growth among the hundred thousand southern blacks who had migrated into the Harlem neighborhood of New York City by the turn of the 20th century. By aiming his ministry at that group, he created the largest black congregation in the world and was one of the most successful leaders of his time in articulating and advocating for the concerns of urban African Americans.

Powell was born on May 5, 1865, in a one-room log cabin near Martin's Mill, Virginia. His father was a German farmer whom he knew only as Powell and who was killed in the last days of the Civil War before Adam's birth. His mother, Sally Powell, was of African-American and Indian descent. Powell, his mother, and 16 siblings lived for several years with Antony Dunn, a tenant farmer, before migrating to Paint Creek, West Virginia, in 1875.

Although he was a bright student, Powell was able to attend school for only three years during his childhood. In 1884, he was forced to flee the state for fear of being lynched because of his role in the shooting of an influential white resident while he was guarding a melon patch. He moved to Rendville, Ohio, where he found work in the coal mines, although he gambled away most of his earnings. In 1885, he attended a religious revival in town that instilled in him a passionate religious conviction. Powell changed his life and began attending Rendville Academy.

In 1887, he moved to Washington, D.C., with hopes of studying law at Howard University. But Powell's academic background was not nearly good enough for him to qualify. While he was working in a hotel, trying to decide what to do next, he was "seized with an unquenchable desire to preach," according to his recollections. He enrolled at the Baptist Wayland Academy, supporting himself as a janitor and waiter.

Shortly after graduating in 1882, he was assigned to Immanuel Baptist Church, a small black congregation in New Haven, Connecticut. Powell served there for 15 years along with his wife, the former Mattie Fletcher Schaffer (whom he had married in 1889). In 1908 he was called to the historic Abyssinian Baptist Church in New York City. The church had been established in the previous century by a group of African Americans and Ethiopian merchants who protested against discriminatory seating in a white Baptist church and began their own church a few blocks away.

Powell wasted no time in exercising leadership in his new position. Moral issues were of prime importance to him. He was strongly opposed to drinking and, incensed by the proliferation of houses of prostitution around the church, he led a successful campaign to drive them from the neighborhood. Theologically, he was driven by his belief that the second coming of Jesus Christ was imminent.

But Powell's rise to prominence can be traced to his awareness of the significance of the black migration from the South. Powell observed two tremendous challenges in this migration, which had drawn more than 100,000 blacks to New York City, primarily to Harlem, in search of economic advancement. First, as he put it, the black influx "scared the white people almost to death." Secondly, the church had virtually no presence among this huge group of people. Powell began to argue strenuously for relocating his church into this area to take up the challenge of providing spiritual and social direction to these people. When congregation members balked, Powell threatened to resign as pastor and carry out the mission himself as a full-time evangelist. Finally, on June 17, 1923, the church moved to a location in Harlem, on 138th Street between Lenox Avenue and Seventh Avenue. There it constructed a 2,000-seat sanctuary.

Powell's vision for this church encompassed far more than merely worship services. Powell was a believer in self help. In his mind, Abyssinian Baptist was to be a community center where black people could find stability and encouragement to improve themselves and their neighborhood. He preached that his congregation needed to get away from the preoccupation with their own struggles. "Work for others will heal our sorrows and make us forget most of our trouble," he declared. To that end, Abyssinian Baptist set up housing for the elderly, organized a mission to Africa, developed a skills training center, and created an endowment to assist blacks in attending college. The church soon offered the nation's largest adult education program and became a leader in sponsoring evangelical crusades. When the Great Depression began in 1929, Powell created a large soup kitchen to help feed the destitute.

Powell was active in civil rights, and his stance on racial issues was conciliatory, asking only that white Americans grant blacks "the right of equal opportunity with all other American people." He viewed blacks and whites in the United States as having a shared destiny. Over the years, he became increasingly active in politics as he sought to steer this destiny to positive ends. Powell was one of the founders of the Urban League, and in 1910 he served on the first board of directors for the National Association for the Advancement of Colored People (NAACP). His affiliations were remarkably diverse. Originally, he was heavily committed to Republican Party politics, and he remained politically conservative on many issues. But he gradually shifted over to supporting Franklin D. Roosevelt as the Democratic Party became more closely identified with the working class.

Powell recruited his son, ADAM CLAYTON POWELL, JR., to work with him in the 1920s and groomed him to take over leadership of his church. When the senior Powell was ready to retire in 1937, the son was ready to step in and he assumed a fame during his career exceeding that of his father. Powell, Sr., however, was the one who created his son's base of power by building Abyssinian Baptist to between 10,000 and 14,000 members by the time of his retirement. He was successful in withdrawing into the background and not infringing on his son's leadership. During his later years, Powell, Sr., wrote a book entitled *Riots and Ruins*, which documented the history of the Harlem race riots of 1943 and offered suggestions for improving race relations in New York City. Powell died in New York City on June 12, 1953.

Further Reading

Gore, Bob, Robert L. Gore. Jesse Jackson, and Calvin O. Butts. *We've Come This Far: Abyssinian Baptist Church: A Photo Journal.* New York: Stewart, Tabori and Chang, 2001.
Powell, Adam Clayton, Sr. *Against the Tide: An Autobiography.* New York: Richard R. Smith, 1938.

Price, Frederick K. C.
(1932–   ) *nondenominational evangelist*

Relying on a philosophy of "teaching, not preaching," Frederick Price has been the most successful black televangelist in history. Beginning with a nine-member congregation made up primarily of his family members, he has built a bustling megachurch in Los Angeles, and his *Everlasting Faith* grew to become the fifth most popular religious TV show in the world.

Price was born on January 3, 1932, in Santa Monica, California, where his parents, Fred and Winifred Price, owned a janitorial service. His parents were former Jehovah's Witnesses who had soured on organized religion. Therefore, Frederick had little contact with religion until he met Betty Scott while attending Dorsey High

School. Eager to impress her parents, he regularly attended her church until he and Betty were married. At that time, he dropped out of church life until his wife attended a weeklong tent revival. Price visited the event out of curiosity and experienced a dramatic conversion. Soon afterward, he joined a local Baptist church, and felt a call to become a minister. After completing two years at Los Angeles City College, Price worked as an assistant pastor in the Baptist church in 1955, supplementing his income with work as a paper cutter.

Price, however, had difficulty finding a comfort zone within one denomination. He moved away from the Baptist Church in 1957 to take a position as pastor at an African Methodist Episcopal church in Val Verde, California. In 1959, he moved back into mainstream white Christianity as a pastor of a Presbyterian church, and a few years later drifted away from the larger denominations to work in a community church in the Christian and Missionary Alliance. Price spent more than a decade in this search for his niche in ministry, a process made more difficult by the death of his eight-year-old son in an automobile accident in 1962.

Still looking for focus, Price started a new church in West Los Angeles in 1969. Five of the original nine members were family. A short time later, he found the direction he had been lacking when he veered into the Pentecostal tradition. Price received his baptism of the Holy Spirit and spoke in tongues on February 2, 1970. At that time, he felt that God was calling him to establish a new nondenominational church in which he could preach his message unfettered by hierarchical or traditional concerns. His theology was a blend of Pentecostalism and the prosperity teachings of Kenneth E. Hagin. "When faith is added to the power of God, there is an explosion of healing or whatever you want," Price declared. He viewed himself not as a preacher supplying inspiration, but as a teacher whose job was merely to provide information. "When you

get the right information, inspiration will automatically follow," he said. He developed a style of preaching that depended heavily on simple analogies that vividly illustrated to parishioners the concepts he was conveying.

By November 1973, his message had attracted 300 new members to his congregation. At that time Price moved his congregation, now called Crenshaw Community Church, into a new location in the Inglewood area of Los Angeles. Thinking optimistically, he installed the church into a facility with a seating capacity of 1,400, more than four times the size of the present membership. In the meantime, he returned to school to acquire more expertise in religious matters. In 1978, he earned a bachelor's degree in biblical studies from Friends International Christian University in Merced, California. Later, he would go on to acquire a doctorate in ministry in 1988 and a doctorate in religious studies in 1992, both from Friends International.

While caring for his rapidly growing congregation, Price sought ways to bring his message to a wider audience. In the early 1970s, he reached people using a radio show that aired several times a week. A short time later, he moved into television on local Los Angeles stations, then expanded to five major cities. As the popularity of his *Everlasting Faith* program increased, it was picked up by dozens of stations across the nation.

Hewing to his teaching philosophy, Price made no effort to interject entertainment value or flamboyance into his show. Basically, he did nothing but preach a sermon. Yet this seemed to be exactly what a large segment of the audience was looking for. Following the highly publicized scandals of televangelists Jim Bakker and Jimmy Swaggart, Price was one of only two major TV evangelists to increase their ratings during the 1980s.

Crenshaw Community Church, in the meantime, continued to grow at a breathtaking rate. By 1982, Price had to expand to three services because of the lack of room for the congregation in his huge facility. As membership continued to swell, Price recognized that he had to expand to an even larger facility. Rather than succumb to the temptation to build a plush palace in a nicer neighborhood, Price stayed in the inner city, buying a 32-acre parcel of land that had been the original site of Pepperdine University in South Los Angeles. Initially, the price tag for a sanctuary of the size Price wanted was more than $16 million. While mulling the feasibility of this, he happened to visit the huge dome that housed Howard Hughes's famous "Spruce Goose" airplane in Long Beach. He immediately recognized that such a dome would allow him to build a huge auditorium more cheaply than conventional methods, with the added advantage of removing pillars that would obstruct parishioners' views. The resulting Crenshaw Center Christian Faith Dome cost approximately $9 million. The cavernous building's seating capacity of more than 10,000 made it the largest house of worship in the United States. While some decried the building as a monument to excess, Price explained his action in typical analogous form. "You've got to have a boat to get the folks in so you can get out there in the middle of the lake where the fish are," he said.

By the turn of the 21st century, Price's church had more than 18,000 members, and his television show reached an average audience of 33 million viewers. In addition, he founded the Fellowship of Inner City Word of Faith Ministries in 1990 to share ideas with independent parishes around the country on meeting the challenges of urban churches, and in 1997 he launched a long series of sermons aimed at getting churches to live up to their responsibilities in matters of race.

Further Reading

Collier, Aldore. "A Grand Slam Homer for Jesus," *Ebony*, December 1989, p. 40.

Phelps, Shirelle. *Contemporary Black Biography.* Vol. 17. Detroit, Mich.: Gale Research, 1998.

Price, Frederick K. C. *Religion and Racism: Perverting the Gospel to Subjugate a People.* Los Angeles: Faith One, 2002.

Proctor, Henry Hugh

(1868–1933) *Congregational clergy, writer, lecturer*

Hugh Proctor was an effective pastor who built two thriving churches and exercised a calming influence on Atlanta with his message of racial conciliation and advocacy of improved opportunities for African Americans.

Proctor was born on December 8, 1868, on a farm near Fayetteville, Tennessee. He was the youngest of four children of Richard and Hannah Proctor, both of whom were former slaves. His childhood was limited to his farm and the rural school he attended three months of the year; Proctor was 12 before he visited his first town.

Eventually, he became a public school teacher at Pea Ridge, Tennessee, and then served as principal of a school near his hometown. In 1884, he decided to pursue further education, beginning with a term at Central Tennessee College. He then transferred to Fisk University, where he supported himself digging ditches. While at Fisk, he came under the influence of Henry Bennett, a Congregational professor, and decided to pursue a calling in the ministry. Upon graduation with a B.A. degree in 1891, he enrolled at Yale Divinity School, where he joined the three other black students in a quartet that performed at local churches. "I sometimes say I dug my way through Fisk and sang it through Yale," he observed. He obtained his bachelor of divinity degree from Yale in 1894, shortly after his marriage to Adeline Davis. Proctor was ordained on July 1, 1894, and accepted a call to the newly formed First

Congregational Church in Atlanta. Under his leadership, the congregation moved from a mission-supported church of 100 to a self-sufficient congregation of more than 1,000.

In 1903 Proctor joined George W. Henderson in organizing the National Convention of Congregational Workers among Colored People, an organization that brought blacks together from all over the country to support each other in ministry. Three years later, on September 22, 1906, he was visiting Memphis when he heard news of terrible race riots back in Atlanta. Returning home, he developed a twofold plan for easing racial discord in the city. First, he called together a group of 20 whites and 20 blacks to form the Interracial Council of Atlanta to promote harmony and defuse tension. Secondly, operating on the belief that a contributing factor to unrest was blacks' lack of access to arts, recreation, and entertainment, he began looking for ways to increase this access. When his congregation outgrew their building and erected a new structure in 1908, Proctor included such amenities as a gymnasium, sewing room, and library. In response to blacks being denied admission to the opera in Atlanta, Proctor initiated the Atlanta Colored Music Festival, bringing in the best black musicians in the United States. Proctor also initiated the first kindergarten in the city, the first temperance society in Georgia, and the first orphanage in the nation sponsored by a black church.

In 1919, at the request of the U.S. War Department, Proctor sailed to Europe to minister to black troops stationed there after World War I. After traveling 4,000 miles and visiting 100,000 soldiers, he returned to the United States and accepted a call to Nazarene Congregational Church in Brooklyn, New York, in 1920. In his later years, he wrote *Between Black and White*, a collection of autobiographical sketches published in 1925, and procured funding that pulled Fisk University out of financial peril. Proctor died on May 12, 1933.

Further Reading

Luker, Ralph E. *The Social Gospel and Black and White*. Chapel Hill: University of North Carolina Press, 1991.

Proctor, H. *Between Black and White: Autobiographical Sketches*. 1925. Reprint, Freeport, N.Y.: Books for Libraries Press, 1972.

Prophet Jones
(James Francis Marion Jones)
(1908–1971) *cult leader*

Prophet Jones was one of the most flamboyant of the black religious personality cult leaders who flourished briefly in the United States during the mid-20th century.

He was born James Francis Marion Jones in a Birmingham ghetto in 1908. He claimed to have received the gift of prophecy at two, when he predicted his father would come home bloody from a slight accident. Jones grew close to his mother, a schoolteacher, rather than his abusive father, who worked as a brakeman on the railroad. She raised him in a Holiness church called the Triumph Church and Kingdom of God in Christ, where he began preaching at the age of 11. His religious fervor hampered his schooling because he insisted that God forbade him to read any book written by humans.

Little is known about the years he spent evangelizing for his church in the Midwest and South. He apparently achieved limited success until he moved to Detroit in 1938 and found a receptive audience. After building a new church in that city, his theology grew more and more inwardly focused, to the point where in 1944 he broke off from his former denomination. Declaring that God told him to start his own church, he organized the Church of the Universal Triumph/the Dominion of God.

Prophet Jones's church was, strictly speaking, a cult rather than a church. It had no social program; the benefits it offered to followers were healing and, in exchange for hefty contributions, personal access to Jones's prophetic powers on Thursdays. Jones began exalting himself, referring to himself at times as God's prophet and even as God himself. He structured his organization as a tiny kingdom, even installing a throne in the sanctuary (a replica of King Solomon's) on which he sat during services.

During the 1950s, Jones announced that all persons alive in the year 2000 would be immortal. He provided his followers with a strict code of moral and ritual regulations, known as the 50 Decrees, to help them reach that goal. The regulations ranged from abstinence from coffee, tea, and alcohol, to rules on how to bow or curtsy before the "royal family" (his own). His followers, whom he called citizens, were not to mingle with "noncitizens." He replaced the Christmas celebration with a seven-day feast of Philamathya in honor of his own birth.

Jones's sermons could run as long as five hours. If the offerings were not what he expected, he sometimes locked parishioners in the sanctuary until his goal was reached. He often dressed in colorful robes decorated with feathers, or in a white mink coat given him by a follower, and lived in an opulent mansion known as the "French Castle."

Jones claimed a following of more than 2 million people at one time, but historians consider those numbers exaggerated. Most of his adherents were women, and about 10 percent nationally were white. His ministry disintegrated after two morals charges were brought against him in 1956, including indecent solicitation of an officer. While Jones was never convicted, the incidents ruined his credibility and cost him all but his most fanatical supporters. Thereafter, he was in constant financial trouble and lost his house and his mink coat to creditors. Jones spent most of his later years in Chicago, suffered a stroke in September 1970, and died in Detroit on August 12, 1971.

Further Reading

Kobler, J. "Messiah in Mink," *Saturday Evening Post,* March 5, 1955, pp. 20–1.

Melton, J. Gordon. *Religious Leaders of America.* 2d ed. Detroit, Mich.: Gale Research, 1999.

Smith, Jesse Carney, ed. *Notable Black American Men.* Vol. 1. Detroit, Mich.: Gale Research, 1999.

Washington, Joseph R., Jr. *Black Sects and Cults.* New York: Doubleday, 1972.

Q

Quinn, William Paul

(1788–1873) *African Methodist Episcopal bishop*

William Paul Quinn was one of the most energetic and longest-serving of the early African Methodist Episcopal (AME) bishops.

He was born on April 19, 1788, although there is wide discrepancy in reports of his birthplace, ranging from Calcutta, India, to Honduras. By the age of 20, he had come to the United States and settled in Bucks County, Pennsylvania. After being converted by black Methodist preachers in 1808, he became active in the church. Quinn obtained a license to preach in 1812 and was in attendance at the conception of the AME Church in Philadelphia in 1816. Quinn was ordained a deacon in the AME Church in 1818 and began his formal ministry at small communities in New Jersey: Bushtown, Gouldtown, Salem, and Springton. He returned to Bucks County in 1826 and quarreled so vehemently with AME bishop RICHARD ALLEN that he withdrew from the denomination. He soon had a change of heart and petitioned to return in June 1828, but was not officially welcomed back until 1833. At that time, he became the AME's first itinerant pastor working west of the Allegheny Mountains. He was instrumental in the formation of the denomination's Western

Conference in 1838, the year in which he was ordained an elder and assigned to the Pittsburgh–Philadelphia–District of Columbia circuit. In 1840, Quinn was appointed to a circuit in Illinois in the newly formed Indiana Conference.

Quinn's energy and organizational skills were in much demand. In 1841, he accepted a position as assistant to AME bishop MORRIS BROWN. Quinn was responsible for overseeing expansion in the western regions, and his success was such that he was dubbed the Saint Paul of the AME Church. Between 1841 and 1844 he helped initiate 72 new congregations and 47 churches. His report of his activities so impressed delegates to the AME general conference in 1844 that they elected him the denomination's fourth bishop. Quinn went on to take charge of AME organizational operations in Ohio, Indiana, Illinois, Michigan, Kentucky, and Missouri. His work in Kentucky and Missouri entailed considerable risk, as the recruitment by churches of slaves in those states was deemed a capital offense.

In an attempt to improve the AME's governing structure, Quinn proposed in 1848 a system giving authority to a group of presiding elders. His idea was rejected at the time but was later adopted and became an integral part of the church's operating structure. Morris Brown died on May 9, 1849, at which time Quinn succeeded him as the AME's senior bishop. He retained the post for nearly 25 years, far longer than his predecessors, until his death on February 2, 1873. The memory of Quinn's service to the AME has been honored by naming Paul Quinn College in Waco, Texas, as well as churches in 15 states, after him.

Further Reading

Murphy, Larry G., ed. *Encyclopedia of African American Religious Biography.* New York: Garland Publishing, 1993.

"William Paul Quinn." AMEC Net web site. Available online. URL: http://www.amecnet.org/quinn.htm. Downloaded February 18, 2003.

R

Randolph, Florence Spearing

(1866–1951) *African Methodist Episcopal Zion evangelist*

Florence Spearing Randolph grew up believing that the pulpit was no place for a woman. But she found herself drawn against her will into active ministry in the African Methodist Episcopal Zion Church (AMEZ Church). Randolph became one of the earliest female clergy and one of the few granted appointment to serve parishes, including a prestigious position at Wallace Chapel in New Jersey.

She was born Florence Spearing on August 9, 1866, in Charleston, South Carolina. Her mother, Anna, died when Florence was young, and she was raised by her father, John, a cabinetmaker and painter, with help from his mother. Her grandmother made a great impression on Florence as she accompanied the woman on her rounds visiting the sick and conducting Bible studies. They attended the local Episcopal church, where Florence experienced her conversion at the age of 13.

Florence Spearing attended public schools in Charleston. She was attending Avery Normal School when, in 1880, her father became ill and she was forced to work as a dressmaker to earn money. Two years later, the 16-year-old Spearing moved north where the pay for dressmakers was considerably higher. She lived first in New York

and then settled in Jersey City, New Jersey. There she met Hugh Randolph, a cook who worked for a railroad. The two were married in 1886 and had one child together.

That same year, Florence Randolph became active at Monmouth Street AMEZ Church. After a period of time as a Sunday school teacher, she attended a Holiness revival meeting and experienced such a strong presence of the spirit that she was rendered unconscious. Randolph began studying under the Reverend E. George Biddle, a Yale scholar and leader of a Holiness movement, and assisted him at meetings. By 1888, her faith was strong enough that she decided to take one work day off each week to do missionary work in the city. In 1892, Randolph also began lecturing and organizing for the Women's Christian Temperance Union.

Some time later, a pastor who was supposed to officiate at a revival meeting became ill. Randolph had no choice but to fill in for him. The meeting was such a success and drew such positive press coverage that her services were soon in great demand. She appeared well-suited to becoming a minister, which was now possible since the AMEZ Church had taken the bold step in 1894 of allowing women to be ordained. A traditionalist who found the notion of women pastors offensive, Randolph refused to consider it until her pastor noted that, technically, she needed a preacher's license to do the kind of public speaking she was already doing. She began to consider ordination, "not that I wanted the honors, nor sought them but pressure was brought to bear by the pastor."

Still leery of taking such a step, Randolph sought divine guidance. After a long, prayerful struggle, she decided that she would consider herself called by God if her dress business failed. When it proceeded to fail soon afterwards, Randolph took up her new career, leaving her home and family. She was licensed to preach in 1897 and began working without a salary. Randolph was ordained a deacon in Atlantic City, New Jersey, in May 1900, and was ordained an elder in 1902.

For the first part of her ministry, Randolph was assigned to small, floundering congregations, beginning with Pennington Street AMEZ Church in Newark, New Jersey, in 1901. From there she moved on to a small church in New York City and then to Poughkeepsie, New York. In each case, as soon as Randolph nurtured the congregation to health, she was reassigned.

Opposition to women pastors was still strong within the church, but Randolph bore the pressure with grace. In 1905, a male observer wrote of her, "In the pulpit, or on the platform, she is always a woman, and when she speaks she has something to say."

Randolph maintained an active role in both church and civic organizations throughout her ministry. She served for 25 years as president of the New Jersey chapter of the Women's Home and Foreign Missionary Society and served as president of the national organization from 1916 to 1920. She presided over the New Jersey State Federation of Colored Women's Clubs, which she helped found in 1915, for 12 years and served as its chaplain for four years. In addition, she maintained a high profile with the Women's Christian Temperance Union. In 1922, Randolph traveled abroad, first speaking in England and then assisting missionaries in West Africa. She returned to the United States with a young African girl for whom she took the responsibility of education.

In 1926, Randolph was rewarded for her long record of accomplishment with the pastorate of Wallace Chapel AMEZ Church, a large congregation in Summit, New Jersey. For 20 years she served as one of the few women pastors entrusted to lead a large congregation in a mainstream denominational church. During her pastorate, Randolph sought to improve her theological understanding by taking courses at the Moody Bible Institute and studying for two terms at Drew Theological Seminary in New Jersey. In 1933, Livingstone College presented her with an honorary doctor of divinity degree, which made her the first African-American woman given such a degree.

Randolph retired from ministry at Wallace Chapel in 1946, and died on December 28, 1951.

Further Reading

Collier-Thomas, Bettye. *Daughters of Thunder: Black Women Preachers and Their Sermons.* San Francisco: Jossey-Bass Publishers, 1998.

Weisenfeld, Judith, and Richard Newman, eds. *This Far by Faith: Readings in African American Women's Religious Biography.* New York: Routledge, 1995.

Ransom, Reverdy Cassius
(1861–1959) *African Methodist Episcopal pastor, bishop, editor*

Reverdy Ransom wielded great influence as a minister in the African Methodist Episcopal Church (AME Church) and as editor of its most prominent periodical, the *AME Review.*

He was born on January 16, 1861, in Flushing, Ohio. His mother, Harriet, the daughter of an ex-slave mother and Native American father, was unwed, and no father came forward to claim responsibility. In 1865, she boarded her son with the parents of George Ransom, in nearby Washington, Ohio, while she worked as a domestic. She eventually married Ransom, who adopted Reverdy.

Harriet Ransom viewed education as the key to success and was determined her son would be learned. In 1869, the family moved to Cambridge, Ohio, a few miles to the west, where Reverdy enrolled in an AME school for black children. By the age of 13 he had completed the school's curriculum and requested to attend the town's white school but was denied. His mother and he bartered laundry and janitorial services in exchange for lessons from private teachers.

Ransom planned to attend Wilberforce College in pursuit of a law career in 1881 after his marriage to Leann Watkins. His wife's pregnancy at this time might have prevented him from going, but his mother took in the child and obtained money for her son to attend school.

In his first year at Wilberforce, Ransom went through a painful divorce and felt stifled by the school's authoritarian, conservative atmosphere. He transferred to Oberlin College in 1882 on a scholarship, which was revoked after he tried to integrate the school's dining hall. Ransom returned to Wilberforce, where he experienced a call that he described as "so vividly clear and impressive as to leave no doubt." He squelched his disagreement with the school's theology and graduated in 1886. Observers regarded his graduation speech as the most inspiring they had ever heard.

Ransom was then assigned to some of the poorest parishes in the AME Church, including one in Altoona, Pennsylvania, that had only 13 members. After four years of struggle, he was called to a larger church in Springfield, Ohio, in 1890. He served there until called to a Cleveland congregation in 1893. There he recognized the importance of urban ministry, and limited his work to large northern cities for the rest of his career. In 1896, he accepted the pastorship at Bethel AME Church in Chicago, where he made a name for himself with social action projects such as the Men's Sunday Club, which worked

with migrant laborers and helped out with Jane Addams's social work at the famous Hull-House. From there he moved on to Charles Street AME in Boston in 1905, where he joined W. E. B. DuBois in opposition to the accomodationist racial strategies of Booker T. Washington. He served there but a short time before moving on to Bethel AME Church in New York City in 1907.

Ransom advocated a nation based on the teachings of Jesus, saying, "There should be no race problem in a Christian state." His independent nature and aggressive social policies often produced friction with AME leadership. Nonetheless, Ransom was so highly regarded nationally that in 1912 he was elected to the job of editor of the *AME Review*. Twelve years later he was elevated to the post of bishop. Ransom retired as bishop in 1952 and died in Wilberforce in 1959.

Further Reading

Burkett, Randall K., and Richard Newman. *Black Apostles: Afro-American Clergy Confront the Twentieth Century*. Boston: G. K. Hall and Company, 1978.

Luker, Ralph E. *The Social Gospel and Black and White*. Chapel Hill: University of North Carolina Press, 1991.

Morris, Calvin S. *Reverdy C. Ransom: Black Advocate of the Social Gospel*. Lanham, Md.: University Press of America, 1990.

Pinn, Anthony, ed. *Making the Gospel Plain: The Writings of Bishop Reverdy C. Ransom*. Harrisburg, Pa.: Trinity Press, 1999.

Revels, Hiram Rhoades

(1827–1901) *African Methodist Episcopal clergy, U.S. senator*

Hiram Revels holds the distinction of being the first black U.S. senator. It was an honor that the dedicated African Methodist Episcopal (AME) minister never sought, but was indicative of the trust he earned during his lifetime of ministry.

Hiram Rhoades Revels was born on September 27, 1827, in Fayetteville, North Carolina, to free parents of mixed African, Scottish, and Native American background. Educational and employment opportunities for blacks were limited in the South in the aftermath of the NAT TURNER rebellion, and Hiram Revels's education was limited to snatches of schooling at private elementary schools. In 1838, he was apprenticed to his older brother, a barber, in Lincolntown, North Carolina. But when his brother suddenly died in 1841, Revels headed north in search of educational opportunities.

After a period of wandering, he found a place at Beech Grove Seminary, a Quaker school in Liberty, Indiana. Revels was no stranger to religion—his father had been a Baptist minister. During his studies he became committed to the idea of becoming a preacher. In 1845, he attended a seminary that admitted blacks, variously listed by historians as being in Drake County, Ohio, or Union County, Indiana, where, at the age of 18, he received his preaching license. Revels then lived in Baltimore, where his preaching attracted a great deal of attention by the time he was ordained an elder in the AME Church in 1849.

Revels spent the next several years as an itinerant preacher, traveling among black congregations in Illinois, Indiana, Kansas, Kentucky, Missouri, and Ohio. Along the way he studied for two years at Knox College in Galesburg, Illinois, where he met his future wife, Phoebe Bass. There were plenty of challenges and problems in store for Revels, both within the church and without. While preaching in Saint Louis in 1853, he fell into a quarrel with AME Bishop DANIEL PAYNE that was so bitter it led Revels to withdraw from the AME Church for several years. He ended up serving at a Presbyterian church until reconciling with Payne two years later. Revels also met with stiff resistance from whites, especially when he preached in slave states. "At times I met with a great deal of opposition," he recalled later in life. "I was imprisoned in Missouri in 1854 for preaching

the gospel to Negroes, though I was never subjected to violence."

In 1857, Revels finally settled into a permanent position as pastor of an AME church and principal of a school for blacks. The onset of the Civil War, however, kindled his activist spirit. Revels recruited two regiments of black troops in Maryland early in the war. Sent by the AME to organize a school for blacks in St. Louis, he recruited another regiment of black volunteers. Not content with that, he joined the Union army as a chaplain, serving a regiment of free black soldiers from Mississippi. The authorities, impressed with his conduct during the war, appointed him provost marshal of the key southern fortress of Vicksburg, Mississippi.

At the war's end, Revels returned to parish ministry, focusing primarily on bringing newly freed slaves into the denominational fold. After briefly serving congregations in Leavenworth, Kansas, and New Orleans, Louisiana, Revels ended up in Natchez, Mississippi, in 1868. His work there as a pastor of a growing AME congregation and founder of a school again impressed political leaders, particularly those of the Republican Party.

Revels found himself drawn into the political arena somewhat against his will because of his trustworthy reputation. In late 1868, the region's military governor appointed him to the Natchez Board of Aldermen. The following year, the Republican Party drafted him as a compromise candidate for state senator when supporters of the two front-running candidates were deadlocked. He opened the legislative session with a prayer so inspiring that author John R. Lynch wrote, "That prayer . . . made Revels a U.S. Senator. He made a profound impression on all who heard him."

One of the tasks of the state senate was to fill the unexpired term of its U.S. senator, Jefferson Davis, former president of the Confederate States of America. Again, despite no effort in pursuing this job, Revels was nominated for the position. Following a heated debate, the legislature elected him on January 20, 1870, by a vote of 81 to 15. Revels's selection as a U.S. senator created indignant opposition in the Senate, where his credentials were immediately challenged. His opponents argued that blacks were not considered citizens in the South prior to passage of the Fourteenth Amendment in 1868. Therefore, Revels had not been a citizen long enough to qualify for the office. Revels's supporters, however, won the argument with another technicality: The citizenship law included an exception for mulattoes, which qualified Revels. On February 25, 1870, following a vote of 48 in favor and eight opposed, Revels took his seat as the nation's first African-American senator.

Hiram Revels, a minister of the African Methodist Episcopal Church, poses for his senate portrait as the first black senator in U.S. history. *(Library of Congress)*

During his term, Revels took a moderate, conciliatory stand on most issues, arguing for amnesty and the restoration of full citizenship for former Confederate soldiers. While he made some eloquent pleas in favor of equal rights for blacks, he was not fully accepted by all Senate members and was unable to get any of his legislative proposals passed. His major accomplishment was using his senate office to get blacks jobs in the previously whites-only U.S. Navy Yard.

Revels's term lasted only until March 3, 1871. He returned home to Mississippi and accepted a job as president of the new Alcorn A & M University, the first land-grant college for African Americans in the United States. He continued to serve in a political capacity, taking over as Mississippi's interim secretary of state in 1873. He became disgruntled with the Republican Party at that time, particularly the governor, and resigned before the governor could fire him. Revels further alienated his former party by campaigning for Democrats in 1875 and testifying on their behalf in election inquiries. The Democrats rewarded him by reappointing him to his previous post when they took over the statehouse in 1876. However, the backlash against Revels was so severe that he was forced to surrender his pastorate in Holly Springs, Mississippi.

Revels served as secretary of state until his retirement in 1882. He remained active, however, as the editor of the *Southwestern Christian Advocate*, and taught theology courses at Shaw College in Holly Springs. He died while attending a church conference in Aberdeen, Mississippi, on January 16, 1901.

Further Reading

Haskins, Jim. *Distinguished African-American Political and Government Leaders.* Phoenix, Ariz.: Oryx Press, 1999.

Montgomery, William E. *Under Their Own Vine and Fig Tree: The African-American Church in the South, 1865–1900.* Baton Rouge: Louisiana State University Press, 1993.

S

Seal, Catherine
(Catherine Seals, Nanny Cowans)
(ca. 1874–1930) *cult leader*

Despite her illiteracy, Catherine Seal (some-times spelled Seals) founded and controlled one of the largest religious cults in the United States during the 1920s. Her interracial Church of the Innocent Blood was particularly popular among women of the New Orleans area.

She was born Nanny Cowans in Hustonville, Kentucky, on a date variously cited as anywhere from 1874 to 1887. Her birth mother is not recorded; apparently she was raised by her father, Bill Cowans, and her stepmother Lue Cowans. It does not appear that Nanny ever attended school before arriving in New Orleans at the age of 16. She married three times, taking her last name from one of her husbands, although the circumstances of the change from Nanny to Catherine are unclear.

Her call to the ministry came as a result of physical abuse by her third husband. In severe pain and partially paralyzed on one side after being kicked in the stomach, Seal sought relief from a white faith healer. The man, however, refused to heal a "colored" person. Seal limped away, pleading, "Sweet Jesus, help me! Only give me the power to heal and I'll help colored and white just the same."

Eventually her health improved and Seal embarked on her mission of healing. As word of her powers spread, she left her job as a cook in 1922, and founded the Church of the Innocent Blood. She attended classes taught by the famed New Orleans spiritualist LEAFY ANDERSON, but her refusal to abide by a dress code caused a permanent rift between them.

Seal's message, which she claimed was inspired by the Holy Spirit, was a mixture of mysticism, compassion, and parts of the Biblical message she had gleaned from others over the years. She had a remarkable ability to transcend race and soon attracted thousands of followers, both black and white. Her special focus was on caring for unmarried pregnant women. She placed a high value on life and preventing abortions, and little value on male involvement in the family process. A feminist well before her time, she believed that women naturally made better leaders.

From 1923 to 1928, Seal spoke to huge crowds in the streets of New Orleans, to the increasing irritation of the authorities. Concerned that police harassment would lead to an incident that would damage her movement, Seal relocated her operations to an out-of-the-way spot on the edge of town. There she began constructing a building that was a combination church, refuge, and hospital for pregnant women, as well as a personal residence. Completed on January 4, 1930, the red-roofed building was dominated by a raised platform at its center. On this platform was the bed and chair on which Seal slept in full view of her congregation. According to one observer, "Catherine of Russia would not have been more impressive on her throne than was this black Catherine sitting upon an ordinary chair at the edge of the platform." Seal had a flair for the dramatic, choosing to make her entrance into the church through a hole in the roof of a side room.

Although she came to regard herself as divine, Seal's health failed in the summer of 1930. On August 11, only seven months after the completion of her building, Seal died. Her successors were unable to match her charisma, and the Church of the Innocent Blood quickly faded away.

Further Reading

Smith, Jesse Carney, ed. *Notable Black American Women.* Vol. 2. Detroit, Mich.: Gale Research, 1996.

Smith, Michael Proctor. *Spirit World: Patterns in Expressive Folk Culture of African Americans in New Orleans.* Gretna, La.: Pelican, 1992.

Seymour, William Joseph
(1870–1922) *founder, Pentecostal movement*

William J. Seymour is proof that the power of religious conviction can take the most unassuming person and use him to transform literally millions of people. The tiny church Seymour founded in Los Angeles shook the city like an earthquake at the turn of the 20th century. Although the church lasted but a few decades, the Pentecostal movement that arose from Seymour's work has produced the fastest-growing religious denominations in the United States.

Seymour was born on May 2, 1870, in Centerville, Louisiana, to former slaves Simon and Phillis Seymour. Little is known of his early life, other than that he was raised Baptist and experienced dreams and visions at an early age. Eventually, he settled in Indianapolis, Indiana, where he found work as a waiter at an upscale restaurant.

Somewhat unsettled religiously, he switched from his Baptist roots to the African Methodist Episcopal Church (AME Church) in Indianapolis. Around 1900, he then joined the Church of God one of the Holiness denominations that emphasized sanctification of the believer through the activity of the Holy Spirit. At about this time, Seymour contracted a severe case of smallpox that cost him his left eye. This experience caused him to reflect further on his religious situation and he concluded that he was meant to be a preacher. Seymour obtained his preaching license and was ordained as a minister of a small Holiness church known as the Evening Lights Saints.

In 1903, Seymour moved to Houston, Texas, where he pastored another small Holiness church. There, two years later, he encountered Charles Fox Parham, a Methodist preacher who was the dynamic leader of the fledgling Pentecostal movement. After having been dramatically healed from an invalid state, Parham had founded a small Bible school in Topeka, Kansas, which emphasized speaking in tongues as "initial evidence" of having received baptism through the Holy Spirit. Encouraged by a pastor from Houston who had attended his school, Parham had recently moved his school to Houston. Seymour was one of 60 preachers who enrolled at the new school.

Parham's doctrine was accepting of all races, but southeast Texas was not. In order to mollify a community that would not abide blacks and whites learning together in a classroom, Seymour had to sit in a hall and listen to Parham's teachings through the doorway. He became an enthusiastic supporter of Parham's views on the Holy Spirit.

At the school, Seymour met Neely Terry, a young woman pastor of a black Holiness church, the Church of the Nazarene, in Los Angeles, that was looking for a new associate pastor. She was so impressed with Seymour that she encouraged her church to extend him a call. The church did, and Seymour accepted, with assistance from Parham, who helped him raise the money to make the trip.

The church got far more than it bargained for. Seymour preached his first sermon using Acts 2:4, "Anyone who does not speak in tongues is not baptized with the Holy Spirit," as his text. His assertion that his parishioners had not received the Holy Spirit upset the congregation, which accused him of spreading false doctrine. They not only asked him to leave but barred the doors against his return.

At this point, Seymour did not have the means to return home. But a few sympathetic congregation members, together with some Baptists, asked him to conduct prayer meetings in their homes. At one of these meetings in early April 1906, the group experienced an intense influx of the Holy Spirit; in the words of participating members, "the fire came down." The first to receive the gift of speaking in tongues was an eight-year-old boy, followed by several other members.

News of this experience spread and brought a large crowd to a revival meeting on the front porch of Richard Asberry's home. The enthusiasm of the mixed black and white crowd crescendoed into outbursts of ecstasy. According to reports, "They shouted until the foundation of the house gave way, but no one was hurt." There were reports that Jennie Moore, who would eventually become Seymour's wife, "spoke in tongues and then went to the piano and for the first time in her life began to play beautiful music and sing in an unknown, beautiful language."

The collapsed house incident demonstrated the need for a larger, permanent place to conduct services. Seymour and his followers found such a place, an old, two-story AME church at 312 Azusa Street that had been converted into a

William Seymour touched off one of the greatest religious explosions of the 20th century when he transformed the Azusa Street Mission into a house of spiritual fervor. *(Flower Pentecostal Heritage Center)*

stable and warehouse, now partially gutted by fire, surrounded by a lumberyard and a tombstone factory. They cleaned up the broken glass and debris and, using planks set upon empty nail kegs, began to worship there.

Services at the Azusa Street Mission began on April 14, 1906. Word had spread of miraculous happenings among Seymour's group: conversions, speaking in tongues, healings, and inexplicable acquisitions of gifts. According to observers, "Men and women would shout, weep, dance, fall into trances, speak and sing in tongues and interpret messages in English."

Thousands of people tried to cram into the small building to learn what this dynamic church group was all about. The Azusa Street Mission became a whirlwind of activity, with three services a day, seven days a week, the first starting at 10 A.M. and the last often continuing past midnight. Day after day, the church was swamped with seekers of religious fervor, the curious, skeptics, and even laborers on their lunch hour.

Seymour's church drew plenty of criticism. Newspapers published cynical reports of the "wild scenes" going on. Some of the city's Holiness churches denounced Seymour as an "instrument of Satan." But such reports only fanned the flames of curiosity. And many witnesses attested to the extraordinary power of Seymour's church. One visitor, A. G. Osterberg, reported, "I am witness to the fact that the Holy Spirit can and does make folk sing who otherwise cannot sing."

As the Azusa Street Mission's fame spread, thousands of fervent Christians from throughout the United States and foreign lands traveled on pilgrimages to Los Angeles to witness for themselves what was happening. Along with intense enthusiasm, they discovered a church that was completely color-blind regarding race. Here was one of the few places in the world where African Americans from the inner city could worship alongside whites. As one participant observed,

"The color line has been washed away by the blood (of Christ)."

In contrast to the flamboyant church over which he presided, Seymour was a quiet, humble man with no pretensions of personal glory. He was a restrained preacher who emphasized teaching. His leadership was open and relaxed, encouraging his people to follow where the Spirit led them. Seymour continued to regard himself as a student of Parham, and, as the burden of shepherding the huge numbers of people worshiping at Azusa Street began to overwhelm him, he wrote to Parham, asking him to come out and oversee the situation.

When Parham arrived in October 1906, however, he was distressed by the frenzied activity. He preached a few times and tried to instruct Seymour in some matters of procedure and doctrine. Seymour, however, believed that the Holy Spirit was guiding the mission in all things, and he refused to accept Parham's teachings. Parham then urged Seymour to resign, at which time Seymour broke with him completely and informed Parham that he was no longer welcome at the church. Seymour incorporated his ministry that year as the entirely independent Pacific Apostolic Faith Movement.

The Azusa Street Mission enjoyed a spectacular but brief period of success. By the end of its first year, it had spawned nine Pentecostal assemblies in the Los Angeles areas. But problems began appearing on several fronts in 1908. According to one member, the mission's reputation brought "all the religious sore-heads and crooks and cranks, seeking a place in the work. We had the most to fear from these." Racial unity also began to disintegrate under the discomfort of whites who denigrated the proceedings at Azusa Street as "disgustingly similar to Southern darkey camp meetings." By 1908, whites began leaving Seymour's mission. Within six years, it was almost exclusively black, which undercut its appeal as a beacon of interracial harmony. Among those whites who left were influential backers Clara Lunn and Florence Crawford, who confiscated Seymour's entire mailing list upon leaving. Unable to communicate with his members, Seymour saw his congregation gradually slip into disorganization.

Seymour continued to lead his declining Azusa Street Mission while also traveling across the country leading revival campaigns, until his death on September 28, 1922. His wife, Jenny, (whom he had married in 1908) attempted to continue his work, but the mission closed its doors in 1923. After her death in 1936, it was sold and torn down to make room for a parking lot.

While his own church disappeared and he has been largely ignored by historians, the movement Seymour started spread widely. Due to the evolved nature of the Azusa Street Mission, most people came to regard the Pentecostal movement as a black movement, and today most Pentecostals are African American. But Seymour's movement also inspired visitors such as William H. Durham, who went on to found the Assembly of God Movement in 1914 and who has written, "Practically every early Pentecostal movement in the world can trace its origins directly or indirectly to Seymour's Azusa Street Mission."

Further Reading

Burgess, Stanley M., et al., eds. *Dictionary of Pentecostal and Charismatic Movements.* Grand Rapids, Mich.: Zondervan, 1988.

Burkett, Randall K., and Richard Newman. *Black Apostles: Afro-American Clergy Confront the Twentieth Century.* Boston: G. K. Hall and Company, 1978.

Durasoff, Steve. *Bright Wind of the Spirit: Pentecostalism Today.* Englewood Cliffs, N.J.: Prentice Hall, 1972.

Melton, J. Gordon, ed. *Biographical Dictionary of American Cult and Sect Leaders.* New York: Garland, 1986.

Paris, Arthur. *Black Pentecostalism: Southern Religion in an Urban World.* Amherst: University of Massachusetts Press, 1982.

Synan, Vinson. *The Holiness-Pentecostal Tradition.* Grand Rapids, Mich.: Eerdmans, 1997.

Tucker, David M. *Black Pastors and Leaders.* Memphis, Tenn.: Memphis State University Press, 1975.

Sharpton, Al
(Alfred Charles Sharpton, Jr.)
(1954–   ) *Pentecostal minister, Baptist clergy, political activist*

Once dismissed by a majority of the public as merely a publicity seeker, Al Sharpton has matured into one of the most influential African-American leaders of the late 20th and early 21st centuries. A devoted follower of MARTIN LUTHER KING, JR., and JESSE LOUIS JACKSON, Sharpton assumed their mantle as a champion of the poor and oppressed in society.

He was born Alfred Charles Sharpton, Jr., in Brooklyn, New York, on October 3, 1954, the son of Alfred, Sr., and Ada Sharpton. His father was a carpenter and contractor who became so successful that he moved the family to a 10-room house in Queens shortly after Al, Jr.'s, birth, and traded in his Cadillac for a new one every year.

Sharpton's early life was centered on religion. The family were active members of Washington Temple Church of God in Brooklyn. Young Al was so interested in religious matters that he was preaching sermons before he could read and write. When he did learn those skills, he began reading the Bible in his spare time. By the age of nine he was preaching so often and so well that he was tagged "the Wonder Boy Preacher." That year he joined the tour of famed gospel singer MAHALIA JACKSON, where he preached a sermon during intermission. At the age of 10, Sharpton was a fully ordained Pentecostal minister.

The same year, however, Sharpton's life was shattered when his father suddenly abandoned the family. Left with little money or income, his mother moved back to Brooklyn, supporting the family as best she could as a seamstress and later as a machinist. Sharpton and his family lived for a year in a housing project before moving into a rundown apartment. The sudden plunge from affluence to poverty gave Sharpton a unique perspective on living among the underclass, one far different from many of his neighbors, who had no expectations of a life different from the one they were living. "In the project, I thought, 'No, I don't have to accept this,'" remembers Sharpton. "'I know there is a better life.'"

Almost immediately, he became politically active. At the age of 12 he was recruited as a youth leader in the Civil Rights movement. Sharpton fell under the influence of a variety of activists including ADAM CLAYTON POWELL, JR., Martin Luther King, Jr., and eventually Jesse Jackson, whom he came to admire as a father figure. In 1968, Sharpton took on the role of youth coordinator of civil rights leader James Farmer's unsuccessful run for Congress in Brooklyn. A year later, he was recruited by Jackson's organization to serve as youth director of the New York City branch of Operation Breadbasket. In 1970, Sharpton founded his own political organization, the National Youth Movement. As further evidence of his leadership skills, he was elected student council president at Tilden High School. Upon graduation in 1972, he accepted the position of youth director for the presidential campaign of black congresswoman Shirley Chisholm.

Along the way, he became friends with soul music legend James Brown, and the lure of celebrity drew him away from politics in 1973. Sharpton became Brown's protégé and assistant, promoting his tours and arranging his schedule. The two became so close that Sharpton adopted Brown's wavy hairstyle as a pledge of solidarity. He also married one of Brown's backup singers, Kathy Jordan, with whom he had two daughters.

The onetime boy preacher remained out of the public eye until the mid-1980s, when he served as a community relations adviser for Jesse Jackson's presidential campaign. Sharpton first achieved national attention for his involvement in inquiries into the death of Michael Griffith, a black construction worker who was chased onto a freeway in Queens, New York, by a group of whites and killed by a car on December 20, 1986. During the trial a year later, the whites were convicted only of manslaughter. Sharpton orchestrated a protest that tied up traffic in New York City for hours, rallying crowds under the slogan "No Justice, No Peace."

Shortly thereafter, a black teenage girl charged that she had been abducted and raped by a group of whites. Sharpton served as spokesman for the girl's family and offered the media numerous unsubstantiated, sensational charges claiming a massive cover-up by government authorities. His credibility took a severe hit from what the press regarded as showboating, particularly when a grand jury declared the story to be a hoax in October 1988.

Sharpton's image suffered further from revelations that he had been an informant for the Federal Bureau of Investigation in drug cases that targeted blacks in the mid-1980s, from charges of income tax evasion that were settled when he pled guilty to a lesser charge, and from strident accusations questioning the integrity of a white female jogger who was beaten severely by black youths in 1990. As a result, a *New York Daily News* poll conducted in 1990 found that 90 percent of whites and 73 percent of blacks believed that Sharpton was a negative influence on race relations. Despite such low trust among voters, Sharpton ran for U.S. Senate in the 1992 Democratic primary. He was defeated handily.

In 1991, Sharpton was stabbed in the chest while leading a demonstration in a schoolyard in Bensonhurst, Brooklyn, protesting the racially motivated murder of Yusuf Hawkins. According to Sharpton, the stark confrontation with lethal hatred caused him to take stock of himself. He began to wonder if some of his statements had contributed to an environment of hatred rather than the social justice message of King and Jackson that he had hoped to emulate. He came to the conclusion that he had allowed himself to be distracted by the trappings of celebrity. "I realized I was nowhere near being the person that I would want to be," Sharpton admitted.

Sharpton then backed off from the political scene for a time. In February 1994, he was rebaptized into the Baptist faith and began to spend more of his time preaching. But social activism was in his blood. A photograph of King and Jackson taken the day before King's assassination stood in his office, reminding him of the seriousness of the fight for equality and freedom. As a result, he returned as a champion of the rights of the powerless in a series of highly publicized episodes of alleged police brutality against blacks in New York City, and in drawing attention to slavery rings operating in the Sudan. Sharpton, however, had changed considerably from his early days. He shed 100 pounds, and appeared in public in a suit and tie, rather than baggy sweat suits and gold medallions.

Sharpton has received the National Action Network Award for keeping the legacy of Jackson and King alive. He remains one of the most prominent black activists in the nation, is frequently mentioned as a potential political candidate, and campaigned for the 2004 Democratic presidential nomination.

Further Reading

Chappell, Kevin. "The New Al Sharpton." *Ebony,* July 2001, pp. 124–129.

Graham, Judith, ed. *Current Biography Yearbook, 1995.* New York: H. W. Wilson, 1995.

Mitchell-Powell, Brenda. *African American Biography.* Vol. 4. Detroit, Mich.: Gale, 1994.

Newfield, Jack. "An Interview with Al Sharpton." *Tikkun,* July 1998, pp. 22–24.

Shuttlesworth, Fred
(1922–   ) *Baptist pastor, civil rights leader*

Utterly fearless in the face of threats, intimidation, and violence, Fred Shuttlesworth was the most outspoken and action-oriented leader in the Civil Rights movement of the 1950s and early 1960s. Although largely unheralded today, Shuttlesworth provided the dynamic leadership that ensured the success of the famous campaign against segregation in Birmingham in 1962.

Shuttlesworth was born on March 18, 1922, in Mugler, Alabama, and grew up near the city of Birmingham. He attended Selma College, where he received a B.A. degree, and Alabama State University, where he earned a B.S. degree. Shuttlesworth became a Baptist preacher in 1949, serving two rural churches in the Selma, Alabama, area. In 1953, he became the pastor at Bethel Baptist in Birmingham, Alabama, and it was there that he made plans to meet segregation head on. In the words of one contemporary, "He would willingly stride into an arena jam-packed with hungry lions if he knew the lions believed in segregation."

Shuttlesworth's first efforts accomplished little. He made an unsuccessful attempt to urge the city to hire more blacks on the police force. When, in an effort to build his political strength, he joined the National Association for the Advancement of Colored People (NAACP), Alabama outlawed the organization. Undaunted, he helped found an alternative group called the Alabama Christian Movement for Human Rights (ACMHR) in 1956, and served as its president.

Shuttlesworth's willingness to stand out made him a prime target of racists. After he called for an end to segregated seating on the city's buses in December 1956, his home was blown up with dynamite. Undaunted, he showed up to lead a group of 20 blacks who took "white" seats on buses and was arrested. Shuttlesworth forced the issue into the courts, where it lingered for years. It was not until November 1961 that a federal court finally ordered the desegregation of the buses. In the meantime, Shuttlesworth attempted to integrate the schools by enrolling four black students, including two of his children, at a white high school in Birmingham in September 1957. Shuttlesworth was attacked by a mob and beaten, and the children were refused entrance.

Fred Shuttlesworth's raw courage and tenacity as a Birmingham pastor made him the unsung hero of the Civil Rights movement. *(Birmingham Public Library Department of Archives and Manuscripts)*

That same year he joined with several other Alabama clergymen, including MARTIN LUTHER KING, JR., to plan a more effective campaign for integration. All of them agreed that the best solution was a nonviolent strategy of confronting hatred and bigotry and getting them out in the open. Once that happened, they believed, the conscience of the American people would not allow the injustice to continue. They believed that the best way to accomplish this was with an organization that was both Christian and led by African Americans. To that end, they formed the Southern Christian Leadership Conference (SCLC), with King as president and Shuttlesworth as secretary.

A man of action, Shuttlesworth often grew impatient with the strategizing and discussions of his associates. "A rattlesnake don't commit suicide and ball teams don't put themselves out," he declared. "You got to put them out." He kept up the pressure on segregationists by helping organize student sit-ins at segregated institutions in 1960, for which he was again arrested. That same year, he was called to Revelation Baptist Church in Cincinnati, Ohio. The call out would have been a convenient excuse for Shuttlesworth to take a break from danger and hardship, but he returned frequently to the South and took a leadership role in the Freedom Riders, a group of blacks and whites who rode interstate buses together in an attempt to desegregate them. The Freedom Riders were frequent victims of vicious attacks. At one point, concerned about Shuttlesworth's safety, U.S. Attorney General Robert Kennedy urged him to stay away. "Mr. Kennedy, don't you know I'm a battlefield general?" replied Shuttlesworth. "I lead my troops into battle." Nonetheless, he believes that Kennedy arranged his arrest in May 1962 to prevent him from being killed.

At about that time, Shuttlesworth suggested that the ACMHR and the SCLC join forces in a major civil rights demonstration. He suggested Birmingham, often described as the most segregated city in the South, as a target. If they could force a confrontation and win concessions there, it would be a major symbolic victory for the movement. SCLC officials agreed, largely because they knew they could count on Shuttlesworth to make arrangements for a well-run campaign in that city. When Birmingham merchants learned what was being planned, they approached Shuttlesworth to work out a deal to avoid bad publicity. The merchants agreed to desegregate water fountains and rest rooms, but their negotiations were thwarted by police chief Theophilus Eugene "Bull" Connor, who threatened to arrest anyone who accommodated the agitators. The demonstration went on, with Shuttlesworth vowing to fill up the jails if necessary. At one point, in fact, more than 4,000 demonstrators were locked up. But as SCLC leaders predicted, Connor's vicious response to the peaceful demonstrators, aired on national television, produced a groundswell of sympathy for the Civil Rights movement. In one of the landmark achievements of the SCLC, Birmingham officials ended up making meaningful concessions toward dismantling public discrimination.

Shuttlesworth continued to find active ways to fight discrimination. He directed a nonviolent training center in Birmingham in the early 1960s. In the summer of 1964, he was arrested while marching for integration in Saint Augustine, Florida. The following year he helped organize the highly publicized Selma-Montgomery march to end discrimination in voting. Altogether, from 1958 to 1969, he took part in 10 civil rights challenges that went before the U.S. Supreme Court.

During this activity, Shuttlesworth's opponents attacked him on another front. He was accused of misappropriation of funds and tyrannical behavior at his Cincinnati church. Shuttlesworth believed it was part of a broad effort to discredit civil rights leaders. In the end

he resigned from the church, but several hundred of his supporters formed a new church and called him to be pastor of it.

In 1970, at the age of 58, Shuttlesworth stepped down from leadership in the ACMHR and the SCLC, although he remained active in civil rights causes. He remembers the turbulent years of the 1950s and 1960s as being dangerous, yet exhilarating. "It was thrilling, in that you were challenging the system, and you knew something had to move," he said. "We knew that God was with us, because you take the religion out of it, it would be nothing."

Further Reading

Fairclough, Adam. *To Redeem the Soul of America: The SCLC and Martin Luther King, Jr.* Athens: University of Georgia Press, 1987.

Manis, Andrew M. "Birmingham's Fred Shuttlesworth: Unsung Hero of the Civil Rights Movement." *Baptist History and Heritage* (summer-fall 2000): 67–78.

Powledge, Fred. *Free At Last? The Civil Rights Movement and the People Who Made It.* Boston: Little, Brown, 1991.

Skinner, Tom
(1942–1994) *Baptist evangelist*

Tom Skinner made a remarkable transformation from the leader of one of Harlem's most violent gangs to a passionate evangelist. Through his radio ministry, numerous outreach programs, and high-profile service as an informal chaplain to professional sports teams, he has made an impact on the lives of thousands.

Skinner was born in the Harlem neighborhood of New York City during a World War II air raid drill on June 6, 1942. He was the oldest of five children of Alester and Georgia Skinner. Alester Skinner was a highly educated Baptist minister with more of an intellectual apprecia-

Tom Skinner rose from the Harlem ghetto to become a dynamic religious speaker. *(Billy Graham Center)*

tion of the Bible than faith in its central message. He insisted that his children educate themselves, telling them that in order to make it in the world, they had to be twice as good as whites. He assigned them a list of 100 books to read by the age of 16, which Tom Skinner completed well ahead of time. Georgia Skinner, despite having only a fourth-grade education, provided the boy with his strongest spiritual support.

Skinner appeared on the surface to be a model child. He was active in church, did well in school, and excelled at sports, with Jackie Robinson as his idol. But inside, he rebelled against his status as a preacher's son. Under the influence of black nationalists who argued that

Christianity was nothing but a sham to keep African Americans in line, he dismissed his father's work entirely. The Christian message of hope and forgiveness seemed completely out of place in a crowded, rat-infested, crime-ridden neighborhood in which, by the age of three, he had seen a man stabbed to death. "I could not reconcile the things I was hearing in church with what was going on in the street."

Skinner drifted into bad company and by the age of 15 was the leader of the Harlem Lords, one of the most notorious gangs in the area. One night he was plotting strategy for a major rumble involving five other gangs, when an unscheduled program came over the radio station to which he was listening. A man began reading from the Bible, in II Corinthians, where it spoke of sin being an absence of God in one's life. Skinner was surprised by what he was hearing. It was the first time he had heard that sin was not something a person did, but something that a person was. He tried to dismiss what he heard, but then was drawn to the promise of God that any person who comes to Christ will not be rejected. Skinner decided that he was living in sin, completely apart from God. He found himself praying and, as he remembered, "That night Jesus Christ did take over my life."

Skinner went to his gang the next day and told them that he had made a commitment to Christ and could no longer be part of the gang. The gang was so stunned that none of them made a move to stop him as he walked away. Skinner became involved with an informal Christian study and discussion group. He renewed his efforts in school and in sports, making all-city teams in football, baseball, and fencing. One youth conference took him to Kansas City, where he met MARTIN LUTHER KING, JR., and committed himself to working for the cause of civil rights.

Skinner graduated from high school in 1959 and on June 2, 1959, was ordained as a minister by the United Missionary Baptist Association. He went on to attend Wagner College in Staten Island, New York, where he starred in three sports and majored in history and philosophy. While still a student in October 1961, he helped found the Harlem Evangelism Association. During the summer of 1962, this group organized the largest evangelism crusade in the history of New York.

After completing his degree at Wagner, Skinner attended the Manhattan Bible Institute. While he was there, he took his message to the airways, forming a corporation called the Tom Skinner Radio Crusades. Skinner finished his studies at Manhattan Bible Institute in 1966, and threw himself into his ministry, which he renamed the Tom Skinner Crusades to better reflect the multiple programs that he initiated. He preached his gospel message in various crusades around the country, often joining forces with white evangelists such as Billy Graham in an attempt to help form a bridge between the black and white communities. He also became involved in a ministry aimed at college students, in giving motivational speeches and sermons, and in working as a consultant on community development projects.

In the late 1960s, Skinner's interest in sports opened a new door for his ministry. He began serving as a volunteer team chaplain for several professional sports teams, most notably the Washington Redskins of the National Football League, with whom he worked for a dozen years. Skinner was a leader in cultivating outspoken testimonies of faith and in the evangelical organizing of professional athletes, particularly among football teams.

Skinner's message of faith in Jesus did not ignore the racial inequities of society. He wrote a number of hard-hitting books in the late 1960s and early 1970s that explored the subject of race in the context of Christianity, including *Black and Free* (1968), *Words of Revolution* (1970), and *How Black Is the Gospel?* (1970). He spoke so aggressively for civil rights, in fact, that his radio program was dropped by a major station in 1971 for being too political.

In 1976, he moved his organization, now known as Tom Skinner Associates, to East Orange, New Jersey. Continuing to expand his ministry into new areas of need, he founded the Tom Skinner Associates Learning Center for spiritual and vocational guidance, in Newark, New Jersey. Despite a life lived primarily in the inner city, he opened the Skinner Farm Leadership Institute in Maryland in 1992. Skinner died of leukemia in Norfolk, Virginia, on June 17, 1994.

Further Reading

Galbreath, Edward. "A Prophet Out of Harlem: Willing to Tell the Hard Truth; Evangelist Tom Skinner Represents a Generation of Christian Leaders." *Christianity Today*, September 16, 1996, 36–43.

Murphy, Larry G., ed. *Encyclopedia of African American Religious Biography.* New York: Garland Publishing, 1993.

Skinner, Tom. *Black and Free.* Grand Rapids, Mich.: Zondervan, 1968.

———. *How Black Is the Gospel?* Philadelphia: Lippincott, 1970.

Smith, Amanda Berry
(1837–1915) *mission leader*

Amanda Berry Smith was one of the leaders of the influential Holiness movement that sprang up in the United States in the late 19th century. Dubbed "the Singing Pilgrim," she was a world-famous evangelist and missionary who inspired with her spoken message and her published autobiography.

She was born Amanda Berry on January 23, 1837, in Long Green, Maryland, near Baltimore.

Her parents, Samuel and Marion Berry, were slaves on adjacent farms. Samuel was a favorite of his master's daughter, who extracted a promise from her parents on her deathbed that they would allow him to buy his freedom and that of his family. Earning money by staying up late and making brooms and mats for sale, he purchased their freedom in 1840. Eventually the Berry family moved to a farm in York County, Pennsylvania. Their home became a station on the Underground Railroad.

Both parents were literate. On Sunday mornings, Samuel read the Bible to the family. Although Amanda received virtually no formal education, her parents taught her to read. But the difficulty of providing for a large family forced her to begin working as a domestic at the age of 13. Four years later, in September 1854, she married Calvin Devine and joined him at his home in Columbia, Pennsylvania. Unfortunately, the marriage was difficult, and the two were already separated by the time Devine died fighting in the Union army during the Civil War.

A short time later, she married James Henry Smith, an ordained deacon at the historic Bethel African Methodist Episcopal Church in Philadelphia, who was 20 years her senior. The couple moved to New York City in 1868, where Smith earned money by taking in laundry. That year she happened to visit a church where a preacher gave a sermon on the doctrine of sanctification—the receiving of a second blessing of the Holy Spirit.

The message inspired Smith, who had been a faithful Christian for many years. She was frustrated by her husband's lack of interest in her new conviction, despite his status as a deacon. But he died of cancer in 1869, and a year later Smith experienced a blessing of sanctification that changed her life. While attending a Brooklyn revival in 1870, she beheld a vision and a voice telling her to preach. In November of that year, she was called upon by a minister to give a

sermon before a standing-room-only crowd at a revival, a task that frightened her terribly. As she later testified, she leaned on the Lord for strength and discovered that her beautiful singing voice, together with her passionate conviction, moved her listeners in a way that they had never previously experienced.

Smith began traveling and preaching at revivals, an activity that met with resistance from the men in her African Methodist Episcopal (AME) denomination. When they questioned the appropriateness of a woman preacher and disparaged her lack of education and ordination, she replied that she had received her ordination from God. Although Smith was discouraged from attending, she spent much of her savings traveling to the AME convention in 1872. There she heard from several missionaries about the church's activities overseas and the need for more dedicated missionaries. Smith was convinced that she did not have the education or the intelligence to perform such a task herself. Instead, she began training her daughter Mazie, the only one of her five children to survive to adulthood, for the task. However, after six years of intensive instruction for the task, Mazie fell in love with a young man and decided to get married rather than be a missionary.

In the meantime, Smith had been one of the founding members of the Woman's Christian Temperance Union, organized in 1874. The group's national secretary asked her to come to England to join a revival it was sponsoring. Smith did so, and soon won crowds with her magnetic personality and captivating voice. Her fame spread as the group moved on to France and Italy. This success convinced Smith that she could handle mission work, and in 1879 she agreed to travel to India on another revival tour. Again, her preaching and singing were highly successful.

After a brief period of recovery in the United States, Smith finally realized a life-long dream by sailing to Africa as a missionary. She was a thoroughly Americanized Christian with little regard for ancient traditions or other cultural viewpoints. In her mind, the Christian basis of western civilization made it superior to all others. Yet there was an element of the emotional intensity that her ancestors had carried with them from Africa that appealed to her. "May God save us from the formalism of the day, and bring us back to the old time spirituality and power of the fathers and mothers," she once wrote. Smith's efforts in Africa, primarily in Liberia, won the admiration of the African bishop, William Taylor, who claimed that she had a far greater impact on African lives in her eight years of service than all the previous missionaries combined.

After a brief stopover in England, Smith returned to the United States in 1890. She spent the next several years working on her autobiography, which was published in 1893, and establishing a newspaper called *The Helper*, which promoted her Holiness spirituality. Wanting to produce something of a lasting nature, she relocated to Chicago and spent all of her earnings from the book and the newspaper in establishing a home for orphans. The Amanda Smith Industrial Home opened in 1899 in Harvey, Illinois, as the only Protestant-run home for black children in the state. Smith worked diligently to keep the home functioning despite constant financial shortages until deteriorating health forced her to retire to Sebring, Florida, in 1912. She suffered a stroke and died on February 24, 1915.

Smith was therefore unaware that her legacy was not tied up in the orphanage, which burned down in 1918. Rather, it was her work in promoting the Holiness doctrine of sanctification that lived on. Smith had the uncanny ability to appeal to people of various races and both genders. Her autobiography was one of the key influences in steering CHARLES HARRISON MASON into his brand of Holiness theology that culminated in the founding of the Church of God in Christ. In the words of one contempo-

The Christian witness of missionary Amanda Berry Smith profoundly influenced the black Pentecostal movement that developed at the end of the 19th century. *(Courtesy of the Illinois State Historical Library)*

rary, "She was not only a woman of faith . . . she possessed a clearness of vision which I have seldom found equaled."

Further Reading

Loewenberg, Bert James, and Ruth Bogues. *Black Women in Nineteenth Century American Life: Their Words, Their Thoughts, Their Feelings.* University Park: Pennsylvania State University Press, 1976.

Smith, Amanda B. *The Story of the Lord's Dealings with Mrs. Amanda Smith, the Colored Evangelist.* 1893. Reprint, Northbrook, Ill.: Metro Books, 1969.

Sernett, Milton, ed. *African-American Religious History: A Documentary Witness.* Durham, N.C.: Duke University Press, 1999.

Smith, Lucy
(1874–1952) *faith healer*

Lucy Smith was perhaps the best known of the black Holiness preachers who attracted large congregations from among the rural blacks who migrated from the South to the northern cities in the early part of the century.

She was born on January 14, 1874, on a plantation near Woodstock, Georgia. She never knew her father, and grew up in severe poverty with her mother and five siblings in a tiny one-room cabin. The necessities of survival forced her to begin working in the fields at an early age. Not until she was 13 did she first step into a schoolhouse, and then for only four months out of the year.

She continued the farming life after marrying William Smith in 1896, and after bearing nine children. In 1908, she and her husband finally gave up trying to scratch a living off the farm and moved to Athens, Georgia. William Smith could not handle the adjustment and abandoned his wife within a year, leaving Lucy Smith with a huge family to support by herself. She moved to Atlanta in 1909 and then joined a large migration of rural Southern blacks to Chicago in 1910, supporting her family by sewing dresses.

An active member of the Baptist church since the age of 12, Smith joined Olivet Baptist Church shortly after moving to Chicago. She switched to Ebenezer Baptist in 1912 and then began drifting into the Holiness/Pentecostal movement, where black women who felt the call to preach found a much more receptive audience. Despite her churchgoing background, she claimed that, in 1914, "I received my baptism and came in to the works of the Lord." After spending time at the Stone Church, a white Pentecostal congregation, she began prayer meetings in her house in 1916.

The more emotional, demonstrative Holiness style of religion had great appeal to the masses of homesick southern blacks who had grown up with that tradition rather than the more staid mainstream denominational style. After three years of home preaching and healing, Smith needed larger buildings to accommodate her followers. In 1926, after moving around from place to place, Elder Lucy Smith, as she called herself, began constructing a permanent church in one of Chicago's poorest neighborhoods. She was always proud of the fact that her All Nations Pentecostal Church was "no second-hand white church, but one built from the ground up," and that it was the only church in Chicago founded by a woman.

A large person who spoke in a comfortable style with little regard for standard grammar, Smith attracted attention primarily due to her gift of healing. She began offering healing services three times a week for those affected with a variety of afflictions. "I takes the blind and the deaf, and the crippled, and all kinds of strokes and lame of all kind on Wednesday afternoon," she explained in the 1930s. "The minor ones come Wednesday night." Smith claimed to have cured more than 200,000 people during her 38 years of ministry. Under her direction, All Nations Pentecostal Church also began serving free meals to destitute neighbors, and Smith delivered an address on local radio twice a week.

Smith sold her church and rebuilt in 1938. Eventually, membership in All Nations Pentecostal Church reached 3,000. Upon her death on June 18, 1952, more than 60,000 mourners came to pay their respects, and her funeral was estimated to be the largest in Chicago up to that time.

Further Reading
"Faith Healer." *Ebony*, January 1950, pp. 37–39.
Smith, Jesse Carney, ed. *Notable Black American Women*. Vol. 2. Detroit, Mich.: Gale Research, 1996.

Smith, Willie Mae Ford See MOTHER SMITH.

Spottswood, Stephen Gill

(1897–1974) *African Methodist Episcopal bishop*

Stephen Spottswood was an effective pastor and bishop in the African Methodist Episcopal Zion Church (AMEZ Church), and a longtime leader of the National Association for the Advancement of Colored People (NAACP).

He was born Stephen Gill Spottswood on July 18, 1897, in Boston, Massachusetts, the only child of Abraham Lincoln Spottswood and Mary Elizabeth Spottswood. He attended a variety of integrated schools during his youth, including Cambridge Latin School in Massachusetts and Freeport High School in Maine. He then attended Albright College in Reading, Pennsylvania, where he earned a B.A. degree in history in 1917.

Spottswood, who had been religiously inclined since he was a boy, then returned to Boston and entered the service of the AMEZ Church as an assistant pastor at Columbus Avenue African Methodist Episcopal Church. At the same time, he attended Gordon Divinity School, where he was awarded his bachelors degree in theology in 1919. That same year he married Viola Booker, with whom he would have five children.

Spottswood took on the role of an itinerant pastor in the New England Conference of the AMEZ Church. He was largely responsible for the creation of First African Methodist Episcopal Church in Lowell, Massachusetts. Spottswood was ordained as a deacon in early 1920 and as an elder later that year. He served briefly at Green Memorial AMEZ Church in Portland, Maine, before assuming duties as pastor of Varick Memorial AMEZ Church in New Haven, Connecticut. While in that city, he continued his education at Yale Divinity School.

Spottswood moved around a great deal during his early ministry. In 1925, he became pastor of Goler Memorial AMEZ Church in Winston-Salem, North Carolina. From there he moved on to Jones Tabernacle AMEZ Church in Indianapolis, Indiana, in 1928; Saint Luke's AMEZ Church in Buffalo, New York, in 1932; and then John Wesley AMEZ Church in Washington, D.C., in 1936. There, Spottswood finally was able to put down roots, serving that church for 16 years. During his ministry, the congregation increased its membership from 600 to more than 3,000.

While in Washington, Spottswood increased his commitment to the Civil Rights movement. A member of the NAACP since 1919, he became president of the organization's Washington branch in 1947. As a result of his increasing prominence, Spottswood was elected an AMEZ bishop in 1952 and spent much of the following two decades supervising congregations throughout the nation. He also served as head of his denomination's Home Missions Department. He carried a heavy load of grief, however, due to his wife's death in a fire in 1953.

In 1954, Spottswood was named to the board of directors of the NAACP. He became vice president of the organization in 1959 and was elected its president on April 10, 1961. It was Spottswood's belief that the most effective protests were those involving economic issues, and he promoted a strategy of boycotts and sit-ins to combat segregation. In July 1961, he led a 22-car Freedom Train to Washington to highlight the need for more civil rights legislation. Although moderate in his positions, he was a dynamic speaker who gained particular attention in 1970 for his keynote speech at the 1970 NAACP convention in which he accused the Nixon administration of being antiblack and declared, "Killing black Americans has been the 20th-century pastime of our police."

Spottswood retired as bishop in 1972 and died at his home in Washington on December 2, 1974.

Further Reading

"Stephen Gill Spottswood." The African American Registry. Available online. URL: http://www.aaregistry/comafrican_american_history/544/stephen_spottswood. Downloaded February 18, 2003.

Garrity, John A., and Mark C. Carnes, eds. *American National Biography*. Vol. 20. New York: Oxford University Press, 2002.

Stallings, George Augustus, Jr.

(1948–) *Roman Catholic priest*

George Stallings earned a reputation as the most radical black priest in the Roman Catholic Church. His establishment, without the approval of authorities, of a Catholic church tailored to the needs of African Americans resulted in his official excommunication by the church.

George Augustus Stallings, Jr., was born on March 17, 1948, in New Bern, North Carolina, the son of Dorothy and George Augustus Stallings, Sr. Although he was baptized in the Catholic church of his mother, Stallings was also exposed to the black Baptist tradition by his grandmother. While still a young boy, Stallings decided he wanted to be a preacher, but his mother and a local priest steered him into the priesthood.

Stallings left home to attend Asheville Catholic High School, then enrolled at Saint Pius X Seminary in Garrison, New York. Upon earning his bachelor's degree in philosophy, he went to Rome, Italy, to study at Pontifical University of St. Thomas Aquinas in 1970. There he challenged the status quo by advocating for more student input in designing the school's program of study. Stallings earned three postgraduate degrees in five years at Pontifical University. He was ordained into the priesthood on July 20, 1974, and assigned to the position of associate pastor at a parish in Washington, D.C. Two years later, he became the youngest head pastor in the history of the diocese when he was appointed to lead St. Teresa of Avila, in Washington, D.C.

Stallings wasted little time in establishing his rebellious nature. In defiance of expectations, he refused to live in the church rectory. He gained a widespread reputation for his thundering sermons that were more reminiscent of the Pentecostal than the Catholic tradition. Stallings introduced gospel music into the church service and at one point hung a painting of a black Jesus in the sanctuary. These actions proved enormously popular, and his congregation increased from 200 to more than 2,000 by the time he left in 1988 to become the director of evangelism for the District of Columbia diocese.

The Catholic Church hoped that Stallings could continue to attract new parishioners in his new position. But instead, he became increasingly disillusioned with what he saw as the church's inability to meet the needs of blacks. "The reality is that a split exists in the American church just as it exists in American society, and its cause is racism," he declared. In defiance of his superiors, he organized a separate church called Imani Temple African American Congregation. The church's inaugural service at the Howard University chapel on July 2, 1989, attracted 2,300 worshipers. The Catholic Church responded by prohibiting Stallings from delivering the sacraments. In January 1990, Stallings announced on national television that his church was declaring its independence from the Roman Catholic Church and would engage in practices contrary to Catholic doctrine, such as ordaining women, allowing priests to marry, and accepting homosexuality and contraception. This time, the Catholic Church excommunicated Stallings. Its threat to also excommunicate his followers caused a large number of defections back to the traditional church.

That same year, in an act of defiance, Archbishop Richard Bridges of California consecrated Stallings as a bishop, which enabled him to ordain his own priests. He went on to establish satellite congregations in Baltimore, Maryland; Philadelphia, Pennsylvania; Norfolk, Virginia; and Lagos, Nigeria. Reactions to Stallings among black Catholics have been mixed. While many black clergy denounced him, Emerson Moore credited him with raising important issues and "putting black Catholics on the map."

Further Reading

Bigelow, Barbara Carlisle. *Contemporary Black Biography.* Vol. 6. Detroit, Mich.: Gale Research, 1994.

Melton, J. Gordon. *Religious Leaders of America.* 2d ed. Detroit, Mich.: Gale Research, 1999.

Mitchell-Powell, Brenda. *African American Biography.* Vol. 4. Detroit, Mich.: Gale, 1994.

"Stallings Dedicates a Cathedral." *Christian Century,* September 7, 1994, pp. 809–810.

Sullivan, Leon Howard

(1922–2001) *Baptist clergy, executive*

While serving a large congregation in North Philadelphia, Leon Sullivan established some of the most far-reaching social programs in the United States. He also developed the Sullivan Principles, a set of criteria to guide businesses in operating in a socially responsible way.

Sullivan was born on October 16, 1922, in Charleston, West Virginia. His early childhood was unstable, as his parents were separated and Sullivan had to move nearly a dozen times. He was primarily reared by his grandmother. Sullivan was an unusually introspective and perceptive boy, often wandering the hills by himself meditating and writing poetry. He found the racial segregation of his life—the poor, black neighborhood, the black schools—galling. At the age of 10, he was informed that he could not sit at a restaurant counter because of his race. As Sullivan remembered the incident, "At that moment as I stood there glaring at the big man's burning eyes, I decided that I would stand on my feet against this kind of thing as long as I lived."

He began with a personal campaign to visit every public eating and entertainment spot in Charleston until he received equal treatment. Sullivan had no success until the time when, upon being asked to leave, he stood and recited the Preamble to the U.S. Constitution. The restaurant owner was so impressed that he not only agreed to serve Sullivan but also gave him a free meal.

Leon Sullivan's vision for social justice yielded significant results on the local, national, and international levels. *(Urban Archives, Temple University, Philadelphia Pennsylvania)*

Sullivan's coordination and 6-foot, 5-inch height enabled him to attend West Virginia State College on a football and basketball scholarship. However, a serious knee injury soon ended his athletic career. Sullivan's scholarship was withdrawn, and he was forced to work nights at a steel mill to pay for his education. During his sophomore year, his grandmother died in extreme poverty. On her deathbed, she urged him to help his people so that they would not end up in the same circumstances. Sullivan, who had been ordained into the Baptist church at 17, took up the challenge. While still in school, and laboring at the mill, he worked part time at two small local churches.

During Sullivan's senior year, he met ADAM CLAYTON POWELL, JR., who encouraged him to come to New York City. Sullivan did so and, with Powell's influence, got a job as the first black coinbox collector in the history of Bell Telephone Company while he attended Union Theological Seminary. He also met A. Philip Randolph, president of the first black trade union in the United States, who taught him a great deal about nonviolent negotiating techniques.

In 1945, Sullivan finished his schooling and married Grace Banks, who served as his confidante and adviser throughout his life. He accepted a call that same year to First Baptist Church in South Orange, New Jersey, where he served for five years. In 1950, he moved on to Zion Baptist, a church in a crumbling neighborhood in North Philadelphia, Pennsylvania. After taking stock of the situation, Sullivan swung into action. In March 1953 he called a meeting at city hall of all residents interested in reclaiming their neighborhood. Out of this meeting came the Philadelphia Committee, a joint effort of citizens and police to fight crime. More than 20,000 people would eventually volunteer their time in this group. Largely based on this effort, the National Junior Chamber of Commerce named Sullivan one of the nation's 10 outstanding men in 1955.

Sullivan believed, however, that to fight crime was to treat the symptoms and not the causes of inner-city problems. He thought that economic conditions were the key. In the mid-1950s he initiated a youth employment service in the basement of Zion Church. The program pioneered the way for similar efforts across the nation in succeeding decades. Continuing his efforts, Sullivan delivered a dynamic sermon entitled "The Walls of Jericho Must Come Down," in which he inspired his followers to take an active part in promoting the economic interests of the poor. His congregation used its buying power as a tool for justice in selectively patronizing only those establishments that engaged in fair hiring practices toward minorities. MARTIN LUTHER KING, JR., later used this program as a template for his Operation Breadbasket.

In the early 1960s, Sullivan decided that his next step was to train African Americans so that they would be better positioned to take advantage of job opportunities. Under his leadership, the Opportunities Industrialization Center (OIC) opened on January 24, 1964. Within a short time, the OIC was the fastest growing employment training program in the United States. By 1980, it had procured $130 million a year in funding. By 1993, the program had trained more than 1 million workers and spread into 80 cities. A seemingly bottomless well of initiative for improving lives, Sullivan founded Adult Armchair Education to provide educational services for people in their homes, followed by the Zion Investment Association, which financed the first shopping center owned and operated by African Americans.

Sullivan's leadership in the area of economic opportunity won the admiration of large corporations such as General Motors, which in 1971 made him the first black member of its board of directors. Sullivan used that position to lobby for action on behalf of South African blacks living under apartheid. After succeeding in getting General Motors to cease doing business with

South Africa, he developed the Sullivan Principles, a code of responsibility for U.S. businesses operating in places such as South Africa. The Sullivan Principles became widely adopted by corporations around the world.

Sullivan then pushed for more aggressive action against South Africa's apartheid government. He called for U.S. divestment of business concerns in the country, coupled with aid projects for South African blacks. In order to devote himself full-time to African-American concerns, Sullivan retired to Phoenix, Arizona, in 1988. By the end of his 38 years, he had increased his congregation ten-fold to 6,000 members. In 1991 he initiated a series of African and African-American Summits to explore mutual cooperation between blacks in the two continents. Later that decade, his tireless opposition to apartheid was rewarded when South Africa freed imprisoned black leader Nelson Mandela and dismantled apartheid.

Sullivan continued searching for ways to infuse morality into business practices. At a meeting of the United Nations in 1999, he introduced the Global Sullivan Principles for socially responsible business. After a lifetime of working for the betterment of his people, Sullivan died on April 24, 2001.

Further Reading

Haskins, Jim. *Distinguished African-American Political and Government Leaders.* Phoenix, Ariz.: Oryx Press, 1999.

Lincoln, C. Eric, and Lawrence H. Mayima. *The Black Church in the African American Experience.* Durham, N.C.: Duke University Press, 1990.

Roberts, J. Deotis. *A Theological Commentary on the Sullivan Principles.* Philadelphia: International Council for Equality of Opportunity Principle, 1980.

Sullivan, Leon. *Build, Brother, Build.* Philadelphia: Macrae Smith, 1969.

T

Tanner, Benjamin Tucker

(1835–1923) *African Methodist Episcopal Church leader, editor*

Benjamin Tucker Tanner was regarded by his contemporaries as "King of the Negro editors." In addition to editing two highly regarded periodicals, he authored several books and served the African Methodist Episcopal Church (AME Church) as bishop.

Tanner was born on December 25, 1835, one of four children of Hugh and Isabel Tanner, free blacks of Pittsburgh, Pennsylvania. After his father's death, Tanner took over the family barber business while attending school at Avery College in Allegheny, Pennsylvania, from 1852 to 1857. Avery offered to pay his expenses at the time, but Tanner insisted on financing his own education. During those years, Tanner accepted the Christian faith and decided to become a minister. He attended Western Theological Seminary beginning in 1857, and married Sara Miller a year later.

After completing his education at Western in 1860, Tanner was ordained a deacon and an elder by the AME Church. He was assigned to a church in Sacramento, California, but when he could not come up with the funds for travel, he was called instead to Fifteenth Street Presbyterian Church in Washington, D.C. Tanner founded a Sunday school for freed blacks in the naval yard in 1861. A year later he worked at the Alexander Mission, a situation that so upset white neighbors that he frequently worked under military guard. He moved on to a congregation in Georgetown in 1863 and then to a church in Baltimore in 1866, where he helped organize and served as principal of a new school for blacks in Frederickstown, Maryland.

Tanner's writing career took off in 1867 when he published a lengthy history entitled *An Apology for African Methodism.* This, along with his reputation as an educator, brought about his election in 1868 as the chief secretary and elder of *The Christian Recorder,* the official publication of the AME Church and the oldest continuously published black periodical in the United States. Tanner moved to the church headquarters in Philadelphia, where he held the position as editor for 16 years. BENJAMIN WILLIAM ARNETT remarked of Tanner's work, "His pen is sharper than his razor, and his editorial chair is finer than the barber chair."

In the 1880s, Tanner was the key figure behind the creation of the *AME Church Review,* which he built into the nation's leading public forum for African-American religious scholarship. He continued to write books, including the provocatively titled *The Negro's Origin: and Is He Cursed by God?*

The AME Church honored Tanner by electing him bishop in 1892. He spent the next 16 years traveling extensively, under the AME's system of reassigning bishops to different geographical areas every four years. He retired in 1908 and died on January 15, 1923. In addition to his legacy as the most respected black editor of his time, Benjamin and Sara Tanner raised a family of distinguished children, seven of whom lived to adulthood. The most famous of these was Henry Ossawa, a widely respected African-American painter.

Further Reading

Bowden, Henry Warden. *Dictionary of American Religious Biography.* Westport, Conn.: Greenwood Press, 1993.

Montgomery, William E. *Under Their Own Vine and Fig Tree: The African-American Church in the South, 1865–1900.* Baton Rouge: Louisiana State University Press, 1993.

Seraile, William. *Fire in His Heart: Bishop Benjamin Tucker Tanner and the AME Church.* Knoxville: University of Tennessee Press, 1998.

Tate, Mary Magdalena Lewis
(Mother Tate, Mary Lena Street)
(1871–1930) *Pentecostal leader*

Mary Magdalena Tate was one of the leaders of the spirit-filled Holiness movement that percolated up from African religious roots into the Christian religion in the late 19th century. She was responsible for the first great Pentecostal revival that blazed a trail for one of today's most popular religious denominations.

Few details are recorded about her early days other than that she was born Mary Lena Street on January 3, 1871, and had such a penchant for pure living as a child that she was nicknamed "Miss Do Right." She eventually married David Lewis and lived with him in Dickson, Tennessee, where she became the mother of two boys.

In 1903, she was overcome with the desire to preach. Leaving her family at home, she traveled to Steel Springs, Tennessee, to proclaim the gospel, and met with such success that she continued on to Paducah, Kentucky. From there she journeyed to Brooklyn, Illinois, where she preached her first sermon. Her husband's reaction to her calling can only be inferred from the fact that the two apparently had no contact with each other after this time. She began going by the name of Mary Magdalena Tate, and was popularly known as Mother Tate.

Taking her sons in tow, she embarked on a second mission trip, this time beginning in Paris, Tennessee. Speaking to black audiences in the streets and in their homes, she established the Church of the Living God the Pillar and Ground of Truth without Controversy, commonly shortened to the Church of the Living God or House of God. She achieved spectacular success in Alabama from 1905 to 1907, conducting more than 300 conversions to her church.

Her ministry took on a more intense, spiritual nature following a severe illness in 1908. One day, Mother Tate declared herself "healed and sealed," and began speaking in tongues. Most of her followers thought she was mentally ill, but she quickly recovered from her illness and began to proclaim the value of "Baptism by the Holy Ghost and Fire." That year she formally affiliated her church with the Pentecostal movement. On June 25, 1908, she organized a large Pentecostal revival in Greenville, Tennessee, in which nearly 100 new members were baptized.

In addition to preaching and conducting revivals, Tate spent much time writing and editing the "Constitution, Government and General Decree" for her denomination, which was adopted at the 1914 general assembly. In 1923, she founded a publishing house in Nashville, Tennessee, to reach a larger audience.

Tate's movement spread rapidly throughout the South and then across the United States. By 1910, she had ordained preachers in her church in Tennessee, Kentucky, and Georgia. By 1924, she had established churches in 20 states and the District of Columbia, and her movement had even spread into foreign countries. Her church, however, was plagued by internal squabbles and defections, to the point where Tate declared, "Because of sin and jealousy, so much trouble will come on the church that I'll be glad that I'm asleep in Christ." She died on December 28, 1930. The Church of the Living God continued to thrive on a modest scale and is presently active in nearly every state in the Union.

Further Reading

Lewis, Meharry H. "Mary Lena Tate: VISION." Church of the Living God, The Pillar and Ground of the Truth web site. Available online. URL: http://clgpgt1915.freeyellow.com/page2.html. Downloaded February 18, 2003.

Melton, J. Gordon. *Religious Leaders of America. 2nd ed.* Detroit, Mich.: Gale Research, 1999.

Smith, Jesse Carney, ed. *Black American Women.* Vol. 2. Detroit, Mich.: Gale Research, 1996.

Taylor, Gardner Calvin
(1918–   ) *Baptist preacher*

Gardner Taylor is widely regarded as one of the finest preachers in U.S. history. James Coston, president of Interdenominational Theological Seminary, has said of him, "Hearing him preach gives me the impression that he has a direct pipeline to God. If I could only hear one sermon, it would be a Taylor sermon."

Taylor was born on June 6, 1918, in Baton Rouge, Louisiana, to W. M. and Selma Taylor. He was an excellent student who dreamed of becoming a lawyer. After earning a B.A. degree from Leland College in 1937, he was accepted into the University of Michigan Law School. Before he began classes, however, he experienced a terrifying accident. While he was driving along the highway, a car suddenly veered across the road in front of him. Taylor slammed into it and one of the two white men in the car was killed. In such situations in the South, blacks were routinely assumed to be at fault regardless of the circumstances, and Taylor feared that he would be lynched. He was saved, however, by the testimony of two white witnesses to the accident who supported his story. Taylor felt the presence of God so strongly throughout the incident that he made the decision to abandon law and dedicate his life to the service of God.

Instead of attending the University of Michigan, he enrolled at Oberlin Theological Seminary in Ohio. While a student there, he was ordained a Baptist minister and served a congregation in Elyria, Ohio, from 1938 to 1940. He earned his bachelor of divinity degree in 1940, the same year he married Laura Scott, a schoolteacher. Taylor was then called to a parish in New Orleans, where he served until 1943, before moving on to a congregation in Baton Rouge, Louisiana. Taylor's reputation as a spellbinding and inspiring speaker led to his call to one of the nation's largest congregations, Concord Baptist Church of Christ in Brooklyn, New York, in 1948.

Taylor experienced some adversity at the nearly 4,000-member church, particularly in 1952, when the church burned to the ground. But he was able to rebuild a sanctuary in 1956 and raised enough money to pay off the $1.7 million mortgage within six years. Under Taylor's leadership, Concord Baptist expanded its ministry to include a large nursing home, a credit union, and a clothing exchange. His wife guided the organization of an elementary school known for its innovative teaching methods.

In 1958, Taylor was appointed by Mayor Robert Wagner to the New York City Board of

Education, making him only the second African American since 1917 to serve in that capacity. Gardner used the position to advocate strongly for minorities and for dismantling discriminatory practices within the district. Not only did he insist on equal funding for predominantly minority districts, but Gardner took the side of a group of parents calling for a citywide boycott of the public schools because of the neglected facilities for minority students.

While serving a congregation that eventually grew in the 1960s to surpass Abyssinian Baptist as the largest black Protestant church in the United States, with more than 12,000 members, Gardner took a leadership role in the Civil Rights movement. He was actively involved in the Congress of Racial Equality (CORE). He marched and was arrested with MARTIN LUTHER KING, JR., on several occasions when protesting racial discrimination in the South.

Taylor's support of King's nonviolent civil disobedience campaign put him in the center of a major denominational dispute in 1960. The National Baptist Convention (NBC), of which he and King were members, was controlled by JOSEPH HARRISON JACKSON of Chicago, who strongly opposed King's tactics. That led to a split among the membership at the group's 1960 annual convention. The civil rights activists selected Taylor as their candidate to oppose Jackson's reelection. A controversial series of political maneuvers ensued. The NBC's nominating committee recommended that Jackson be reelected to another term. The Taylor forces responded with 45 minutes of boisterous protest. During the demonstration, the committee chair, a strong Jackson supporter, ruled that the report of the nominating committee was adopted and that Jackson was reelected. He then adjourned the proceedings. Furious at the high-handed action, the Taylor supporters occupied the podium and held a state-by-state vote for president, which Taylor won by more than a three-to-one

margin among those who were still present. Both sides then declared their candidate the NBC president, a situation that eventually was decided by courts, which ruled in Jackson's favor.

The Taylor supporters were so incensed that they pulled out of the denomination and formed their own group, which they called the Progressive National Baptist Convention (PNBC). Taylor served as both president and vice president of the new denomination. During his term as president in 1967–68, the PNBC made headlines by becoming the first predominantly black religious body to condemn the U.S. prosecution of the war in Vietnam.

While all this was going on, Taylor found time to teach classes at Colgate-Rochester Theological Seminary. In 1962, he also took over as president of the Protestant Council of New York City, becoming the first African American ever to hold that position. In addition, he wrote a book called *How Shall They Preach*, in which he shared his insights on the art of delivering sermons.

Taylor remained as lead pastor of Concord Baptist for 42 years until his retirement in June 1990. He remained in high demand as a preacher at conventions and conferences and was given a presidential medal of honor for his long years of service.

Further Reading

Galbreath, Edward. "The Pulpit King: The Passion and Eloquence of Gardner Taylor, a Legend Among Preachers," *Christianity Today*, December 11, 1995, pp. 25–28.

Hamilton, Charles V. *The Black Preacher in America.* New York: William Morrow, 1972.

Lincoln, C. Eric, and Lawrence H. Mayima. *The Black Church in the African American Experience.* Durham, N.C.: Duke University Press, 1990.

Taylor, Gardner. *The Words of Gardner Taylor.* Valley Forge, Pa.: Judson Press, 1999.

Thurman, Howard

(1900–1981) *Baptist clergy, theologian*

Howard Thurman, whom *Life* magazine ranked as one of the top 15 preachers of the 20th century, profoundly influenced the course of the Civil Rights movement as an ethicist and educator. In the words of JESSE LOUIS JACKSON, "He sowed the seeds that bred a generation of activists who tore down the walls of oppression."

Thurman was born on November 18, 1900, in Daytona, Florida, where he was raised by his grandmother, a former slave. Public school for blacks went only through the seventh grade, but Thurman showed such outstanding academic ability that the principal volunteered to teach him eighth-grade subject matter so that he could qualify for high school. He was then sent to live with cousins in Jacksonville, which had a high school for blacks. However, at the train station he discovered that there was an extra charge for carrying his baggage. Having no money to cover the charge, Thurman thought his dream of an education was over. But as he sat in tears, an anonymous black man paid his baggage fare and was never seen again. Given this unexpected reprieve, Thurman worked hard in school and graduated as his school's valedictorian.

He then attended Morehouse College in Atlanta, from which he graduated in 1923. Planning for a career in ministry, he enrolled in Colgate-Rochester Theological Seminary in New York. He was ordained in the Baptist Church in 1925, received his theological degree in 1926, and accepted a call to Mount Zion Baptist Church in Oberlin, Ohio, the same year. So inspiring were Thurman's sermons that he drew many white listeners, and Mount Zion was a rare case of an all-black congregation that became interracial.

While in Oberlin, Thurman became aware of the writings of a Quaker mystic, Rufus Jones. He left Mount Zion in 1929 and traveled to Haverford, Pennsylvania, where he studied for a

Howard Thurman's philosophy of nonviolent Christian love strongly influenced the thinking of Martin Luther King, Jr. *(Boston University)*

short time under Jones. He regarded this as a pivotal time in his career. Jones opened his eyes to the universality of the human condition. But whereas Jones focused on a global application, Thurman, who had grown up in a racist society, centered his thought on how African Americans could shield themselves and their spirituality from a destructive and demeaning environment.

Thurman then left the parish ministry for an academic career. He began teaching religious studies at Morehouse College in 1929. He married Sue E. Bailey, a writer and historian, in 1932, and then moved on to teach at Howard University in Washington, D.C. Continuing his exploration into philosophy and theology, he learned of the works of Mohandas K. Gandhi, an Indian who advocated a form of social justice activism based on nonviolent, passive resistance. Gandhi was a Hindu, not a Christian, and yet his teachings seemed to mirror much of what Jesus taught. Intrigued by this, Thurman began a quest to discover the relationship of Christians to non-Christians, and to understand the equality of all before God. He and his wife traveled to India in 1935 to meet with Gandhi, observe his philosophy in action, and question him about how the nonviolent method of protest could be used by blacks to combat racism in the United States. He concluded, despite his experiences with discrimination, that blacks and whites shared a great deal in common.

> The burden of being black and the burden of being white is so heavy that it is rare in our society to experience oneself as a human being. As a human being, he belongs to the life and the whole kingdom of life that includes all that lives and perhaps, also, all that has ever lived. And knowing all that, I also know that all human beings are one.

Thurman returned to Howard University where he taught and served as dean until 1944. He also began the first of many widely acclaimed theological books, *The Greatest of These*, published in 1944. Eventually, he would write 20 books and publish more than 800 tapes of sermons and lectures. His publications demonstrated his keen insight, sense of humility and humor, and touch of mysticism that tinged his Christian beliefs. "I have always felt that a word was being spoken through me," he once said. "Three-fourths of the time I didn't get it right." He disliked the label of a theologian and preferred to describe himself as an ethicist.

Long before JAMES H. CONE developed his black liberation theology, Thurman taught along similar lines. He saw Jesus' teachings as techniques of survival for the oppressed. It was his view that a person could not live a good life in a spirit of fear or hatred. He came to believe that people, created in the image of God, have within themselves a presence and power of the divine—a sort of built-in Creator that moves them to transform their environment for the good of the community.

It was Thurman who steered MARTIN LUTHER KING, JR., in the direction of the nonviolent resistance that would characterize his ministry. Before he left Howard University, Thurman conveyed his discoveries of Gandhi to the school's president, MORDECAI WYATT JOHNSON. King then heard a sermon by Johnson in which he presented Gandhi's point of view. King was intrigued and began his own exploration of Thurman and Gandhi. It was said that he always carried a copy of Thurman's 1949 book *Jesus and the Disinherited* wherever he went. King paid special attention to Thurman's words: "Anyone who permits another to determine the quality of his inner life gives into the hands of the other the keys to his destiny."

In 1944, Thurman moved to San Francisco, where he cofounded an interracial congregation called the Church for the Fellowship of All Believers. He continued to be one of the most articulate spokesmen for the cause of the universality of Christianity and was a popular speaker nationwide. Even in his later years, he continued to expound his understanding of religion in books such as *With Head and Heart: The Autobiography of Howard Thurman*, published in 1980, and *For the Inward Journey: The Writings of Howard Thurman*, published posthumously in 1984. Thurman died on April 10, 1981.

Further Reading

Fluker, Walter. *They Looked for a City: A Comparison of the Ideal of Community in the Thought of Howard Thurman and Martin Luther King, Jr.* Lanham, Md.: University Press of America, 1989.
Harding Vincent. "Dangerous Spirituality." *Sojourners*, January 1999, pp. 28–31.

Thurman, Howard. *A Strange Freedom: The Best of Howard Thurman on Religious Experience and Public Life.* Boston: Beacon Press, 1998.

———. *With Head and Heart: The Autobiography of Howard Thurman.* San Diego: Harcourt Brace Jovanovich, 1979.

Tolton, Augustus
(1854–1897) *Roman Catholic priest*

Augustus Tolton was an early African-American Roman Catholic priest who overcame great prejudice to establish a ministry in Illinois in the 1880s.

Tolton was born on April 11, 1854, on a plantation near Brush Creek in northeastern Missouri. His parents, Martha Chisley and Peter Tolton, were Catholic slaves from neighboring plantations. At the beginning of the Civil War in 1861, Peter Tolton escaped from the plantation to join the Union army, and apparently died during the war. His wife ran away shortly thereafter, taking their four children with her. They were caught by Missouri residents but rescued by a group of Union soldiers and settled in Quincy, Illinois.

Augustus, his mother, and his older brother worked at a tobacco factory. During the off season, when the factory was closed, Augustus attempted to go to school. At first, the Catholic schools in Quincy would not accept him, and when the decision was later made to allow him to attend, many whites were upset. In 1875, the family moved back to Missouri, where his mother found a better job as housekeeper to a priest. Augustus studied briefly under the tutelage of a priest. But even 10 years after the Civil War, the area was still unsafe for blacks, and they returned to Quincy within a year.

By this time, Tolton had decided on the priesthood as his vocation. Unfortunately, no Catholic seminary in the United States would admit him. From 1873 to 1878 he studied under tutors in between working hours at the tobacco factory. In 1878, he began attending Quincy College, newly established by the Franciscans, before and after work. With the help of this order, Tolton traveled to Rome to study at the College of the Propagation of the Faith. After nearly six years of study, he was ordained a priest on April 24, 1886.

The Roman Catholic Church's original intention was to send Tolton to Africa as a missionary. It had come to the church's attention, however, that there were many black Catholics in the United States, and at that time there were no black priests to serve them. Tolton's new commission was to fill this void. According to Tolton, one of the cardinals responded to concerns over acceptance of a black priest by saying, "America has been called the most enlightened nation; we shall see if it deserves that honor."

In July 1886, Tolton assumed his duties as priest of Saint Joseph's Catholic Church for Negroes in his home town of Quincy. Although the church was a black congregation, the quality of the school that Tolton ran at the church was such that more than 200 white children enrolled there.

Feeling persecuted by fellow priests and even the bishop in his locality, Tolton requested a transfer. In 1889, he was assigned to the archdiocese of Chicago. He had made such an impact on new converts in his Quincy parish that 19 of them followed him to Chicago. There he took over a poor black congregation that worshiped in the basement of a white church. A wealthy white woman then contributed $10,000 for him to establish Saint Monica's Church for Negro Catholics, which was opened in 1893. While in the prime of his ministry, Tolton fell victim to heatstroke and died on July 9, 1897.

Further Reading
Adams, Russell L. *Great Negroes Past and Present.* Chicago: Afro-American Publishing Company, 1969.

Augustus Tolton battled overt prejudice as the first African-American Roman Catholic priest in the United States. *(Josephite Archives)*

Garrity, John A., and Mark C. Carnes, eds. *American National Biography*. Vol. 21. New York: Oxford University Press, 2002.

Melton, J. Gordon. *Religious Leaders of America*. 2d ed. Detroit, Mich.: Gale Research, 1999.

Truth, Sojourner
(Isabella Van Wagener, Isabella Bornefree)
(ca. 1797–1883) *lecturer*

Although she could neither read nor write, Sojourner Truth was perhaps the most highly regarded and widely quoted African-American woman of her generation. The self-proclaimed Pilgrim of God was a powerful orator who combined religious fervor and abolitionist passion to spellbind her audiences. In the words of James Miller McKim of the Pennsylvania Anti-Slavery Society, a person could "as well attempt to report the seven apocalyptic thunders as recapture her eloquence."

The woman who came to be known as Sojourner Truth was born Isabella Bornefree, a name which belied her status as the child of slave parents James and Elizabeth Bornefree, sometime around 1797. Her first owner was the Dutch colonel Johannes Hardenburgh of a well-established family in Ulster County, New York. When she was young, her family became the property of Johannes's son Charles. Isabella grew up in a close-knit extended family that was shattered upon the death of Charles Hardenburgh when she was nine or 10. At that time, her father and mother, who were too frail for hard labor, were given their freedom. However, Isabella and her younger brother Peter were sold for $100 and a flock of sheep to a neighbor, John Nealy. Nealy was a cruel master who subjected her to severe whippings because of her apparent slowness, not taking into account that she had grown up in a Dutch house and so had a poor understanding of English. She appealed to her father, who managed to facilitate a move to a new owner. Eventually, she ended up as the property of John Dumont. While working for Dumont, she had a relationship with Bob, a slave from a nearby estate, with whom she had a child. Attempts to establish a permanent marriage bond, however, were severed by Bob's brutal master. In the words of one historian, after Bob made a last attempt to see her, the master whipped him so savagely that his "blood flowed till it could be traced a mile in the snow."

In 1817, she married Thomas, one of Dumont's older slaves. For the first time, she enter-

Although illiterate, Sojourner Truth spoke against the evils of slavery with unmatched eloquence in the pre–Civil War years. *(Schomburg Center for Research in Black Culture)*

free her a year before the legal deadline, but reneged on the promise. Unable to bear the situation any longer, she ran away to New York City with her youngest child in the fall of 1826. It was this episode that led to her first serious contact with religion. Previously, her mother had told her stories of a God who lived in the sky and had talked to this God in prayers. But Isabella's only association with religion was a hope that "God would kill all the white people and not leave one for seed." Now she came to believe that God had inspired her escape and had led her to seek refuge with a generous family, the Van Wageners.

In order to keep Isabella from harm because of her escape, the Van Wageners purchased her services from her previous owner for the coming year for $20. They also paid her wages for her work as a servant. Isabella was so grateful that she took on the family's last name as her own. While she lived with the Van Wageners, she discovered that her son, Peter, had been illegally sold to a plantation in the Deep South. With the help of some Quakers, she initiated a legal battle to have him returned, which she won.

While returning to the Dumont farm for a reunion with some of the former slaves with whom she had worked for many years, Isabella experienced an extraordinary vision in which she saw Jesus protecting her from God's wrath. She felt his love so strongly and deeply that suddenly she discovered her hatred of slave-owning whites had disappeared. In a search for a religious home, she joined an African Methodist Episcopal (AME) church in 1829, and then drifted into a commune to which she contributed her life's savings in the 1830s. She was publicly accused of murdering the commune's leader, filed suit for libel, and won.

In 1843, at the age of 46, she felt an irresistible call to go out and preach independently throughout the North. In response to the continuing voices she heard, she changed her name to Sojourner Truth, the name by which she

tained hopes of freedom as, in that same year, the New York legislature passed a law decreeing that slavery would end in the state by July 24, 1827. The couple had four children, whom Isabella tried to keep in the fields with her as long as possible while she worked. They were quickly taken from her, however, and sold as slaves.

Isabella worked for 18 years in the Dumont household, both as a field hand and a domestic. For most of that time, she worked so hard and loyally, despite her treatment, that she was ridiculed by her fellow slaves. In exchange for her continued hard work, Dumont promised to would gain lasting fame. Sleeping wherever she could find shelter, she proclaimed a mystical message of God. Although her original intent was to be a wandering preacher, her main message soon evolved into an antislavery, social justice, nonviolence, and brotherhood-of-man philosophy, based on her interpretation of the Bible. Since she was illiterate, she had to have the Bible read to her, and she dictated her rapidly growing network of correspondence to others.

Sojourner Truth did not view the Bible as the literal words of God. Rather, she believed it to be an inspired book that contained the "spirit of truth" but also contained the sometimes errant ideas and opinions of those who had recorded the words. She preferred having children read the Bible for her because they were the only ones who would read it without adding any of their own interpretations, and they would reread any passage she wanted as many times as she asked. When people tried to dismiss her as illiterate, she responded, "I don't read such small stuff as letters; I read men and natures."

When Sojourner Truth spoke, she combined the storytelling tradition of her African heritage with an oratory power that was as tangible to her as it was obvious to others. "I felt so tall within," she said about her speaking, "as if the power of the nation was within me." Indeed, she was an extraordinarily tall, strong woman with a voice so deep and resonating that an article in the *St. Louis Dispatch* alleged that she was a man. The falsehood was widely spread, despite the fact that she had borne five children. Fearless and uninhibited in her proclamation of the truth, she once removed her shirt in public to prove her sex to skeptics, noting that the shame was not hers but theirs for doubting.

Contemporaries regarded her with a mixture of curiosity and admiration. Frederick Douglass, while not always approving of or understanding her, described her as "a strange compound of wit and wisdom, of wild enthusiasm and flintlike common sense." While some news reports of her were respectful, others often contained a note of ridicule.

Sojourner Truth depended on the generosity of others for her survival until the publication of her book, *The Narrative of Sojourner Truth*. Dictated to Olive Gilbert, it appeared in print in 1850. Her work during the Civil War in caring for former slaves in the Washington, D.C., area attracted the attention of famed author Harriet Beecher Stowe, who wrote an article on her that was published in the *Atlantic Monthly*. The article spread her fame throughout much of the land. Even President Lincoln arranged for a personal interview with her in 1864.

Sojourner Truth suffered a great deal of physical abuse from racists throughout her travels. She was beaten countless times and was frequently the target of stone-throwing. On one occasion, a mob beat her so savagely that she had to walk with a cane for the rest of her life. Shortly after the end of the Civil War, she defiantly boarded a "whites only" streetcar in Washington, D.C., and was thrown off so roughly that she separated her shoulder. In this instance, however, she prevailed in her cause, as streetcars in the nation's capital were desegregated. Sojourner Truth also worked hard for the cause of black voting rights and earned respect in becoming the first African American to win a slander suit against a prominent white person.

In 1870, she promoted a plan to resettle African Americans in a state set aside for them in the western United States. Although the plan never gained enough political support to advance, a large number of blacks migrated to the West in response. Sojourner Truth continued to preach into the 1880s, despite declining health. She died in her home in Battle Creek, Michigan, in 1883.

Further Reading

Ortiz, Victoria. *Sojourner Truth: A Self-Made Woman.* Philadelphia: J. B. Lippincott, 1974.

Painter, Nell Irvin. *Sojourner Truth: A Life, A Symbol.* New York: W. W. Norton, 1996.

Stetson, Erlene, and Linda David. *Glorifying in Tribulation: The Life Work of Sojourner Truth.* East Lansing: Michigan State University Press, 1994.

Washington, Margaret, ed. *The Narrative of Sojourner Truth.* New York: Vintage, 1993.

Turner, Henry McNeil
(1834–1915) *African Methodist Episcopal bishop*

Henry McNeil Turner was perhaps the most dominant African-American religious leader of the late 19th century. An innovative and daring thinker, he was the first high-profile clergyman to speak of God as black. It was largely through his efforts that African Methodist Episcopal Church (AME Church) membership multiplied rapidly following the Civil War.

Turner was born on February 1, 1834, in Newberry Court House, South Carolina, in somewhat unusual circumstances for an African American in the South at the time. Both his teenage mother, Sarah Turner, and his father, Hardy, were free blacks. Hardy died when Henry was young, and the boy was largely brought up by his grandmother, Hannah Green. It was she who raised Henry's interest in his African roots with her tales of his grandfather, who she claimed was an African king.

Although he was not a slave, Henry spent much of his youth performing hard labor in the cotton fields. As he grew older, he was apprenticed to a blacksmith and a carriage maker, but he disliked both professions and once ran away from home to escape the commitment. At the age of 12, he was shaken by a vivid dream of being the leader of a vast crowd of people. Along with the tales of his royal heritage, it caused him to wonder if he was destined for great things.

In 1848, Sarah Turner married Jabez Story and moved the family to Story's home in Abbeville, South Carolina. State laws forbidding the teaching of reading and writing to blacks prevented Henry from obtaining an education. But he was able to teach himself a great deal and then found a way to circumvent the restriction when he took on work as a janitor for a law firm. The attorneys were so fascinated by Turner's memory and intelligence that they secretly taught him about many subjects, including law and theology. In 1857, Turner, who had begun working as a carpenter, also took private instruction from an African American who ran a secret school for blacks in Savannah.

His religious interests developed gradually. Although the family seldom attended church when he was young, Turner's mother experienced a conversion at a revival in 1844. Henry, who at one time thought of himself as "the worst boy at the Abbeville Court House," surprised and elated her by joining the Methodist Church in Abbeville four years later. In 1851, he had a deep and emotional personal encounter with God that prompted him to take up the ministry. With his mother's encouragement, he became an exhorter that year and was licensed to preach in 1853. For the next five years, Turner traveled throughout the South, preaching the gospel. His quick mind and the knowledge he had picked up from the lawyers gave him a presence and authority well beyond what people expected from an uneducated black man.

In 1856, Turner married Eliza Ann Peacher, a woman from a wealthy black family in Columbia, South Carolina. A year later, his work took him to New Orleans. There he heard for the first time the story of RICHARD ALLEN and the AME Church. At that time, there was no greater position in the Methodist Church to which a black person could aspire beyond preacher. Only white ministers were allowed to distribute the sacraments. Turner was intrigued by the idea of an all-black denomination in which blacks could hold any position and choose their own pastors.

For a time, however, he remained a pastor in the Methodist Church. His greatest success as an evangelist for this denomination came in 1858, when he helped organize a revival in Athens, Georgia. Turner made such an impression on listeners that he was invited to preach to the white students and professors at the nearby state university.

With the escalation of the conflict that would culminate in the Civil War, however, it had become a dangerous time for free blacks in the South. Partly out of fear for his family's safety and partly because of his discomfort with the slavery accommodations being made by the Methodist Church in the South, Turner moved north and was admitted as a clergyman to the AME Church in August 1858.

He was immediately assigned to take over two struggling parishes in Baltimore. Turner not only rebuilt the congregations but became actively involved in politics, particularly on the issue of slavery. Early in the Civil War, he was furious with President Lincoln for his slowness in freeing the slaves. After Lincoln signed the Emancipation Proclamation in 1863, Turner was among the leading advocates of black participation in the Union army. He was an effective recruiter for the military and himself enlisted as a chaplain. In that capacity, he worked hard and passionately at converting any nonreligious troops to Christianity. Although he did not see combat, his war experience nonetheless nearly killed him when he contracted smallpox.

Near the end of the war, Turner's regiment was stationed in North Carolina. He discovered that JAMES W. HOOD and other ministers of the AME's rival, the African Methodist Episcopal Zion Church (AMEZ Church), had already begun work organizing churches in that state. Turner began organizing for the AME Church

and brought a number of churches into the fold. Although he attempted to do so in a spirit of cooperation with the AMEZ Church, the two denominations engaged in a sometimes bitter "turf war" over the congregations that Turner found disheartening.

Turner moved on to Georgia in 1865, where he made his most influential contributions to the church. From 1865 to 1871, Turner worked an exhausting schedule that included as many as 15,000 miles of travel in a year, three sermons every Sunday, and one sermon every other night

Henry McNeil Turner, a leader in establishing the African Methodist Episcopal Church in the South, was among the first to identify God as black. *(Schomburg Center for Research in Black Culture)*

of the week. "I have had to pass through blood and fire," he later commented of his grueling labors.

Turner drew a great deal of criticism for his unconventional method in ordaining ministers. He was accused of ordaining men on street corners and on railroad cars—men with no particular training or even inclination for the ministry. Sometimes he accepted them on a trial basis, and sometimes he even had to talk them into accepting ordination. In his defense, Turner pointed to the severe shortage of black pastors in the South. The church needed someone to serve the thousands of people crying out for leaders, and Turner was determined to provide them. His ideas on ordination were so radical that in 1888 he defied ecclesiastical tradition by ordaining a woman, only to have the act revoked by a scandalized AME general conference.

Whatever the academic or doctrinal defects of Turner's ordination procedures, they proved to be an astounding success. By getting pastors into hundreds of new AME churches, Turner helped to establish the denomination throughout the state and later throughout the South. When he joined the AME Church in 1858, the denomination had only 20,000 members, virtually none in the South. By 1869, Turner had recruited that many new members in Georgia alone, at a rate of 5,000 per year. The momentum he created continued until, by 1896, the AME Church had swelled to 452,725 members, nearly 80 percent of whom lived in the South. Contemporary black religious leader REVERDY CASSIUS RANSOM credited Turner with having achieved the nearly impossible task of "transforming an impoverished, scattered people into a disciplined organization with great collective power."

Turner's obvious abilities as a churchman impressed his white neighbors, who urged him to limit his work to spiritual matters alone. They told him he would do well as long as he left politics alone. Turner, however, could not divorce religion from the well-being of his parishioners. Ignoring the warnings, he leapt headlong into politics. After helping to organize the Republican Party in Georgia and serving as a delegate at the Atlanta Constitutional Convention, he won election to the Georgia House of Representatives in April 1868. The white majority in the legislature, however, voted to unseat him and 23 other elected black legislators on the basis of their race. Turner responded with an eloquent and impassioned speech in which he declared, "God has weaved and tissued variety and versatility throughout the boundless space of his creation." He called the efforts to diminish people's worth on the basis of race a "thrust at the God of the Universe for making a man and not finishing him; it is simply calling the great Jehovah a fool." Nearly a century before the Civil Rights movement of the 1950 and 1960s, Turner led a march demanding voting rights for black citizens.

Turner's strong advocacy did not change many minds among whites, and it focused a great deal of animosity toward him. He once remarked, "If I had not secreted myself in houses at times, in the woods at other times, in a hollow log at another time, I would have been assassinated" by such groups as the Ku Klux Klan.

After years on the front lines of activism for racial equality, Turner grew pessimistic about the possibility of blacks being accepted as equals in white society. "As long as we remain among whites, the Negro will believe that the devil is black . . . and that God is white and that he bears no resemblance to him." This point of view led him to favor emigration to Africa. Turner became increasingly radical in his theological stance in his later years as he sought ways to free blacks from many generations of forced inferiority. In an 1898 address, he made the stunning pronouncement that, "We had rather . . . believe in no God, or . . . believe that all nature is God than to believe in the person of

God, and not to believe he is a Negro." Turner died on May 9, 1915.

Further Reading

Angell, Stephen Ward. *Bishop Henry McNeil Turner and African-American Religion in the South.* Knoxville: University of Tennessee, 1992.

Burkett, Randall K., and Richard Newman. *Black Apostles: Afro-American Clergy Confront the Twentieth Century.* Boston: G. K. Hall and Company, 1978.

Litwack, Leon, and August Meier, ed. *Black Leaders of the Nineteenth Century.* Urbana: University of Illinois Press, 1988.

Luken, Ralph E. *The Social Gospel in Black and White.* Chapel Hill: University of North Carolina Press, 1991.

Montgomery, William E. *Under Their Own Vine and Fig Tree: The African-American Church in the South, 1865–1900.* Baton Rouge: LSU Press, 1993.

Ponton, M. M. *The Life and Times of Henry M. Turner.* New York: Negro Universities Press, 1970.

Turner, Nat

(1800–1831) *slave rebellion leader*

No man struck terror into the hearts of white Southerners in the United States more than Nat Turner. Considered an instrument of God by some and an instrument of the devil by others, Turner had religious visions that inspired the greatest slave uprising in U.S. history.

Turner was born on October 2, 1800, on a slave plantation in Virginia. As is the case with most slaves, little information exists on his childhood. Apparently he was originally the property of a successful farmer named Benjamin Turner. His mother's name was Nancy but his father's name is not recorded. His father evidently escaped from slavery when Nat when nine. The boy and his mother were passed on to the nearby plantation of Benjamin Turner's son,

Samuel, at about that time. Nat Turner eventually married a woman named Cherry. In 1822, he and his wife were sold to Thomas Moore in the western part of Southhampton County for $400.

His various masters seemed satisfied, even pleased, with his industriousness and intelligence. Turner appears to have had an exceptional intellect and memory, and a pleasant personality that even whites found engaging. Although teaching slaves to read was taboo or illegal in most slave states, Turner's parents apparently had acquired the ability to read and passed along this skill to their son. By some accounts, Nat Turner's exceptional abilities made him something of an outsider among his fellow slaves, who regarded him with respect bordering on awe. His reputation in this regard has grown over the years to the point where some accounts speak of him as exercising a form of psychic control over other slaves and even his master, which most historians write off as an exaggeration.

Turner was exposed to Christianity at an early age, as Benjamin Turner was known to be a devout Methodist. Nat Turner spent a good deal of time reading and meditating on the Bible. Over time, he became well versed in Christianity and a firm believer, and some accounts say this put him in especially good stead with his masters. Details of Turner's life begin to emerge in the 1820s, when he first reported seeing religious visions. He was initially somewhat confused as to the meaning of these strange visions. In 1825, he escaped from the plantation and hid in the nearby woods for 30 days, only to return voluntarily some time later out of a Christian sense of duty. This baffling behavior apparently increased the distance between himself and other slaves.

Historian Thomas Gray argues that Turner's ultimate decision to stage a slave revolt was not prompted by revenge or anger but was the culmination of a long process of deliberation. According to Turner's later accounts, he received a particularly vivid vision on May 28, 1829. As he described it, "I heard a loud noise in the heavens, and the Spirit instantly appeared to me and said the Serpent was loosen, and Christ had laid down the yoke he had borne for the sins of men, and I should take it on and fight against the Serpent." Turner came to regard this as a command to preach the gospel and bring freedom to God's captive people on the plantations. He wrestled with this command for a long time, and in the end concluded, reluctantly, that he was to lead a violent revolt against slave owners.

Before he would do so, he awaited a sure sign from God. He regarded a solar eclipse that occurred in February 1831 as such a sign. At that time, he told four trusted companions of his

This artist's rendition shows the capture of Nat Turner in a swamp following his failed slave revolt. *(Schomburg Center for Research in Black Culture)*

plan, and set July 4 as the date for the slave revolt. At the appointed time, however, Turner was too sick to undertake the plan, and he put it off again while awaiting another sign. This came in the form of a strange discoloration of the sky in early August.

On August 21, Turner and his companions set out to begin the great liberation. They approached the home of Turner's owner at about 2 A.M., where they met other slaves who joined the group. Turner climbed a ladder and entered the house through an upper window, then let in the others. They killed the master and all the other occupants of the house and then moved on to neighboring farms, armed primarily with swords and clubs. Turner's rampaging army grew to 60 members who attacked one white dwelling after another. Over the course of the next 24 to 48 hours they killed 55 whites without suffering any losses. Panic, however, had spread throughout the countryside. The slaves found the houses they attacked empty; meanwhile, the whites were gathering in force to put down the murderous rebellion.

Turner's band was on its way to collect supplies of guns and ammunition to continue the destruction when it was met by a small militia. The band scattered after a brief skirmish, but then ran into a much larger militia. Several of Turner's men were wounded in the encounter, and he retreated with his army to a large plantation. Having been awake for 36 consecutive hours, Turner finally succumbed to sleep, which marked the end of his rebellion. By the time he awoke, half of his force had yielded to second thoughts and fled. Turner tried to rally the remaining force, but they were scattered after the second of two failed attacks. Turner obtained survival provisions and fled to the Great Dismal Swamp, where he hid in a cave and eluded capture for six weeks.

Turner's views on his slave insurrection were captured by interviewers and published in a book called *Nat Turner's Confessions*, but historians have cast doubt on the reliability of the proslavery authors. When asked whether the failure of his plot and his subsequent condemnation to death were proof that his actions were not divinely inspired, Turner reportedly responded, simply, "Was not Christ crucified?" Turner was hanged on November 11, 1831. Seventeen others also were hanged in connection with the uprising. Harsh reprisals followed against slaves in general in the succeeding months, followed by repressive laws to prevent such a thing from happening again.

Further Reading

Litwack, Leon, and August Meier, eds. *Black Religious Leaders of the Nineteenth Century*. Urbana: University of Illinois Press, 1988.

Ogbar, Jeffrey. "Prophet Nat and God's Children of Darkness," *Journal of Religious Thought* (winter 1997): 51–71.

Turner, Nat. *The Confessions of Nat Turner*. New York: AMS Press, 1973.

Young, Henry J. *Major Black Religious Leaders, 1755–1940*. Nashville, Tenn.: Abingdon, 1977.

Vanzant, Iyanla
(Rhonda Harris)
(1953–) *author, spiritual counselor*

Iyanla Vanzant arose from a horrendous childhood to become a best-selling author and internationally known motivational speaker on issues of spirituality. In 1992, Los Angeles mayor Tom Bradley described her as "an inspiration to all women, particularly young African-American women growing up through hardship in the inner city." She virtually created a market for inspirational religious literature and is considered the leading spiritual self-help authority for African-American women.

She was born Rhonda Harris on September 13, 1953, in the back of a taxicab in Brooklyn, New York. Her father, Horace Harris, worked in an underworld gambling operation. She was only two when her mother, Sarah Jefferson, died. Thereafter, she was in the care of various relatives who had little time or interest for the duty. Although she did well in school, she received no encouragement at home to excel. At the age of nine, Harris was raped by an uncle. Desperately seeking love and attention, she became pregnant by 15, married at 18, and had three children by age 23. Her husband had a violent temper and beat her severely on numerous occasions. The situation finally drove her to at-tempt suicide, and she spent time in a hospital psychiatric ward. After she was released, she and her children went on welfare. After eight years of barely subsisting, Vanzant got in touch with her spiritual side. She had grown up with an understanding of religion as a series of traditions and rules that instilled a fear of God. But she discovered that God was a loving God who was personally interested in her. "The thing that has reaped the greatest benefit for me," she has said, "was the day I finally said, 'Okay God, I don't know how to do this. You do it. Just tell me what to do whatever it is.'"

Deciding that she needed to take responsibility for finding a purpose to her life, Vanzant ignored family protests and enrolled at Medgar Evers College. She graduated in the summer of 1983 with a degree in public administration and immediately entertained job offers for more money than she had ever dreamed of making. That same year she was ordained as a Yoruba priestess in a religion that combined ancient African traditions of spirituality with contemporary African-American culture.

Vanzant went on to study law at Queens College Law School and obtained her degree in 1988. She then worked as a public defender in Philadelphia, Pennsylvania, for four years. In the meantime, she began putting together her life experience, her education, and her spiritual curiosity into a coherent package of inspirational enlightenment. She was heavily influenced in her thinking by a book called *Practicing the Presence* by Joel Goldsmith. Opening herself to the presence of God, Vanzant found that "God told me to do four things: tell my story, teach His law, write books, and make people laugh." To that end, in 1988, she founded the Inner Visions Network, an organization of spiritual and holistic practitioners dedicated to the idea that empowerment is a function of self-knowledge. It is Vanzant's view that the core issues in life revolve around an image of self. "Racism and sexism in and of themselves are not what limits Black women in America," she has said. "It is our perception of them." Vanzant wrote a book entitled *Tapping the Power Within,* but found that there was virtually no record of success for publishers trying to market inspirational books to African Americans. As a result, the only publisher that would accept her work was a small Harlem company called Writers and Readers, which published the book in 1992. The book sold so well that Vanzant had no trouble publishing subsequent books, particularly after Oprah Winfrey invited her to make several promotional appearances on her television show.

Vanzant employed the unusual writing method of developing an inspirational title that described what she was trying to say and then writing with the title in mind. In 1993, she published the first of her best-sellers, *Acts of Faith,* which described her healing journey from poverty and hopelessness to joy and self-reliance. The book sold more than 400,000 copies in a previously nonexistent market. She followed this success with 1995's *Faith in the Valley,* an examination of how a person's behavior can cause problems in life. Vanzant's title was a reminder that in order to reach peaks in life, one must also go through the valleys, and she gave advice on how to let the power of God enable one to do the work necessary to get through those difficult times.

Over the next several years, she wrote *Interiors: A Black Woman's Healing in Progress,* which used her own experience of mental illness and recovery as an inspiration to readers; *The Spirit of Man: A Vision of Transformation for Black Men and the Women Who Love Them,* which was one of her few ventures away from her female audience; and *Yesterday I Cried: Celebrating the Lessons of Living and Loving,* which she wrote as a reminder to readers that one does not attain a level of joy and peace but that life is an ongoing process of rediscovering and renewing these things.

Vanzant's popularity as an author and motivational speaker has made her a celebrity worldwide. Her Inner Visions Network has evolved over the years into Inner Visions Worldwide. She has expanded her audience to prison inmates, whom she sees as particularly in need of her religious philosophy. As of 2001, her prison ministry had attracted 3,000 followers, eight of whom were on death row. Trying to balance the time commitments of her ministry with the demands of her family, which grew to include a new husband, Adeyemi Bendele, in 1996, and grandchildren, Vanzant has attempted to implement a tour schedule that allows her to visit 20 cities annually. She often spends time teaching inner growth classes and workshops at her Inner Visions Spiritual Life Maintenance Center in Silver Spring, Maryland.

Further Reading

Phelps, Shirelle. *Contemporary Black Biography.* Vol. 17. Detroit, Mich.: Gale Research, 1998.

Vanzant, Iyanla. *Faith in the Valley: Lessons for Women in the Journey to Peace.* New York: Simon & Schuster, 1998.

———. *In the Meantime: Finding Yourself and the Love That You Want.* New York: Simon & Schuster, 1998.

———. *Yesterday I Cried.* New York: Simon & Schuster, 1998.

Varick, James

(1750–1827) *cofounder of African Methodist Episcopal Zion Church*

James Varick was the most prominent founding member of what came to be known as the African Methodist Episcopal Zion Church (AMEZ Church), which emerged as a rival to RICHARD ALLEN's African Methodist Episcopal Church (AME Church) in the 19th century. Varick was also one of the leaders of the black community in New York City during his lifetime.

Varick was born in 1750 near Newburgh, New York, to a slave mother and Richard Varick, her white owner. Set free when James was young, she took her children to live in New York City. There Varick spent at least some time in the black schools run by churches in the city. At the age of 16, Varick joined John Street Methodist Episcopal Church. Although the membership was primarily white, and the leaders exclusively so, he eventually obtained a license to preach at the church. However, black preachers were paid little, if anything, and he made his living as a shoemaker and tobacco cutter. In 1796, he married Aurelia Jones, with whom he had seven children, four of whom survived infancy.

As early as 1780, black members of the John Street church had felt the need to band together to hold separate prayer meetings and classes. With the black membership of the church growing rapidly, the whites kept control by increasing restrictions on blacks, shunting them off to limited seating in the very back rows. Irritated by this practice, Varick and about 30 other blacks pulled away from the church. They began meeting for their own services on Sunday afternoons and Wednesday evenings in a remodeled house.

By 1800, the group was ready to take the next step and build their own house of worship. That year they purchased a lot and built a wooden building for their church, which they named the Zion Church. In 1801, an independent charter was granted to the congregation, under the name of the African Methodist Episcopal Church.

This church, however, continued to be affiliated with the white Methodist Episcopal Church, which was slow in recognizing the need for and the qualifications of blacks as ordained ministers. It supplied ordained whites to serve a morning communion service on the second Sunday of the month. The African Americans, however, wanted to ordain their own pastors and initiated a protracted battle to free themselves from the authority of the high church. In 1806, Varick and two other blacks were ordained as deacons in New York. Even so, while white pastors generally were paid a living salary, Varick had to continue in his other businesses, as well as serving as a teacher in a school sponsored by his church. His leadership experience in organizing the New York church proved invaluable, and in 1818, he was asked to come to New Haven, Connecticut, to help start a similar separation effort.

Varick's name does not appear on the Zion Church's documents until 1820, when the congregation approved his resolution for formal separation from the white denomination. Aware that this was imminent, black church organizer Richard Allen of Philadelphia traveled to New York in an attempt to persuade Zion to join his fledgling denomination, the AME Church. Leery of handing over control of their destiny to anyone, white or black, after their experience with the Methodist Episcopal Church hierarchy, and put off by Allen's abrasive manner, Varick's congregation voted to remain an independent movement despite having no noticeable differences with Allen in theology. The two church organizations became rivals in the attempt to organize a growing African denomination, a competition that was especially confusing due to the fact that both claimed the name African Methodist Episcopal Church. Eventually, in 1848, the name Zion was added to the New York–based group's name to distinguish the two.

The congregation at Zion passed Varick's resolution and on September 13, 1820, named him and Abraham Thompson as the church's elders. The declaration of independence, however, did not achieve independence. The white Methodist Episcopal leadership continued to challenge the right of the congregation to govern itself outside of Methodist Episcopal rules. After two years of struggle, Varick's group finally succeeded in establishing legal recognition of its independence. That year Varick was elected and ordained as the denomination's first supervisor; he was reelected to the post in 1824.

Varick presided over the establishment of his denomination, which continues as a viable black denomination to this day, although it fell behind Allen's denomination early and has never caught up. On a larger scale, he was one of the leaders of the New York African Bible Society, and he was active in social improvement efforts of New York blacks through the establishment of the African Society for Mutual Relief and through his work in creating an African-American Masonic lodge.

Varick was also active politically. In 1821, he joined with other leading New York blacks in petitioning the state's constitutional convention to secure voting rights for African Americans. He was a staunch opponent of the African colonization movement, which he and his friends viewed as a white strategy for depriving African Americans of their rights and citizenship in the United States. Varick was one of the founders of *Freedom's Journal*, the nation's first black newspaper, which was printed at his church, and he made the church a popular meeting spot for the black community wishing to discuss any issue.

In July 1827, Zion Church held a rousing celebration of thanksgiving over the abolition of slavery in New York. Less than three weeks later, on July 22, 1827, Varick died.

Further Reading

Broadnav, Reginald. "Was James Varick the Founder of the AME Zion Church?" *AMEZ Quarterly* (January 1997): 33–50.

Garrity, John A., and Mark C. Carnes, eds. *American National Biography*. Vol. 22. New York: Oxford University Press, 2002.

Hamilton, Charles V. *The Black Preacher in America*. New York: William Morrow, 1972.

Lincoln, C. Eric, and Lawrence H. Mayima. *The Black Church in the African American Experience*. Durham, N.C.: Duke University Press, 1990.

Vesey, Denmark

(ca. 1767–1822) *African Methodist Episcopal preacher, insurrectionist*

The first black regiment organized to fight for the Union in the Civil War adopted as its battle cry "Remember Denmark Vesey of Charleston!" Vesey was a carpenter and African Methodist Episcopal Church (AME Church) preacher who masterminded the largest slave uprising conspiracy in U.S. history.

Details of Vesey's birth are not known, but historians believe he was born in 1767, possibly in West Africa. At some point, he was taken captive and transported to the West Indies, where he became the personal slave of Capt. Joseph Vesey, a professional slaver, in 1781. Through the captain's activities over the next two years, Vesey witnessed the horror and destruction of life caused by slave raiders.

Captain Vesey retired to Charleston, South Carolina, in 1883. Denmark Vesey continued as his slave and heard from the captain's contacts in the West Indies about a bloody but successful slave uprising in Haiti. The incident apparently weighed on his mind for several decades. But he was in no position to do anything about it until he had the tremendous fortune to win $1,500 in a lottery in 1799 or 1800. With that money he was able to purchase his freedom, although not that of his family. He set up a carpenter shop and became one of the more prosperous black tradesmen in the city.

Vesey then became active in the AME Church of MORRIS BROWN, later a bishop, and became a preacher himself. With the injustices of the slave trade seared into his memory, he constantly preached against the evils of the practice, citing Bible passages to support his position. Vesey grew bolder as time went on, even daring to argue openly with white supporters of slavery. Although he was free and living comfortably, he gradually became committed to the idea of leading an insurrection such as occurred in Haiti. He traveled to plantations and preached his message among slaves, trying to raise their receptivity to overt action.

By 1821, Vesey had recruited four trusted lieutenants committed to carrying out a slave rebellion. They built a complex, secret organization of some 9,000 slaves, each assigned to various units, but with limited communication so that few people knew many of the details of the plan. They raised money to buy weapons smuggled in from Haiti and developed a battle plan.

The strike date was set for July 14, a Sunday, when slaves could be about town without drawing suspicion and few whites would be supervising their slaves. At midnight, one group was to seize the guardhouse, others would capture the bridges, while still others were to be rampaging through town, killing whites.

Vesey and his lieutenants were adamant that no house slaves be included in the plan because of their tendency to be more loyal to their masters. The rule was violated, however, and a house slave warned his master of the plot. The leaders barely managed to hide incriminating evidence of the plan. Vesey moved up the target date, only to have another house slave betray the plan before it could be launched. Realizing the plan was now hopeless, Vesey burned his list of supporters before he was caught. Nonetheless, details of the plot frightened white southerners into a series of draconian laws persecuting blacks. Vesey was hanged on July 2, 1822; 35 others were executed for participating in the conspiracy; and Brown's church was closed. He was considered a martyr among abolitionists, and his aborted uprising inspired white abolitionist John Brown to try a similar effort more than 35 years later.

Further Reading

Adams, Russell L. *Great Negroes Past and Present.* Chicago: Afro-American Publishing Company, 1969.

Higginson, Thomas Wentworth. "Denmark Vesey," *Atlantic Monthly* online. Available online. URL: http://www.theatlantic.com.issues/1861/june/higgin.htm.

Kranz, Rachel, and Philip J. Koslow. *The Biographical Dictionary of African Americans.* New York: Facts On File, 1999.

"The Vesey Conspiracy," Africans in America web site. Available online. URL: http://www.amenet.org/quinn.htm. Downloaded February 18, 2003.

Waddles, Charleszetta
(Mother Waddles, Charleszetta Lina Campbell)
(1912–2001) *visionary, humanitarian*

Despite less than an eighth grade education and no theological training, Charleszetta Waddles became ordained at the age of 44 and went on to win recognition as one of the nation's most celebrated Christian warriors in the fight against poverty. Her Perpetual Mission for Saving Souls of All Nations has provided timely aid for countless desperate people throughout the world.

She was born Charleszetta Lina Campbell on October 7, 1912, in Saint Louis, Missouri, the oldest of seven children of Henry and Ella Campbell. She learned first-hand the toll that destitution can take on a family when her father lost his job as a barber. Deserted by his friends and gripped by despair, he never fully recovered from the ordeal and died when Charleszetta was 12. Ella Campbell's weak heart prevented her from assuming a heavier burden of responsibilities, and so Charleszetta quit school in eighth grade to support the family. The income from her jobs as a maid, cook, factory worker, and dishwasher were not adequate to fill the family's needs, and they had to go on federal assistance.

She became pregnant at 14 and married Clifford Walker, who died five years later. At 21 she married again, to LeRoy Wash, a truck driver. They moved to Detroit with their children seeking job opportunities. The couple divorced in the late 1940s, leaving her with nine children, back on welfare, and living in a friend's basement.

Throughout all of life's troubles, she remained upbeat. Despite her desperate situation in Detroit, she initiated a neighborhood women's prayer group. All of the participants had felt the sting of poverty and yet, rather than dwell on their own problems, they tried to think of ways to alleviate the miseries of others. By 1948, she had come to believe that God was calling her to "create a church that had a social conscience, that would feed the hungry, clothe the naked and take folk in from outdoors." She and her group began by asking everyone who came to their prayer meetings to bring a can of food. She collected the cans in her basement for distribution to the needy. As she warmed to the task of feeding the hungry, she opened a restaurant that charged only 35 cents for a meal. Charleszetta did all the cooking and cleaning.

As her work drew praise and support, she decided to form the church about which she had been dreaming. She became ordained in the

Pentecostal tradition in 1956 and soon afterward founded the Perpetual Mission for Saving Lost Souls. The following year she married Payton Waddles, a Ford Motor Company worker who encouraged her efforts.

Over the years, Mother Waddles, as she liked to be known, provided emergency relief for hundreds of thousands of desperate people. By the 1970s, she was providing food, clothing, shelter, legal services, and job placement in more than a dozen U.S. cities as well as 10 African nations. She relied totally on donations and accepted no government funds. Her work was publicized and partially funded by her two autobiographies and two cookbooks, and she also wrote a training manual for missions. In her lifetime, she won more than 300 awards for community service, including a special humanitarian award from President Nixon, and was the subject of a 1989 Public Broadcasting Service documentary entitled *Ya Done Good*. Waddles died on July 12, 2001. Known for her perpetual smile, Waddles shrugged off all accolades with the comment, "It's not me that's doing it, it's God."

Further Reading

Hine, Darlene Clarke. *Black Women in America*, M–Z. Brooklyn, N.Y.: Carlson Publishing, 1993.

Mabunda, L. Mpho. *Contemporary Black Biography.* Vol. 10. Detroit, Mich.: Gale Research, 1996.

"Mother Waddles: One Woman's War on Poverty," *Essence*, October 1990, p. 48.

"Mother Waddles: Perpetual Mission," Mother Waddles: Perpetual Mission web site. Available online. URL: http://www.motherwaddles.org/faq.htm. Posted August 30, 2002.

Walker, David

(1785–1830) *author, abolitionist*

David Walker was the first person to publish a treatise calling for armed black resistance to slavery. Although he was not a clergyman, he relied heavily on biblical imagery to prophesy the destruction of the United States unless the nation rid itself of slavery.

Walker was born in 1785 to a free mother in Wilmington, North Carolina. His father was a slave, and Walker grew up with such a hatred of the institution that he left the South to get away from it. He ended up in Boston in the 1820s, taught himself to read and write, and opened a secondhand clothing shop near the harbor.

Walker became obsessed with the issue of slavery and began thinking and writing on the subject. He was one of the founders of and main contributors to the abolitionist *Freedom's Journal,* the first black newspaper in the United States. His early positions amounted to a testing of the water as he wrote with caution and moderation. As late as autumn 1828, he published an article in which he urged readers to seek freedom but only within the constraints of the U.S. Constitution.

During that year, Walker married a fugitive slave, whom he referred to only as Eliza to protect her identity. Sometime in the next year, Walker became more radical in his opposition to slavery. In September 1829, he wrote, with the speed and passion of a man possessed, a work commonly known as *Appeal to the Coloured Citizens of the World*. Walker had it printed at his expense and found ways to distribute it.

At the core of Walker's arguments were two religious beliefs: first, that slavery was an abomination before God, and second, that Jesus would come again one day to judge the world. Walker warned, "When God Almighty commences his battle in the continent of America for the oppression of his people, tyrants will wish they were never born."

Such an argument was incendiary enough, but Walker carried it to conclusions that even abolitionists found shocking. He urged slaves to band together. "Do not two hundred and eight years of very intolerable suffering teach us the actual necessity of a general union among us?" Furthermore, he declared it the duty of every Christian, particularly black, to fight against slavery, because submission to slavery was seen as opposing God. "It is no more harm for you to kill the man who is trying to kill you than it is for you to take a drink of water," he declared.

While his entire argument was based on biblical ideas, Walker had little good to say about U.S. religious institutions. He titled one of the articles of his *Appeal*, "Out Wretchedness in consequence of the preachers of the Religion of Jesus Christ." In his view, the whites' perversion of the Christian doctrine was the very thing that brought about the blacks' condition of slavery. Walker's work triggered an immediate and violent reaction in the South. Several states made it a crime to possess the document, and there were groups that offered large sums of money for his capture, dead or alive.

Walker's wife and friends begged him to flee to Canada, but Walker refused. He was preparing material for a third edition of his *Appeal* when he was found dead in the doorway of his shop on June 28, 1830. It was widely believed that he had been poisoned. Walker's *Appeal* remained one of the most widely read books of its time and was a strong influence on the generation of abolitionists who followed him.

Further Reading

Newman, Richard, et al., eds. *Pamphlets of Protest: An Anthology of Early African American Protest Literature, 1790–1860.* New York: Routledge, 2001.

Walker, David. *David Walker's Appeal, in Four Articles, Together with a Preamble, to the Colored Citizens of the World, But in Particular, and Very Expressly, to Those of the United States of America.* Reprint, New York: Hill and Wang, 1965.

Wimbush, Vincent. "Reading Texts Through Worlds, Worlds Through Texts," *Semeia* 2 (1993): 129–140.

Young, Henry J. *Major Black Religious Leaders, 1755–1940.* Nashville, Tenn.: Abingdon, 1977.

Walker, Hezekiah Xzavier, Jr.
(1962–) *musician, clergy*

Hezekiah Walker is part of the tradition of black preacher-musicians who have brought their message of salvation through the fusion of traditional gospel with a contemporary genre. Nicknamed the "Pastor of Hip Hop," Walker has a long line of Grammy nominations to his credit and has built a thriving church in a neglected neighborhood of New York City.

Hezekiah Xzavier Walker, Jr., was born in 1962, in Brooklyn, New York. He was one of five children of extremely strict parents who banned them from dancing and going to movies. Church was a large part of their life; Walker joined the choir at the age of eight. As a teen, he began writing songs for a gospel ensemble group in which he participated.

When Walker was 14, his father died. He kept at his studies and eventually obtained a job with the Xerox Corporation in Stamford, Connecticut. However, when he was 21, his mother died as well, leaving Walker severely depressed. He quit his job and did nothing for two months while his savings disappeared. One day, he found the courage to pray about his situation. "When I finished, I sat down and wrote the song, 'I'll Make It,'" he remembers. That song formed the foundation for a 12-member gospel ensemble group he formed called the Love Fellowship Crusade Choir, which made it the title song of their first record album, released in 1986.

The group struggled for a while until they were able to sign a contract with Benson Records, an established gospel label. They achieved their breakthrough in 1993 when *Live in Toronto* produced brisk sales. In that same year, Walker decided to turn his personal ministry to homeless persons and prison inmates into something larger. He became an ordained minister and in 1994 opened a storefront church, the Love Fellowship Tabernacle, in a ravaged neighborhood in the East New York section of Brooklyn that he believed was in special need of a spiritual presence. Love Fellowship Tabernacle had only eight members at its first service, but Walker's charisma, energy, and infusion of urban culture, including rap music, into standard Pentecostal-style worship drew crowds, especially among the young.

Not wishing to exploit the success of his Love Fellowship Crusade Choir, Walker at first refused to have a choir at his church. But the success of his music drew many music lovers, including talented musicians, who were looking for an outlet to praise the Lord. Walker abandoned his objections and formed the Love Fellowship Tabernacle Church Choir in 1995.

The choir proved to be one of the best in the nation. In 1995 it won a Grammy Award for Best Gospel Album by a Choir or Chorus with its *Live in Atlanta at Morehouse College.* The choir, which grew to more than 200 members, followed this achievement with Grammy nominations in 1996, 1997, and 1998, gaining such fame that they were invited to back up such performing artists as Whitney Houston and the group Hootie and the Blowfish in concert.

The Love Fellowship Tabernacle grew so quickly that it had to relocate to an 850-seat facility in 1996. It outgrew that facility a few years later, and the congregation completed work on a plush 1,500-seat sanctuary in 2001.

Walker has been criticized for using the proceeds of his profession to finance a luxurious lifestyle that includes a 22-room mansion. But he prefers to concentrate on the work that his Love Fellowship Tabernacle and choirs are carrying out. "This is my baby," he said, "and I have the joy and contentment of a father who's seen his children growing up strong, straight, true and doing great things for the Lord."

Further Reading
Hedges, Chris. "Gospel Message, Rap Style," *The New York Times*, April 21, 2001, B1–4.

Henderson, Ashyia N. *Contemporary Black Biography.* Vol. 34. Detroit, Mich.: Gale Research, 2002.

Walker, Hezekiah. *Hezekiah Walker and the Love Fellowship Crusade Choirs.* New York: Warner Books, 1998.

West, Cornel
(Cornel Ronald West)
(1953–   ) *philosopher, theologian*

Cornel West has been called the Black Jeremiah, a prophet for modern times. One of the most prominent and respected critics of American society in recent years, he has written several significant books addressing current social issues through the lens of a black intellectual.

West was born on June 2, 1953, in Tulsa, Oklahoma, the son of Clifton, Jr., an air force civilian administrator, and Irene West, an elementary-school teacher. In the late 1950s the family moved to Sacramento, California. There West, the grandson of a pastor, grew up in a stable, close-knit, Christian home.

He became active in social issues when, at the age of 10, he marched with his family in a civil rights demonstration in their city. In high school, he and three other black Sacramento students orchestrated a successful citywide school strike over their demands to have a black studies course added to the curriculum. West's early heroes were the Black Panthers, liberation theologian JAMES H. CONE, and especially MARTIN LUTHER KING, JR.

A brilliant student, West enrolled at Harvard University at the age of 17. There he took such heavy course loads that he was able to complete the four-year curriculum in three years, with majors in Near Eastern languages and literature. One of his professors described him as "the most intellectually aggressive and highly cerebral student I have taught in my 30 years."

West came to the conclusion that there were three basic components to the Christian life: Christian ethical service, humility, and political striving for social improvement. Therefore, West never was content to simply explore the intellectual issues at stake, but involved himself in social causes, including prison visitation, and political and social causes, such as protesting U.S. policy toward African nations. West came to describe himself as a "non-Marxist socialist," who believed that the beliefs of Christianity and socialism could be reconciled. He eventually joined the Democratic Socialists of America.

West graduated from Harvard in 1973, and went on to obtain a master's degree from Princeton in 1975. He then continued to study at Harvard, earning his Ph.D. in 1980 while working as assistant professor of religion at Union Theological Seminary in New York. He wrote profusely during that decade, and many of his writings eventually made their way into published books. The first of these was *Prophesy Deliverance! An Afro-American Revolutionary Christianity,* in which he argued that prophetic Christianity had great potential as a framework for combating racism and oppression.

In 1984, West moved from Union Theological Seminary to a teaching position at Yale Divinity School. Continuing to put his beliefs into action, he demonstrated in protest against Yale's financial investments in companies that did business with the apartheid government of South Africa, and he was jailed. The Yale administration disciplined him for his actions by revoking his scheduled leave of absence. Having already made arrangements to teach at the University of Paris during that time, West spent the months between February and April of 1987 commuting across the Atlantic Ocean to fulfill his two commitments.

He soon left the Yale faculty and spent a year teaching at Union Theological Seminary. While he was there in 1988, his book *Prophetic*

Fragments, a critique of contemporary culture, was published. In 1989, West took a position as professor of religion and African American Studies at Princeton University. In that year, his book entitled *The American Evasion of Philosophy: A Genealogy of Pragmatism* was published. In this work, West advocated what he saw as the two primary values in culture: individualism and democracy. West presented his own vision of pragmatism in support of democracy based on his understanding of the biblical prophetic tradition.

In 1991, West had two important books published. One of them, *Ethical Dimensions of Marxist Thought,* was actually written during the 1970s. In it, West integrated the best of socialist and Christian thought. The other book, which he coedited, was *Breaking Bread: Insurgent Black Intellectual Life,* in which he compiled some of the most thought-provoking writings of contemporary black intellectuals as part of his overall goal to help foster a new generation of effective, progressive black leadership.

West's most widely known and accessible book was *Race Matters,* published in 1993. His stated purpose in the book was

> to be as bold and defiant in my criticism of any form of xenophobia, as honest and candid about the need for civil response and social accountability of each one of us, and as charitable and compassionate toward any political perspective from which we can gain insight and wisdom to empower us.

The book was damning in its criticism of the way Americans, including the churches, have inculcated race into the fabric of society. "To engage in a serious discussion of race in America," wrote West, "we must begin not with the problems of black people but with the flaws of American society." He saw the application of love as the only answer to a bleak future and pulled no punches in describing what he saw as the consequences of inadequate response: "Either we learn a new language of empathy and compassion or the fire this time will consume us all."

West has put into practice elements of his compassionate solution, most notably his attempts to create understanding between blacks and Jews by writing a regular column in the Jewish journal *Tikkun*. West has been married three times and has one child from his first marriage. He currently holds the position of professor of African American Studies and Philosophy of Religion at Harvard University.

Further Reading

Boynton, Robert. "Princeton's Public Intellectual," *The New York Times Magazine*, September 15, 1991, p. 39.

Henderson, Ashyia N. *Contemporary Black Biography*. Vol. 33. Detroit, Mich.: Gale Research, 2002.

West, Cornel. *Keeping Faith: Philosophy and Race in America*. New York: Routledge, 1993.

———. *Race Matters*. Boston: Beacon Press, 1993.

Young, George, ed. *Cornel West: A Critical Reader*. Malden, Mass.: Blackwell Publishers, 2001.

White, Reggie
(1961–) *football player, minister*

For most of his career, the Reverend Reggie White was equally at home pounding on offensive tackles or preaching the gospel. White won fame as the most devastating pass rusher of his era and one of the most colorful, outspoken evangelical figures in all of sports.

White was born on December 19, 1961, in Chattanooga, Tennessee, to Thelma White, a single parent, and grew up in a multiracial neighborhood in that city. Baseball was his passion until he saw O. J. Simpson play in a football game on television, and he then switched his allegiance to football.

At the age of 13, White experienced a profound religious revelation. From that point, he carried his Bible with him wherever he went. He

declared that he wanted to be a football player and a minister, and he set about fulfilling that dream. In high school, White developed into an all-American football lineman, an all-state basketball center, and a third-place finisher in the shot put at the state meet. At the University of Tennessee, White recorded 15 sacks and more than 100 tackles in his senior year to earn Southeastern Conference Player of the Year honors.

White played two seasons with the Memphis Showboats of the United States Football League before signing with the Philadelphia Eagles of the National Football League (NFL) in 1985. Despite missing four games, he finished the season among the league leaders in sacks, with 13, and earned the NFL's Defensive Rookie of the Year award. For the next several years, White was as terrifying a defensive lineman as the league had seen. In 1986, White recorded 18 sacks, and he increased that total to 21 the following year. Meanwhile, he became so vocal both on and off the field about his Christianity that he was given the nickname "Minister of Defense."

Frustrated by team controversies and contract disputes, White played out his option in Philadelphia and became a free agent in 1992. NFL teams wooed White so lavishly that his "Reggie Tour" of NFL cities became national news. White shocked even himself by choosing Wisconsin's Green Bay Packers in the end, but he was convinced that God was calling him to play for the team. With the veteran defensive end serving as inspirational leader of the defense, the Packers improved each year. During the off-season, White founded and worked for an inner-city church in Knoxville, Tennessee, and organized an urban renewal project in Green Bay called Urban Hope. Regarding his outspoken Christian witness, White responded, "I'm not a religious man. I am a man that's seeking a purpose and I'm a man that's seeking the will of God."

In 1996, White's long quest for a championship finally came to fruition. He anchored a defense that allowed the fewest points in the NFL as the Packers swept through the playoffs and into the Super Bowl, where White recorded three sacks in the team's 35–21 victory. That year, an arsonist destroyed his East Knoxville church. Due to generous donations, largely from Packer fans, White set about rebuilding the church.

He continued to play at a high level through 1998, when he notched 16 sacks and was named the NFL's Defensive Player of the Year. That year he created a storm of controversy with his religiously based, antihomosexual remarks before the Wisconsin legislature. White retired from football, only to yield to the urge to get back on the field in 2000 with the Carolina Panthers. In this final season, White sacked quarterbacks five times to bring his NFL-record sack total to 198.

Further Reading

White, Reggie. *In the Trenches*. Nashville, Tenn.: Thomas Nelson, 1996.

———, with Steve Hubbard. *God's Playbook: The Bible's Game Plan for Life*. Nashville, Tenn.: Thomas Nelson, 1988.

Williams, Cecil
(1929–   ) *Methodist clergy*

Cecil Williams has transformed Glide United Methodist Church from a small, staid middle-class congregation on the edge of a dangerous neighborhood to one of the largest, most radically innovative congregations in the United States. As reported by *Life* magazine, "Visitors, from liberal community activists to Republican philanthropists, from Oprah [Winfrey] to [President Bill] Clinton have come away speaking of Glide as a model religious institution, a church for the 21st century."

Cecil Williams was born on September 22, 1929, in San Angelo, Texas, the youngest in a family of six children. He was a hardworking, intelligent student who, from an early age, was pegged for greatness by members of the black Methodist church that his family attended faithfully. But he was also marked by the overt racism of the community and bore memories of his mother being ridiculed for presuming to shop at a white grocery store. The last straw for him came when his grandfather, a local cowboy legend known as Papa Jack, died in 1938. Despite his esteemed reputation, Papa Jack was buried in the crowded, poorly maintained section of the cemetery reserved for blacks.

Something about this injustice pushed Williams to the edge of insanity. For weeks he hid in bed, shivering under the covers as what he thought were aliens disguised as humans told him to die. According to Williams, the resolution to this horrifying nightmare came to him in a flash one night. He saw that his destiny was not to die but to build a church where Jesus' words of love would be lived out in a way the world had never before seen. Unlike all the churches he knew, this would be an integrated church.

Williams set about fulfilling his mission by attending Sam Houston College in Austin, Texas, where he showed such ability that he was chosen class president. Upon graduating in 1952, Williams was one of the first five African Americans admitted to Perkins School of Theology at Southern Methodist University in Dallas. While studying there, he experienced an acceptance that reaffirmed his commitment to a colorblind community of faith.

Williams earned his bachelor of divinity degree at the school in 1955 and was assigned to the lowliest of Methodist congregations in Hobbs, New Mexico, where a total of six members met in a schoolhouse. The experience proved valuable to Williams, who in such a small, informal setting learned to discard his

Cecil Williams's unconventional approach to ministry transformed struggling Glide Memorial Methodist Church of San Francisco into a prototype of modern inner-city ministry. *(Corbis)*

prepared manuscript sermons and preach directly to the congregation without notes. After building the congregation up to 45 members in one year, he left to take a multifaceted position as dean, chaplain, and instructor at Huston-Tillotson College. There he acquired a reputation as a radical when he helped lead a successful student revolt over lack of student input in their own education.

In 1959, Williams received a fellowship for a postgraduate program at the Pacific School of Religion in Berkeley, California. Two years later, he was called to revive the dispirited Saint

James United Methodist Church in Kansas City, Missouri. Williams presided over a stunning reversal of fortune, attracting an integrated influx of new members that boosted the church's membership from about three dozen to more than 700 in four years. While impressive, however, it only foreshadowed William's plans.

Williams moved to San Francisco in 1964 to become director of community involvement at the Glide Urban Center, a program run under the auspices of Glide Memorial Methodist Church. Despite a solid endowment, the primarily white, middle-class church struggled for survival. In 1966, Williams was a surprise choice as the church's new pastor.

Glide was where Williams would attempt to make his dream come true. On his third Sunday in the pulpit, he tore off his ministerial robes and thundered, "We're gonna make these walls come down!" To many longtime members, it seemed that what Williams had in mind was destroying the church altogether. Under his direction, in the summer of 1967 the church hosted an event called the Invisible Circus, which attracted a host of San Francisco's counterculture. Not only did the event spiral out of control, with rampant drug use and obscenities scrawled on the church walls, but Williams then invited many of these impolite visitors back for worship on Sunday. Williams then took the even more radical move of taking down the giant cross on the church's rear wall, declaring that he wanted the church to be a symbol of life, not death. Williams brought in rock bands and celebrities to appeal to people who were suspicious of normal church traditions.

These actions prompted the departure of many of the congregation's members. But in their place, Williams brought in even larger numbers of nontraditional worshipers, including street people, hippies, drug addicts, prostitutes, and people from non-Christian religions such as Jews and Muslims. Williams had the integrated congregation he had sought, filled with people from all walks of life and nationalities. Glide Memorial soon had standing room only, as people flocked to experience a kind of spiritual welcome they had never before received. Said one Jewish member, "I don't think I ever understood what a family was until I came here."

Williams mobilized his congregation to make a difference in the community, showing the love of Jesus. He led a march to a drug-infested neighborhood, invited users to share their stories and to join the congregation. He made it clear that he expected everyone in the congregation to join in with some part of the church's

mission, whether it was in substance-abuse programs, domestic-violence programs, providing food and shelter, anger management, or job and computer skills. "If your power of the Spirit does not lead you outward, then the power of your Spirit does not count," he declared.

Glide Memorial became so closely associated with social justice that even the notorious Symbionese Liberation Army designated it as the community organization it wanted to administer its radical social program in exchange for the release of its kidnap victim, Patty Hearst. In 1980, Williams published a book relating his experiences in building his church, entitled *I'm Alive: An Autobiography.* The following year, he founded an organization called the New Moral Minority to counter the effects of the right-leaning religious Moral Majority.

Since then, Williams's program of integrated social action has attracted curious government officials and celebrities wishing to see firsthand what it has accomplished. At the turn of the 21st century, Glide Memorial was the largest provider of social services in San Francisco.

Further Reading

Miller, Kenneth. "A Church for the 21st Century," *Life,* April 1997, pp. 47–55.
Murphy, Larry G., ed. *Encyclopedia of African American Religious Biography.* New York: Garland Publishing, 1993.
Williams, Cecil. *No Hiding Place: Empowerment and Recovery for Our Troubled Communities.* New York: HarperCollins, 1992.

Wilmore, Gayraud Stephen, Jr.

(1921–) *Presbyterian clergy, cocreator of National Commission of Black Churchmen*

Gayraud Wilmore is a Presbyterian clergyman and theologian who was one of the primary spokesmen for Black Power concerns in mainstream U.S. denominations during the 1970s.

Gayraud Stephen Wilmore, Jr., was born on January 20, 1921, in Philadelphia, Pennsylvania, one of three sons of Gayraud Wilmore, Sr., and Patricia Wilmore. While fighting with the 92nd Infantry of the United States Army in Italy during World War II, he observed at close quarters the cruelty of which humans are capable, and this was a key factor in his decision to go into the ministry. Wilmore attended Lincoln University in Pennsylvania and, upon graduation in 1947, continued at the Lincoln University Theological Seminary. In 1950, he obtained his bachelor of divinity degree and married Lee Wilson, with whom he would have four children.

While still in seminary, Wilmore began his service in the Presbyterian Church, the denomination of his family, as a student pastor at Faith Presbyterian Church in York, Pennsylvania. Once out of school, he assumed leadership of Second Presbyterian Church in West Chester, Pennsylvania. During his four years there, he earned a master's degree at Temple University in Philadelphia.

In 1953, Wilmore accepted a position on the executive staff of the Middle Atlantic region of the Student Christian Movement, a group that worked with college students. A few years later he moved to a leadership position with the Presbyterian Church's Board of Christian Education. In the late 1950s, he was the major force behind the organization of the National Committee of Negro Churchmen. Wilmore then taught social ethics at the Pittsburgh Theological Seminary, beginning in 1960. During this time he wrote a book called *The Secular Relevance of the Church*. In 1963, he was asked to serve as executive director of the United Presbyterian Church's Commission on Religion and Race.

While serving in this position, Wilmore drew national attention for his response to a challenge to white denominations from Black Power advocates in the form of James Forman's *Black Manifesto*. The *Black Manifesto* challenged white churches to pay hundreds of millions of dollars in reparations to African Americans for their role in contributing to segregation and the resulting economic loss to blacks. Wilmore supported the manifesto's demands for a more intentional sharing of power with blacks and lent the document credibility by virtue of his position in the higher ranks of a mainstream denomination. Wilmore wrote "The Churches' Response to the Black Manifesto," in which he said, "It may well be that James Forman is being used by God to declare to the churches, 'this night your soul is required of you; and the things you have prepared, whose will they be?'"

Wilmore was one of the primary creators of the National Commission of Black Churches, which he saw as representing "the beginning of Black reflection in the racial situation in America independent of the white theologians and ethicists." In 1970, he published a highly acclaimed history entitled *Black Religion and Black Radicalism*. Two years later he joined the faculty of Boston University, then moved on to Colgate-Rochester Seminary in 1974. In 1983 Wilmore was named Dean of the Master of Divinity Program and Professor of Afro-American Studies at New York Theological Seminary. He moved on to Interdenominational Theological Seminary in Atlanta, from which he retired in 1990.

Further Reading

Findlay, James F., Jr. *Church People in the Struggle*. New York: Oxford University Press, 1993.

Turner, Eugene. *Dissent and Empowerment: Essays in Honor of Gayraud Wilmore*. Louisville, Ky.: Witherspoon Press, 1999.

Wilmore, Gayraud. *Black and Presbyterian: The Heritage and the Hope*. Philadelphia: Geneva Press, 1983.

———. *Black Religion and Black Radicalism*. 3d ed. Maryknoll, N.Y.: Orbis Books, 1998.

Wright, Jeremiah, Jr.

(1941–   ) United Church of Christ clergy, theologian

Through passionate and effective preaching and special attention to presenting the gospel in the context of the black community, Jeremiah Wright has helped his congregation on Chicago's South Side grow from a tiny, struggling community into the largest United Church of Christ (UCC) congregation in the United States.

Wright was born on September 22, 1941, in Philadelphia, Pennsylvania, the son and grandson of preachers. For much of his youth he was openly rebellious against his upbringing and was even arrested for grand larceny at age 15. During his senior year of college at Howard University, he suddenly quit school and joined the U.S. Marines, followed by a stint in the U.S. Navy. In 1967, he was sitting on the steps of a church drinking alcoholic beverages when he was confronted by the pastor, who asked him a simple question: "When you love something as much as I suspect you love the church, where do you think you'll do the most good? On the outside throwing stones or on the inside making it what God wants?"

The message hit home with Wright, who joined the church the next morning. He was ordained eight months later and returned to Howard, where he earned both his bachelor's and master's degrees by 1969. During the next few years, as he worked toward an advanced degree at the University of Chicago, Wright served as an assistant pastor and a researcher for the American Association of Theological Schools. He expected his calling to be in an academic setting until he encountered the church in the inner city of Chicago. Trinity United Church of Christ, which had once ministered largely to upscale, educated blacks, was disintegrating during the Black Power movement of the 1960s. In 1971, the congregation's 87 remaining active members took a bold stand, declaring their church to be "unashamedly black and unapologetically Christian," and sought a pastor who could lead them in that direction. It was exactly the calling that Wright felt he was created for.

Wright found he had to jettison much of what he had learned in seminary. "The way we were taught to preach in seminary prior to the 70s, they should have changed the course to 'How to Destroy a Black Church,'" he said. Thundering from the pulpit or wandering among the pews, Wright's messages spoke directly to the hearts of African Americans. He showed a rare ability to relate the spiritual message of the Bible to contemporary issues, particularly in the area of civil rights.

At the same time, he took issue with what he saw as the exclusive nature of mainline Christianity. "Contrary to what Jesus talks about in terms of 'whosoever will, let them come,'" he said, "mainline denominations say 'our kind of Christian.'" Fighting against that image, he began building a ministry of outreach to draw in the lost and afflicted of the neighborhood. Over time, Trinity UCC has developed 60 ministries of support and outreach.

Wright is widely considered one of the nation's finest preachers, and he works hard at the task, delivering three different sermons every Sunday. Largely as a result of his vision and leadership, the services are packed. At a time when mainstream denominations have been experiencing steady decline, Trinity UCC has experienced explosive growth and now has the largest membership of any UCC church in the nation.

Further Reading

Wright, Jeremiah, Jr. *Good News: Sermons of Hope for Today's Families.* Valley Forge, Pa.: Judson Press, 1995.

———. *What Makes You Strong: Sermons of Joy and Strength from Jeremiah Wright.* Valley Forge, Pa.: Judson Press, 1998.

Wright, Richard Robert, Jr.
(1878–1967) *African Methodist Episcopal bishop, editor*

Richard Wright is regarded as the most famous and highly educated bishop of the African Methodist Episcopal Church (AME Church) in the 20th century.

He was born Richard Robert Wright on April 16, 1878, in Cuthbert, Georgia, the son of Major Richard Robert and Lydia Wright. His father was widely known as the "black boy of Atlanta" for his highly publicized remark to Freedmen's Bureau director O. O. Howard, "Tell them we are rising." The elder Wright, a former slave, advanced to a position as president of the Georgia State Industrial College and was a prominent member of the Republican Party.

The younger Wright dedicated himself to the AME Church during his youth. He attended Georgia State College while working in a lay capacity at Bethel AME Church in Augusta, Georgia. In 1898, he obtained his degree as well as an exhorter's license. Wright went on to enroll at the University of Chicago Theological Seminary, where he earned a bachelor of divinity degree in 1901. Now an ordained elder in the church, he spent two years lecturing in Hebrew and Greek at Payne Theological Seminary before resuming his studies at the University of Chicago and assisting at REVERDY CASSIUS RANSOM's church. In 1903, he sailed to Germany to study for two years at the University of Berlin and the University of Leipzig.

When he returned to the United States, Wright became interested in the banking business and founded the Eighth Ward Building and Loan Association in 1906. In 1909, he began editing the *Christian Recorder,* the official periodical of the AME Church, and performing editing duties for the denomination's publishing house. He became intensely interested in urban issues, and pursued a doctorate in sociology at the University of Pennsylvania, which he completed in 1911.

As an editor, Wright was a strong advocate of black migration from the rural South to northern cities. Seeing this migration as a golden opportunity for blacks to come together in such numbers and with such purpose as to assume an important role in American society, he asked his readers to "throw open the arms of welcome to every Negro who desires to come." Putting into practice what he preached, Wright turned to his banking expertise to create the Citizens and Southern Banking Company in 1920, specifically to serve the needs of African-American migrants to Philadelphia. Eventually, this operation became the largest black-owned bank in the nation.

Wright continued as editor of the *Christian Recorder* even after he took over the position of president at Wilberforce University in Ohio. Only when he was named an AME bishop in 1936 did he relinquish those duties. His first four years as bishop were spent in South Africa, where he led the formation of more than 50 new schools. Returning to the United States, Wright served another brief term as president at Wilberforce in addition to his duties as bishop.

Wright gained notice for the number and quality of his writings, which included a study guide for prospective missionaries and several books, most notably a biographical history, *The Bishops of the African Methodist Episcopal Church.* He spent his later years serving as historiographer of his denomination before his death in Philadelphia on December 12, 1967.

Further Reading
Campbell, James T. *Songs of Zion.* Chapel Hill: University of North Carolina Press, 1998.

Wright, Richard R. *87 Years behind the Black Curtain: An Autobiography.* Philadelphia: Rare Book Company, 1965.

X–Y

X, Malcolm See MALCOLM X.

Young, Andrew Jackson
(1932–   ) *United Church of Christ clergy, politician*

Andrew Young began his career as a United Church of Christ (UCC) pastor and ended up as a groundbreaking and influential politician, statesman, and civic organizer.

He was born Andrew Jackson Young, Jr., in New Orleans, Louisiana, on March 12, 1932, to Andrew, Sr., and Daisy Young. A bright student, Young graduated from high school at the age of 15. He attended Howard University in Washington, D.C., where he majored in biology in preparation for following in his father's footsteps as a dentist. However, inspired by the college president, MORDECAI WYATT JOHNSON, he opted instead to enroll at Hartford Theological Seminary in Connecticut. Young completed his studies at the seminary in 1955 and headed south to serve as a pastor in Marion, Alabama. Soon afterwards, he moved on to Beachton, Georgia, where he attempted to emulate the strategy of the Southern Christian Leadership Conference (SCLC) in organizing black voter registration and desegregation campaigns and opposing the Ku Klux Klan.

In 1957, Young accepted a position as associate director of the National Council of Churches' Department of Youth Work, which brought him to New York City. Four years later, he took an assignment with the UCC as director of its voter education program in the South. While working in Atlanta in that job, he became involved with the SCLC, and in 1962 became MARTIN LUTHER KING, JR.'s, administrative assistant. For the next several years, he took care of many of the organizational details of the SCLC's civil rights struggle. Black congressman Julian Bond claimed, "King was the spearthrower and Andy came behind and put it all together." Young was named the SCLC's executive director in 1964. He was on the balcony in Memphis when King was assassinated on April 4, 1968.

After working hard to help the organization regroup after the loss of King, Young decided to move in a different direction in the fight for equality. In 1970, he ran for Congress in Georgia's Fifth District. He won the Democratic primary but lost in the general election. The defeat allowed him to accept an appointment as chair of Atlanta's Community Relations Committee, where he gained experience and voter recognition. Young then tried again in the 1972 election and won, making him the first African-American representative from a southern state in 70 years.

official policy. "I have always seen my role as a thermostat, rather than a thermometer," he said. In 1979, however, he violated State Department rules prohibiting unauthorized contact with the Palestinian Liberation Organization (PLO), and was forced to resign.

Young rebounded by winning the mayoral election in Atlanta in 1981. During his term in office, Atlanta enjoyed unprecedented business growth, and Young was reelected by a large margin in 1985. He set his sights on the governorship in 1990 but was defeated in the primary. Again, Young landed on his feet after a loss, guiding the Atlanta Olympic Program Committee in its successful sponsorship of the 1996 Olympic Games. In 1999 he was named president of the National Council of Churches.

Further Reading

"Andrew Young to NCC post," *Christian Century,* November 1999, pp. 1048–49.

Fairclough, Adam. *To Redeem the Soul of America: The SCLC and Martin Luther King, Jr.* Athens: University of Georgia Press, 1987.

Hamilton, Charles V. *The Black Preacher in America.* New York: William Morrow, 1972.

Young, Andrew. *An Easy Burden.* New York: HarperCollins, 1992.

United Church of Christ pastor Andrew Young fashioned a remarkable career in politics as a United Nations ambassador and mayor of Atlanta. *(Library of Congress)*

Despite being such an outsider, Young proved adept at learning the rules and traditions and working within the system to get things done. He was easily reelected in 1974 and 1976. His strong endorsement of Jimmy Carter in 1976 helped provide momentum for the campaign that carried Carter into the White House. Carter then named Young the U.S. ambassador to the United Nations (UN). In his two and a half years of service at the UN, Young often strayed outside the normal job description for an ambassador, rendering his own opinion and forcing discussion of issues even when it did not fit

Youngblood, Johnny Ray
(1948–   ) *Baptist clergy*

Johnny Youngblood faced the challenge of revitalizing a dying church in one of New York's most violent neighborhoods. Not only did he succeed spectacularly, but he did so by focusing on the church's most neglected and antagonistic constituency, the young African-American male.

Johnny Ray Youngblood was born in New Orleans, Louisiana, on June 23, 1948. Neither of his parents, Palmon and Ottie Mae Youngblood, were high school graduates. Palmon, who worked as a laborer at a sugar refinery, had little to do with rearing their three children and was often away gambling and drinking. Ottie Mae worked hard as a maid and a nanny to put the children through Catholic school. She also exposed Johnny to a heavy dose of religion at Holy Family, a Spiritualist congregation run by a pastor named Mother Jordan. The pastor convinced Johnny Youngblood that he was called to preach and began grooming him to follow in her footsteps. By the age of 12, Youngblood obtained a license to preach and was locally famous as the "boy preacher" on Jordan's weekly radio show. He also organized a 35-member youth choir that performed throughout the region.

Youngblood, however, had doubts about some of Holy Family's doctrine, and he was especially bothered by the lack of males in the church. Upon graduation from high school, he enrolled at Dillard University with plans to become a teacher, not a pastor. While in school, however, he found himself in a moral quandary when he got a girl pregnant. Reluctant to turn to his church for support, he instead leaned on his college friend, Eli Wilson. Wilson introduced him to his father, a Baptist minister who also worked as a longshoreman. Intrigued by this masculine presence in religion, Youngblood attended services at Wilson's church and was so moved that he was baptized and licensed to preach in the Baptist faith. Shortly thereafter, Youngblood left home after a heated argument with his father about money for his college tuition.

For a time he supported himself as an itinerant preacher but was still unclear about his path in life when Reverend Wilson urged him to make use of his exceptional speaking ability and presence. "Man, if I had what you have, couldn't nobody touch me," he declared. Youngblood agreed to continue in school and attend seminary at least on a trial basis. In 1970, he enrolled at Colgate-Rochester Theological Seminary in Rochester, New York, and

Johnny Ray Youngblood's energy, vision, and emphasis on male involvement transformed a dying church into a significant community presence. *(St. Paul Community Baptist Church)*

accepted that this was his career calling. While at the seminary, he took a course entitled "The Gospel and the Ghetto," taught by Reverend William Augustus Jones, a pastor in Brooklyn. Jones recognized Youngblood's potential for inner-city ministry, and when Youngblood graduated in 1973, he invited him to join him as an assistant pastor. Youngblood was pleased to discover a context in which the Christian gospel was not merely "empty utterances of Christian brotherhood," but could have a dynamic effect in bringing hope to a violent, despairing neighborhood. It meshed with what he read in the book of Luke about preaching the gospel to the poor and healing the brokenhearted, about restoring hope in people's lives as well as saving their souls.

After a year with Jones, Youngblood was ready to try inner-city ministry on his own. In the spring of 1974 he accepted a call to St. Paul Community Baptist Church in the Bedford-Stuyvesant section of Brooklyn. Located in one of the city's most violent, impoverished, and drug-ridden neighborhoods, St. Paul's was a dying church of fewer than 100 worshipers that had little hope for the future. Youngblood noticed immediately the absence of black males, other than some longtime members of the board of trustees who controlled the congregation. Sensing the board's antagonism to his assertion of authority, Youngblood decided to risk a major confrontation on his third Sunday on the job. In a volatile meeting, he forced the resignations of half the board. Then he set about rebuilding the church.

Youngblood stressed the importance of the biblical tithe, the concept of giving the first tenth of one's earnings to the church. He cleared up the congregation's debt and then began the process of buying land and buildings in the neighborhood and replacing the illegal businesses that had been taking place in them with family-owned, community-minded businesses. Under his leadership, St. Paul joined with Bedford-Stuyvesant congregations and a group called the Industrial Areas Foundation to create an ambitious program to provide decent housing for area families. Known as the Nehemiah Housing Project, this effort constructed 2,300 two-story, single-family homes in some of Brooklyn's most dilapidated areas, and was so successful that the federal government used it as

a model for a program of its own. Youngblood also started a school within the church and initiated a program that helped pay college tuition for congregation members.

Youngblood's greatest focus was on increasing male participation in the church. "This country is not going to live up to its potential until the black man lives up to his," he said. Based on the example of Timothy, he set up an all-male board of elders, formed a men's chorus, and inaugurated an annual Father's Day Conference at the church. In 1987, he formed the Eldad-Medad men's Bible study group, which soon regularly attracted 120 to 150 men on a weekday evening.

Eschewing traditional church language, operating with swashbuckling disregard for "safe" church politics, and stressing that "good" did not equal "weak," Youngblood appealed to many young African-American men who had previously been discounted as unworthy material for the church because of their lifestyle. "If you look into the Bible," noted Youngblood, "when God got moving, he worked with the people on the bottom of the social order. And that's why we're here." Many were impressed by Youngblood's courage in not accepting any salary but relying purely on "Love Offerings" for his income.

The result of his efforts was a startling transformation of both the church and the community. By the mid-1990s, St. Paul had more than 5,000 members, a staff of more than 50, and a budget that topped $3 million.

Further Reading

Freedman, Samuel G. *Upon This Rock: The Miracles of a Black Church.* New York: HarperCollins, 1993.

Mabunda, L. Mpho. *Contemporary Black Biography.* Vol. 8. Detroit, Mich.: Gale Research, 1995.

Bibliography and Recommended Sources

Adams, Russell L. *Great Negroes Past and Present.* Chicago: Afro-American Publishing Company, 1969.

Andrews, William L., ed. *Sisters of the Spirit.* Bloomington: Indiana University Press, 1986.

Bowden, Henry Warden. *Dictionary of American Religious Biography.* Westport, Conn.: Greenwood Press, 1993.

Broughton, Viv. *Black Gospel: An Illustrated History of the Gospel Sound.* Poole, Dorset, England: Blandford Press, 1985.

Burgess, Stanley M., et al., eds. *Dictionary of Pentecostal and Charismatic Movements.* Grand Rapids, Mich.: Zondervan, 1988.

Burkett, Randall K., and Richard Newman. *Black Apostles: Afro-American Clergy Confront the Twentieth Century.* Boston: G. K. Hall and Company, 1978.

Carson, Clayborn, et al., eds. *Eyes on the Prize: Documents, Speeches and First-Hand Accounts from the Black Freedom Struggle, 1954–1990.* New York: Penguin Books, 1991.

Collier-Thomas, Bettye. *Daughters of Thunder: Black Women Preachers and Their Sermons.* San Francisco: Jossey-Bass, 1998.

Durasoff, Steve. *Bright Wind of the Spirit: Pentecostalism Today.* Englewood Cliffs, N.J.: Prentice Hall, 1972.

Fairclough, Adam. *To Redeem the Soul of America: The SCLC and Martin Luther King, Jr.* Athens: University of Georgia Press, 1987.

Faucet, Arthur Huff. *Black Gods of the Metropolis: Negro Religious Cults of the Urban North.* New York: Octagon Books, 1970.

Franklin, John Hope, and August Meier, eds. *Black Leaders of the Twentieth Century.* Urbana: University of Illinois Press, 1982.

Garrity, John A., and Mark C. Carnes, eds. *American National Biography.* Vol. 3. New York: Oxford University Press, 2002.

Hamilton, Charles V. *The Black Preacher in America.* New York: William Morrow, 1972.

Haskins, Jim. *Distinguished African-American Political and Government Leaders.* Phoenix, Ariz.: Oryx Press, 1999.

Hine, Darlene Clarke. *Black Women in America, A–L.* Brooklyn, N.Y.: Carlson Publishing, 1993.

Hine, Darlene Clarke. *Black Women in America, M–Z.* Brooklyn, N.Y.: Carlson Publishing, 1993.

Kluger, Richard. *Simple Justice: The History of Brown v. Board of Education and Black America's Struggle for Equality.* New York: Vintage Books, 1977.

Kyle, Richard. *The Religious Fringe.* Downers Grove, Ill.: Intervarsity Press, 1993.

Lincoln, C. Eric, and Lawrence H. Mayima. *The Black Church in the African American Experience.* Durham, N.C.: Duke University Press, 1990.

Litwack, Leon and August Meier, eds. *Black Leaders of the Nineteenth Century.* Urbana: University of Illinois Press, 1988.

Lippy, Charles, ed. *Twentieth Century Shapers of American Popular Religion.* New York: Greenwood, 1989.

Loewenberg, Bert James, and Ruth Bogues. *Black Women in Nineteenth Century American Life: Their Words, Their Thoughts, Their Feelings.* University Park: Pennsylvania State University Press, 1976.

Melton, J. Gordon. *Religious Leaders of America.* 2d ed. Detroit, Mich.: Gale Research, 1999.

Mitchell-Powell, Brenda. *African American Biography.* Vol. 1. Detroit, Mich.: Gale Research, 1994.

Montgomery, William E. *Under Their Own Vine and Fig Tree: The African-American Church in the South, 1865–1900.* Baton Rouge: Louisiana State University Press, 1993.

Moses, Wilson Jeremiah. *Black Messiahs and Uncle Toms: The Social and Literary Manipulations of a Religious Myth.* University Park: Pennsylvania State University Press, 1982.

Murphy, Larry G., ed. *Encyclopedia of African American Religious Biography.* New York: Garland Publishing, 1993.

Newman, Richard, et al., eds. *Pamphlets of Protest: An Anthology of Early African American Protest Literature, 1790–1860.* New York: Routledge, 2001.

Paris, Arthur. *Black Pentecostalism: Southern Religion in an Urban World.* Amherst: University of Massachusetts Press, 1982.

Paris, Peter J. *Black Religious Leaders: Conflict in Unity.* Louisville, Ky.: John Knox Press, 1991.

Powledge, Fred. *Free at Last? The Civil Rights Movement and the People Who Made It.* Boston: Little, Brown, 1991.

Sernett, Milton, ed. *African-American Religious History: A Documentary Witness.* Durham, N.C.: Duke University Press, 1999.

Smith, Jesse Carney, ed. *Notable Black American Men.* Detroit, Mich.: Gale Research, 1999.

———. *Notable Black American Women.* Vol. 1. Detroit, Mich.: Gale Research, 1996.

———. *Notable Black American Women.* Vol. 2. Detroit, Mich.: Gale Research, 1996.

Swift, David E. *Black Prophets of Justice: Activist Clergy before the Civil War.* Baton Rouge: Louisiana State University Press, 1989.

Synan, Vinson. *The Holiness-Pentecostal Tradition.* Grand Rapids, Mich.: Eerdmans, 1997.

Wagner, Clarence M. *Profiles of Black Georgia Baptists.* Gainesville, Ga.: privately published, 1980.

Washington, Joseph R., Jr. *Black Sects and Cults.* New York: Doubleday, 1972.

Weisenfeld, Judith, and Richard Newman, eds. *This Far by Faith: Readings in African-American Women's Religious Biography.* New York: Routledge, 1995.

Young, Henry J. *Major Black Religious Leaders, 1755–1940.* Nashville, Tenn.: Abingdon, 1977.

Entries by Religious Affiliation

African Methodist Episcopal (AME)
Allen, Richard
Arnett, Benjamin William
Brown, Morris
Brown, Oliver
Coker, Daniel
Flake, Floyd
Jones, Robert Elijah
Lee, Jarena
McKenzie, Vashti Murphy
Payne, Daniel
Quinn, William Paul
Ransom, Reverdy Cassius
Revels, Hiram Rhoades
Tanner, Benjamin Tucker
Turner, Henry McNeil
Vesey, Denmark
Wright, Richard Robert, Jr.

African Methodist Episcopal Zion (AMEZ)
Gardner, Eliza Ann
Hood, James, Walker
Moore, John Jamison
Mother Smith
Randolph, Florence Spearing
Spottswood, Stephen Gill
Varick, James

Baptist
Abernathy, Ralph
Adams, Charles
Boyd, Richard Henry
Broughton, Virginia E. Walker
Bryan, Andrew
Burroughs, Nannie Helen
Butts, Calvin Otis
Cary, Lott
Cleveland, James
Dorsey, Thomas Andrew
Dyson, Michael Eric
Fauntroy, Walter Edward
Fisher, Elijah John
Forbes, James
Gomes, Peter John
Gray, William Herbert, III
Hooks, Benjamin Lawson
Howard, M. William, Jr.
Jackson, Jesse Louis
Jackson, Joseph Harrison
Jackson, Mahalia
Johnson, Mordecai Wyatt
King, Martin Luther, Jr.
King, Martin Luther, Sr.
Lee, George
Liele, George
Lyons, Henry
Mays, Benjamin Elijah
Paul, Thomas
Powell, Adam Clayton, Jr.
Powell, Adam Clayton, Sr.
Shuttlesworth, Fred
Skinner, Tom
Sullivan, Leon Howard
Taylor, Gardner Calvin
Thurman, Howard
Youngblood, Johnny Ray

Black Nationalist
Agyeman, Jaramogi Abebe
Ali, Noble Drew
Ben-Israel, Ben Ami
McGuire, George Alexander

Church of God (Holiness)
Barrow, Willie B.
Jones, Charles Price
Michaux, Lightfoot Solomon

Church of God in Christ
Blake, Charles Edward, Sr.
Crouch, Andrae
Ford, Louis H.
Franklin, Robert M.
Mason, Charles Harrison

Colored Methodist Episcopal
Coleman, Mattie E.

Disciples of Christ
Barnes, Carnella Jamison

Episcopal (Methodist Episcopal)
Bragg, George Freeman

Burgess, John Melville
Crummell, Alexander
Harris, Barbara Clementine
Jones, Absalom
Murray, Pauli

LUTHERAN
Jones, Jehu, Jr.

METHODIST
Elaw, Zilpha
Evans, Henry
Hosier, Harry
Kelly, Leontine Turpeau
Lowery, Joseph Echols
Mason, Lena Doolin
Williams, Cecil

NATION OF ISLAM
Fard, W. D.
Farrakhan, Louis
Malcolm X
Muhammad, Elijah
Muhammad, Wallace D.

NONDENOMINATIONAL *
Anthony, Wendell
Bell, Ralph S.
Bethune, Mary McLeod
Colemon, Johnnie
Cone, James Hal
Daddy Grace
Elmore, Ronn
Father Divine
Foreman, George

Green, Al
Grier, Rosey
Jakes, T. D.
King, Barbara Lewis
Kofey, Laura Adorkor
Perkins, John
Price, Frederick K. C.
Prophet Jones
Smith, Amanda Berry
Smith, Lucy
Truth, Sojourner
Vanzant, Iyanla
Waddles, Charleszetta
Walker, Hezekiah Xzavier, Jr.
West, Cornel
White, Reggie

PENTECOSTAL
Forbes, James
Seymour, William Joseph
Sharpton, Al
Tate, Mary Magdalena Lewis

PRESBYTERIAN
Cannon, Katie Geneva
Chavis, John
Ferguson, Catherine Williams
Garnet, Henry Highland
Gloucester, John
Grimké, Francis
Wilmore, Gayraud Stephen, Jr.

ROMAN CATHOLIC
Clements, George
Delille, Henrietta

Healy, Eliza
Healy, James Augustine
Healy, Patrick
Marino, Eugene Antonio
Perry, Harold Robert
Stallings, George Augustus, Jr.
Tolton, Augustus

SHAKER
Jackson, Rebecca Cox

SPIRITUALIST
Anderson, Leafy
Laveau, Marie
Seal, Catherine

UNAFFILIATED *
Garvey, Marcus Mosiah
Turner, Nat
Walker, David

UNITED CHURCH OF CHRIST (CONGREGATIONAL)
Agyeman, Jaramogi Abebe
Beman, Amos
Chavis, Ben
Delk, Yvonne V.
Haynes, Lemuel
Pennington, James William Charles
Proctor, Henry Hugh
Wright, Jeremiah, Jr.
Young, Andrew Jackson

---

* *Nondenominational* refers to a specific church or church organization that is outside (F. Price's church) or transcendent of (The Billy Graham Association) the mainstream denominations. *Unaffiliated* refers to a person such as David Walker who used religious themes and influenced religious thought while unaffiliated with any organized religious group.

ENTRIES BY YEAR OF BIRTH

PRE-1760
Bryan, Andrew
Evans, Henry
Haynes, Lemuel
Hosier, Harry
Jones, Absalom
Liele, George
Varick, James

1760–1779
Allen, Richard
Brown, Morris
Cary, Lott
Chavis, John
Ferguson, Catherine Williams
Gloucester, John
Paul, Thomas
Vesey, Denmark

1780–1799
Coker, Daniel
Elaw, Zilpha
Jackson, Rebecca Cox
Jones, Jehu, Jr.
Laveau, Marie
Lee, Jarena
Quinn, William Paul
Truth, Sojourner
Walker, David

1800–1819
Beman, Amos
Crummell, Alexander
Delille, Henrietta
Garnet, Henry Highland
Moore, John Jamison
Payne, Daniel
Pennington, James William
    Charles
Turner, Nat

1820–1839
Arnett, Benjamin William
Boyd, Richard Henry
Gardner, Eliza Ann
Healy, James Augustine
Healy, Patrick
Hood, James Walker
Revels, Hiram Rhoades
Smith, Amanda Berry
Tanner, Benjamin Tucker
Turner, Henry McNeil

1840–1859
Broughton, Virginia E. Walker
Fisher, Elijah John
Grimké, Francis
Healy, Eliza
Tolton, Augustus

1860–1879
Bethune, Mary McLeod
Bragg, George Freeman
Burroughs, Nannie Helen
Coleman, Mattie E.
Fard, W. D.
Jones, Charles Price
Jones, Robert Elijah
Kofey, Laura Adorkor
Mason, Charles Harrison
Mason, Lena Doolin
McGuire, George Alexander
Powell, Adam Clayton, Sr.
Proctor, Henry Hugh
Randolph, Florence Spearing
Ransom, Reverdy Cassius
Seal, Catherine
Seymour, William Joseph
Smith, Lucy
Tate, Mary Magdalena Lewis
Wright, Richard Robert, Jr.

1880–1899
Ali, Noble Drew
Anderson, Leafy
Daddy Grace
Dorsey, Thomas Andrew
Father Divine
Garvey, Marcus Mosiah
Johnson, Mordecai Wyatt
King, Martin Luther, Sr.

Mays, Benjamin Elijah
Michaux, Lightfoot Solomon
Muhammad, Elijah
Spottswood, Stephen Gill

1900–1909
Burgess, John Melville
Jackson, Joseph Harrison
Lee, George
Mother Smith
Powell, Adam Clayton, Jr.
Prophet Jones
Thurman, Howard

1910–1919
Agyeman, Jaramogi Abebe
Barnes, Carnella Jamison
Brown, Oliver
Ford, Louis H.
Jackson, Mahalia
Murray, Pauli
Perry, Harold Robert
Taylor, Gardner Calvin
Waddles, Charleszetta

1920–1929
Abernathy, Ralph
Barrow, Willie B.
Colemon, Johnnie
Hooks, Benjamin Lawson
Kelly, Leontine Turpeau

King, Martin Luther, Jr.
Lowery, Joseph Echols
Malcolm X
Shuttlesworth, Fred
Sullivan, Leon Howard
Williams, Cecil
Wilmore, Gayraud Stephen, Jr.

1930–1939
Adams, Charles
Bell, Ralph S.
Clements, George
Cleveland, James
Cone, James Hal
Delk, Yvonne V.
Farrakhan, Louis
Fauntroy, Walter Edward
Forbes, James
Grier, Rosey
Harris, Barbara Clementine
King, Barbara Lewis
Marino, Eugene Antonio
Muhammad, Wallace D.
Perkins, John
Price, Frederick K. C.
Young, Andrew Jackson

1940–1949
Ben-Israel, Ben Ami
Blake, Charles Edward, Sr.

Butts, Calvin Otis
Chavis, Ben
Crouch, Andrae
Flake, Floyd
Foreman, George
Gomes, Peter John
Gray, William Herbert, III
Green, Al
Howard, M. William, Jr.
Jackson, Jesse Louis
Lyons, Henry
McKenzie, Vashti Murphy
Skinner, Tom
Stallings, George Augustus, Jr.
Wright, Jeremiah, Jr.
Youngblood, Johnny Ray

1950–1959
Anthony, Wendell
Cannon, Katie Geneva
Dyson, Michael Eric
Elmore, Ronn
Franklin, Robert M.
Jakes, T. D.
Sharpton, Al
Vanzant, Iyanla
West, Cornel

1960–
Walker, Hezekiah Xzavier, Jr.
White, Reggie

Index

Boldface locators indicate main entries. *Italic* locators indicate photographs.

DISCARD